Bc

DICTIONARY OF
CONCEPTS IN
GENERAL PSYCHOLOGY

DICTIONARY OF CONCEPTS IN GENERAL PSYCHOLOGY

John A. Popplestone and
Marion White McPherson

Reference Sources for the Social Sciences and Humanities, Number 7

Greenwood Press
New York • Westport, Connecticut • London

Library of Congress Cataloging-in-Publication Data

Popplestone, John A.
    Dictionary of concepts in general psychology / John A. Popplestone
and Marion White McPherson.
        p. cm. — (Reference sources for the social sciences and
humanities, ISSN 0730-3335 ; no. 7)
    Bibliography: p.
    Includes index.
    ISBN 0-313-23190-7 (lib. bdg. : alk. paper)
    1. Psychology—Dictionaries.   I. McPherson, Marion White.
II. Title.   III. Series.
BF31. P665 1988
150'. 3'21—dc 19   88-3120

British Library Cataloguing in Publication Data is available.

Library of Congress Catalog Card Number: 88-3120
ISBN: 0-313-23190-7
ISSN: 0730-3335

First published in 1988

Greenwood Press, Inc.
88 Post Road West, Westport, Connecticut 06881

Printed in the United States of America

The paper used in this book complies with the
Permanent Paper Standard issued by the National
Information Standards Organization (Z39.48-1984).

10 9 8 7 6 5 4 3 2 1

Contents

Series Foreword

In all disciplines, scholars seek to understand and explain the subject matter in their area of specialization. The object of their activity is to produce a body of knowledge about specific fields of inquiry. As they achieve an understanding of their subject, scholars publish the results of their interpretations (that is, their research findings) in the form of explanations. Explanation, then, can be said to organize and communicate understanding. When reduced to agreed-upon theoretical principles, the explanations that emerge from this process of organizing understanding are called concepts.

Concepts serve many functions. They help us identify topics that we think about, help classify these topics into related sets, help relate them to specific times and places, and provide us with definitions. Someone has observed that without concepts, "man could hardly be said to think."

Like knowledge itself, the meanings of concepts are fluid. From the moment an authority introduces one into a discipline's vocabulary and gives it specific significance, that concept has the potential to acquire a variety of meanings. As new understandings develop in a discipline, inevitably the concepts change.

Although this pattern in the formation of the meaning of concepts is widely recognized, few dictionaries—certainly none in a consistent manner—trace the path a concept takes as it becomes embedded in a research topic's literature. This dictionary makes accessible brief, authoritative discussions of major concepts in general psychology. Like all other concept dictionaries in this series, entries uniformly consist of four parts.

The first briefly defines a concept's current meaning and/or meanings. The second locates a concept's origins in the vocabulary of psychology and, paragraph by paragraph, traces to the present how its various meanings developed. The third cites fully all references discussed in the preceding part.

For needs not met by information in parts one through three, the fourth part provides sources of additional information for further investigation about the concept. Primarily these additional information sources consist of references for extensive literature reviews, major articles, and other specific discussions considered essential to a comprehensive understanding of the concept.

Entries in this dictionary are deliberately designed to meet different levels of needs. Among the four parts of each entry, the first is perhaps characteristic of what we associate with most specialized, or "subject field," dictionaries. When you need only to learn the current meaning of a concept, you can confine your use of the dictionary to this part of an entry.

Other, more comprehensive research needs are met in parts two and three of each entry. In these parts, you can "tune in," so to speak, at the level of discussion of the concept you wish, and then proceed to the level of understanding that meets your particular needs. Parts two and three of each entry make up this dictionary's major contributions. That is, each entry's second and third part add, uniquely, a significant feature about how meanings of concepts develop and evolve. This feature has heretofore only been included in a few reference works, and if they occur at all it's more by accident than design. Yet, when we consider how desirable these characteristics of dictionaries are, we can only wonder why, in the past, these characteristics have not been featured in subject-field dictionaries.

Finally, as a departure point for more intense investigation, the last part of each entry gives suggestions you need to explore the discussions in the literature of specific concepts to whatever detail required.

Raymond G. McInnis

Preface

The subject matter of science is typically depersonalized and is carefully ordered and expressed in formal, regulated ways—often in formulae. This orderliness, in contrast, is not characteristic of the science of psychology because the subject matter is not confined to logical reactions but includes many that are fragmented and erratic. Some reactions are clearly appreciated (''I hate cats, can't stand the sight of them''), but others are sensed only vaguely or incompletely and their implications are usually not conscious, and thus not readily verbalized (''People who admire me are worthwhile and those who do not are worthless''). These combinations neither emerge from nor follow organized patterns, but are the product of associations among parts, aspects of experience. They are combined because they *happened to be encountered* at the same time and/or in the same place. Some of them are frequently repeated, others are colored by emotional distress, and still others are rewarded. In spite of their casual, contiguous origins many of these associations acquire the power of convictions, and in fact some are believed to be axiomatic and infallible, with the result that criticisms that they are illogical and the products of chance are defeated. The certainty about them is due to the genesis in personal experiences. What has been learned at firsthand has a persuasive authenticity.

People became curious about the mind and its vagaries long before there was a scientific psychology, and the explanations that emerged were then provided by religion and philosophy. The attempts that began in the late nineteenth century to move psychology away from these supernatural and mentalistic traditions in the direction of science included recommendations for conceptualizing the field so that it would deal only with natural, tangible factors. Some of these proposals, or at least residuals of them, are part of the modern scene, and thus they influence the content of this volume.

One of the most famous of these prescriptions is behaviorism, a theory that was first promulgated in the 1910s and one that proclaims that the only legitimate subject matter for psychology is observed behavior. Research within this frame of reference also brought to light an intimate relationship between behavior and experience, with most of the information about the latter formalized in the study of learning.

Learning, of course, modifies responses, and the resulting diversity distinguishes psychological behavior from biological behavior. To illustrate—as a stimulus that induces biological reactivity a cup of tea is ingested, digested, absorbed, and excreted. But as a stimulus that induces psychological reactivity a cup of tea may be handled in a variety of ways—it may be consumed, served, passed, sold, purchased, discarded, or even thrown. Each one of these psychological responses is concomitant with a composite of biological ones. In hackneyed terms—biology is necessary but not sufficient for psychological behavior, and it must be supplemented by learning. Even a brief consideration of proficiency calls attention to the indispensable nature of acquisition. The skill of a pilot, the competency of a surgeon, the scholarship of a medievalist, and the art of a classical musician are impossible without experience, without practice. Learning is also requisite for less intricate tasks. A young child, for example, may be unable to explain the difference between a fraction of one quarter and one of three quarters, but prior encounters with both candy and sharing may well allow a ready perception of the inequality between one quarter and three quarters of a candy bar. This specificity is generalized only after the child masters additional skills.

Biology is an important and crucial field, but we do not view it as the sole basis of or as a substitute for psychology. As a result the information that is included in this book features explanations of behavior in behavioral terms. An experiment, for example, that treats changes in the level of anxiety as it is sensed is preferred to one that reports changes in heart rate and blood pressure. An experiment that probes the differences in awareness between running away from the feared and running toward the desired is considered more relevant than one that continues the (as yet unsuccessful) search for physiological differences in running under these two conditions.

Modern psychology is founded on research, and we describe experiments that illustrate how the information is acquired. The techniques that are used are astonishingly diverse. The data range from the differentiated reactivity of nonverbal, primitive organisms, such as single-cell animals, through the creative thinking of eminent scientists. Some of the experimental strategies are the same or similar to those used in other sciences, but many are applicable only to psychology. For example, unwitting descriptions of the self were obtained by asking research participants to describe the personality they thought was disclosed in mirror images of specimens of handwriting, including a sample of the writing of each participant. In animal research the white rat and the pigeon are famous, or infamous. Experiments have disclosed a psychological attribute even in the Venus's-flytrap, specifically "learning" in that the plant will close in response to mechanical stimulation for a few trials, and after them it reacts only to normally adequate stimulation.

Laboratory research is supplemented by observations that are made in the field and in clinical situations. Psychologists ascertain the incidence of disclosures of youthful aspirations by the aged and participate in specialized interest groups in order to learn about the personality of the members. They plot the time and frequency of tree climbing and wrestling in orphaned bear cubs raised in a protective pen. They administer tests of personality and intellectual skills to academically superior children, to academic failures, to emotionally disturbed individuals, and to immigrants struggling to learn an unfamiliar culture.

Space limits do not allow an enumeration, or an evaluation, of the methods used in psychology. In order to accommodate to this forced selection we have omitted discussions both of statistical criteria and of detailed criticisms of the strengths and weaknesses in the experimental designs. What we do include, however, are accounts of investigations that are defensible. Scientific information is always accumulating, and as a result what is condoned by some is condemned by others, either today or in the future. Science is an ongoing process and the knowledge it yields is always tentative, but according to current criteria the research reviewed in this volume is, at this time, valid. It should be noted that cross references to other entries in this dictionary are designated by the use of SMALL CAPITALS which indicates that the discussion THERE is relevant to the discussion *here*.

Inasmuch as the discussion has come around to errors we would like to comment that we have struggled mightily to minimize, if not utterly prevent, mistakes in reporting. This goal has led to a change of "reverence" to "reference" and "in significant ways" to "insignificant ways." We would prefer to indicate that any mistakes that remain are "yours," but proofreading indicates that they are "ours."

THE DICTIONARY

A

ACHIEVEMENT. An outcome, the result of numerous variables—educational, economic, political, and social, as well as psychological. This heterogeneity has led to two different but related concepts. One deals with a personal disposition or need and the second deals with the techniques that link this motive with the educational, social and economic circumstances that determine the level of achievement that is realized. These concepts are presented in the order in which they were devised.

Need for Achievement. 1. A desire to improve the quality of performance as shown by planning, thinking about, and working energetically and persistently on tasks that are difficult and important.

Achievement Motivation. 1. The study of relationships among the psychological and cultural variables that determine the level of accomplishment that is actually obtained.

The need for achievement does not, despite its name, designate the actual attaining of success, but rather refers to a motive. The strength of this is inferred both from behavior and from mentation, but the latter is probably the more frequently used source in research on this topic. The thoughts of a person in whom the need for achievement is strong typically disclose careful planning of the most effective ways of managing challenging and consequential jobs. There is an attraction to assignments that are formidable and important, with the focus on long-term enterprises. The individual would like to surpass previous records, including ones that have been set personally. More attention is given to the solving of a problem than to ultimate success, and teamwork is oriented more toward task completion than toward socializing. The rewards of achievement are satisfaction with oneself rather than the praise of others, and excellence is given more weight than prestige. In other words, this motive is technically defined and there are no synonyms for it, although sometimes it is referred to as the achievement motive and even as *n* Ach.

The need for achievement was the first variety of SOCIAL MOTIVATION to be investigated by means of a special experimental design that became a standard format for research on this topic. Let us begin with the procedure: It involves comparing the responses of people—who vary in the strength of their need for achievement—to a request to describe each picture in a series of ambiguous ones, to imagine what happened prior to the scene, and what will happen next. The assumption is made that both the thoughts and the actions of the characters in the stories are determined by their motives, and the way the environment reacts to these—called the press—discloses the narrator's apperception, that is, beliefs about the long-term consequences of environmental actions. Each need-press interaction is called a *thema*, and the procedure is referred to as the thematic apperception method. The ambiguity of the scenes as well as the lack of any information about the sequence of events fosters content that originates within each subject, and hence the characters' needs and apperception are those of the narrator. Explicit criteria are developed for judging—that is, scoring—the presence of the need in the storyteller's thoughts. These principles allow different investigators to agree with one another, and they also provide an empirically based and detailed definition of the concept.

McClelland, Clark, Roby, and Atkinson (1949) started the initial experiment on the need for achievement by asking male undergraduates, when working under different motivational conditions, to perform a few simple tasks, such as solving anagrams and unscrambling words. One group was led to believe that they were merely assisting a graduate student in developing a test and that the test items rather than the participants were on trial. In a second group attempts were made to arouse the need for achievement by exposing the subjects to a competitive atmosphere and informing them that the purpose of the experiment was to identify colleges with the highest incidence of potential leaders. These subjects were also told that their performance on the initial tasks was inadequate. All participants were then asked to make up stories to four pictures, each vague but relevant to achievement. Analyses of the differences in the narratives indicated a stronger need for achievement in the individuals who had been led to believe that they were in competition and also inept. This difference encouraged further experimentation, and the guidelines for judging or scoring the presence of the need for achievement were refined (McClelland, Atkinson, Clark, & Lowell, 1953/1976).

Additional experimental work not only confirmed the original results, but also indicated that an alertness to accomplishment influences thinking and behavior in a variety of ways (Heckhausen, 1967). This dispersion is illustrated in an experiment by Knapp and Garbutt, who hypothesized that individuals with a high need for achievement would not want to waste time because that would limit how much could be achieved. They asked male undergraduates who had made up stories for a series of pictures to evaluate time-related similes, such as "a fleeing thief" and "drifting clouds" (1958, p. 429). Students with high need for achievement scores were found to prefer figures of speech that suggest rapidity rather than those that imply slowness.

Another example of the effect of the need for achievement on other responses is found in a propensity to take independent action. This has been demonstrated in various investigations, but one of the more intriguing of these is a by-product of research on resistance to conformity. To illustrate this McClelland et al. (1953/1976) refer to an experiment in which groups of seven students, six of them in collusion, were shown a line and asked to compare its length with that of three unequal ones. A member of each group was instructed to declare that one of the obviously discrepant lines was equal to the standard and the conspirators were told to concur. Thus one participant, consistently the last to be questioned, was confronted with the choice of either conforming by following the group (and error) or upholding his own nonconforming (but accurate) perception. A review of thematic apperception stories of the "yielders" and "nonyielders" disclosed that the majority of those with a high need for achievement made independent judgments, whereas the majority of those with a low need concurred with the group opinion.

Early in the research program McClelland observed that students who are motivated for achievement tend to become involved in entrepreneurial positions and to procure jobs that demand initiative and risk taking. He pursued this correlation in formal experiments, including a comparison of adult occupations with the need for achievement scores that had been obtained fourteen years earlier, when the subjects were undergraduates (McClelland, 1965). An analysis disclosed that 83 percent of the men who hold entrepreneurial positions had obtained high scores as undergraduates, and 79 percent of those in nonentrepreneurial positions had received low scores.

There have been numerous cross-cultural comparisons of the need for achievement, and the nature of these experiments is illustrated in LeVine's (1966) research on Nigerian tribes that vary in the way they seek success. At one extreme is a group whose behavior is aggressively competitive, and at the other is one who practices subservience to a benefactor. These samples were found to differ in the amount of achievement imagery in their dreams, with a high level characteristic of aggressors and a low level characteristic of the recipients of favors.

Overt expressions of the need for achievement are the result of a complex of socioeconomic factors. A person can neither attempt nor manage a challenge unless the environment provides an opportunity to do so, and on the other hand, tasks will not be undertaken unless there is a need or motive to do so. The concept of achievement motivation is concerned with techniques of connecting these personal and social variables, and McClelland and his colleagues, working both in the laboratory and in field situations, have investigated various procedures (McClelland, 1961/1976). In many of these extralaboratory studies the data are extracted from public as well as personal documents. An example of this approach is deCharms and Moeller's comparison (1962) of the relationship between the need for achievement and indices of output in America between 1800 and 1950. The motive was inferred from the content of samples of children's literature, and accomplishment was inferred from the number of patents issued per 1 million population. The curves for these two sets of data are parallel.

There are various methods of helping people to recognize and take advantage of opportunities. One of the preferred ways is by first alerting them to the nature and level of their own need for achievement. The individual is taught to calculate his or her personal score because learning to do this calls attention to the extent and focus of the interest. This differentiated information then helps to transform previously vague ideas into specific ones and to disclose strong and weak aspects of the achievement thema. It also promotes an increasing number of relevant associations, and the more intimate the connections between motives and other events, the higher the probability that opportunities will be discerned and seized.

Accurate measurements of the effectiveness of these programs are hindered by the impossibility, in field research, of controlling all relevant variables. Changes in achievement motivation may be obscured by financial crises, war, natural disasters, and the like. Despite these drawbacks some evidence has been accumulated that suggests that training fosters improvement but gradually and subtly rather than dramatically. McClelland and Winter comment about some of these effects on residents of an undeveloped country four years after the instruction: "In no sense has the course led to instant and continued success for all, or for even a small proportion of men. Rather, it has led to some improvement for many . . . we feel that an existing process—innovation and entrepreneurial success—has been accelerated among several men" (1971, p. 398).

Astonishingly, the people who participated in the research on the need for achievement during the initial twenty years were, with extremely few exceptions, white male college students. This restriction prevented generalizing about the concept to the population at large, but critics tended to disregard both the ethnic exclusion and the socioeconomic homogeneity. The neglect of women, however, did elicit strong protests. The compensation for this slighting, once under way, has been vigorous and has resulted in the formulation of an additional concept, FEAR OF SUCCESS. Several experiments point to the probability of sex differences in the need for achievement, but some of the evidence is inconsistent and inconclusive. Stewart and Chester, after completing a critical review of the research conducted in the thematic apperception tradition, conclude that there is no adequate experimental support for sex differences. They acknowledge some confusion in the results and attribute this in part to variations in the procedures used by different experimenters. They also comment on an intrusion of the popular culture that clouds the understanding of the laboratory data: "It is hard to resist the interpretation that researchers were eager to see the arousal of the achievement motive in women as especially problematic" (1982, p. 181). Stewart and Chester speculate that differences, should they be confirmed, may not be due to sex role per se, but may be due to variations in attitudes toward competitiveness. They suggest that men may restrict their orientation to achievement to the domain of work, whereas women may be sensitized to excellence in a variety of situations.

In summary, research has disclosed many facts about the need for achievement as well as various effects of this motive on other kinds of behavior. But the research is not yet sufficiently conclusive to allow consensus about some aspects of its influence, with the deficits particularly large in relation both to sex differences and to methods of strengthening achievement motivation.

References

deCharms, R., & Moeller, G. H. (1962). Values expressed in American children's readers: 1800–1950. *Journal of Abnormal and Social Psychology, 64*, 136–142.

Heckhausen, H. (1967). *The anatomy of achievement motivation* (K. F. Butler, R. C. Birney, & D. C. McClelland, Trans.). New York: Academic Press. This volume details research on achievement, and selected facets of the concept are given individual attention.

Knapp, R. H., & Garbutt, J. T. (1958). Time imagery and the achievement motive. *Journal of Personality, 26*, 426–434.

LeVine, R. A. (1966). *Dreams and deeds: Achievement motivation in Nigeria.* Chicago: University of Chicago Press.

McClelland, D. C. (1965). N Achievement and entrepreneurship: A longitudinal study. *Journal of Personality and Social Psychology, 1*, 389–392.

McClelland, D. C. (1976). *The achieving society.* New York: Irvington. (Original work published 1961). The current printing has a new Introduction.

McClelland, D. C., Atkinson, J. W., Clark, R. A., & Lowell, E. L. (1976). *The achievement motive.* New York: Irvington. (Original work published 1953). The 1976 printing varies from the first in that there is a Preface that outlines much of the research activity that took place after the initial publication. One chapter, "Analysis of imaginative stories for motivational content," provides a scoring manual for the need for achievement.

McClelland, D. C., Clark, R. A., Roby, T. B., & Atkinson, J. W. (1949). The projective expression of needs: 4. The effect of the need for achievement on thematic apperception. *Journal of Experimental Psychology, 39*, 242–255.

McClelland, D. C., & Winter, D. G. (1971). *Motivating economic achievement.* New York: Macmillan. Discusses the influence of achievement motivation in different business and community situations.

Stewart, A. J., & Chester, N. L. (1982). Sex differences in human social motives: Achievement, affiliation, and power. In A. J. Stewart (Ed.) *Motivation and society: A volume in honor of David C. McClelland* (pp. 172–218). San Francisco: Jossey-Bass.

Sources of Additional Information

Atkinson, J. W. (1974). The mainsprings of achievement-oriented activity. In J. W. Atkinson & J. O. Raynor (Eds.), *Motivation and achievement* (pp. 13–42). New York: John Wiley. This article provides a perspective on the state of the art, including fear of failure as well as achievement motivation. Entwisle, D. R. (1972). To dispel fantasies about fantasy-based measures of achievement motivation. *Psychological Bulletin, 77*, 377–391. In this technical article the author discusses what she believes are the weaknesses in the thematic apperception method of studying the need for achievement. Meade, R. D. (1966). Achievement motivation, achievement, and psychological time. *Journal of Personality and Social Psychology, 4*, 577–580. This research is designed to test the hypothesis that individuals with a high need for achievement value time. The results concur with previous studies and indicate an intolerance for slow motion as well as an attraction to fast action; Minor, C. A. & Neel, R. G. (1958). The relationship between achievement motive and occupational preference. *Journal of Counseling Psychology, 5*, 39–43. Many male veterans with high need-for-achievement scores indicate a preference for high-status civilian positions, whereas those with moderate or low scores tend to choose occupations for which they have skills. Stewart, A. J. (Ed.). (1982). *Motivation and society: A volume in honor of David C. McClelland.* San Francisco: Jossey-Bass. This volume provides a perspective on the work on achievement. A chapter by McClelland is included. Winter, D. G. & Wiecking, F. A. (1971). The new Puritans: Achievement and power motives of new left radicals. *Behavioral Science, 16*, 523–530. This article offers some research data and provocative speculations about the social motives of undergraduate radical activists.

ADAPTATION.   See HABITUATION and ADAPTATION.

ADJUSTMENT.   1. A synonym for the psychophysical method of average error and the method of reproduction. 2. Promoting harmonious relationships between the self and the environment. 3. Tempering relationships between private preferences and social demands. 4. A synonym for adaptation and habituation.

   The first of these definitions is a very early one in psychology, but it is still in circulation and is used to designate a procedure in PSYCHOPHYSICS, the study of the relationships between the physical attributes of stimuli and the sensing of them. The relationship is frequently expressed as a THRESHOLD, the statistically determined minimal amount of physical stimulation or the minimal change in energy that can be appreciated. One group of similar procedures for ascertaining the threshold is called the method of adjustment. The general format of this method is one in which an individual is asked to adjust a variable stimulus, such as a circle of light, until it appears equal—in this instance in size—to a standard. Because the subject tries to reproduce the standard, the technique is sometimes called the method of reproduction, and because the discrepancies between the judged and the actual size are also measured, it is also referred to as the method of average error (Avery & Cross, 1978).

   The concept of adjustment suggests a state of equilibrium, but a sustained balance is rare and a more appropriate referent is that of making changes. In the field of psychology these most often occur in efforts to improve the relationship between an organism and its environment, both the physical and the social one. The term was initially used to indicate biological modifications that were the result of evolutionary changes, and it is difficult to pinpoint the exact time when psychologists began to use the word adjustment in relation to their own subject matter. It is not included in a turn-of-the-century dictionary (Baldwin, 1901/1940), but it is in one published in 1934 (Warren).

There were a few early specialized meanings, but these were short-lived, and possibly some were idiosyncratic. For example, a 1917 text (Hollingworth & Poffenberger) uses the word adjustment to describe institutional, as opposed to individual, actions. Occasionally the concept appeared as equivalent to attitude and SET (Bolton, 1908; Thorndike, 1931/1968). More commonly it was used as a synonym for HABITUATION and ADAPTATION.

The term was also linked to particular contexts, such as school (Zachry, 1929), social relationships (Dexter, 1927; Symonds, 1934), and vocational endeavors (Hollingworth, 1920). This developing specificity, however, was soon counteracted by expansion, and accommodation, adaptation, and habituation all came to be used as synonyms. The cloudiness of the term is illustrated in a treatise edited by Murchison (1934/1969) in which the field of experimental psychology is divided into the two large categories of receptive and adjustive processes. Warren defines the latter as "*any* [italics added] operation whereby an organism or organ becomes more favorably related to the environment" (1934, p. 6).

At the same time that the contraction and expansion were going on, a growing amount of attention was being paid to efforts to increase the compatibility between inner, private wishes and outer, social demands. Laurance F. Shaffer (1903–1976), one of the pioneer proponents of this interpretation, was the first to give an academic course on this topic. The custom spread so extensively that a class in the Psychology of Adjustment became a sequel to the Introduction to Psychology in many undergraduate curricula. As a result the word adjustment came into wide circulation. Shaffer initially offered the course in the academic year 1929–1930 under the title Mental Adjustments (The Psychology of the Student), but in 1932 the name was changed to the one that endured: the Psychology of Adjustment.

At first Shaffer used a lithoprinted volume, *The Psychology of Adjustment*, that he had written. In 1936 a version of this was published in regular textbook form. In the Preface to the book Shaffer comments that "every person expects psychology to contribute to an understanding of his own life problems" (p. ix). The text caters to this expectation by discussing a variety of common personal and interpersonal difficulties and describing how normal people manage them. Shaffer's lecture notes indicate that the tenor of the instruction was upbeat, and he offered the class a motto: "More fun for more people" (Shaffer Papers, M 763). The notes also convey some of the culture of the era, in that the traditional reliance on biological explanations of difficulties is downplayed: "Don't place too much emphasis on the physical" (M 763). The class was also advised that the information about the causes and treatment of difficulties in adjustment would be pursued in an atmosphere free of the indignation and censure that at that time often accompanied consideration of this subject matter.

Shaffer endeavors to bridge the gap between academic psychology and everyday problems, but the success with which this goal is met is somewhat limited. The volume can be described as consisting of two embankments, each of which is stronger than the connections between them. On one side are surveys of traditional topics in general psychology, such as learning, motivation, and emotion, and on the other side are overviews of a broad spectrum of such negatives as frustration, anxiety, "demeaning roles," and "unobtainable goals." The bridging takes the form of trying to relate the quandaries to relevant systematic knowledge, for example, thwarting to motivation and repression to memory.

Many courses and a plethora of textbooks followed, but the unrelenting efforts of textbook writers to keep abreast of the times had little effect on the purposes of the instruction, nor did the writers achieve marked improvement in linking formal psychology with personal concerns. A review of two texts that were written forty-three years after Shaffer's first volume is clearly tuned to the prototype: "The authors of both of these texts are attempting to make psychology meaningful and relevant to the concerns of introductory-level students. Both books have strengths, but neither provides a workable blend of relevant research bases with discussions of adjustment" (Donelson, 1979, p. 1037).

The most commonly repeated content in books on the psychology of adjustment is probably the DEFENSE MECHANISMS, and for a multitude of students the term adjustment is probably a generic one for a list of intrapersonal strategies that modulate motives. Such words as compensation, rationalization, regression, and repression have come into common use. These and other defense mechanisms, originally formulated by psychoanalysts and ascribed to the psychiatrically disabled, have come to be perceived as tactics that normals use when their personal, private experiences induce distress.

Thus, except in the nomenclature of psychophysics, adjustment is neither a technical nor an organized concept, but it has become a durable and conspicuous component of everyday vocabulary. This free circulation retains the connotation of making changes that smooth the way, but it also, on occasion, revives the early but misleading implication of equilibrium. This reappearance takes the form of a statement about the success, or lack thereof, of attempts to improve adjustment, commonly expressed as a dichotomy: maladjusted or unadjusted versus adjusted.

References

Avery, D. D., & Cross, H. A., Jr. (1978). *Experimental methodology in psychology.* Monterey, CA: Brooks/Cole.

Baldwin, J. M. (Ed.). (1940). *Dictionary of philosophy and psychology* (Vol. 1). New York: Peter Smith. (Original work published 1901.)

Bolton, T. L. (1908). Meaning as adjustment. *Psychological Review, 15,* 169–172. This article illustrates the struggles in turn-of-the-century psychology to organize various concepts. The author implies that adjustment in humans is analogous to instincts in animals.

Dexter, R. C. (1927). *Social adjustment.* New York: Alfred Knopf.

Donelson, E. (1979). In search of adjustment [Review of *Dynamics of personal adjustment* (3rd ed.) and *Personal adjustment: The psychology of everyday life*]. *Contemporary Psychology, 24,* 1036–1038.

Hollingworth, H. L. (1920). *The psychology of functional neuroses*. New York: Appleton. An account of the maladjustments of soldiers in the first World War. One short section deals with the attempts to improve "vocational adjustment" (p. 240).

Hollingworth, H. L., & Poffenberger, A. T. (1917). *Applied psychology*. New York: Appleton. This volume reviews much of basic psychology and relates that knowledge to occupational variables.

Murchison, C. A. (Ed.). (1969). *A handbook of general experimental psychology: Pt. 1. Adjustive processes*. New York: Russell & Russell. (Original work published 1934). Each chapter is written by a different author. The volume constitutes a comprehensive account of basic psychology in the 1930s. More space is devoted to sense organs than in contemporary treatises. The documentation is impressive.

Shaffer, L. F. Papers. Archives of the History of American Psychology, Bierce Library, University of Akron, Akron, Ohio.

Shaffer, L. F. (1936). *The psychology of adjustment: An objective approach to mental hygiene*. Cambridge, MA: Houghton Mifflin.

Symonds, P. M. (1934). *Psychological diagnosis in social adjustment*. New York: American Book.

Thorndike, E. L. (Ed.). (1968). *Human learning*. New York: Johnson Reprint. (Original work published in 1931). The author was a pioneer in research on learning both in animals and in humans. This volume contains essays on human learning that reflect Thorndike's belief that some acquisition can be facilitated.

Warren, H. C. (1934). *Dictionary of psychology*. Cambridge, MA: Houghton Mifflin.

Zachry, C. B. (1929). *Personality adjustments of school children*. New York: Charles Scribner's Sons.

Sources of Additional Information

Goodstein, L. D., & Lanyon, R. I. (1975). *Adjustment, behavior, and personality*. Reading, MA: Addison-Wesley. This title illustrates the preference, at the time of publication, that psychology be identified as a behavioral science. Shaffer, L. F., & Shoben, E. J., Jr. (1956). *The psychology of adjustment: A dynamic and experimental approach to personality and mental hygiene*. Cambridge, MA: Houghton Mifflin. This volume is one in a series that was written under the editorship of Leonard Carmichael, then Secretary of the Smithsonian Institution, who refers to the first edition as one of the "landmarks in the evolution of psychology as an organized science" (p. v). Weight, D. G. (1984). Six adjustment texts [Review of *Personal adjustment and growth, Psychology of adjustment and human relationships, Contemporary psychology and effective behavior, Understanding human adjustment, Adjustment and growth, Psychology applied to modern life*]. *Contemporary Psychology, 29*, 871–873. Weight comments on the increasing number of textbooks in the area, and adds: "The psychology of adjustment is becoming a much more viable teaching subject" (p. 871). Still gaining momentum fifty-five years after Shaffer's first course. Wolff, W. (1947). *What is psychology: A basic survey*. New York: Grune & Stratton. This book is intended to present psychology as a developing discipline, to provoke more questions than answers. The word adjustment is seldom used, but much of the discussion resembles the content of adjustment texts.

AFFILIATION. See NEED FOR AFFILIATION.

AGGRESSION. 1. Overt behavior, both verbal and physical, that is intended to hurt others and/or damage property. 2. A synonym for hostility.

The concept of aggression is selective in that it emphasizes actions that are intended to degrade, harm, injure, or destroy. Behavior that is aggressive in the sense of competitive or enterprising is typically referred to by means of the adjective aggresive, but a variety of technical words are also used. To illustrate— a person with a strong desire to surpass earlier levels of accomplishment may be described as having a high NEED FOR ACHIEVEMENT. The words COMPETENCE and effectance are applied to those who enjoy making diligent efforts to elaborate and develop numerous aspects of their experiences. They are the people who find the process or the means gratifying, and they undertake tasks with vigor and enthusiasm.

Some psychologists have attempted to specify the differences between being aggressive and enterprising by distinguishing ''hostile'' aggression from other varieties (Feshbach, 1964). Many discussions of this topic, however, contain so many references to force that the distinction becomes questionable. ''Instrumental'' aggression, for example, is defined as assaultive behavior that is carried out in order to achieve socially acceptable goals. Combat personnel are said to display ''instrumental'' aggression because their behavior is ''primarily oriented toward the attainment of some goal other than doing injury (such as winning the war)'' (Berkowitz, 1962, p. 31). Buss points out that ''the son who wins a street fight with a peer is likely to be rewarded by the approval of his father ('He's a real boy, some fighter!')'' (1961, p. 3).

The including of an *intention* to damage in the definition of aggression differentiates it from accidents and from intervention that is a function of social role, such as an instructor assigning a failing grade or a farmer harvesting livestock (Kaufmann, 1965). Instances in which the difference between aggression and performing one's ''duty'' is clouded can sometimes be clarified by observing the source of gratification. A parent who gets pleasure from punishing a child is not motivated solely by the desire to instill more acceptable behavior. A police officer whose self-esteem is raised when he or she makes a large number of arrests may be displaying more interest in ego enhancement than in keeping the peace.

The fact that aggression overlaps with other kinds of attacks leads to inconsistency in the vocabulary, particularly in the use of the terms ANGER, assertiveness, and HOSTILITY. Anger stands apart from these reactions in that it is of brief duration and the muscular concomitants are more apt to be expressive than mobilized. Aggression, assertiveness, and hostility are better integrated, more sustained sequences. Assertiveness varies from the other reactions in that its purpose is not so much to criticize or damage as it is to assure respect for one's status, a recognition of one's rights. Of these three terms, hostility and aggression are the most often confused. Many authors do not make any distinction between the two, and the disorder is further increased by the fact that the two responses are often concomitant. In precise terminology, hostility is reserved for oblique, indirect attacks, and aggression for open confrontations. This distinction is important because it brings differences in response styles to the forefront, specifically the amount of personal exposure—a hostile antagonist is obscured but an aggressor stands in bold relief.

In the inaugural era of experimental psychology, aggression was considered to be an instinct and to be a reaction to *any* interference. William McDougall, one of the founders of the field of social psychology, asserted that "pugnacity" differs from other instincts in that it is activated not by the perception of specific objects, but by "any opposition to the free exercise of any impulse, any obstruction to the activity to which the creature is impelled . . . its excitement . . . is apt to be intense in proportion to the strength of the obstructed impulse" (1912, pp. 59–60).

This opinion was reflected in some of the first research on aggression. This began in 1939, when Dollard, Doob, Miller, Mowrer, and Sears published *Frustration and Aggression*, a landmark volume. The researchers initially assumed "a universal causal relation between frustration and aggression" (p. 10). They first investigated the details of this relationship by testing a series of hypotheses that were based in part on McDougall's belief about the role of *any* thwarting agent as well as the equality of strength between frustration and aggression. These experiments led to several modifications. They disclosed, for example, differential effects among various antecedents of aggression, and thereby helped to dissolve the idea that aggression is an instinct. The research was also interpreted as strengthening rather than weakening the assumption that aggression is an inevitable reaction. This firming up came about despite some experimental failures to elicit expected aggressive responses, and it was promoted merely by interpreting the episodes as instances of deflected or disguised rather than dissipated aggression. Psychoanalysis had previously portrayed aggression as strong and cunning (Freud 1920/1938), but the theory was criticized as unscientific, and hence much of its teaching was ignored. Some weakening of this censure was initiated by the Dollard team when they also began to see aggression as furtive, and in fact their interpretation was one of the first steps in a movement in scientific psychology—one that is still going on—to identify displaced forms of aggression.

The early research also made it clear that aggression is not the only response to FRUSTRATION and that frustration is only one of several causes of aggression (Miller, 1941). This discovery fostered a separation of the two concepts, and gradually the frustration-aggression hypothesis of Dollard et al. changed from a central position to one that is primarily historic.

One line of research in the extension of the concept included probing life histories in search of the origins of aggression. There is evidence that the level of aggression shown in adulthood is strongly influenced by childhood experiences, and the more powerful variables appear to be corporal punishment and growing up in poverty (DeWit & Hartup, 1974; Parke & Slaby, 1983). Some controversy exists about the course of the development of aggression. There is opinion that no known *configuration* of experiences, or of personality traits, accurately predicts those children who will be the most prone to aggression in adulthood. Others believe that aggression is a stable personality trait, and that a program for its control must address such specifics as "television programming, gender role expectations, and child rearing practices" (Eron & Huesmann, 1984, p. 140).

The study of human aggression is supplemented by work on animals, both in the laboratory and in natural habitats (Scott, 1975; Washburn & Hamburg, 1968). These efforts bring to light several variables that modify the intensity of aggression, such as the level of male hormones, crowding, and even the temperature. The animal data also indicate that aggression in free-roaming animals may, in some instances at least, be beneficial. For example, the warding off of intruders disperses the population and thus protects the food supply. Fighting may also leave the strongest and the healthiest to reproduce.

In contrast, recent research on human aggression is colored by a sense of misfortune and of futility. Numerous factors can be blamed for this, but contemporary television programming is probably the most frequently indicted contributor, even though brutality has been a part of children's literature for a long time. It has existed from the classic fairy tales through the popular comic strips to modern animated cartoons, but surveys indicate that twentieth-century children may now spend more time watching a video screen than they do pursuing any other activity.

Measuring the possible (mal)effects of this is difficult. In the first place, ascertaining the exact amount of influential contact is elusive because what is on the screen and what the viewer perceives are not identical. There is a substantial amount of evidence that watching current programs increases both the spectator's own aggression and the tolerance for assaultiveness in others, but difficulties are encountered when efforts are made to measure exactly how long the postviewing effects last, how much of the video content carries over into behavior in other situations, how often it is imitated or how often it emerges in aggressive action that is different from what was seen, and how much aggression is weakened because of the vicarious experience of witnessing violence. No satisfactory way has been found to distinguish between children who are the most reactive and those who see telecasts as encapsulated and quite disparate from everyday affairs. At this point in time the belief that consequences of television are unfortunate seems to be stronger than the actual information supporting this conclusion (Byrne & Kelley, 1981).

The fact that aggression and a more intense form of it, violence, are telecast points to at least a tolerance, if not a sanction, of aggression. A moment's reflection indicates that this acceptance is not confined to the media, but that it is institutionalized in other segments of society. It is a conspicuous component of recreation. In the modern world, hunting is more often a sport than a necessity. Boxing, wrestling, and bullfighting attract large audiences. There is an unwillingness to restrict the distribution of firearms or to adopt measures that will assure safe driving. Violence is even disguised as obedience. Those who are ordered to maintain law and order are authorized to behave aggressively, and war may be glorified (Feshbach, 1971; Rule & Nesdale, 1976). To date, psychology has not formulated a persuasive explanation for this approbation, and the deficit serves as a reminder that the concept of aggression is in itself only partially comprehended.

References

Berkowitz, L. (1962). *Aggression: A social psychological analysis*. New York: McGraw-Hill. Berkowitz covers the history of the concept, and organizes and interprets the experimental literature up to the date of publication.

Buss, A. H. (1961). *The psychology of aggression*. New York: John Wiley. Buss' original intention was to review all of the research, but this turned out to be too voluminous for one book. He manages, however, to present a great deal of information about the topic, including materials that are not readily accessible in print, such as doctoral dissertations and papers read at professional meetings.

Byrne, D., & Kelley, K. (1981). *An introduction to personality* (3rd ed.). Englewood Cliffs, NJ: Prentice-Hall. In this textbook there is a review of the literature on "Exposure to Violence and Aggression: TV and the Movies" (pp. 393–399).

DeWit, J., & Hartup, W. W. (Eds.). (1974). *Determinants and origins of aggressive behavior*. The Hague: Mouton. This is a collection of papers read at a 1973 conference held in Monte Carlo, sponsored by the Scientific Affairs Division of the North Atlantic Treaty Organization. About one hundred representatives of various disciplines attended. The forty-four articles constitute the different papers that were read. The forty-fifth article reviews the status of the information.

Dollard, J., Doob, L. W., Miller, N. E., Mowrer, O. H., & Sears, R. R. (1939). *Frustration and aggression*. New Haven, CT: Yale University Press. This book is a classic. It illustrates the problems encountered in formulating comprehensive, logic-tight theories about the diffuse and elusive concepts of frustration and aggression.

Eron, L. D., & Huesmann, L. R. (1984). The control of aggressive behavior by changes in attitudes, values, and the conditions of learning. In R. J. Blanchard & D. C. Blanchard (Eds.), *Advances in the study of aggression* (Vol. 1, pp. 139–171). Orlando, FL: Academic Press.

Feshbach, S. (1964). The function of aggression and the regulation of aggressive drive. *Psychological Review, 71*, 257–272.

Feshbach, S. (1971). Dynamics and morality of violence and aggression: Some psychological considerations. *American Psychologist, 26*, 281–292. Feshbach discusses the variables that reduce the condemnation of violence.

Freud, S. (1938). *A general introduction to psychoanalysis* (rev. ed.; J. Riviere, Trans.). New York: Garden City. Original work published 1920.

Kaufmann, H. (1965). Definitions and methodology in the study of aggression. *Psychological Bulletin, 64*, 351–364. Kaufmann's account of the difficulties of arriving at a definition of aggression clarifies several issues.

McDougall, W. (1912). *An introduction to social psychology* (6th ed.). Boston: John W. Luce. The first edition was published in 1908.

Miller, N. E. (1941). The frustration-aggression hypothesis. *Psychological Review, 48*, 337–342.

Parke, R. D., & Slaby, R. G. (1983). The development of aggression. In P. H. Mussen (Ed.), *Handbook of child psychology* (Vol. 4, pp. 547–641, 4th ed.). New York:

John Wiley. The authors survey the literature on aggression in childhood and offer an informative perspective on the current state of the knowledge. The coverage of the effects of television violence is comprehensive and commendably objective.

Rule, B. G., & Nesdale, A. R. (1976). Moral judgment of aggressive behavior. In R. G. Geen & E. C. O'Neal (Eds.), *Perspectives on aggression* (pp. 37–60). New York: Academic Press. This is an excellent review of a generally neglected topic. The authors conclude that the criticism of aggression is reduced when the aggressor's goal is corrective rather than punitive, when good intentions are inferred, when the consequences are minor, when the characteristics of the victim are negative, and when the provocation is social rather than personal.

Scott, J. P. (1975). *Aggression* (2nd ed.). Chicago: University of Chicago Press. The first edition, published in 1958, was widely accepted. Scott's goal is to learn about aggression in humans, but he includes animal research that is relevant to the problem.

Washburn, S. L., & Hamburg, D. A. (1968). Aggressive behavior in Old World monkeys and apes. In P. C. Jay (Ed.), *Primates: Studies in adaptation and variability* (pp. 458–478). New York: Holt, Rinehart, & Winston. The authors emphasize the benefits of aggression. "In summary, in Old World monkeys and apes aggression is an essential adaptive mechanism" (p. 478).

Sources of Additional Information

Johnson, R. N. (1972). *Aggression in man and animals*. Philadelphia: W. B. Saunders. This review of the literature is often cited because of its thoroughness. Kaufmann, H. (1970). *Aggression and altruism: A psychological analysis*. New York: Holt, Rinehart, & Winston. Kaufmann deals with the psychology of both aggression and altruism, including ways to reduce the former and increase the latter. "It is unrealistic, cowardly, and in all probability, incorrect to assign our present desperate dilemmas to 'human nature.' We do not know what human nature is" (p. 142). Milgram, S. (1974). *Obedience to authority: An experimental view*. New York: Harper & Row. Milgram ascertained the maximum amount of electric shock that subjects, following orders, will administer to a victim. The volume reviews this research, discusses allied topics, and provides a skeletal but accurate history of research on obedience. Milgram states: "The essence of obedience consists in the fact that a person comes to view himself as the instrument for carrying out another person's wishes, and he therefore no longer regards himself as responsible for his actions" (p. xii). Samuel, W. (1981). *Personality: Searching for the sources of human behavior*. New York: McGraw-Hill. Chapter 12 of this textbook, "Causes of aggression and antisocial behavior," is an easy to read, yet comprehensive review of various explanations of aggression. Ulrich, R. E., Hutchinson, R. R., & Azrin, N. H. (1965). Pain-elicited aggression. *The Psychological Record, 15*, 111–126. The authors construct a strong argument and present evidence that punishment may provoke aggression rather than compliance.

ANDROGYNY.   See MASCULINITY, FEMININITY, and ANDROGYNY.

ANGER.   1. A transitory emotional reaction that is subjectively compelling, often unpleasant, and varying in intensity from mild to distressingly strong.

Anger consists of two components: disquieting subjective feelings and an awareness of physiological reactions that is characteristic of all EMOTION. The muscular reactions that accompany anger are more apt to be inhibited or symbolic than assaultive, but they range from merely a clenched fist through temper tantrums (McKellar, 1949).

Anger, in and of itself, is of brief duration, but it often precedes a series of different responses, and because these resemble one another there is confusion in terminology. The following distinctions are offered as a means of minimizing this disorder. HOSTILITY is more extended in time than anger, and it is the appropriate term when the antagonism involves oblique or disguised retaliation. AGGRESSION is the preferred word when describing direct, open attacks, both verbal and physical. Assertiveness, a term that has recently increased in popularity, also designates confrontation, but the purpose of assertiveness is to assure a recognition of one's rights and it lacks the destructive ingredient that is typical of aggression and hostility (Alberti, 1977). FRUSTRATION connotes thwarting that is experienced when activity that is considered to be important is interrupted. To summarize the differences—anger is a short-lived, spurt-like response, whereas hostility, aggression, frustration, and assertiveness are more enduring. In hostility and frustration implicit attitudes are salient, but in aggression and assertion explicit behavior is often dominant.

Psychologists began work on anger just before the turn of the century, and during the first three decades most of the effort centered around ascertaining such details of the response as its provocation, amenability to control, and/or inhibition. This pattern is readily apparent in one of the pioneer studies, an 1899 investigation by G. Stanley Hall, one of the first psychologists to be interested in children and adolescence. Because of the problems involved in experimentally arousing anger in the laboratory Hall preferred to use a questionnaire, and the one he devised inquired about numerous aspects of anger. He assembled more than 2,000 replies, apparently from both children and adults, and reported on the variations in the physical expression of anger, such as tension, clenched fists, crying, scratching, and kicking. He also listed specific irritants, some of which are quite dated: "Thumb rings . . . bangs . . . short hair in women . . . flashy ties, heavy watch chains" (p. 543). Hall's recommendations for the control of anger included the simultaneous application of various strategies, emphasizing particularly the fending off of the reaction by diverting attention to other topics, reflecting on moral and ethical matters, or even reciting some biblical text. He also advised relaxation because "if one can assume even approximately the muscular expressions of the opposite state, anger cannot long persist" (p. 574).

The last recommendation predicts modern advice with such fidelity that it licenses interrupting the chronology in order to look briefly at present-day prescriptions. Psychologists seldom advised relaxation until the early 1960s, when they began to explore the feasibility of using it as a means of controlling affect. The procedures that have been designed vary somewhat, but typically they include having the subject identify specific stimuli that lead to a buildup of affect and then learning to interrupt that sequence by responding in ways that are antagonistic to emotion. In resonance with Hall's 1899 statement, Warren and McLellarn commented in 1982 that "relaxation can serve as an incompatible response to anger" (p. 1095).

To return to the early days of the study of anger—in 1918 Richardson requested a group of young men to record their outbursts of anger in diaries. He analyzed these records and wrote a qualitative account of various kinds of subjective experiences, of the nature of events that triggered the episodes of anger, of the speed with which the emotion developed, its rate of disappearance as well as some of the fantasy that accompanies the outbursts.

Gates, in 1926, also summarized descriptions of anger recorded, in this instance, by a group of undergraduate women. These entries agree with those of Richardson in indicating that an important provocation of anger, particularly when the feeling is intense, is a sense of being imposed upon, especially when there is a blocking of self-assertiveness. Gates reported that anger is provoked much more frequently by people than by objects. A tabulation of the frequency and duration of the incidents indicated that episodes of anger are brief.

Goodenough (1931/1975) collected and synthesized mothers' descriptions of displays of anger by their children ranging in age from less than one through seven years of age. The volume is a combination of quantified, tabular data and qualitative accounts of everyday events. Goodenough observed, for example, that children whose parents grant their wishes in order to induce them to stop an outburst are the children who have the largest number of tantrums. As a psychologist of her era, Goodenough had no satisfactory explanation for this, but modern OPERANT CONDITIONING would, without hesitation, attribute the increased frequency to the fact that the tantrums are rewarded, or, in technical terms, to the REINFORCEMENT.

These descriptive studies were supplemented by similar ones, and the concept of anger remained essentially that of a fleeting, disorganizing reaction that precedes a diversity of activities, but little attention was paid to these sequels. This shortcircuiting is paradoxical, since people know from their own experience that anger leads to other actions. The reasons for the psychologists' failure to develop these behavioral sequences are complex, but they hinge on the authority of a theory that was rarely questioned until the recent past. This asserts that any MOTIVE or activator other than a biological one must be learned. FEAR was demonstrated experimentally to be a learned DRIVE but with rare exceptions, such as Dollard and Miller's *Personality and Psychotherapy* (1950), the role of anger in instigating behavior has been slighted. As late as 1970, Feshbach, who apparently accepts the validity of the theory, commented on the researcher's neglect: "The mechanism by which anger acquires aggressive drive properties, in the sense of performance of the act in order to bring about injurious consequences, is an intriguing developmental problem about which we have few empirical data" (p. 162).

Even though the consequences of anger are not often singled out for independent observation, research on behavioral sequences that include anger is conducted, and these topics include AGGRESSION, antisocial behavior, conflict, FRUSTRATION, HOSTILITY, and prejudice. Each of these produced such a large amount of research that extracting the information about anger per se has become a prodigious, maybe impossible, task. It is feasible, however, to illustrate two levels of appreciation of the concept. In one, anger is actually more influential than is generally recognized, and in the second, its role is quite readily apparent, although in some instances not fully appreciated.

A study by Hoffman (1970) represents an area in which the role of anger has been shown to exceed the general perception of its importance. In this experiment Hoffman compared two groups of parents: one whose children are said to have a "flexible" conscience because they weigh the circumstances or reasons when judging the seriousness of antisocial behavior, and a second group whose children are labeled "conventional" because their judgments are rigid, in that they are primarily based on legality. "Conventional" children, for example, consider the stealing of cash (breaking a law) to be more reprehensible than lying to a benefactor (breaking a trust), whereas flexible children arrived at the opposite conclusion.

Various differences between the two groups of parents were uncovered, with one of the more critical ones involving anger. The mothers and fathers of children with a legalistic bias are prone, when reacting to an angry child, to suspend the expression of affection. Families whose offspring take circumstances into account are more likely, when a child's irritation is directed toward them, to focus on the circumstances that precede the episode rather than on the expression of emotion. A consideration of these and other differences led Hoffman to conclude that the parents of the "flexible" subjects convey an idea that animosity can be understood and need not permanently impair a relationship. In quite a different vein the parents of "rigid" offspring allow expression of anger to be followed by a diminution of love. Hoffman proposes that this prompts children to try to inhibit the reaction rather than to deal with it, and thus rules become more important than understanding circumstances.

Biopathology is one of the numerous contexts in which anger plays a role. An influence on health has long been suspected by experimenters (Stratton, 1929), and as the evidence of a correlation between anger and biopathology accumulated, a specialty known as psychosomatic medicine came into existence. Much of the vast amount of work on this topic is concerned with isolating the kinds of psychological and biopathological reactions that covary, and much is also concerned with trying to establish mechanisms that connect them. The information obtained in the first variety of inquiry is more authoritative than that coming from the second, with the data indicating that emotions such as aggression, anger, and hostility are contributors to some disorders and absent, or as yet undiscovered, in others. Adding to the complexity is increasing evidence that inhibiting affect may be as unhealthy as indulging in it. Diamond (1982) reviewed the literature on anger in hypertension and heart disease, and concludes: "The literature . . . supports the view that at least a subset of hypertensives are . . . conflicted about anger expression" (p. 428).

The probability that the effects of aborted responses are important points to an intricacy of the subject matter that may not as yet have been fully comprehended. In other words, available experimental sophistication about the topic may be merely a "tip of the iceberg" and the present formulation of the concept of anger, a mere prelude.

References

Alberti, R. E. (1977). Assertive behavior training: Definitions, overview, contributions. In R. E. Alberti (Ed.), *Assertiveness: Inovations, applications, issues* (pp. 19–32). San Luis Obispo, CA: Impact Publishers. A multiauthored volume that documents the confidence in and lack of restraint about assertiveness training.

Diamond, E. L. (1982). The role of anger and hostility in essential hypertension and coronary heart disease. *Psychological Bulletin, 92,* 410–433. This is a review of the literature from the 1930s to the present, with the concentration on recent work.

Dollard, J., & Miller, N. E. (1950). *Personality and psychotherapy: An analysis in terms of learning, thinking, and culture.* New York: McGraw-Hill. This book illustrates the struggles of the era to align anger and theory. The theorists believed that anger is a learned drive, and they labored to establish that point.

Feshbach, S. (1970). Agression. In P. H. Musen (Ed.), *Carmichael's manual of child psychology.* Vol. 11, pp. 159–260; 3rd ed. New York: John Wiley.

Gates, G. S. (1926). An observational study of anger. *Journal of Experimental Psychology, 9,* 325–336.

Goodenough, F. L. (1975). *Anger in young children.* Westport, CT: Greenwood Press. (Original work published 1931). Although this is a formal, scientific account, the author's style is readily intelligible. Her discussion of intrafamilial conflicts is penetrating. The bibliography of technical literature is supplemented by references to important philosophical discussions of the topic. The references are annotated.

Hall, G. S. (1899). A study of anger. *American Journal of Psychology, 10,* 516–591.

Hoffman, M. L. (1970). Moral development. In P. H. Mussen (Ed.), *Carmichael's manual of child psychology.* Vol. 2, pp. 261–360; 3rd ed. New York: John Wiley. Hoffman is a productive and active contributor to the research on the influence of various aspects of parental behavior on moral development.

McKellar, P. (1949). The emotion of anger in the expressionof human aggressiveness. *British Journal of Psychology, 39,* 148–155.

Richardson, R. F. (1918). *The psychology and pedagogy of anger* [Educational Psychology Monographs, *19*] Baltimore: Warwick & York.

Stratton, G. M. (1929). Emotion and the incidence of disease: The influence of the number of diseases, and of the age at which they occur. *Psychological Review, 36,* 242–253. The author compares medical histories with self-reports of fear and anger, and concludes that having been ill, particularly in childhood, and having suffered from a variety of diseases leads to reports of more intense emotional responses. This paper represents an early approach to psychosomatic medicine.

Warren, R., & McLellarn, R. W. (1982). Systematic desensitization as a treatment for maladaptive anger and aggression: A review. *Psychological Reports, 150,* 1095–

1102. Desensitization is a procedure that demands that subjects rank emotion-inducing stimuli in order from the highest to the least disturbing. They are then trained to relax and to imagine the anger excitants, progressively, from the least to the most upsetting, without lessening the relaxation. The authors conclude that desensitization should be augmented by an alertness to the stimuli that instigate anger and by learning other ways of handling problems.

Sources of Additional Information

Anastasi, A., Cohen, N., & Spatz, D. (1948). A study of fear and anger in college students through the controlled diary method. *Journal of Genetic Psychology, 73*, 243–249. The title conveys the core of the research. The results are in essential agreement with similar studies, but the authors make the interesting observation that fear is often triggered by anticipated situations and anger by present ones. Gesell, A. L. (1906). Jealousy. *American Journal of Psychology, 17*, 437–496. This is a review of the concept at the date of publications, and is interesting—even though possibly at the same time a bit boring—because it discloses the matter-of-fact, readily discernible responses that psychologists of the era tended to accept at face value. Gesell concludes that jealousy typically includes anger, grief, and self-pity. Margolin, G. (1979). Conjoint marital therapy to enhance anger management and reduce spouse abuse. *American Journal of Family Therapy, 7*, 13–23. The author's goal is to teach antagonists to learn how to avoid and deal with anger so that unfortunate physical and psychological damage is avoided. O'Donnell, C. R., & Worell, L. (1973). Motor and cognitive relaxation in the desensitization of anger. *Behaviour Research and Therapy, 11*, 473–481. Although the authors identify their topic as anger, prejudice might be more correct. "Anger" in white males was aroused by exposing them to "black racial stimuli." The effectiveness of desensitization was measured in several ways, including changes in anxiety, disgust, and ethnocentrism. A reminder to the reader to *search* out the concept of interest without being misled by the vocabulary.

ANXIETY. 1. An emotion or feeling that is dominated by apprehension even though neither the cause nor the nature of the danger is known. 2. A synonym for fear.

The experiences of anxiety and of fear are sometimes defined as equivalent although they have different causes and their similarity consists of merely a feeling of apprehension and an awareness of those physiological reactions that are part of EMOTION. The instigators of fear are generally clearly recognized, and their effects are predictable. But an anxious individual does not know what the danger is or how to deal with it. In fact, vagueness is such an integral part of the experience that reactions in which the individual *does* recognize the cause are singled out and labeled separately as "manifest anxiety" (Lewis, 1980; Moore & Fine, 1968). The anxious person's uncertainty about the danger is complemented by a certainty that it will materialize and that it is inescapable. A frightened person knows what is threatening, and hence knows where to look for protection. An anxious person, lacking information about the nature of the menace but convinced that it is unavoidable, may not even attempt to deflect the cause, but may search for ways of minimizing or avoiding the anxiety per se.

Guilt is another reaction that is sometimes confused with anxiety. Both may include regret about having violated a moral or ethical principle, but the two responses are otherwise different. Guilt focuses on personal initiative, and anxiety on imminent danger. Anxiety is also sometimes, but again should not be, confused with depression, an experience that is dominated by dejection, sorrow, and debilitation. These reactions may be concurrent, but feeling unhappy or depressed is not the same as feeling frightened or apprehensive.

Anxiety is reputed to be so pervasive in contemporary culture that the modern era is sometimes called "the age of anxiety." It is not, however, a recent phenomenon, and there is opinion that the human has always experienced anxiety (McReynolds, 1975). Both philosophers and literary people have addressed the topic, and systematic accounts of the psychology of anxiety first appeared in discussions of psychopathology. Freud (1894/1953) described a condition that he called "neurotic anxiety," and he postulated several features that remain in the modern concept. One of these asserts that anxiety results from repression, that is, from the exclusion from consciousness of impulses that violate the social or ethical code. Originally these impulses were identified only as erotic or sexual, but later he added aggressive and destructive ones. The displacement of these impulses from awareness does not devitalize them, but it does render them both inescapable because they remain within the person and unrecognizable because they are unconscious. Psychoanalysis proposes that these impulses provoke anxiety. In this framework the individual is anxious about the self, about what he or she would like to do.

Freud depicted a second condition that he called "chronic anxiety" and that he described as "free floating" because it is triggered by a multitude of different stimuli. He also defined an "anxiety attack." This is an episode of acute distress that is usually sudden in onset, variable in severity, but frequently acutely oppressive, and generally self-terminating. During an attack the person may focus on somatic components ("heart spasms," "trembling knees"), on subjective reactions of dread ("I can't stand the fear, it hurts too much"), or on impulses ("I can't do anything but run, run fast, there is no choice"; "I'm scared I'm going to hurt someone").

Interest in anxiety spread beyond the domain of psychoanalysis into the fields of psychiatry and clinical psychology and then into studies of the normal personality. Enough anxiety was discovered in normals to remove any idea that it is uniquely a pathological phenomenon, and this pervasiveness prompted psychologists to ask why foreboding about the unknown is so common. They attempted to answer this by seeking explanations in a framework of individual differences in experiences instead of in the more traditional psychiatric framework of conjectured psychic forces. It is not possible to review all these efforts, but one interpretation is outlined in order to illustrate a behavioral explanation of the origin of anxiety.

Cameron and Magaret (1951) assert that certain child-rearing practices are important sources but certainly not the only generators of anxiety. Among the parental practices that they indict is the combination of threatening children while making demands that they will not or cannot meet. A youngster is told, for instance, that one's hands must always be washed before eating and that failures to comply will result in the contracting of disease. But the child does eat with unwashed hands and the illness that has been forecast, and which the child apprehensively expects, fails to develop, and so the child continues to associate dread with some impending misfortune. In this sense, he or she practices being anxious. Another parental custom that nourishes anxiety is that of putting off-spring through inquisitions in a manner that assumes guilt, a kind of interrogation that trains the child to look for negatives within the self.

Even though psychology's concern with theory is vigorous, it takes second place to the addiction of the discipline to test construction and administration. The concept of anxiety did not escape this treatment, but the original measurements did not come from an expected source, such as research on PERSONALITY, but came enexpectedly from a search for variables that facilitate CLASSICAL CONDITIONING. Welch and Kubis (1947) became interested in the truth of an observation by the pioneer experimenter Pavlov, that active, excitable dogs form conditioned responses more readily than do passive, quiet ones. They reasoned that since anxiety is an excitant, it might facilitate learning. In order to check the accuracy of this belief, they compared the rate and stability of conditioning in a group of normal adults and a group of anxious patients. As predicted, the latter did learn more rapidly and their conditioned responses were the most stable.

These empirical demonstrations provoked a need for a method of selecting people with varying levels of anxiety to participate in learning experiments. In order to do this, Taylor (1951) asked clinicians to identify individual items on a pencil-and-paper test of personality that they believed measured anxiety. These items were combined into a single scale, and this was quickly adopted for a number of purposes in addition to research on learning (Taylor, 1953). Some researchers were content to use Taylor's items, but others compiled different ones, and they began, and are still continuing, to measure the effects of anxiety in this way on a wide variety of responses, including decision making, intelligence, learning, memory, problem solving, perception, and vigilance. Diverse individuals are examined: the old, the young; the normal, the neurotic, the psychotic; the introvert, the extrovert; the dominant, the submissive; the bright, the dull; the obedient, the rebel. Investigations are made of anxiety-inducing events, and the most common of these is probably academic examinations, but there are also studies of anxiety aroused by physical illness, separation, stress, and various other kinds of discomfort.

By 1969 the research productivity had reached such a level that Adelson reported that "anxiety was the most popular single topic in personality this year" (p. 231). He also dubbed the study of its effects on performance as "a hardy perennial" (p. 234). There still appears to be no marked decline of interest in the topic. Sims, Dana, and Bolton (1983) note, for example, in relation to research on drawing, that the original Taylor scale continues to be the most popular test used to determine the level of anxiety.

A questionnaire about anxiety can be administered to groups, and since it is scored both quickly and mechanically it does not demand clinical sophistication of the experimenters (Greene, 1952). Some researchers assume that a score on a test of a manifest anxiety is a valid measure, but critics of these self-reports are less satisfied. They comment that these tests assess only what is consciously experienced and what the individual is willing to report. Among the more crucial variables that are neglected are the experiential antecedents that are inherent in anxiety (Sarason, 1950). These omissions are exemplified by a brief description of people who sense a great deal of trepidation at the prospect of having to take a classroom test. The traditional concept of anxiety postulates that these are people whose parents assessed them in an unduly harsh manner during childhood and that even years later the thoughts of taking an examination arouse this earlier foreboding which in turn incites retaliative impulses. In this framework the anxiety is due to the reactivation of the past, and not to the forthcoming examination.

Many simply disregard these residuals and deal only with immediate provocation. As a result much of the research on the subject that is called anxiety is, strictly speaking, research on FEAR, an assessment of merely known, and disclosed, variables. Large portions of the concept seem to many to have been sacrificed.

References

Adelson, J. (1969). Personality. In P. H. Mussen & M. R. Rosenzweig (Eds.), *Annual Review of Psychology*, *20*, 217–252.

Cameron, N., & Magaret, A. (1951). *Behavior pathology*. Boston: Houghton Mifflin. A revision of Cameron's 1947 text, one of the earliest texts in psychopathology to stress the crucial role of culture and personal experience in determining aberrations in psychological behavior. It acknowledges the influences of biology, but it insists on the importance of other variables.

Freud, S. (1953). The justification for detaching from neurasthenia a particular syndrome: The anxiety-neurosis (1894). In *Sigmund Freud: Collected papers* (Vol. 1, 7th impression, pp. 76–106). E. Jones (Ed.). (J. Rickman, Trans., 1895). London: Hogarth. (Originally published 1924). The date immediately following the title of the article is apparently the year of authorship and 1895, the year of publication.

Greene, E. B. (1952). *Measurements of human behavior* (rev. ed.). New York: Odyssey Press. An account of the psychological tests of the era. The presentation is both accurate and critical.

Lewis, A. (1980). Problems presented by the ambiguous word "anxiety" as used in psychopathology. In G. D. Burrows & B. Davies (Eds.), *Handbook of studies on anxiety* (pp. 1–16). Amsterdam: Elsevier/North-Holland Biomedical Press.

McReynolds, P. (1975). Changing conceptions of anxiety: A historical review and a proposed integration. In I. G. Sarason & C. D. Spielberger (Eds.), *Stress and anxiety* (Vol. 2, pp. 1–26). New York: John Wiley. The concept of anxiety from the earliest philosophers to the present is reviewed. The emphasis is on the pre-scientific era.

Moore, B. E., & Fine, B. D. (Eds.). (1968). *A glossary of psychoanalytic terms and concepts* (2nd ed.). New York: American Psychoanalytic Association. (Third printing 1975). This glossary is the work of many contributors, and it is written for the general public.

Sarason, S. B. (1950). The test-situation and the problem of prediction. *Journal of Clinical Psychology, 6*, 387–392.

Sims, J., Dana, R. H., & Bolton, B. (1983). The validity of the Draw-A-Person Test as an anxiety measure. *Journal of Personality Assessment, 47*, 250–257.

Taylor, J. A. (1951). The relationship of anxiety to the conditioned eyelid response. *Journal of Experimental Psychology, 41*, 81–92. This article is based on the author's doctoral dissertation. At the time it was completed there were no indications that the methods she used to identify subjects would set off such a large amount of research on anxiety.

Taylor, J. A. (1953). A personality scale of manifest anxiety. *Journal of Abnormal and Social Psychology, 48*, 285–290.

Welch, L., & Kubis, J. (1947). The effect of anxiety on the conditioning rate and stability of the PGR. *Journal of Psychology, 23*, 83–91.

Sources of Additional Information

Alpert, R., & Haber, R. N. (1960). Anxiety in academic achievement situations. *Journal of Abnormal and Social Psychology, 61*, 207–215. This experiment compares different pencil-and-paper tests of anxiety—a good illustration of the unduly heavy traffic in this topic. Dustin, D. S. (1969). *How psychologists do research: The example of anxiety.* Englewood Cliffs, NJ: Prentice-Hall. The main purpose of this brief volume is to illustrate research procedures, but the choice of anxiety as the example results in portrayal of the concept. Hamilton, V. (1975). Socialization anxiety and information processing: A capacity model of anxiety-induced performance deficits. In I. G. Sarason & C. D. Spielberger (Eds.), *Stress and anxiety* (Vol. 2, pp. 45–68). New York: Wiley. Hamilton casts anxiety as analogous to information processing: "The greater the impairment of potential processing capacity and the greater the intrusion of task-irrelevant information, the smaller will be the capacity of the information-processing system to cope with increases in externally presented information" (p. 61). Korchin, S. J. (1964). Anxiety and cognition. In C. Scheerer (Ed.), *Cognition: Theory, research, promise* (pp. 58–78). New York: Harper & Row. The author identifies how some aspects of anxiety increase cognitive skills and others decrease them. Mandler, G., & Sarason, S. B. (1952). A study of anxiety and learning. *Journal of Abnormal and Social Psychology, 47*, 166–173. The purpose of this experiment was to assess the effects of anxiety on intelligence test scores. The authors were unable to arrive at a definitive answer because anxiety appears under certain conditions to increase scores and under others to decrease them.

ASPIRATION. See LEVEL OF ASPIRATION.

ATTENTION. 1. A selective awareness of components in a stimulus complex. 2. Sensory and postural responses that facilitate some psychological reactions and attenuate others. 3. A system analogous to electronics that selects information to be processed.

Psychologists devote a great deal of effort, with only limited linguistic restraint, to considerations of how people, surrounded by a myriad of stimuli,
come to react only to particular ones. For example, individuals become absorbed
with a painting in a museum and ignore the ceiling, floor, and lighting of the
room in which it is hung, and while looking at the picture they are drawn more
to some parts than to others. Because this kind of differentiated reactivity is
universal, it has attracted a great deal of discourse, and various terms are used
either as equivalent to or as a particular variety of attention. These names include
concentration, CONSCIOUSNESS, CURIOSITY, EXPLORATION, PERCEPTION, SET,
VIGILANCE, and even RESPONSE. Following is a sample of statements that documents the profusion: "The study of attention is essentially the study of selectivity
in perception and cognition and of variations in overall responsiveness to stimulation" (Wachtel, 1967, p. 417); "Attention can be defined as the selective
aspect of perception and response" (Treisman, 1969, p. 283); "We would assert
that those behaviors labeled 'exploration,' 'curiosity,' etc., belong to the general
class of behavior, *attention*" (Dember & Earl, 1957, p. 91); "The old notion
of attention or set" (Lazarus & McCleary, 1951, p. 114); "Attention and consciousness are almost synonyms, and selection is the fundamental principle of
both" (Boring, 1933, pp. 231–232); "The question of diffused versus concentrated attention" (Paschal, 1941, p. 387); "Vigilance research concerns the
attentiveness of the subject" (Frankmann & Adams, 1962, p. 257).

In 1955 Deese expressed pessimism about restricting this diffusion: "These
words—attention, vigilance, and set—by no means refer to the same things, but
they have common origins in a class of psychological problems, and it is a
fruitless and arbitrary task to attempt to distinguish clearly between them"
(p. 359). Nineteen years later Berlyne joined Deese in deploring the persisting
disarray. After referring to a complaint about linguistic confusion that was made
in 1896, as well as a second one made in 1937, Berlyne observed: "If these
two authors had been writing at the beginning of the 1970's, they would have
found even more grounds for their doleful observations. The difficulties are
compounded by the fact that contemporary writers on attention, like the work
gang of the original Tower of Babel, often fail to realize that they are speaking
different languages" (1974, p. 123).

Attention was a central topic in early scientific psychology. As early as 1890
William James, one of the trailblazers of modern psychology, expressed the
opinion that attention is too well known to require a definition but then proceeded
to formulate one in which attention is depicted as dynamic and includes still
persisting but nonetheless erroneous belief that an appropriate application of
attention can underwrite success: "Every one knows what attention is. It is the
taking possession by the mind, in clear and vivid form, of one out of what seem
several simultaneously possible objects or trains of thought. Focalization, concentration of consciousness are of its essence. It implies withdrawal from some
things in order to deal effectively with others" (pp. 403–404).

Titchener tried to integrate the concept into the theory of STRUCTURAL PSY-CHOLOGY, and in contrast to James' formulation, he characterized attention as an attribute of sensation, one of the basic elements of the mind. Titchener was adamant that the task of psychology is to discover the elements that constitute the mind, and he endeavored to procure this information by the method of INTROSPECTION, an esoteric technique for observing the details of consciousness. He first identified attention as clearness, and in an attempt to convey just what he meant he invoked the word vividness and finally "attensity," that is, a power to compel attention that is analogous to intensity. These attempts to elucidate were not successful, and the introspective results pointed to variations in the clarity of sensations. Titchener's emphasis on the basic structure of the mind did not allow a satisfactory treatment of the selective property of attention, and the importance of this particular formulation soon lost ground (Boring, 1970).

This defeat of theory was followed by a reduction of interest in the broad topic of attention in favor of continuing with some prior investigations of specific aspects of the concept, particularly those that feature momentary rather than sustained attention. One of these is the range, or what later was called the span, of attention. About the middle of the nineteenth century philosophers became curious as to whether the mind can grasp more than one object at a time, and in order to determine this they threw small objects onto a flat surface and reported the number immediately comprehended. This technique is intrinsically flawed because it does not prevent more than one sighting. The difficulty was not overcome until the invention of the tachistoscope, an instrument that exposes stimuli so briefly that only one glance is possible. Laboratory use of this apparatus indicated that the number of stimuli that can be attended varies from trial to trial within each individual, among different individuals, and with such contextual factors as the nature of the stimuli and their dispersion in the visual field (Pillsbury, 1908).

Introspective data disclosed disagreement between the number of stimuli that are sensed as clear and the number that are sensed with agreement emerging when attensity is ignored (Glanville & Dallenbach, 1929). Dallenbach, as early as 1920, proposed acknowledging the discrepancy by reserving the word attention for the number of clearly appreciated stimuli and the word apprehension for the total number that is sensed. The reactions to this proposal are paradoxical in that the label range, or span, of apprehension came into use, but many interpret it as the range, or span, of attention and ignore the reasons for the change in name.

The chronology of the study of fluctuations in attention parallels the chronology of the study of the span of apprehension to the extent that each topic was investigated before psychology became a formal laboratory discipline, and each evolved into a classic topic within the field. In 1875 a specialist in diseases of the ear discovered that, in the absence of any changes in the physical environment, the barely audible ticking of a watch is experienced as waxing and waning. This led to the discovery of analogous oscillations in reactions to weak visual and tactile stimuli. The phrase "fluctuation of attention" was applied to these involuntary variations, so brief and so lacking in intensity that they are generally not noticed. As in the span of apprehension, the psychological variables combine with contextual ones to prevent specifying any single interval as characteristic of the duration of the fluctuation (Pillsbury, 1908; Woodworth & Schlosberg, 1954).

At one time there was considerable interest in the human's ability "to do two things at once." The situation arises when there is an unintended or unwelcome interruption in attention and when there is a conscious effort to deal with more than one task. The experimentation, as in the case of studies of the span of apprehension and fluctuations of attention, started early, in this instance in 1887, when a French scholar found that it is possible to recite one familiar poem while writing a second. Modern research designs follow the general pattern of eliminating introspective accounts, and they rely on changes in performance to indicate changes in attention. The distractors are experimenter-induced, and the effects of intrusions of personal thought and wishes are rarely taken into account.

Requesting subjects to pursue more than one task at a time typically results in a loss of efficiency in both tasks, and similar decrements are also found when the experimental procedure relies on materials that have built-in distractors. An example of this kind of interference is found in the word and color stimuli material designed in 1935 by Stroop and still in use (Tzeng & Wang, 1983). Subjects are presented with words and color that are incongruous. The names of colors, for example, are printed in a hue that is different from the script (the word red is in blue ink, the word blue is in green ink, and so on). The discrepancy between the time required to read colored names and the time required to read those that are printed in black provides an index of the amount of interference. Although there have been some very well designed experiments on distraction there has been no satisfactory control of rapid shifts in attention. As a result conclusive evidence that attention is divided among tasks or that it shifts among them is lacking. One favored interpretation holds that attention shifts from one undertaking to another; that is there is probably no simultaneous focusing, but rather diversion from one operation to another.

The investigations of variations in attention were initiated when attention was conceptualized as a mental phenomenon, and its substance was assumed to be based on some undiscovered alignment with the nervous system. When BEHAVIORISM began to dominate the field of psychology, this ethereal formulation was stigmatized in a very conspicuous manner. This led to a decrease in experimentation on the elusive properties of attention (Paschal, 1941). At the same time, however, the concept was strengthened, but this was carried out in an inconspicuous manner. The recognition that sensory and motor adjustments, clearly palpable variables, intensify some reactions and weaken others made it possible to restructure the concept in a way that gives it credence that is by emphasizing the muscular components of the response, by featuring the activity of attending. Dashiell illustrates the conversion: "Consider the military command of 'Attention!' What is aroused . . . is a certain stance, a fixed position of arms and hands, a poise of head, even a certain directing of the eyeballs; and all of this posturing is designed to render the soldier more sensitive to the next commands heard and . . . less sensitive and reactive to other stimuli, whether extra- or intra-organic'' (1937, p. 322).

A substantial interest in the concept developed in the 1950s, when psychologists began to adopt electronic information processing as a model. In this approach the function of the organism is changed from that of a passive recipient of stimulation to that of an active processor, and the selective function of attention made it highly suitable for incorporation into metaphors between machines and psychological mechanisms. The enthusiasm for computer analogies was so strong that terminology moved away from the conventional ways of identifying organismic events in favor of language that is characteristic of engineering. Broadbent, for example, postulates ''a filter at the entrance to the nervous system which will pass some classes of stimuli but not others'' (1958, p. 42). He explains blocking as ''an interruption in the intake of information from one source. . . . In other words, if we think of a filter selecting some of the information reaching the senses; then this filter ceases for a second or so to select task information, and rather selects some other kind of stimulation.'' (1958, p. 133) This orientation toward variables that influence startup more than erraticism keeps the earlier interest in momentary phenomena of attention still in the background.

The reliance on analogies has been supplemented by some remarkable refinements in research equipment. The apparatus that is currently available allows carefully regulated timing as well as simultaneous recording of numerous events. For example, Lewis (1970), in an experiment designed to evaluate Broadbent's filter hypothesis, required subjects to shadow—in more traditional terminology, to repeat—accurately each word in a list delivered to one ear while a different list was being delivered to the other ear. The equipment allows a reliable synchronizing of the two sets of stimuli, automatic recording of the subject's responses, as well as the measuring of verbal reaction time. Research conducted under these advantages has not yet modified in significant ways the previously available behavioral data, but it is filling in some of the subtleties of the responses. In the Lewis experiment, for example, words in the unattended message were not recalled, but those that are semantically similar to attended words were found to interfere with reaction time. In other words, stimulation that is not appreciated may be subtly influential.

Posner's address—when accepting an award for scientific excellence from the American Psychological Association—includes a review of the development of theories of attention, as well as comments about the gains in sophistication. His concluding remarks are similar to a summary of recent gains in the study of SENSATION. In both instances a respectful acknowledgment of the sophistication of the forefathers is supplemented by a comment about contemporary naiveté: ''Our current knowledge and techniques owe much to Wundt, Helmholtz, Pavlov, and others. I have tried to convince you that we now know more because of current developments in the field. . . . Yet I recognize fully how far we really are from a complete theory at any level or from a deeper theory that ties together the different threads that I have tried to describe here'' (1982, p. 178).

References

Berlyne, D. E. (1974). Attention. In E. C. Carterette & M. P. Friedman (Eds.), *Handbook of perception*. Vol. 1. *Historical and Philosophical Roots of Perception* (pp. 123–147). New York: Academic Press.

Boring, E. G. (1933). *The physical dimensions of consciousness*. New York: Century.

Boring, E. G. (1970). Attention: Research and beliefs concerning the conception in scientific psychology before 1930. In D. I. Mostofsky (Ed.), *Attention: Contemporary theory and analysis*. (pp 5–8). New York: Appleton-Century-Crofts. A posthumous publication. Boring, Titchener's devoted student, rarely criticized the master, but the definition of attention did prompt him to comment that Titchener's attempt to make attention an attribute of sensation "must have retarded the development of the experimental psychology of attention through at least three decades (1890–1920, say)'' (p. 6).

Broadbent, D. E. (1958). *Perception and communication*. Oxford: Pergamon Press. An important work on selective listening, a classic in the field of attention.

Dashiell, J. F. (1937). *Fundamentals of general psychology*. Boston: Houghton Mifflin.

Deese, J. (1955). Some problems in the theory of vigilance. *Psychological Review, 62*, 359–368.

Dember, W. N., & Earl, R. W. (1957). Analysis of exploratory, manipulatory, and curiosity behaviors. *Psychological Review, 64*, 91–96.

Frankmann, J. P. & Adams, J. A. (1962). Theories of vigilance. *Psychological Bulletin, 59*, 257–272.

Glanville, A. D. & Dallenbach, K. M. (1929). The range of attention. *American Journal of Psychology, 41*, 207–236. Dallenbach suggested as early as 1920 that the "range" that is measured is that of apprehension rather than attention. The experiments described in this article provide data that strengthen that proposal.

James, W. (1890). *The principles of psychology*. Vol. 1. New York: Henry Holt. "*My experience is what I agree to attend to*" 402.

Lazarus, R. S. & McCleary, R. A. (1951). Autonomic discrimination without awareness: A study of subception. *Psychological Review, 58*, 113–122.

Lewis, J. L. (1970). Semantic processing of unattended messages using dichotic listening. *Journal of Experimental Psychology, 85*, 225–228.

Paschal, F. C. (1941). The trend in theories of attention. *Psychological Review, 48*, 383–403.

Pillsbury, W. B. (1908). *Attention*. London: Swan Sonneschein. One of the first textbooks devoted to this topic. A comprehensive and authoritative treatment.

Posner, M. I. (1982). Cumulative development of attentional theory. *American Psychologist, 37*, 168–179.

Stroop, J. R. (1935). Studies of interference in serial verbal reactions. *Journal of Experimental Psychology, 18*, 643–661. Stroop's main interest was in learning, but the materials he devised provide a research tool that distracts, and thus is useful in research on attention.

Treisman, A. M. (1969). Strategies and models of selective attention. *Psychological Review, 76*, 282–299. An integration of empirical results and theory.

Tzeng, O. J. L., & Wang, W. S. Y. (1983). The first two R's. *American Scientist, 71*, 238–243. There are pictures of the Stroop materials in this article.

Wachtel, P. L. (1967). Conceptions of broad and narrow attention. *Psychological Bulletin, 68*, 417–429.

Woodworth, R. S., & Schlosberg, H. (1954). *Experimental psychology* (rev. ed.). New York: Henry Holt.

Sources of Additional Information

Berlyne, D. E. (1969). The development of the concept of attention in psychology. In C. R. Evans & T. B. Mulholland (Eds.), *Attention in Neurophysiology: An International Conference* (pp. 1–26). New York: Appleton-Century-Crofts. Berlyne's history of the concept includes some of the reasons for the renewed interest in the topic. Duncan, J. (1980). The locus of interference in the perception of simultaneous stimuli. *Psychological Review, 87*, 272–300. An illustration of the contemporary approach to attention, written with such terms as capacity, storage, and communication channels. Kagan, J. (1970). Attention and psychological change in the young child. *Science, 170* (No. 3960), 826–832. An interesting account of studies of attention in young children. MacKay, D. G. (1973). Aspects of the theory of comprehension, memory, and attention. *Quarterly Journal of Experimental Psychology, 25*, 22–40. This article deals with the specific nature of some of the relationships among understanding, recall, and attention.

AUTHORITARIAN PERSONALITY. 1. An individual who perceives selected authorities as infallible, willingly carries out their orders, seeks security by courting their approval, and is subservient to the dictates of tradition.

Outside the field of psychology the terms authoritarian and authoritarianism often refer to value-laden political concepts. Within the field of psychology "authoritarian personality" designates a personality pattern that evolved from research on prejudice (Sanford, 1956). Many authors shorten the label to "authoritarian" or "authoritarianism," but the reference in such instances is to personality rather than to ideology.

The groundwork for the psychological concept was initiated in the 1920s in Germany by personnel at the Frankfurt Institute, and after their emigration to the United States it was continued with the cooperation of American colleagues. At that time the bulk of the work was carried on at the University of California at Berkeley, and it was then clearly focused as research on anti-Semitism with the intention of identifying a specific kind of personality, a potential fascist. The investigators made intensive probes of life histories and also administered various psychological tests. The yield was a personality configuration that was labeled and published as *The Authoritarian Personality* (1950) under the joint authorship of Adorno, Frenkel-Brunswik, Levinson, and Sanford.

The book describes a constellation of interrelated beliefs that authoritarians endorse. Important among these is a conviction that society is arranged in a hierarchy and that wisdom increases with the height of the ladder. There is a certainty about the correctness of authority that leads these people to respond in a submissive fashion to superiors and in aggressive ways to inferiors, attitudes so distinctive that they are singled out as "authoritarian submission" and "authoritarian aggression." The authoritarian personality also relies heavily on tradition. The conventionalism not only resembles DOGMATISM, but also equates the familiar and the norm to yield the corollary: What is different is *wrong*. There is opinion that wild and dangerous events are going on almost everywhere. These perils make it necessary to be alert to the evils of others, but this is a difficult task because authoritarians are obtuse about psychological behavior. As a means of compensation they depend on readily observable objective cues and signals rather than subjective signs. A well-written manual that describes how to operate a machine provides the authoritarian personality with "trustworthy" information, but a poem "signifies nothing."

Drawing extensively from histories of numerous individuals, Adorno et al. (1950) concluded that these convictions generally emerge in a family in which the parents are tradition bound, advocate the virtues of hard work and "self-control," and adhere to clearly delineated, traditional sex roles. They believe that misfortune is probably due either to supernatural intervention or to failure to adhere to the rules. A paramount parental duty is to make sure that one's offspring are conformists, and this is promoted by the ready use of punishment. This is often severe, but the parent is rarely criticized and is described and remembered merely as "strict but fair." There are several maleffects of such familial attitudes, and these include a devitalization of the self as well as a protective concentration on acquiescence with authority. Accommodation to the demands of parents is facilitated by keeping an eye out for explicit directives, and these are most readily discernible in familiar surroundings and in routines. This reliance on the known feeds the notion that any group that varies from one's own is unsound, unpredictable, and deviant.

The Authoritarian Personality was saluted, and it led to a voluminous amount of research. The discovery that there are individuals who are receptive to directives to be punitive, particularly to members of an outgroup, offered a plausible explanation to many of those who were deeply perplexed by the extreme events that had occurred in Nazi Germany. Plaudits for the research are still continuing, and Byrne and Kelley, for example, writing in the current decade (1981), inform undergraduate students that the volume is a "classic."

On the other hand critics were also at work, and in some instances with even more fervor and persuasion than the supporters. Hyman and Sheatsley (1954), for example, spelled out some methodological weaknesses, but even in the face of these they conclude their discussion with praise for the concept. The ways in which opinions and beliefs were measured is one of the more common targets of the criticisms. When Adorno et al. (1950) began they lacked satisfactory tools, and in the course of the research program they compiled various scales. One measures anti-Semitism, the A-S scale. This consists of a series of items on which the respondent rates the level of agreement or disagreement with statements that pervade the writings and conversation of individuals who are known to be prejudiced against Jews. The authors also devised an E or ethnocentrism scale that consists of items that disclose cultural narrowness that is, hostility to various groups there cover a broad spectrum, including non-Caucasians, "foreigners," criminals, and the now dated "Zoot suiters" and "Okies."

The discovery that scores on the A-S and the E scales tend to agree with one another strengthened impressions that reactions to specific groups might be merely an example of a more generalized personality trend. For example, agreement with the remark that Jews are objectionable because they violate conventional values might be due to a belief in the wisdom of tradition, and this opinion can be stated in a generalized and neutral form: "Although leisure is a fine thing, it is good hard work that makes life interesting and worthwhile" (Adorno et al., 1950, p. 229). This format improves a questionnaire because subjects are not apt to edit replies to socially inoffensive items. This gain prompted restating some of the specific items on the earlier scales and combining them to make what is called the fascist scale or, more commonly, the F scale.

The F scale came into such widespread use that much of what is labeled research on authoritarianism is actually research on the F scale. This led some researchers to equate authoritarianism with the score on the scale, and LeVine and Campbell, for example, refer to "the concept as operationalized in the F-Scale" (1971, p. 148).

This equivalence is attenuated, however, by the use of numerous revisions of the original measure. Titus and Hollander (1957) report that more than sixty studies using some form of the F scale were published between 1950 and 1955. As a result individuals have been identified as authoritarian or nonauthoritarian on the basis of questionnaires that vary from merely a few items to more than one hundred (Kirscht & Dillehay, 1967). The authors of each of these modifications typically assert that their innovations refine the original instrument but also retain the same psychological properties.

Some appraisers of the art believe that the concept of the authoritarian personality has been submerged in the methodology: "The F scale correlates most systematically with other paper-and-pencil measures, and least systematically with interpersonal behaviors, particularly as situational conditions are varied" (Titus & Hollander, 1957, p. 62). A decade later Samelson and Yates agree that "what the F scale really measures remains unfortunately unclear" (1967, p. 102). The ambiguity persists to the present.

Controversy has not, however, obliterated the concept of the authoritarian personality, and pursuit of the topic has included the compiling of tests that assess various beliefs that the authoritarian personality accepts. One of the more interesting of these, and one of the earliest, is the Traditional Family Ideology scale, or TFI, an inventory of "appropriate" behavior and attitudes for different members of the family. The important components, in the authors' terms, are "conventionalism," "authoritarian submission," "exaggerated masculinity and femininity," "extreme emphasis on discipline," and "moralistic rejection of impulse life" (Levinson & Huffman, 1955).

In perspective, several of the original conclusions of the Adorno team have survived the criticisms. Altemeyer, in the recent past, comments on the staying power of authoritarian aggression, authoritarian submission, and conventionalism, and combines them into a measurement of "right-wing authoritarianism." He presents this as a methodological refinement of prior methods and as relevant to the contemporary political climate: "Even after all the setbacks, research on authoritarianism will not finally die, for one so often senses that there is a vast, continuing authoritarian sentiment dwelling in the land . . . and we had better come to understand and learn to control it" (1981, p. 11).

References

Adorno, T. W., Frenkel-Brunswik, E., Levinson, D. J., & Sanford, R. N. (1950). *The authoritarian personality*. New York: Harper & Bros. This volume of almost 1,000 pages is a major source of information, and the serious student will read it.

Altemeyer, B. (1981). *Right-wing authoritarianism*. Winnipeg: University of Manitoba Press. In the course of presenting his own research the author offers a lengthy account of the research on the original concept as well as a particularly detailed discussion of the attenuating effects of a set to respond in an acquiescent manner.

Byrne, D., & Kelley, K. (1981). *An introduction to personality* (3rd ed.). Englewood Cliffs, NJ: Prentice-Hall. This undergraduate textbook describes the authoritarian in less technical language than that found in Adorno et al.

Hyman, H. H., & Sheatsley, P. B. (1954). "The authoritarian personality"—A methodological critique. In R. Christie & M. Jahoda (Eds.), *Studies in the scope and method of the authoritarian personality* (pp. 50–122). Glencoe, IL: Free Press. The errors in methodology cited in this early article are numerous, but the authors still see virtues in the work.

Kirscht, J. P., & Dillehay, R. C. (1967). *Dimensions of authoritarianism: A review of research and theory*. Lexington: University Press of Kentucky. An excellent review of the research literature on the concept. There is a lengthy reference list.

LeVine, R. A., & Campbell, D. T. (1971). *Ethnocentrism: Theories of conflict, ethnic attitudes, and group behavior*. New York: John Wiley.

Levinson, D. J., & Huffman, P. E. (1955). Traditional family ideology and its relation to personality. *Journal of Personality, 23*, 251–273.

Samelson, F., & Yates, J. F. (1967). Acquiescence and the F Scale: Old assumptions and new data. *Psychological Bulletin, 68*, 91–103.

Sanford, N. (1956). The approach of the authoritarian personality. In J. L. McCary (Ed.), *Psychology of personality: Six modern approaches* (pp. 255–319). New York: Logos Press. An early "restatement" of the concept of the authoritarian personality by one of the original authors.

Titus, H. E., & Hollander, E. P. (1957). The California F scale in psychological research: 1950–1955. *Psychological Bulletin, 54*, 47–64.

Sources of Additional Information

Jay, M. (1973). *The dialectical imagination: A history of the Frankfurt School and the Institute of Social Research 1923–1950*. Boston: Little, Brown. An account of the intellectual and social matrix that gave rise to *The Authoritarian Personality*. Masling,

J. M. (1954). How neurotic is the authoritarian? *Journal of Abnormal Social Psychology,* *49*, 316–318. The author contends that the personal values of social scientists have influenced their view of the authoritarian personality. This is deplored, and greater objectivity is urged. Melikian, L. H. (1959). Authoritarianism and its correlates in the Egyptian culture and in the United States. *Journal of Social Issues, 15*, 58–68. Cross-cultural studies of the authoritarian personality have helped illuminate the results found in the United States. This is a good sample of the benefits that cross-cultural studies provide. Sanford, N. (1973). Authoritarian personality in contemporary perspective. In J. N. Knutson (Ed.), *Handbook of political psychology* (pp. 139–170). San Francisco, CA: Jossey-Bass. This is a short history of the concept and a proposal for future directions.

B

BEHAVIOR. See STIMULUS, RESPONSE, and BEHAVIOR.

BEHAVIORISM. These are four versions of behaviorism, a viewpoint that strives for objectivity in psychology and specifies that behavior is the only appropriate subject matter. The variations follow in the temporal order of their formulation:

Radical Behaviorism. 1. The view that there is no mind and that scientific psychology is devoted to the study of behavior. 2. A synonym for classical, naive, extreme, or Watsonian behaviorism, and, more recently, Skinnerian behaviorism.

Methodological Behaviorism. 1. The opinion that only subject matter that can be described in a behavioral frame of reference is suitable in psychology.

Neobehaviorism. 1. An orientation that strives to relate intraorganismic variables to overt responses.

Skinnerian or Operant Behaviorism. 1. The interpretation of behavior as under the control of reinforcement, that is, as molded by the consequences that behavior induces. 2. A synonym for radical behaviorism.

The emergence of behaviorism as a system of psychology is dated 1912–1913, years in which John B. Watson (1878–1958) delivered lectures on animal psychology at the Johns Hopkins University and at Columbia University (Harrell & Harrison, 1938; Samelson, 1981). The publication of one of these lectures, "Psychology as the Behaviorist Views It" (Watson, 1913), is identified as the first significant paper on behaviorism. Although this primacy has been challenged (Titchener, 1914), Watson is the person who is generally given the credit for disseminating a behavioristic interpretation of psychology and for attracting a following. His major writings span the period from 1903 through 1930, and they are supplemented by an autobiography (Watson, 1936).

Early in his career Watson decided that psychology could become a science if it would adopt the perspective and methods of comparative (animal) psychology and restrict the subject matter of psychology to behavior because this is palpable. He was relentlessly disdainful of any mentalism in psychology, and he asserted, for example, that consciousness, the mind, and mental life are merely different labels for the soul, a supernatural concept and therefore inappropriate in a scientific enterprise. Watson insisted that INTROSPECTION, an abstruse but at the time an esteemed experimental procedure for observing one's own consciousness, must be replaced by objective methods, that is, by procedures that can be replicated, made public, and that are independent of the experimenter. He proposed that these qualifications would broaden the field of psychology by allowing it to include animals and infants, organisms that cannot introspect. He dismissed those who criticized his exclusion of mental events as irrelevant inasmuch as the intangible psyche is of no consequence. The renunciation of consciousness led Watson's colleagues to label this theory radical behaviorism (Schneider & Morris, 1987).

Watson specified that behavior included both gross, readily apparent muscular responses as well as smaller internal ones, with the latter in some instances so minute that observations are possible only when they are amplified. But he also proposed that what is most relevant to psychology consists of integrated response: "The behavior of the whole man. . . . 'What is he doing and why is he doing it?' " (1925, p. 14).

Watson converted many psychological reactions into behavioral terms. To illustrate—he characterized visual images as the activity of the visual motor apparatus, and he identified thinking with various implicit muscular movements, particularly laryngeal ones, which he interpreted as residuals in the adult of the overt speech of childhood. For Watson, behavior was seen as always elicited by stimuli, and he proposed that psychology's task is to understand the relationship between specific responses and specific stimuli. He believed that one of the major goals of psychology is that of predicting a response when the stimulus is known, as well as predicting a stimulus when the response is known.

Watson was curious about the origins of behavior. Relying on observations of infants, he concluded that innate variables are limited, that the more potent determiners are experiential, and that learning is the significant determiner. This experiential track is important for many reasons, and probably the most important among them is the fact that it releases psychological events from a rigid alignment with physiological events. For Watson, CLASSICAL CONDITIONING is the chief mechanism by which learning takes place. His stalwart faith led to extreme statements, and the following is one of the better-known passages: "Give me a dozen healthy infants, well-formed, and my own specified world to bring them up in and I'll guarantee to take any one at random and train him to become any type of specialist I might select—a doctor, lawyer, artist, merchant-chief, and, yes, even into beggar-man and thief, regardless of his talents, penchants, tendencies, abilities, vocations, and race of his ancestors'' (1926, p. 10).

Watson was not reluctant to put his trust to practical use, and in 1928 he published a manual of child-rearing practices. The manual instructs parents on the handling of such everyday problems as temper tantrums, thumb sucking, and the selection of toys. It was an important book in its era in that it promoted the notion that the course of growth is not inevitable and may be manipulated.

Many psychologists resented Watson's unorthodox definition of psychology, but others listened, in many instances because they harbored suspicions about the validity of introspection or questioned the subjective nature of many of the topics psychologists studied. Furthermore, Watson's ideas were not entirely new, inasmuch as suggestions with a behavioristic flavor were scattered, but not integrated, throughout the psychological literature. In brief, Watson spoke at a time when the audience was prepared, in part at least, for some of his ideas (Burnham, 1968). The attraction is indicated in Haggerty's report of the twenty-second annual meeting of the American Psychological Association, written just one year (1914) after the appearance of Watson's inaugural paper. Haggerty commented that "in spirit the meeting had a decidedly behavioristic tendency. More than half the papers either championed the behavioristic point of view in one or another form or reported experiments pursued through behavioristic methods'' (1914, p. 86).

For many psychologists the gains that might accrue to procedural objectivity were offset by Watson's denial of the mind. A possible solution to this dilemma of how to retain subjectivity and at the same time achieve objectivity emerged in the form of methodological behaviorism, an enterprise that endeavors to convert mentalistic concepts into behavioristic ones. The practice is inflexible in the sense that topics in which this kind of adaptation is impossible are abandoned. Weiss provides an early illustration of this point of view: "Consciousness . . . is a purely personal experience and has no scientific value or validity unless it is *expressed* in some form of behavior, such as speech or other form of representation'' (1917, p. 305).

Methodological behaviorism gained a foothold that grew into a stronghold: "Virtually every American psychologist, whether he knows it or not, is nowadays a methodological behaviorist. That goes for those who glorify John B. Watson as well as for those who belittle him'' (Bergmann, 1956, p. 270).

An additional promotion of methodology came when psychologists adopted operationism, a concept initiated in physics. This holds that scientific credentials are furthered when the subject matter is specified in terms of the operations by which it is studied and measured (Pratt, 1939). Hostile feelings, for example, can be defined operationally as the differences in the level of maliciousness assigned to photographs of people before and after witnessing portrayals of violence. This linkage between response and measurement obviously reduces subjectivity, but it is also restrictive in that operational concepts are always confined to the specific context in which they are examined.

An important phase of the overall concern in psychology with method is referred to as neobehaviorism, a version of behaviorism that began with methodology but culminated in theory. This approach flourished from the 1930s through the 1950s, and during this interval some psychologists became so involved with theory construction that they expended more effort in assessing explanations than in pursuing the original subject matter. Much of their work centered around LEARNING THEORY but there was also some spillover into the broader topic of BEHAVIOR THEORY.

Edward C. Tolman (1886–1959), one of the most conspicuous neobehaviorists, was convinced that animal behavior is goal-directed, that organisms respond selectively and purposefully to the environment. He refers to this theory as purposive behaviorism, and in this he aspired to formulate "a behavioristic psychology which would be able to deal with real organisms in terms of their inner psychological dynamics" (1957, p. 3). Incidentally he did such a masterful job of anchoring the perspective of animals to their behavior that Köhler, an advocate of the psychological method of PHENOMENOLOGY, dubbed him a "cryptophenomenologist" (Tolman, 1957, p. 3).

The theory is too intricate to be reviewed in this discussion, but a few illustrations of it expose the neobehaviorists' stress on aligning covert variables with externals. Tolman defined these "inner psychological dynamics" operationally by assuming, for example, that a rat demonstrates "expectancy" when, on encountering a barrier at the maze area in which it is customarily fed, it *immediately* uses an alternative pathway to the food. Similarly, the act of eating was interpreted as a display of purpose, and a correct running of the maze as evidence that the animal has learned a "cognitive map," an appreciation of the correct turn at each point in a maze. Tolman's formulations are now out of fashion, but these "inner psychological dynamics" are obvious precursors to modern cognitive psychology (MacCorquodale & Meehl, 1954).

Clark L. Hull (1884–1952) epitomizes the neobehaviorists' involvement with theory. In the early part of his career he dealt with a variety of topics but later came to concentrate on learning, and then took on the task of formulating a comprehensive theory of behavior. Hull, revering both formal logic and quantification, formulated a series of postulates, and from each of these he deduced corollaries and then assessed the agreement between the deductions and the experimental results (Hull, 1952).

Although it is not feasible to review the theory, it is feasible to comment on it. Whenever possible, concepts are designated by means of symbols and equations, and formulae are written. Hull is not reluctant to complete these with empirically obtained numerical constants and to use language that simulates the physical sciences as, for example, the law of habit strength formation is expressed as $_sH_r = 1 - 10^{-aN}$ (Marx & Cronan-Hillix, 1987, p. 324). In this equation $_sH_r$ = habit strength, ^{a} is an empirical constant, and ^{N} is the number of trials.

Hull's aura of hard science functioned as a model for a discipline endeavoring to achieve a *bona fide* scientific status: "Few psychologists have had so great an effect on the professional motivation of so many researchers. He popularized the strictly objective behavioristic approach as it had never been popularized previously" (Marx & Cronan-Hillix, 1987, p. 326).

This attraction was countered by the presence of shortcomings in the doctrine, even by an occasional inconsistency (Koch, 1954). One drawback is the dependence on highly specific data: "When Hull was . . . attempting to become precise and quantitative, he became highly particularistic, confining many of the later postulates and corollaries to the results of single experiments done with rats bar-pressing in a Skinner box" (Bower & Hilgard, 1981, p. 131).

The most recent version of behaviorism is the viewpoint advocated by B. F. Skinner, with the initial formulations appearing in print in the 1930s. Skinner reiterated Watson's renunciation of subjective entities, and during the 1940s he referred to his theory as radical behaviorism, the same label that was previously applied to Watsonian behaviorism (Schneider & Morris, 1987). Skinner shared Watson's conviction that behavior is the optimum topic for psychology, and he reestablished experimentation as the central task. Skinner frequently used only a single animal in order to avoid the artificiality that comes when observations from many individuals are combined into a single measure. The results of the laboratory work in OPERANT CONDITIONING strengthened his perception of REINFORCEMENT, the consequences of a response, as the factor that modifies behavior. This appreciation influenced him to endorse the label operant behaviorism for his system (personal communication, August 25, 1986).

Much of the research on operant behaviorism is devoted to reinforcement. This includes studies of the effects of qualitatively different kinds of reinforcement, the influence of both rapidity and delay in its delivery, and the effects of administering it both continuously and intermittently, and in the latter case at both periodic and aperiodic intervals.

Skinner contends that sophistication about these empirical relationships will underwrite both the prediction and the control of behavior, and he has projected similar effects into contexts that are more complicated than those devised in the laboratory. He asserts, for example, that complex human behavior is the product of reinforcement, and the extreme position that he takes is exemplified in the explanation that a child learns to recognize printed words because he or she is rewarded for correct recognition and not reinforced for inaccurate recognition (Skinner, 1978). He suggests that operant conditioning accounts even for the endurance of species. "Survival may be said to be *contingent upon* certain kinds of behavior" (Skinner, 1974, pp. 36–37).

This ascription of power to reinforcement eliminates the need to seek explanations within the organism. This stance makes the system atheoretical, and in that respect it contrasts sharply with neobehaviorism: "A final answer to the problem of lawfulness is to be sought, not in the limits of any hypothetical mechanism within the organism, but in our ability to demonstrate lawfulness in the behavior of the organism as a whole" (Skinner, 1953, p. 17).

COGNITIVE PSYCHOLOGY and the HUMAN POTENTIAL MOVEMENT are now beating drums that are loud and different from those of the behaviorists. Their major attack is on the restricting of psychology to externals, and they are conducting experiments on private, subjective reactions and emphasizing the role of the behaving individual—how information is taken in and how it is processed. The controversy over the efficacy of consequences versus internal phenomena is far from settled. At this date some believe that the heyday of behaviorism is past, whereas others vehemently disagree. Current psychology offers abundant support for both positions.

References

Bergmann, G. (1956). The contribution of John B. Watson. *Psychological Review, 63*, 265–276.

Bower, G. H., & Hilgard, E. R. (1981). *Theories of learning* (5th ed.). Englewood Cliffs, NJ: Prentice-Hall.

Burnham, J. C. (1968). On the origins of behaviorism. *Journal of the History of the Behavioral Sciences, 4*, 143–151.

Haggerty, M. E. (1914). The twenty-second annual meeting of the American Psychological Association. *Journal of Philosophy Psychology and Scientific Methods, 11*, 85–109.

Harrell, W., & Harrison, R. (1938). The rise and fall of behaviorism. *Journal of General Psychology, 18*, 367–421. This article has a 426-item bibliography.

Hull, C. L. (1952). Clark L. Hull. In E. G. Boring, H. S. Langfeld, H. Werner, & R. M. Yerkes (Eds.), *A history of psychology in autobiography* (Vol. 4, 143–162). Worcester, MA: Clark University Press. Hull's definition of neobehaviorism discloses his involvement with theory: "A behaviorism mainly concerned with the determination of the quantitative laws of behavior and their deductive systematization" (p. 154).

Koch, S. (1954). Clark L. Hull. In W. K. Estes, S. Koch, K. MacCorquodale, P. E. Meehl, C. G. Mueller, Jr., W. N. Schoenfeld, & W. S. Verplanck (Eds.), *Modern learning theory. A critical analysis of five examples* (pp. 1–176). New York: Appleton-Century-Crofts. A technical account of Hull's theory.

MacCorquodale, K., & Meehl, P. E. (1954). Edward C. Tolman. In W. K. Estes, S. Koch, K. MacCorquodale, P. E. Meehl, C. G. Mueller, Jr., W. N. Schoenfeld, & W. S. Verplanck, (Eds.) *Modern learning theory: A critical analysis of five examples* (pp. 177–266). New York: Appleton-Century-Crofts. A technical account of Tolman's theory.

Marx, M. H., & Cronan-Hillix, W. A. (1987). *Systems and theories in psychology* (4th ed.). New York: McGraw-Hill.

Pratt, C. C. (1939). *The logic of modern psychology*. New York: Macmillan. This book includes a lucid explanation of the role of operationism in both physics and psychology. There is a discussion of the various kinds of behaviorism. The publication date allows the least amount of attention to the last of these varieties of behaviorism.

Samelson, F. (1981). Struggle for scientific authority: The reception of Watson's behaviorism, 1913–1920. *Journal of the History of the Behavioral Sciences, 17*, 399–425.

Schneider, S. M. & Morris, E. K. (1987). A history of the term *radical behaviorism*: From Watson to Skinner. *The Behavior Analyst, 10*, 27–39.

Skinner, B. F. (1953). *Science and human behavior*. New York: Macmillan.

Skinner, B. F. (1974). *About behaviorism*. New York: Alfred Knopf. One of Skinner's later writings. He starts the treatise with a list of twenty misconceptions about behaviorism.

Skinner, B. F. (1978). *Reflections on behaviorism and society*. Englewood Cliffs, NJ: Prentice-Hall.

Titchener, E. B. (1914). On "Psychology as the behaviorist views it." *Proceedings of the American Philosophical Society, 53* (213), 1–17. One of the main targets of Watson's attacks, Titchener, refers readers to criticisms of introspection that began in the 1800s.

Tolman, E. C. (1957). *Principles of purposive behavior*. Unpublished, mimeographed document. Tolman papers. Archives of the History of American Psychology, University of Akron, Akron, OH. This is one of Tolman's last accounts, and it puts much of his work in perspective.

Watson, J. B. (1913). Psychology as the behaviorist views it. *Psychological Review, 20*, 158–177.

Watson, J. B. (1925). *Behaviorism*. New York: W. W. Norton. This is the second printing. The first was in 1924.

Watson, J. B. (1926). What the nursery has to say about instincts. In C. Murchison (Ed.), *Psychologies of 1925* (pp. 1–35). Worcester, MA: Clark University Press. This volume contains two additional articles by Watson: "Experimental Studies on the Growth of the Emotions" and "Recent Experiments on How We Lose and Change Our Emotional Equipment."

Watson, J. B. (1928). *Psychological care of infant and child*. New York: W. W. Norton. This book is "Dedicated to the first mother who brings up a happy child."

Watson, J. B. (1936). John Broadus Watson. In C. Murchison (Ed.), *A history of psychology in autobiography* (Vol. 3, pp. 271–281). Worcester MA: Clark University Press. Watson's personal life was unconventional and he was asked to resign from an academic position. He then had a career in advertising.

Weiss, A. P. (1917). Relation between structural and behavior psychology. *Psychological Review, 24*, 301–317.

Sources of Additional Information

Amsel, A. (1982). Behaviorism then and now. [Review of *Psychology from the standpoint of a behaviorist*]. *Contemporary Psychology, 27*, 343–346. This is intended to be a "retrospective review" of J. B. Watson's *Psychology from the standpoint of a Behaviorist*, 1919. But the author extends the essay into a chronicle of behaviorism in various forms, including recent criticisms of it. The work of Tolman, Hull, and Skinner is referred to as well as contemporary criticisms by the humanistic psychologists and cognitive scientists. Kendler, H. H., & Spence, J. T. (Eds.). (1971). *Essays in neobehaviorism: A memorial volume to Kenneth W. Spence*. New York: Appleton-Century-Crofts. Kenneth Spence was one of Hull's most productive students. Skinner, B. F. (1932). Drive and reflex strength: 2. *Journal of General Psychology, 6*, 38–47. This article gives the specifications for the Skinner box, a piece of laboratory equipment that has come into general use. It delivers pellets of food when a lever is pushed. The rate of manipulation and eating responses are automatically recorded. The box insulates against noise and regulates temperature and light, controls that minimize the contamination of results. Todd, J. T. & Morris, E. K. (1986). The early research of John B. Watson: Before the behavioral revolution. *The Behavior Analyst, 9,* 71–88. The title is self-explanatory. The article covers Watson's undergraduate and graduate education as well as his early research. Zuriff, G. E. (1985). *Behaviorism: A conceptual reconstruction.* New York: Columbia University Press. The author reviews various forms of behaviorism and both praises and criticizes each viewpoint. The discussion is comprehensive and sophisticated, but at times the philosophical content obscures the psychology.

BEHAVIOR THEORY. See LEARNING THEORY and BEHAVIOR THEORY.

BODY IMAGE. 1. The subjective picture of one's body, typically including its form, size, integrity, strength, and attractiveness.

Body image is an important concept, both in its own right and as a component of the concept of the SELF. The recognition by philosophers of its significance predated the founding of experimental psychology. Lotze, for example, called attention to "our abiding remembrance of the activity of our own body" (1856/1885, p. 584). He observed that it sharpens intelligibility: "Only he who himself moves with toil and effort can know what motion means" (p. 585). He also commented on the subjectivity: "Heels and stilts afford a quite distinct feeling of double contact . . . a lively feeling, not only of being exalted above the ground, but of *filling this whole space upwards with our own increased stature* [italics added] (p. 593).

The history of the scientific study of body image is unusual in that it first emerged in clinical work in neurology, where it was prompted by the distortions that some neurologically damaged patients report about their body image, insisting, for example, that half is missing, proclaiming that a paralyzed anatomical part is as functional as a non-paralyzed one, or complaining about pain in a phantom limb—one that has been amputated. In 1935 Schilder devoted a volume to body image, amending it with a presentation of the aberrations that are described by patients who have psychiatric rather than neurological difficulties.

A second, somewhat unusual area in which research on body image first started is the field of intelligence testing. In 1926 Florence Goodenough devised the Draw-A-Man Test as a measure of intelligence. This procedure is feasible because the number of details that children depict increases with age, and this allows converting the total number of anatomical details that are drawn into an IQ. Goodenough's technique set off an unusually large amount of work, spreading from children to adults and from the study of intelligence to the study of various aspects of personality (Falk, 1981). Body image was included in this program, and numerous conclusions about the topic have been formulated. Unfortunately the merit of these has not been demonstrated because incontrovertible discriminations between drawing skill and body percept have yet to be established.

A lack of adequate evidence is, unfortunately, a handicap to much of the research both on body image and on the concept of the self. The handicap hinges on the fact that there are many different cues about both the self and the body percept, and because these cues are organized implicitly, there is no way of observing how they are arranged. This obstacle is pervasive, and readily discernible in attempts to learn how an image of the body is formed. Many psychologists assume that an infant gradually learns to distinguish between the self and the not self, and that much of this knowledge comes from the different sensations that movements stimulate. An infant is believed to notice, for example, that moving includes changes in the position of the head, the arms, the legs, and the trunk but that the pillow and crib—even though they may shake a bit— are not part of the organic unit. There are, however, no conclusive ways of demonstrating that these associations are made or of finding out which makes a stronger impression—the wide swings of the arms and legs or the head changes, spatially constricted but potentially impressive because they change visual and auditory experiences.

One of the principal ways of compensating for this is investigating the compatibility of measurements and inferences. In some instances these comparisons are straightforward and convincing, but many others are complicated by the intricate interrelationships among different kinds of sensory data. An experiment conducted by McKinney illustrates the complexity even when only two channels—visual and tactile—are considered. In this research on hand scheme, children, aged four through eight years, were asked to close their eyes, and one of their fingers was briefly touched. The participants, their eyes still closed, were asked to indicate which finger had been stimulated, but this request was made under three conditions: one, the subjects merely placed their hand, palm up, on the table; two, the subjects were asked to turn the hand over before identifying the finger; and three, the subjects were asked to turn the hand over and then back again to the original position. Normally sighted children, aged four through six years, made the largest number of errors under condition two, and congenitally blind children made the highest number of mistakes under condition three. In order to explain these results the author infers that in the normally sighted, tactile stimulation elicits visual imagery, and turning the hand interferes with this. He also assumes that blind children do not have visual imagery, and thus this does not become a distraction, but confusion does come from a second turning of the hand. The seven- and eight-year-olds made practically no errors, and the author questions whether this accuracy ''reflects a shift in the importance and dominance of visual imagery, or merely a masking of any real difference on a task that was too simple under all three conditions'' (1964, p. 100).

The many conundrums in research on the formation of body image appear to have discouraged a number of investigators. Pick and Pick comment on a general dearth of information: ''Much of the evidence consists of clinical observations. These are provocative, but they have not been investigated in normal populations. There is even very little clinical literature on the development of body image in children'' (1970, pp. 796–797). They also comment that the deficit occurs even in relation to specific details: "There appear to be no systematic studies of the accuracy with which children perceive their own body dimensions" (1970, pp. 798–799).

Experimentation on normal adults by means of techniques other than drawings was sparse until the 1950s, when two programs of research were initiated, overlapping at certain points but different in emphasis. One features the relationship between body image and self-evaluation, and the second features the relationship between body image and various personality traits. The first of these began with research by Secord and Jourard (1953). These researchers asked subjects to rate their approval or disapproval of various parts and functions of their anatomy (nose, height, voice, etc.) as well as some of their psychological characteristics (ability to lead, capacity for work, conscience, etc.). The results suggested that approval of the physical and the psychological aspects of the self are related.

One of the first extensions of this initial approach involved attempts to identify the anatomical details that are the most important reference points in the body image. As might be predicted, consensus about specific parts has not been achieved, although evidence of a commensurate evaluation of the psychological self and physique continues to accumulate (Mahoney & Finch, 1976; Tucker, 1981).

Some of the experimental literature points to the probability of sex differences in the significance that individuals attach to their bodies (Goldberg & Folkins, 1974: Lerner, Karabenick, & Stuart, 1973), but the laboratory evidence is not as persuasive as the prevalent indictment that society inflicts a "negative body image" on women (Hutchinson, 1982; Kaplan, 1980). The research data that are currently available make it difficult to distinguish confidently between prior convictions and actual sex differences.

The book *Body Image and Personality* by Fisher and Cleveland (1958) was, at the time of publication, in the vanguard of research on the relationship between various aspects of personality and the subjective picture of the body. The book was revised in 1968, and in 1970 Fisher published *Body Experience in Fantasy and Behavior*, and in 1986 he integrated the knowledge of the topic in a two-volume work. These volumes cover the effects of a wide variety of experiences associated with one's physical being. The results are too extensive to be reviewed here, but mentioning a few of them points out some of the numerous ramifications of the body image. One of the pervasive variables is the perception of the limits of the body, with experimental results suggesting that an opinion that the boundary is clearly delineated enhances self-confidence, is conducive to leadership, and promotes a willingness to cope with difficulties. A second line of inquiry concerns variations that are concomitant with differences in the conspicuousness of the body in the perceptual field. The data disclose a tendency for women to be more aware of their bodies, but in both sexes physical salience appears to be correlated with artistic and literary interests, suggesting that an awareness of the soma may carry over to a heightened appreciation of the not self.

These excursions into the relationship between the picture of one's physical build and other psychological domains are being supplemented by probes of the relationship between the concept of body image and various other concepts of current interest. For example, Del Miglio (1984), in a study of a group of adolescent girls, relates the impression of the body to FIELD DEPENDENCE and FIELD INDEPENDENCE (more reliance on cues in the field than on those within the self). The author concludes, in the jargon of the modern era, that "body boundaries, more or less definite and liable to be penetrated, act as an information filter and take a precise role in structuring cognitive processes" (1984, p. 886).

In summary, the personal picture of one's body has eluded direct experimental observation, but thoughtfully evaluated inferences indicate that the nature of the body image probably colors many psychological experiences. The empirical information about the concept suggests that it may well be as basic and multi-faceted as the philosophers originally suggested.

References

Del Miglio, C. (1984). Body boundaries and field dependence of adolescent girls. *Perceptual and Motor Skills, 58*, 883–886.

Falk, J. D. (1981). Understanding children's art: An analysis of the literature. *Journal of Personality Assessment, 45*, 465–472.

Fisher, S. (1970). *Body experience in fantasy and behavior*. New York: Appleton-Century Crofts. The author introduces the topic: "A person's experiences with his body, as a psychological object, intrude widely into his life . . . Being an inevitable accompaniment of his awareness, it has great influence upon him" (p. vii).

Fisher, S. (1986). *Development and structure of the body image* Vols. 1 & 2 Hillsdale, NJ: Lawrence Erlbaum. This is an unusually comprehensive treatise, and it covers both theoretical and clinical issues.

Fisher, S., & Cleveland, S. E. (1958). *Body image and personality*. Princeton, NJ: Van Nostrand. This volume is primarily a research report, but there is also a survey of prior work.

Fisher, S., & Cleveland, S. E. (1968). *Body image and personality* (2nd rev. ed.). New York: Dover Publications.

Goldberg, B., & Folkins, C. (1974). Relationship of body-image to negative emotional attitudes. *Perceptual and Motor Skills, 39*, 1053–1054. The authors consider this research to be exceptional in that the subjects are normals, whereas most of the investigations of the relationship between body image and distressing emotions have involved patients.

Goodenough, F. L. (1926). *Measurement of intelligence by drawings*. Yonkers-on-Hudson: World Book.

Hutchinson, M. G. (1982). Transforming body image: Your body, friend or foe? *Women and Therapy, 1* (3), 59–67. This is not a scientific article. The writing tends to be unduly emphatic, opinion is more prevalent than fact, and belief is promoted but not verified.

Kaplan, J. R. (Ed.). (1980). *A woman's conflict: The special relationship between women and food*. Englewood Cliffs, NJ: Prentice-Hall. This is a popular treatise, with chapters written by different authors. Each seems more interested in defending a particular point of view than in examining the accuracy of it.

Lerner, R. M., Karabenick, S. A., & Stuart, J. L. (1973). Relations among physical attractiveness, body attitudes, and self-concept in male and female college students. *Journal of Psychology, 85*, 119–129.

Lotze, H. (1885). *Microcosmus: An essay concerning man and his relation to the world* (Vol. 1; E. Hamilton & E.E.C. Jones, Trans.). Edinburgh: T. & T. Clark. (Original three-volume work published 1856–1864).

Mahoney, E. R., & Finch, M. D. (1976). Body-cathexis and self-esteem: A reanalysis of the differential contribution of specific body aspects. *Journal of Social Psychology, 99*, 251–258. These authors are critical of previous research, and they report sex differences that are in conflict with the findings of Lerner et al. (see this reference list). They also find that facial details have less effect on self-esteem than other investigators claim.

McKinney, J. P. (1964). Hand schema in children. *Psychonomic Science, 1*, 99–100.

Pick, H. L., Jr., & Pick, A. D. (1970). Sensory and perceptual development. In P. H. Mussen (Ed.), *Carmichael's manual of child psychology* (Vol. 1, pp. 773–847, 3rd ed.). New York: John Wiley. This chapter, like the others in this compendium, is both comprehensive and critical. An excellent reference source.

Schilder, P. (1935). *The image and appearance of the human body*. London: Kegan Paul, Trench, Trubner.

Secord, P. F., & Jourard, S. M. (1953). The appraisal of body-cathexis: Body-cathexis and the self. *Journal of Consulting Psychology, 17*, 343–347.

Tucker, L. A. (1981). Internal structure, factor satisfaction, and reliability of the body cathexis scale. *Perceptual and Motor Skills, 53*, 891–896. Tucker's subjects were undergraduate males. He did not include women so as to avoid any contamination of the data with sex differences.

Sources of Additional Information

Katcher, A., & Levin, M. M. (1955). Children's conceptions of body size. *Child Development, 26*, 103–110. Children, two through five years of age, tend to perceive the opposite sex as larger than themselves. Popplestone, J. A. (1963). A syllabus of the exoskeletal defenses. *The Psychological Record, 13*, 15–25. Exoskeletal defense refers to the modifying or enhancing of the body so as to strengthen it. Such tactics are undertaken by individuals whose body image is believed to be unable to fend off threats they perceive in the world. The article is followed in the same journal by two others, also by Popplestone, that deal with various aspects of the exoskeletal defenses. Popplestone, J. A., & McPherson, M. W. (1972). The exoskeleton, a satisfying and socially acceptable coping mechanism. *Abstract Guide of XXth International Congress of Psychology*, p. 580. This abstract outlines the research that was conducted between the date of writing and the prior entry in this list. Simmel, M. L. (1966). Developmental aspects of the body scheme. *Child Development, 37*, 83–95. This is a review of some of the effects of the loss of body parts on body image.

C

CLASSICAL CONDITIONING. See CONDITIONING.

CLOSED MIND. See DOGMATISM and OPEN MIND.

COGNITION. 1. A composite of responses that includes, but is not limited to, such rational activities as knowing, comprehending, becoming acquainted.

Cognitive Psychology. 1. A modern approach to the study of the psychological processes that are characteristic of rational behavior.

The definitions of cognition that have been formulated in both early and recent eras are unusually consistent in that they are unduly broad: "A generic term for *any* [italics added] process whereby an organism becomes aware or obtains knowledge of an object" (English & English, 1958, p. 92); "*all* [italics added] the processes by which the sensory input is transformed, reduced, elaborated, stored, recovered, and used" (Neisser, 1967, p. 4). Such formulations not only fail to clarify the nature of cognition, but they also neglect the dominant connotation of the rational, nonemotional nature of the phenomenon.

This latitude could well have produced a large accretion of topics, but this was prevented by the belief of many pioneer psychologists that cognition was not an appropriate topic for the laboratory. The "higher mental processes" were considered to be too intricate and at the same time too transient to be brought under experimental control. Wilhelm Wundt (1832–1920), one of the most influential founders of experimental psychology, decided that cognition was so complex that its study should be confined to historical and naturalistic investigations (Blumenthal, 1975). There was also opinion that laboratory treatment might be superfluous in the case of thinking, an important component of cognition, because language constitutes "a faithful mirror of thought" and the laws of thought could be discerned from the principles of formal logic (Woodworth, 1938, p. 783).

One effect of these judgments was the neglect of a generic concept in favor of the pursuit of information about specific cognitive responses, and within this structure masses of laboratory data, segregated into various topics, were collected but seldom interrelated. As a result of this isolation much of the relevant information is not labeled cognition and must be retrieved under such separate entries as ATTENTION, PERCEPTION, LEARNING, MEMORY, THINKING, reasoning, CONCEPT FORMATION, and problem solving. Hilgard's comments reflect the extent of the discrepancy between the actual popularity of the subject matter and the identification of it: "It can be argued that experimental psychology from its start was primarily interested in cognition as represented by the overwhelming interest in sense perception" (1987, p. 237).

A second barrier to a comprehensive concept of cognition came with the assertion of BEHAVIORISM that behavior is the only legitimate subject matter of psychology. For a period of time this ruled out cognition because it primarily consists of implicit responses that have only minimal motor components, but in the 1950s, when the behaviorists' viewpoint began to be challenged, the concept was once again circulating (Leeper, 1951). The adjective cognitive was applied in relation to a variety of responses. To illustrate—the reaction to being confronted with contradictory information was labeled COGNITIVE DISSONANCE. Experimentation on the concepts of FIELD DEPENDENCE and FIELD INDEPENDENCE generated the idea of cognitive style, usually defined as a bias either to analyze or to deal with the totality of the field in which one is functioning. Gradually the popularity of the word reached such a high level that it began to appear as a modifier of many psychological responses. Ability, for example, became cognitive ability and discrimination became cognitive discrimination (Kinkade, 1974). This momentum continued until the entire discipline of psychology was, without any substantial change in definition, presented as cognitive psychology: "A modern approach to the study of the processes by which people come to understand the world, such processes as memory, learning, comprehending language, problem solving, and creativity" (Hayes, 1978, p. 1). Specialized journals were founded: *Cognitive Psychology* in 1970 and *Cognition: International Journal of Cognitive Psychology* in 1972.

This expansion is the result of at least four interacting variables: (1) an increased appreciation of the importance of cognitive functions; (2) the custom, when attempting to gain mastery over something that is perplexing, of drawing analogies between what is and what is not understood; (3) the lack of a recognized motoric structure or basis for cognition; and (4) the emphasis in electronics on sequences. The last two variables are intimately related, in that accomplishments in the area of information processing suggested the feasibility of bypassing the as-yet-unknown structure of cognition in favor of attending to processing per se. Once this shift in perspective was endorsed, the study of cognitive psychology came into full bloom (Neisser, 1976).

Professionals in discipline other than psychology began to take an interest in cognition. Programs were written by computer scientists, and contributions were also made by linguists, mathematicians, and philosophers. These efforts, sweeping in scope, include a suggestion that resonates with Wundt's prior exclusion of experimental work in cognition, specifically that the yield from the laboratory may be less fruitful than theoretical and mathematical contributions. An exuberant attitude and optimism developed, and the field, in the view of many, was enlarged from cognitive psychology to cognitive science. Some extremism also emerged. The psychological profession was informed that "it is likely that many young scientists will give up the tattered name 'psychologist' to wear the as yet unsullied label of 'cognitive scientist' " (Posner & Shulman, 1979, p. 371).

The aggrandizing elicited censure (Kantor, 1971; Skinner, 1984): "Some people think of it more as science fiction than as a science of cognition" (Rayner, 1985, p. 692). "No one would accuse cognitive psychology of being shy or isolated. With origins in communication theory, linguistics, and artificial intelligence, the field acquired early a reputation for intellectual philandering that it continues to flaunt. To many both inside and outside of psychology, it is a diverse and confusing field" (Olson, 1982, p. 100).

Neither the viability nor the merits of cognitive psychology and cognitive science are easy to assess at this date. Much of the research follows the pattern that is characteristic of the history of cognition; that is, the concept is described as an integration of various processes, but understanding the composite continues to be elusive, and as a result there is a sharper focus on a particular kind of response than on relationships among various responses. Even when attention, perception, concept formation, and the like are cast as information-processing models they are apt to be examined as separate topics. Thus the contemporary reader must, like his or her predecessors, search for much of the knowledge about cognitive psychology in a series of separate concepts.

The reliance on analogies has, however, produced some gains, and conspicuous among these is the emphasis on the respondent. Information processing is conceptualized as an active procedure, and thus the individual is no longer seen as a passive recipient of stimulation, but is viewed as a processor, an organizer, an interpreter. This orientation leads researchers to attend more to what the organism does, and this shift has brought to light some of the processing maneuvers. In other words, a few inroads have been made in the difficult task of grasping the relationships among different cognitive processes. There is, for example, more alertness to the importance of memory in thinking, to the intimacy between what is organized at intake and what is recalled, and to the role of meaning as a guide to understanding (Mayer, 1981).

In order to provide the reader with at least a few specifics about research both on cognition and on cognitive psychology, comparisons of the early and recent work on two topics are noted. One of these was made by Estes in a 1981 "Retrospective Review" of Woodworth's authoritative *Experimental Psychology* (1938), dubbed "the bible" at the time of its publication. Estes evaluates Woodworth's treatment of several topics and in relation to his discussion of memory writes: "The thumbnail sketch of the modern view of memorizing . . . is in fact a paraphrase, close to a verbatim transcription, of the summary of the memorizing process given in *Woodworth*" (p. 329). Estes then remarks that refinements have come more in theory than in laboratory information: "Comparing those accounts with those available in the 1980s, we can see that the great change is not in outlook, nor in specific methods, but rather in the emergence over the intervening years of much more powerful theoretical models" (p. 329). Estes also compares some early and recent accounts of reading and arrives at essentially the same conclusion as in the case of memory.

We have chosen to present a few more details about reading because it involves a number of cognitive responses. In 1908 Edmund B. Huey (1870–1913) published a survey of the accumulated research on reading, conducted, of course, with the equipment available in the turn- of-the-century psychology laboratories. Despite this handicap, there is an impressive amount of information in Huey's *The Psychology and Pedagogy of Reading*. For instance, the trailblazers learned that what is read is perceived during brief *fixation* pauses, and not during eye movements. The duration of both the movements and the pauses was measured, and determinations were also made of the effect on the comprehension and speed of reading of such variables as the content of the material and the quality and structure of the print.

An illustrative contribution of contemporary cognitive psychology is a 1975 article, "Errors in Reading: An Analysis Using an Augmented Transition Network Model of Grammar" (Stevens & Rumelhart). In this modern experiment the material that the subjects read is computer-generated and screen-displayed. Responses are automatically recorded and stored in a memory disc, and thus are accessible for review and reappraisal. The subjects' tasks include reading a paragraph and then predicting from fragments of similar material particular words that will next occur. Some of the texts are satisfactorily exposed, whereas others are "degraded," that is, the contrast on the projection screen is decreased. The rationale for this experiment is written in a vocabulary that emphasizes electronic concepts. For example, "While the visual and perceptual system is passing up the results of their analyses to higher-level processes, semantic and syntactic systems are passing their information down to bias the perceptual systems" (Stevens & Rumelhart, 1975, p. 136).

The results of the experimentation in two eras are remarkably similar. For example, Huey concluded that accuracy increases as the contrast between the print and page increases. Stevens and Rumelhart found that a "degraded" condition reduces accuracy. The forefathers learned that the form of letters influences the number of errors and that meaning increases the rapidity of reading. The successors concur but state their conclusion as a reliance on both contextual and visual input.

In a review of some recent research on eye movements Banks makes a reference to Huey, and is explicit about the resemblance between the old and the new:

"Indeed, it was a bit depressing to . . . realize that everything important we knew about reading was known to Huey. The research reported by Huey was conducted largely with equipment that Archimedes could have built" (1985, p. 685).

Similar failures to advance knowledge significantly have been noted by others, but such criticisms are generally explained by the advocates of the new technology as due to the brief time span during which modern research on cognition has been under way. Continued opportunities to experiment may validate this interpretation, but to date much of the yield seems less substantial than the predictions.

References

Banks, W. P. (1985). Eye movements as a handle on cognition in reading [Review of *Eye movements in reading: Perceptual and language processes. Perspectives in neurolinguistics, neuropsychology, and psycholinguistics: A series of monographs and treatises*]. *Contemporary Psychology, 30*, 684–685.

Blumenthal, A. L. (1975). A reappraisal of Wilhelm Wundt. *American Psychologist, 30*, 1081–1088. Blumenthal endeavors to correct several prevalent misconceptions about Wundt. His arguments are persuasive, but some could be seen as incomplete.

English, H. B., & English, A. C. (1958). *A comprehensive dictionary of psychological and psychoanalytical terms.* New York: Longmans, Green.

Estes, W. K. (1981). Retrospective review: The bible is out [Review of *Experimental Psychology*]. *Contemporary Psychology, 26*, 327–330.

Hayes, J. R. (1978). *Cognitive psychology: Thinking and creating.* Homewood, IL: Dorsey Press. The author intends that this volume will make readers aware of the uniqueness and contributions of cognitive psychology to the understanding of "the complex problems of language, problem solving, and creativity" (p. x). There is a considerable amount of historical material.

Hilgard, E. R. (1987). *Psychology in America: A historical survey.* San Diego: Harcourt Brace Jovanovich.

Huey, E. B. (1928). *The psychology and pedagogy of reading.* New York: Macmillan. (Original work published 1908.)

Kantor, J. R. (1971). *The aim and progress of psychology and other sciences: A selection of papers.* Chicago: Principia Press. Kantor's pleas for scientists to rely on direct contact with the events they study have been repeated over and over but until recently, frequently ignored. He advocates interacting with psychological events and not imposing an explanatory model on the events.

Kinkade, R. G. (Ed.). (1974). *Thesaurus of psychological index terms.* Washington, DC: American Psychological Association.

Leeper, R. (1951). Cognitive processes. In S. S. Stevens (Ed.), *Handbook of experimental psychology* (pp. 730–757). New York: John Wiley. This is a single chapter devoted to cognition in a volume that covers the field of experimental psychology. The space devoted to cognition contrasts with Woodworth's 1938 *Experimental Psychology* (see this reference list).

Mayer, R. E. (1981). *The promise of cognitive psychology.* San Francisco: W. H. Freeman. The author argues that behaviorism was not in error, merely incomplete, "too limiting and restricting" (p. 3). Mayer's discussion of the reactivation of interest in internal processes is well written.

Neisser, U. (1967). *Cognitive psychology*. New York: Appleton-Century-Crofts.

Neisser, U. (1976). *Cognition and reality: Principles and implications of cognitive psychology*. San Francisco: W. H. Freeman.

Olson, G. M. (1982). A necessarily personal view [Review of *Cognitive psychology and its implications*.] *Contemporary Psychology, 27*, 99–101.

Posner, M. I., & Shulman, G. L. (1979). Cognitive science. In E. Hearst (Ed.), *The first century of experimental psychology* (pp. 371–405). Hillsdale, NJ: Lawrence Erlbaum. The authors point out that the current recommendation that cognitive science rely more on mathematics and linguistics than on experimentation "suggests that Wundt's judgment is not completely dead" (p. 374).

Rayner, K. (1985). Cognitive science: Reality or passing fancy? [Review of *Method and tactics in cognitive science*.] *Contemporary Psychology, 30*, 692–693.

Skinner, B. F. (1984). The shame of American education. *American Psychologist, 39*, 947–954.

Stevens, A. L., & Rumelhart, D. E. (1975). Errors in reading: An analysis using an augmented transition network model of grammar. In D. A. Norman & D. E. Rumelhart (Eds.), *Explorations in cognition* (pp. 136–155). San Francisco: W. H. Freeman.

Woodworth, R. S. (1938). *Experimental psychology*. New York: Henry Holt. This was for many years the authoritative volume on experimental psychology. The text totals 823 pages, but there is not a single index reference to cognition, even though one chapter is devoted to problem solving, a second to thinking, and eight to learning and memory.

Sources of Additional Information

Hunt, M. (1982). *The universe within: A new science explores the human mind*. New York: Simon & Schuster. A popular, unrestrained presentation of cognitive psychology. Miller, G. A., Galanter, E., & Pribram, K. H. (1960). *Plans and the structure of behavior*. New York: Henry Holt. An attempt to relate cybernetics and behavior. Some consider this volume a landmark publication. Segal, E. M., & Lachman, R. (1972) Complex behavior or higher mental process: Is there a paradigm shift? *American Psychologist, 27*, 46–55. The authors discuss the drop in appeal of neobehaviorism and learning theory in psychology, and describe the recent developments and their influences on cognitive psychology. Wolpe, J. (1978). Cognition and causation in human behavior and its therapy. *American Psychologist, 33*, 437–446. This article discusses briefly, but with clarity, some of the cognitive aspects of emotional difficulties.

COGNITIVE DISSONANCE. 1. The distress that is caused by being confronted with contradictory or inconsistent information, beliefs, or actions.

People have long been aware of the human's intolerance for inconsistency, and certain ways of ameliorating the distress have been built into the culture. One is a custom, when the unusual is encountered, of invoking the maxim "the exception proves the rule." Another is the popular belief that the world is just and all injustices will be compensated, albeit at some unspecified date and in some unidentified way. Despite this wide recognition in the public at large, only a limited amount of professional attention was devoted to the effects of inconsistency (Heider, 1946; Osgood & Tannenbaum, 1955) until 1957, when Festinger formulated the concept of cognitive dissonance.

This concept first emerged out of attempts by Festinger and his colleagues to devise a theory that would integrate a very large body of empirical information concerning "communication and social influence" (Festinger, 1957, p.v). This is a difficult challenge, and the method selected for attacking it was one of dealing separately with relatively narrow problems and endeavoring to devise a theory that would account for each.

One of these starting points was a study of the responses of members of a religious sect at a time when an expected prophecy failed to materialize. When confronted with a discrepancy between the promised and the actual, the members were observed to increase their proselytizing. That is, when confronted with an obvious shortcoming in dogma, the sectarians neither rejected nor revised it, but rather tried to increase the number of believers. This action prompted speculation that they were seeking to buttress their faith by increasing the number who share their convictions (Festinger, Riecken & Schachter, 1956).

The spreading of rumors was another phenomenon singled out for explanation, and in this endeavor the theorists became intrigued with a report that the victims of an earthquake predicted even worse disasters in the near future; that is, they circulated unpleasant, fear-inducing information. In searching for the reasons for this the researchers conjectured that maybe the rumors of further damage offered the already frightened people something more to be frightened about and the dire predictions are sought because they are consonant with the way the victims felt.

Various other perplexing reaction patterns were also assessed, and the unifying concept that emerged was that of cognitive dissonance, a discrepancy between different segments of the belief system or between opinion and action. The research that followed confirmed both the popular impression and that of the early researchers that the phenomenon is widespread and recurrent. In fact, even casual reflection suggests that individuals only rarely perceive issues as consistently either positive or negative, but commonly harbor at least some incompatible evidence.

The task that Festinger then undertook was that of defining the concept. The interpretation of cognitive dissonance as part of the *belief* system distinguishes it from ambivalence, the simultaneous *feelings* of attraction and aversion, for example, liking a person because of the keenness of the wit, but at the same time disliking the hostility toward others that the wit exposes. Festinger reserves the word conflict for decision making or taking of action, and comments that making a choice may intensify dissonance because any attractive ideas that are part and parcel of the rejected are excluded and any negative aspects of the chosen are also retained. This opinion has led some psychologists to emphasize decision making, even to assert that commitment to action is necessary if dissonance is to occur (Brehm & Cohen, 1962; West & Wicklund, 1980).

The assumption that dissonance provokes tension that leads to amelioration induced some psychologists to categorize it as a form of MOTIVATION, and the variables that prompt a person to reduce the distress have been found to vary among individuals in complex and elusive ways (Lawrence & Festinger, 1962; Wicklund & Brehm, 1976). One contribution is the importance of the contradictory information and its relevance to life style. To learn, for example, that a mentor's book is filled with plagiarized material is much more tension-inducing than to learn that the postman is not delivering catalogues. To be told that one's father is guilty of embezzlement can induce agitated searches for explanations, but to be informed that a politician has been found guilty of the same crime becomes just another entry in the log of dishonesty in government.

Dissonance comes from a diversity of sources, and one of the more common of these is the necessity of behaving in a manner that is at variance with personal beliefs. For example, a subordinate's mandatory attendance at a meeting leaves the employee with the reassuring feeling that compliance deflects censure but also with the dissonant opinion that the meeting has delayed the completion of a work that is both pleasant to carry out and important.

New information that clashes with familiar and preferred knowledge is another frequent source of dissonance. Discord ensues, for example, when a person who is convinced that automobile accidents are the result of human error is faced with seemingly irrefutable evidence that mechanical malfunctions occur despite the care with which a car is operated. People who want to exhibit high social status are confounded when they have to acknowledge that the ownership of a limousine is flaunted by racketeers and swindlers.

The research on cognitive dissonance involves a diversity of procedures, and many of them are ingenious: asking students to write essays in which they defend a position with which they do not agree, offering children a prize for eating food they dislike, monitoring the advertisements that owners of new cars read in order to check the prediction that they will attend to those for the model they purchased and slight others, and requiring students to memorize difficult definitions in preparation for an examination they know they may not have to take. Researchers have been faulted for various shortcomings, particularly for interpreting the results as evidence of cognitive dissonance while failing to consider the possible influence of other relevant variables. Some have been censured for failing to procure adequate evidence that the dissonance has been aroused, for failing to inquire about the amount and nature of the dissonance they believe that the experimental manipulations have instilled (Chapanis & Chapanis, 1964). Despite such criticisms the study of the concept continues.

Various strategies that alleviate cognitive dissonance have been investigated, and a few of these are illustrated in different reactions to the combination of a wish to drive at a high rate of speed and the knowledge that this practice is dangerous. One technique is to change the behavior—in this instance reduce the speed at which one drives. A second is to change the cognition by denying the validity of the accident statistics. A third technique is to add ideas and responses that are syntonic with some of the existing ones—strengthen the argument that large cars are safer than small ones and insist on driving only a large car. Variations in the cognitive dissonance aroused by a more abstract matter are illustrated in the different techniques that are used to deflect the discomfort that comes from learning about the Nazi persecutions. The victims can be degraded by invoking even an unknown, unidentified liability: "They must have done something terrible, there has to be a reason for their torment." The tension can also be eased by invoking the future: "They will get even someday." It can be dissipated by denying the event: "It never happened. It's a myth." More important for this discussion than an inventory of strategies is the evidence that "dissonance theory does not rest upon the assumption that man is a *rational* animal; rather, it suggests that man is a rational*izing* animal" (Aronson, 1969, p. 3).

References

Aronson, E. (1969). The theory of cognitive dissonance: A current perspective. In L. Berkowitz (Ed.), *Advances in experimental social psychology* (Vol. 4, pp. 1–34). New York: Academic Press.

Brehm, J. W., & Cohen, A. R. (1962). *Explorations in cognitive dissonance*. New York: John Wiley. The authors suggest that the motivation to resolve dissonance is aroused only when a decision is involved.

Chapanis, N. P., & Chapanis, A. (1964). Cognitive dissonance: Five years later. *Psychological Bulletin, 61*, 1–22. The authors detail many faults in the research design. They are particularly critical of what they interpret as a lack of restraint in ascribing the results to cognitive dissonance: "The most attractive feature of cognitive dissonance theory, its simplicity, is in actual fact a self-defeating limitation" (p. 1).

Festinger, L. (1957). *A theory of cognitive dissonance*. Evanston, Il: Row, Peterson.

Festinger, L., Riecken, H. W., & Schachter, S. (1956). *When prophecy fails: A social and psychological study of a modern group that predicted the destruction of the world*. New York: Harper & Row. This lengthy subtitle describes the topic of the research. The investigators obtained information about the subjects from "participant observers," individuals who assumed the role of ordinary members of the group.

Heider, F. (1946). Attitudes and cognitive organization. *Journal of Psychology, 21*, 107–112. Heider's formulation of the role of the perception of social balance and social imbalance was an antecedent of Festinger's theory.

Lawrence, D. H., & Festinger, L. (1962). *Deterrents and reinforcement: The psychology of insufficient reward*. Stanford, CA: Stanford University Press.

Osgood, C. E., & Tannenbaum, P. H. (1955). The principle of congruity in the prediction of attitude change. *Psychological Review, 62*, 42–55. A formulation of a theory about the conditions under which attitudes change. Congruity is stressed, and the incredulity evoked by incongruity is discussed.

West, S. G., & Wicklund, R. A. (1980). *A primer of social psychological theories*. Monterey, CA: Brooks/Cole. The authors describe cognitive dissonance as dealing with reactions that follow a decision.

Wicklund, R. A., & Brehm, J. W. (1976). *Perspectives on cognitive dissonance*. Hillsdale, NJ: Lawrence Erlbaum.

Sources of Additional Information

Baas, L. R., & Thomas, D. B. (1980). Dissonance and perception during a presidential campaign. *Journal of Social Psychology, 112*, 305–306. This is a report of the "dissonance dynamics" of supporters of the presidential candidates just before and after two elections. It is complex, and illustrates some of the problems in interpreting experimental results. Boring, E. G. (1964). Cognitive dissonance: Its use in science. *Science, 145* , No. 3633, 680–685. Boring indicates that dissonance is commonly preceded by a period in which some of the incompatible beliefs are unconscious, with stress developing when they become conscious. He observes that "the culture still insists, long years after the age of reason, that it is reason which yields truth and that contradiction is rationally insupportable" (p. 680). Festinger, L. (1964). *Conflict, decision, and dissonance*. Stanford, CA: Stanford University Press. A number of different experiments are described. Glass, D. C. (1968). Theories of consistency and the study of personality. In E. F. Borgatta & W. W. Lambert (Eds.), *Handbook of personality theory and research* (pp. 788–854). Chicago: Rand McNally. A comprehensive review of research on the preference for consistency and the ways in which inconsistency is managed. McGuire, W. J. (1966). Attitudes and opinions. In P. R. Farnsworth, O. McNemar, & Q. McNemar (Eds.) *Annual Review of Psychology*, Vol. 17, pp. 475–514. The author comments on the impact of cognitive dissonance on research on beliefs: "Over the past three years dissonance theory continued to generate more research and more hostility than any other one approach" (p. 492).

COGNITIVE PSYCHOLOGY. See COGNITION and COGNITIVE PSYCHOLOGY.

COMPETENCE. 1. A motive to understand selected aspects of the environment. 2. A synonym for effectance.

In everyday speech the word competence denotes skill and adequacy, but not marked superiority. In the recent past competence has been given a technical meaning, one in which it is conceptualized as a motive that is gratified intrinsically by a number of different responses. These responses vary from person to person, but they are unified by virtue of their power to strengthen feelings of personal efficacy and self-esteem. This self-initiated, self-rewarding behavior is not necessarily highly skilled or intricate. At a simple level it underwrites an infant's tracking a moving stimulus, a preschooler's joy in finding out why the name is fire hydrant instead of water hydrant or in learning why an enormous long-coated St. Bernard and a tiny Mexican hairless are both called dogs. At a mature level competence accounts for a statesman who is dedicated to bringing new perspectives to old political problems and a historian who unrelentingly tries to unravel the past.

The pleasure that comes from carrying out these activities is believed to be more gratifying than the consequences of the activities, even though the latter are usually constructive and frequently lead to accomplishment. Acquaintances, colleagues, friends tend to praise results, but the person who is motivated by competence appears to be more affected by exercising his or her interests than by the outcome.

The motivational status of competence adds the attribute of persistence to the behavior, and this distinguishes it from other similar responses. Among these is CURIOSITY and EXPLORATION, reactions that change the unfamiliar into the familiar. Continuance also distinguishes competence from COPING, attempts to manage challenging situations. The curious asks, "What is this?" A person who copes asks, "What must I do to handle this?" The person motivated by competence asks, "How can this be extended, expanded? What else is there in it to develop?"

Concepts of both competence and effectance were devised by Robert W. White and published in a landmark paper in 1959, "Motivation Reconsidered: The Concept of Competence." In this article White points out that single motives cannot account for a great deal of behavior, particularly activities that occur when social and biological needs are satisfied, when the individual is free to pursue personal interests. He asserts that the responses that occur under these conditions cannot be attributed to a DRIVE or a GOAL, but that the behavior is an end in itself in that indulging in the responses enhances self-esteem and feelings of efficacy (White, 1960, 1964, 1971, 1973).

White's distinction between the two concepts that he initially proposed is not always clear. Harter transformed some of the theoretical propositions into hypotheses that could be tested experimentally, and she concluded that White "seemed to vacillate between labelling his new construct as competence motivation and effectance motivation" (1978, p. 35). Harter prefers the label effectance, but she also indicates that it is appropriate to use the terms interchangeably. Few authors follow either of these practices, apparently preferring the word competence.

Laboratory research devoted exclusively to competence is restricted in amount (Harter, 1978), but beginning in the 1970s the concept was incorporated into various endeavors. Some of the researchers who are involved in these enterprises explicitly acknowledge White, but some make only a routine citation. This practice combines with the embedding of the concept in other reactions to reduce its visibility, and it is such a recent arrival on the psychological scene that there had been no opportunity to gain a trustworthy perspective on its significance.

MOTIVATION is one area in which some impact is discernible. The traditional emphasis on the activation of the organism is being amended with analyses of how particular responses lead to specific succeeding ones. The fact that competence is gratified by behavior makes it particularly suitable for these attempts to explain behavior in terms of behavior. An illustration is encountered in Bandura's (1977, 1982) theory of self-efficacy. Bandura suggests that a decision to indulge in defensive retreat or in COPING is based on a sense of personal efficacy, and this variable also influences the amount of enthusiasm and the persistence with which a challenge is pursued. In one study designed to test this theory, arithmetic performance was measured in children who were initially inept and uninterested in computation (Bandura & Schunk, 1981). The subjects were provided with explanations of and opportunities to practice different operations that subtraction requires. They were allowed to proceed by means of printed instructions at their own pace, and the results disclosed that children whose goal is a relatively brief amount of work make the greatest gains in accuracy, in ratings of self-efficacy, in insight into their level of skill, and in interest in arithmetic. Bandura interprets this superiority as evidence that relatively immediate success allows experiencing improvement, and this enrichment helps to change disinterest into interest.

Both motivational and cognitive explanations that self-efficacy and intrinsic rewards are determiners of action have to contend with a longstanding, firm opinion that organisms are directed by extrinsic rewards and punishments. One currently popular way of dealing with this involves constructing an argument, usually a convincing one, about the force of inner gratification and then posing questions about its stability. Deci, in *Intrinsic Motivation* (1975), raises the question: "If a person who is intrinsically motivated to do something begins to receive an extrinsic reward for it, what will happen to his intrinsic motivation?" (p. 129). He furnishes evidence that internally generated satisfaction is weakened when an incentive is introduced, but he also furnishes evidence that it is strengthened. The future resolution of the contrasting results will be interesting, but what is noteworthy at this point is the doubt about the stability of internally generated feelings of satisfaction. There are currently episodes in which one hand affirms the importance of intrinsic motivation at the same time as the other hand downgrades it.

A second and quite unrelated area in which the concept of competence is being brought into service is the field of intelligence testing. McClelland (1973), for example, argues that intelligence is a hypothetical entity and measurements of it should be replaced with measurements of actual competence. In this context he intends the popular meaning of competence, that is, proficiency in performance. McClelland, however, also deals with White's formulation of competence, and he recommends its use to remedy a shortcoming that he perceives in test construction, specifically to correct the discrepancy between the nature of the problems encountered in everyday life and the nature of those on intelligence tests. The latter typically present an examinee with clearly stated questions and request that he or she passively select the best answer for each. This structure contrasts with everyday affairs, in which the person is only rarely informed in advance of all the alternatives, and in order to be effective he or she must actively formulate various possible solutions and think through their implications, that is, must react in a manner that is similar to competence-motivated behavior. McClelland suggests the construction of test problems that require subjects to respond in this fashion.

It is interesting to note—in relation to the integration of the concept of competence with measurement—that Bandura and Schunk, in the previously described study of subtraction, scored the subject's performance in terms of "the number of problems in which the children applied the correct subtraction operation" (1981, p. 588). In other words, the traditional tally of absolute accuracy was replaced by a tally of the way the problem was handled. Accounts of the incidental and dispersed use of techniques such as this strengthen our impression that competence is gaining momentum on the current psychological scene.

References

Bandura, A. (1977). Self-efficacy: Toward a unifying theory of behavioral change. *Psychological Review, 84*, 191–215. In this paper Bandura relates the influence of cognitive processes and reinforcement to what he calls self-efficacy, a sense of one's capabilities to manage problems.

Bandura, A. (1982). Self-efficacy mechanism in human agency. *American Psychologist, 37*, 122–147. An integration of the relevant literature.

Bandura, A., & Schunk, D. H. (1981). Cultivating competence, self-efficacy and intrinsic interest through proximal self-motivation. *Journal of Personality and Social Psychology, 41*, 586–598.

Deci, E. L. (1975). *Intrinsic motivation.* New York: Plenum Press.

Harter, S. (1978). Effectance motivation reconsidered: Toward a developmental model. *Human Development, 21*, 34–64. Harter integrates a series of relevant experiments and suggests ways in which White's concepts can be restated so that they can be investigated in the laboratory.

McClelland, D. C. (1973). Testing for competence rather than for "intelligence." *American Psychologist, 28*, 1–14. "Competency testing" rather than "intelligence testing" is gaining ground.

White, R. W. (1959). Motivation reconsidered: The concept of competence. *Psychological Review, 66*, 297–333. White states that he prefers the term effectance rather than satisfaction because the latter connotes specific rewards. He also stresses the continuous nature of much of behavior and the absence of a "consumatory climax" (p. 322). "Effectance motivation subsides when a situation has been explored to the point that it no longer presents new possibilities" (p. 322).

White, R. W. (1960). Competence and the psychosexual stages of development. In M. R. Jones (Ed.), *Nebraska symposium on motivation* (pp. 97–141). Lincoln: University of Nebraska Press.

White, R. W. (1964). Sense of interpersonal competence: Two case studies and some reflections on origins. In R. W. White (Ed.), *The study of lives: Essays on personality in honor of Henry A. Murray* (pp. 72–93). New York: Atherton. As the title suggests, White traces out the sense of competence in two men as disclosed both in their fantasy and in their behavior. Assessments were made during their college years and a decade later.

White, R. W. (1971). The urge towards competence. *American Journal of Occupational Therapy, 25*, 271–274.

White, R. W. (1973). The concept of healthy personality: What do we really mean? *Counseling Psychologist, 4*(2), 3–12. White chides practitioners for not paying adequate attention to the client's sense of competence. A penetrating discussion of the normal personality.

Sources of Additional Information

Boggiano, A. K., & Ruble, D. N. (1979). Competence and the overjustification effect: A developmental study. *Journal of Personality and Social Psychology, 37,* 1462–1468. The authors report their own research and recommend additional efforts to ascertain more details about the variables that undermine intrinsic interest. Boyatzis, R. E. (1982). Competence at work. In A. J. Stewart (Ed.), *Motivation and society: A volume in honor of David C. McClelland* (pp. 221–243). San Francisco: Jossey-Bass. The author is enthusiastic about the importance of competence. Groos, K. (1901/1919). *The play of man.* New York: Appleton. Parts of this volume represent an early version of competence. It is frequently cited, with particular notice given to the description of the young child's "joy in being a cause" as, for example, in making water splash, tearing paper, pulling drawers open, and turning the handle of a coffee mill (p. 96). Harvey, J. H., Harris, B., & Lightner, J. M. (1979). Perceived freedom as a central concept in psychological theory and research. In L. C. Perlmuter & R. A. Monty Eds. *Choice and perceived control* (pp. 275–300). Hillsdale, NJ: Lawrence Erlbaum. Perceived freedom in the choice of activities is interpreted as fostering learning. The authors refer to White's motivational system as an important theoretical statement. White, B. L., Kaban, B., Shapiro, B. & Attanuci, J. (1977). Competence and experience. In I. Č. Užgiris & F. Weizmann (Eds.), *The structuring of experience* (pp. 115–152). New York: Plenum. This article describes "the competent infant" and experiences that foster growth and development. An illustration of the more common meaning of competence.

CONCEPT FORMATION.   See THINKING and CONCEPT FORMATION.

CONDITIONING.   This specialized kind of learning includes three varieties. These share a nomenclature, and they are also similar in that the learning, initially identified as "conditional," depends on repetitive exposure to the same stimuli. These varieties are presented in the chronological order in which they were formulated.

Classical Conditioning. 1. A form of conditioning in which a response comes to be elicited by a previously ineffectual stimulus. This is the result of repetitive paired presentations of the original, neutral stimulus and an effectual one.

Instrumental Conditioning. 1. A variety of learning in which a response comes to be made quickly and regularly because of recurring reinforcement of the response. 2. A synonym for operant conditioning.

Operant Conditioning. 1. A synonym for instrumental conditioning. 2. A refinement of instrumental conditioning in that a particular feature of the response (a *forceful* lever press) or a specific property of the reinforcing stimulus (a *bright* light) is conditioned.

The scientific study of conditioning was initiated by the Russian physiologist Ivan P. Pavlov (1849–1936), and his career from about the turn of the century until his death was devoted to research on the topic (Beach, 1966; Pavlov, 1927/ 1960). An American report of the phenomenon is also acknowledged (Twitmyer, 1902), but the discovery of the conditioned reflex, or, in early translations, the conditional reflex, is customarily ascribed to Pavlov. While studying the physiology of digestion Pavlov observed that the salivary reflex was stimulated by food-related stimuli as well as by food itself. He referred to the former secretions as "psychic" but was adamant that he was dealing with neurological events, and that he had discovered a naturalistic method of investigation.

The method he devised came to be called classical conditioning, and it can be illustrated in a skeleton account of the conditioning of a dog's salivary reflex to a tone. In order to measure the amount of saliva, a duct in the animal's mouth is diverted so that the secretion can be collected in a container. In order to establish a conditioned response the tone is sounded for a few seconds before and, for maximum effectiveness, during a period in which the dog is allowed to eat a small amount of food. Care is taken to repeat these paired stimuli at irregular intervals in order to avoid adaptation to a time span. After a number of presentations the sound alone is offered. This early test of the progress of conditioning customarily discloses a limited amount of saliva, and as a result the tone-food dyads are continued until increases in the amount of secretion accompany the unpaired sound. This is accepted as evidence that conditioning has taken place.

An extension of this method was initiated by Vladimir M. Bekhterev, a compatriot and contemporary of Pavlov. Bekhterev perceived the conditioning procedures as applicable to more responses than the simple salivary and glandular reflexes that Pavlov was exploring. By pairing sound with electric shock he was able to elicit by means of the sound alone a protective forepaw flexion in a dog as well as finger withdrawal in humans. He referred to each of these as an "association-reflex," but this label implied the mentalism that psychology, particularly BEHAVIORISM, was striving to minimize, and as a result Pavlov's terminology was adopted (Hilgard & Marquis, 1940).

The popular culture has an extended history of promoting learning by delivering rewards and avoiding distress. In fact, the technique was described as early as the thirteenth century and appears in the written record in the sixteenth century in an account of exhibitors training a camel to "dance" on cue (Diamond 1974). While a drum was played the animal was made to stand on a hot surface, where it lifted its feet rapidly and successively. After repeated experiences in this situation the camel was brought before the public, and although standing on a base of normal temperature, it lifted its feet when the drum was played. Thus, in perspective, psychology's contribution consists not so much of discovery as of systematizing and standardizing the procedures used in conditioning.

In this process psychologists have identified four basic components: (1) an unconditioned stimulus (US)—one that elicits the reaction that is being conditioned, for example, food instigating salivating, heat provoking withdrawal, and a puff of air eliciting a blink reflex; (2) the unconditioned response (UR)—the reaction that is elicited by the US; (3) the conditioned stimulus (CS)—an excitant that before the experimental contrivance is neutral, that is, unrelated to the UR; (4) the conditioned response (CR)—designated as conditioned only when it is elicited by the CS, it is similar to but not identical with the UR. The CS is presented just prior to, and concomitant with, the US, and this pairing or reinforcement is repeated until the CS alone elicits the CR. A CR is unstable in that it disappears if it is not episodically reinforced, and in order to prevent this extinction experimenters repeat the paired stimuli at various intervals.

Before Pavlov and Bekhterev the study of association had been mainly concerned with the relationship among ideas, and the establishing of a link between a specific stimulus and a bodily reaction was well received. Because conditioning is obviously related to experience it was also expected to throw light on the mechanisms of LEARNING. These positives attracted many psychologists, conditioning laboratories were established, and the method was applied to many different responses and many different stimuli. The reactions that were conditioned included both external reflexes—eyelid, patellar, and pupillary—and internal ones—pulse rate, vasomotor constriction, and blood sugar changes. In the course of all this research the label "conditioned reflex" was changed to "conditioned response." The reactions were conditioned to a great variety of stimuli—electric shock, flashes of light, different colors, geometric forms, buzzers, metronomes, and even verbal commands. Numerous organisms were conditioned, including human adults, both children and infants, as well as an array of animals—monkeys, rats, sardines, snails, and even single-cell organisms (Hilgard & Marquis, 1940).

The technique provides a method of acquiring information about otherwise inaccessible psychological behavior. The specific applications are too numerous to be reviewed here, but a few of the more important can be mentioned. One is ascertaining the simplest forms of life in which learning occurs, and conditioning in plants (*Mimosa pudica*) has been reported (Armus, 1970). A second, but more complex organism is the planarian, or flatworm. This organism has been found to make an aversive response to a bright light after it is paired with an electric shock (Thompson & McConnell, 1955). The human fetus is known to react to loud sounds, and classical conditioning during the last trimester of pregnancy results in conditioned head, arm, and leg movements in response to vibration of the mother's abdomen (Spelt, 1948).

One additional phenomenon, higher-order conditioning, merits noting because it involves a means of gaining voluntary control over otherwise involuntary processes. In this work the CS, after conditioning is firmly established, is treated as a US, and a second stimulus is also conditioned. In an early demonstration of this by Hudgins (1933), the human pupillary reflex was conditioned to a bell, with light providing the US. Then there was a step-by-step conditioning of a sequence of stimuli. These included first the experimenter's verbal order to "contract" and then self-instructions to "contract," initially verbalized and then merely ideated. In other words, subjects learned to change the size of the pupillary reflex, either by speaking or thinking "contract."

Another area in which classical conditioning sheds light is the sensory acuity of nonverbal organisms. The upper and lower limits of energy at which conditioned responses can be established identify the range of energy within which any particular species is sensitive. Furthermore, the minimal differences between stimuli that do and do not elicit conditioned responses depict an organism's ability to differentiate stimuli. For instance, an animal that responds to a *circle* of light with a conditioned response but does not respond to a *rectangle* of light demonstrates an ability to discriminate between these two forms.

The enthusiasm for classical conditioning prompted a few popularizers to classify it as a form of forced indoctrination or brainwashing (Hunter, 1956; Sargant, 1957). This is unwarranted inasmuch as conditioning develops only under very specialized circumstances, and belief systems originate in much more diverse and less regulated contexts.

It was probably inevitable that the original classical conditioning paradigm would be modified and this came about in the 1930s in an innovative form that Hilgard and Marquis (1940) labeled instrumental conditioning, distinguishing it from the original procedures, which they labeled classical conditioning. These two varieties are different in several ways, and one of these is the technique of reinforcement. In instrumental conditioning the CS is defined as the stimulus, specifically the consequence that follows the target response, and it is not applied consistently, but only when the organism makes the response that is being conditioned. Various reinforcement schemes have been devised for instrumental conditioning, but two of them—reward and avoidance—have been used extensively. The paradigm for instrumental conditioning is clearly illustrated in an inaugural experiment, one in which a guinea pig was fed when it moved its head to the right at the sound of a buzzer. The second popular form of instrumental conditioning allows the avoidance of aversive stimuli, and in one of the more popular designs an electric current in the floor of the cage is terminated when an animal presses a lever.

The person who has done the most to advance this variety of conditioning is B. F. Skinner, who began work in the 1930s. Skinner (1938) pointed out that in classic conditioning the organism is passively reactive, but that in instrumental conditioning the response has an effect on, and in that sense it operates on the environment. This difference led him to propose the term operant conditioning, and this label, now the commonly used one, connotes the refinements in methodology that Skinner and his colleagues have devised.

Much of the work on operant conditioning is based on rats isolated in a cage in which a food pellet (CS) is delivered whenever the animal presses a lever (CR). It is tempting to refer to the delivery of the food as inducing gratification, and even to think of the administration of electric shock as inducing distress, but the champions of SKINNERIAN BEHAVIORISM frown on such interpretations because they violate the behaviorists' prohibition of subjective concepts. In operant conditioning REINFORCEMENT is related only to the presentation of, or to the removal of, a reinforcing stimulus.

Operant conditioning researchers are unusually careful, and as part of their control system reinforcement is applied only to clearly delineated responses, always in prescribed amounts, and scheduled in monitored temporal patterns.

Operant conditioning is often targeted on a small unit of behavior or on a specific property of the response. Thus a rat may initially be reinforced for bar pressing but then reinforced for only a light tap so that it comes to exert a minimal amount of force. A bird is trained to peck a key by reinforcing it for a succession of reactions, initially for any orientation toward the key, then for looking directly at the key, then for bending the head forward to peck, and finally for pecking. This complementing of responses as they approximate the CR is called shaping, and its importance lies in the capability of inducing CRs that were originally not operant. With appropriate reinforcement procedures CRs can be chained or combined. Illustrations of this are seen in the teaching of pigeons to "bowl" or to "play tennis" (Skinner, 1958).

Operant conditioning also includes training in stimulus discrimination. In this procedure a response to only one stimulus, or to one aspect of the stimulus context, is reinforced. For example, reinforcement might be given for reacting only when the extreme right square in a horizontal row is lighted, and withheld for reacting when any other unit in the series is illuminated. In the same vein only a sound from a nearby source, never from a distant one, is reinforced. These procedures provide a second method, in addition to that of classical conditioning, for exploring the sensory equipment of organisms that cannot respond verbally.

Operant conditioning has also been applied to humans, and has resulted in various innovations (Buskist & Miller, 1982). Conspicuous among these is the development of programs of mechanical instruction. Teaching machines ask questions, display alternative answers, allow review and additional choices, and reinforce the student when a correct response is made (Nash, Muczyk, & Vettori, 1971). The reader is reminded that several mechanical devices currently in use do not include all of these steps and, therefore, are, in an operant conditioning frame of reference, not teaching machines.

Reinforcement is also used in a treatment method known popularly as "behavior modification." Although the technique centers around psychopathology, it is also used to change specific components of the behavioral repertoire of the general population. These range from complex overt responses, such as the reinforcement of regulated food intake in the management of human obesity (Levitz, 1975), through biofeedback, a method of gaining control over minute, initially barely perceptible or UNCONSCIOUS reactions, such as heart rate and blood pressure (Miller, 1969).

The devotees of operant conditioning project even more victories, and although the achievements to date are promising, they are not completely successful (Breland & Breland, 1961). One example of the efficacy of reinforcement that is now disputed was first reported in an article, " 'Superstition' in the Pigeon" (Skinner, 1948). Skinner noticed that some birds repeated any reaction that happened to be concomitant with the delivery of a reward, for example, flapping a wing. The bird acted as if this incidental action were endowed with the power of delivering the food, and persisted in making this irrelevant response. Staddon and Simmelhag (1971) attempted to replicate this experiment, and they arrived at an interpretation that varies from Skinner's. It is not necessary to review their lengthy argument, but it is appropriate to note that the potency of reinforcement is, on occasion, questioned.

Whatever the shortcomings, psychologists have learned that there is reinforcement for dealing with small segments of behavior and doing so with precision. As a result of this particularity the field now has a technology that is both effective and distinctly psychological.

References

Armus, H. L. (1970). Conditioning of the sensitive plant, *Mimosa Pudica*. In M. R. Denny & S. C. Ratner (Eds.), *Comparative psychology: Research in animal behavior* (rev. ed., pp. 597–600). Homewood, IL: Dorsey Press. The authors augment the chapters in this book by printing relevant selected studies. Armus' paper is one of these.

Beach, E. L., Jr. (1966). The historical significance of Pavlov's experiments on conditional reflexes. *Conditional Reflex, 1*, 281–287.

Breland, K., & Breland, M. (1961). The misbehavior of organisms. *American Psychologist, 16*, 681–684. An engaging description of instances in which animals do not react to reinforcement in the way theory prescribes. These are exceptions in the course of conditioning "thirty-eight species, totaling over 6,000 individual animals" (p. 681).

Buskist, W. F., & Miller, H. L., Jr. (1982). The study of human operant behavior, 1958–1981: A topical bibliography. *The Psychological Record, 32*, 249–268. Almost 300 reports of research.

Diamond, S. (Ed.). (1974). *The roots of psychology: A sourcebook in the history of ideas*. New York: Basic Books. The section that is pertinent to avoidance conditioning is "Leo Africanus" (p. 302).

Hilgard, E. R., & Marquis, D. G. (1940). *Conditioning and learning*. New York: Appleton-Century.

Hudgins, C. V. (1933). Conditioning and the voluntary control of the pupillary light reflex. *Journal of General Psychology, 8*, 3–51. Hudgins saw this research as a contribution to the study of voluntary behavior. Others have interpreted it as the gaining of conscious control over normally unconscious activity.

Hunter, E. (1956). *Brainwashing: The story of men who defied it*. New York: Pyramid Books.

Levitz, L. S. (1975). Behavior therapy in treating obesity. In B. Q. Hafen (Ed.), *Overweight and obesity: Causes, fallacies, treatment* (pp. 355–359). Provo, UT: Brigham Young University Press. This volume contains additional articles on the use of behavior modification in dieting.

Miller, N. E. (1969). Learning of visceral and glandular responses. *Science, 163* (No. 3865), 434–445.

Nash, A. N., Muczyk, J. P., & Vettori, F. L. (1971). The relative practical effectiveness of programmed instruction. *Personnal Psychology, 24*, 397–418. A review of technology that includes evaluating reducing the time required for training and the effects of this on retention scores. Comparisons between academic and industrial settings are also drawn. There is an extensive reference list.

Pavlov, I. P. (1960). *Conditioned reflexes: An investigation of the physiological activity of the cerebral cortex* (G. V. Anrep, Ed. & Trans.). New York: Dover Publications. (Original work published 1927)

Sargant, W. (1957). *Battle for the mind: A physiology of conversion and brain-washing.* Garden City, NY: Doubleday.

Skinner, B. F. (1938). *The behavior of organisms: An experimental analysis.* New York: Appleton-Century-Crofts.

Skinner, B. F. (1948). "Superstition" in the pigeon. *Journal of Experimental Psychology, 38,* 168–172.

Skinner, B. F. (1958). Reinforcement today. *American Psychologist, 13,* 94–99. There is a discussion of reinforcement in many contexts.

Spelt, D. K. (1948). The conditioning of the human fetus *in utero. Journal of Experimental Psychology, 38,* 338–346. Spelt saw in this methodology a means of investigating environmental influences without disrupting the normal fetal environment. He first reported these results in a paper read at the 1938 meeting of the American Psychological Association.

Staddon, J. E. R., & Simmelhag, V. L. (1971). The "superstition" experiment: A reexamination of its implications for the principles of adaptive behavior. *Psychological Review, 78,* 3–43.

Thompson, R., & McConnell, J. (1955). Classical conditioning in the planarian, *Dugesia Dorotocephala. Journal of Comparative and Physiological Psychology, 48,* 65–68.

Twitmyer, E. B. (1902). *A study of the knee jerk.* Philadelphia: John C. Winston. This is a University of Pennsylvania doctoral thesis, and the experiment was designed without any anticipation of conditioning. A bell was presented just before a tap on the kneecap in order to signal the stimuli, but unexpectedly and after several presentations the bell alone elicited the reflex. No name was given to the phenomenon, and its importance was not recognized.

Sources of Additional Information

Grether, W. F. (1938). Pseudo-conditioning without paired stimulation encountered in attempted backward conditioning. *Journal of Comparative Psychology, 25,* 91–96. In backward conditioning the US precedes the CS. This procedure is complicated, and this experiment illustrates one of the pitfalls, that of obtaining a response that appears to be, but is not really, conditioned. Harris, B. (1979). Whatever happened to Little Albert? *American Psychologist, 34,* 151–160. The author reviews a study conducted in 1920 by J. B. Watson and R. Rayner. This has become a legend in the psychological literature, but during this evolution numerous distortions of the original experiment have been reported. Misceo, G., & Samelson, F. (1983). History of psychology: XXXIII. On textbook lessons from history, or how the conditioned reflex discovered Twitmyer. *Psychological Reports, 52,* 447–454. The authors suggest that Twitmyer's "discovery" of the conditioned reflex is a retrospective appreciation rather than a genuine event. Mountjoy, P. T., Bos, J. H., Duncan, M. O., & Verplank, R. B. (1969). Falconry: Neglected aspect of the history of psychology. *Journal of the History of the Behavioral Sciences, 5,* 59–67. This is a review of falconry, with an emphasis on thirteenth-century training techniques and their similarity to operant conditioning. Watson, J. B. (1916). The place of the conditioned-reflex in psychology. *Psychological Review* 1916, *23,* 89–116. Watson, the protagonist of behaviorism, discusses the relationship between classical conditioning and radical behaviorism. His own research on the topic was influential, even though it was limited in amount.

CONSCIOUS. 1. Awareness that ranges from faint to clear. 2. A synonym for sentient. **CONSCIOUSNESS.** 1. A register of experiences that also function as a regulator of behavior. 2. A synonym for an individual's cumulative awareness, the mind.

The concepts of conscious and consciousness have fluctuated in importance. In the formative period of experimental psychology they were considered by many psychologists to constitute the subject matter of the discipline, but this centrality was followed by a period, starting in the 1920s, in which they were rejected because they were considered to be subjective and hence unscientific. By the middle of the century they began to return to favor, and many of the current assessments of them repeat the original proclamations of their fundamental significance. The definitions of the concepts throughout these swings have been confused and confusing, in part because of shortcomings in linguistic practices and in part because of shortcomings in psychology.

The definitions that are offered here call attention to the fact that these terms embrace two concepts, ones that are analogous to the concepts of UNCONSCIOUS and UNCONSCIOUSNESS. Conscious refers to the clarity and to the number of details in both immediate and remembered experiences as well as those that are phantom-like, for example, IMAGINATION, dreams, and fantasy. To illustrate— "I think about all those tiny bits and pieces—I recall it as clearly as when it happened." The second concept, consciousness, refers to a mental substance, an entity, that functions both as a repository and as a guiding force—"My memory, my mind told me I better do that." The existence of these two formulations suggests reserving the adjective conscious for references to the level of awareness and the noun consciousness for references to the agent, but parts of speech are not consistently honored, and it is commonplace to encounter both terms used both as qualifiers and as substance.

The problems in terminology are compounded by the elusiveness of the topics that comes from their covert and private nature. These attributes are so difficult to capture that a defeatist attitude appears to have developed about the possibility of arriving at a satisfactory definition of one of the most important components of the discipline.

The literature of the era speaks for itself: "Mental facts, or facts of consciousness, constitute the field of psychology. . . . *Consciousness* we can only define in terms of itself" (Angell, 1908, p. 1); "We shall, therefore, consider psychology as that science which has for its primary subject of investigation all the phenomena of human consciousness . . . and one result of all of our subsequent investigations will be to show us that consciousness and its primary phenomena can never be defined" (Ladd & Woodworth, 1911, p. 2); and, "We may define psychology more exactly by naming it science of the self as conscious" (Calkins, 1911, p. 1).

The vagueness about both conscious and consciousness is in full view in a 1916 report by Dunlap of a survey he made of fifty-eight psychologists concerning the meaning of the terms awareness, consciousness, experience, and sensation. Dunlap was impressed with the diversity of opinion. He also quotes respondents' remarks of appreciation of and confusion about the topic. Hall, for example, commented: "Consciousness seems to me the most slippery of all terms and yet we can hardly do without it" (p. 601). There was both agreement and disagreement that the terms are equivalent. Some authorities insisted that conscious and consciousness refer only to reactions of the moment whereas others insisted that they embody the past as well as the future. In both instances the criteria for distinguishing between prior and new experiences are neglected. The idea of two concepts was implied in Judd's references to "the *functional* side of consciousness" and "a *state* of consciousness" (p. 594). Woodworth commented explicitly on the problems posed by the two words: "Conceive consciousness not as an entity, but simply as convenient noun to correspond to adjective 'conscious'; minimize use of this noun, using the adjective wherever possible, to avoid the appearance of hypostatizing consciousness" (p. 612).

Two pioneers represent exceptions to this surrender to ambiguity, and each deals with nuances of conscious experiences. One of these is William James (1890), who proposed that "the stream of thought" or "the stream of consciousness" is the subject matter of psychology. The description of this stream, written with James' customary literary finesse, became a classic. In it he depicts the fluid nature of conscious experiences but also points out that this continuity is selective and ever changing, while at the same time unified and personal.

A second theorist, Edward B. Titchener, advocated STRUCTURAL PSYCHOLOGY, a theory that sought to identify the elements that make up the mind. He chose INTROSPECTION as the appropriate method for this task. For Titchener, this is a rigid, formal procedure in which trained personnel observe their own awareness, taking care to particularize fine shades of differences. Titchener's dominant goal was to support the viewpoint of structural psychology, and these introspective accounts were so burdened with doctrinal and procedural artifacts that they did not endure. They did, however, for a period of time at the beginning of the current century, foster the idea that consciousness can be delineated.

A boycott of both concepts gained momentum during the second decade of the twentieth century after John B. Watson, the founder of BEHAVIORISM, insisted that only tangibles are suitable subject matter for psychology. He wanted to prohibit any consideration of the mind or of mental phenomena, and this recommendation was honored to the extent that the topics were rarely mentioned. The exclusion, particularly in the case of the concept of sensibility, may well, however, have been more institutionalized or more apparent than substantive: "Off the printed page, behaviorism was only a refusal to talk about consciousness. Nobody really believed he was not conscious" (Jaynes, 1976, p. 15).

This duplicity may in part be responsible for the re-entry of both concepts that began about the middle of the 20th century, when the HUMAN POTENTIAL MOVEMENT and COGNITIVE PSYCHOLOGY started a campaign to counteract what they considered to be the aridity of behaviorism. The study of the intact person— reasoning, feeling, enjoying, suffering—began to draw attention away from the laboratory dissection: "Modern psychology is recapturing a sense of the rich, functional complexity of human thought and feeling and the value of individual persons who struggle to learn, to love, and to face the great existential problems" (McKeachie, 1976, p. 831).

In the takeover by the "new mentalism" both conscious and consciousness, as well as the vocabulary used to describe them, were reinstated. James' well-known phrase was chosen as the title of an edited volume, *The Stream of Consciousness* (Pope & Singer, 1978). Previously forbidden terms reappeared in the modern literature, even in conjunction with approved ones, and these combinations were not concealed, but rather were flaunted in that they were incorporated into titles. For example, *Mind and Emotion* (Mandler, 1975) and *The Origin of Consciousness in the Breakdown of the Bicameral Mind* (Jaynes, 1976). The *Journal of Mind and Behavior* was established in 1980.

Techniques of altering consciousness were undertaken both as recreational pursuits and as carefully designed research endeavors, and accounts of narrowed, divided, and altered states of consciousness began to appear in impressive amounts (Hilgard, 1980, 1986; Holmes, 1984; Orne, 1959; Tart, 1972; Turner, 1963). The methods used to induce these modifications range from chemical means to psychological ones, such as hypnosis, meditation, the deprivation of sensory stimulation, and the deprivation of sleep.

Introspection was also brought back into service, but in the form of ad hoc reports that are much less formal and less ritualized than the techniques used in structural psychology. Briefs about the legitimacy and relevance of these introspective-like accounts appeared in the literature, sometimes in a rather forced strained way. Tart, for example, points out that modern science is esoteric and the information about it is neither widely circulated nor understood by the laity: "Public observation . . . always refers to a limited, specifically trained public" (1972, p. 1205). After making this point he argues that descriptions of experiences that are formulated by skilled observers and communicated in specialized, technical terms are as open as other kinds of data.

This reactivation brought with it a sequence of interpretations that culminated in a yoking of the concept of level of awareness with the concept of a regulatory function. This appears to have started with suggestions that attending carefully to conscious experience would increase the probability of personal gratification. For example, "the more completely aware an individual can be of all cues and feelings derived from an object or issue the greater the chances for resultant behavior to be in a direction of maximum representative satisfaction" (Collier, 1955, p. 270).

The theme was amended by a suggestion that enhanced sensitivity be used to help alleviate some societal problems. In an address entitled "Man's Forgotten Weapon" Roe (1959) observed that the neglect of human awareness should be rectified because increased sophistication about one's conscious experience would provide information that would improve the planning of programs of human betterment.

By the 1970s the target of this alertness had been narrowed in that the focus was on unpleasant emotional experiences. The phrase "consciousness raising" came into active circulation, and special interest groups were formed for the purpose of helping or supporting the members and restraining people who are believed to cause their distress. In these meetings self-observations are supplemented by testimonies from various members, and the regulatory function of consciousness is directed toward political and social action as well as toward the self (Kravetz, 1976). Conclusive research on the outcome of "consciousness-raising" groups is sparse (Nassi & Abramowitz, 1978), but more important in this discussion than the effectiveness-ineffectiveness is the attenuation of the original formulations. The word consciousness in the context of support groups has less similarity to the prototypical concepts than either the vocabulary implies or many of the advocates believe.

At the same time that these changes were going on, COGNITIVE PSYCHOLOGY was also modifying the concept of consciousness as an agent. These theorists, prone to interpret the organism as behaving in ways analogous to information processing, describe these functions in terms that are typical of electronics, for example, seeking inputs, transforming them, self-correcting, and yielding outputs (Carr, 1979). One of the main effects of this orientation is the featuring of consciousness as an active processor.

Comparison between the early and recent literature makes it apparent that this amendment has not displaced earlier views, and that, in fact, continuity of the concepts is the order of the day. To illustrate—the reader is reminded of the previously cited 1908 quotation from Angell: "Mental facts, or facts of consciousness, constitute the field of psychology" (p. 1). Seventy years later one reads that "psychology without a lively theory of consciousness is a rather lifeless discipline" (Csikszentmihalyi; 1978, p. 337). Even the relationship of the concepts to ATTENTION appears not to have changed significantly. During the first decade of the current century one finds: "Attention, we shall accordingly discover, represents the very heart of conscious activity, its most important centre of vitality" (Angell, 1908, p. 80). In the modern era one reads: "Attention is the process that regulates states of consciousness" (Csikszentmihalyi; 1978, p. 337).

References

Angell, J. R. (1908). *Psychology: An introductory study of the structure and function of human consciousness* (4th ed. rev.). New York: Henry Holt. The author is one of the foremost proponents of functionalism.

Calkins, M. W. (1911). *A first book in psychology* (2nd rev. ed.). New York: Macmillan.

Carr, T. H. (1979). Consciousness in models of human information processing: Primary memory, executive control and input regulation. In G. Underwood & R. Stevens (Eds.), *Aspects of consciousness: Vol. 1. Psychological issues* (pp. 123–154). London: Academic Press. This chapter illustrates in detail the analogies between information processing and consciousness.

Collier, R. M. (1955). Outline of a theory of consciousness as a regulatory field: Preliminary statement. *Journal of Psychology, 40,* 269–274.

Csikszentmihalyi, M. (1978). Attention and the holistic approach to behavior. In K. S. Pope & J. L. Singer (Eds.), *The stream of consciousness: Scientific investigations into the flow of human experience* (pp. 335–358). New York: Plenum Press.

Dunlap, K. (1916). The results of a questionary on psychological terminology. *The Johns Hopkins University Circular, 5,* 587–639. A period piece.

Hilgard, E. R. (1980). Consciousness in contemporary psychology. In M. R. Rosenzweig & L. W. Porter (Eds.), *Annual Review of Psychology, 31,* 1–26.

Hilgard, E. R. (1986). *Divided consciousness: Multiple controls in human thought and action* (expanded ed.). New York: John Wiley. An excellent account of the mechanism of hypnosis.

Holmes, D. S. (1984). Meditation and somatic arousal reduction: A review of the experimental evidence. *American Psychologist, 39,* 1–10. This article is more critical than many accounts of this topic.

James, W. (1890). *The principles of psychology* (Vol. 1), New York: Henry Holt. An early commentator who is still read and appreciated for being literate and interesting as well as informative.

Jaynes, J. (1976). *The origin of consciousness in the breakdown of the bicameral mind.* Boston: Houghton Mifflin. Jayne's argument is one of the more controversial ones in recent psychology.

Kravetz, D. F. (1976). Consciousness-raising groups and group psychotherapy: Alternate mental health resources for women. *Psychotherapy: Theory, Research, and Practice, 13,* 66–71. A brief, but reasonably complete and objective description of the purposes and procedures.

Ladd, G. T., & Woodworth, R. S. (1911). *Elements of physiological psychology: A treatise of the activities and nature of the mind* (Rev. ed.). New York: Charles Scribner's Sons.

Mandler, G. (1975). *Mind and emotion.* New York: John Wiley. Mandler describes the volume as concerned with "modern mentalism."

McKeachie, W. J. (1976). Psychology in America's bicentennial year. *American Psychologist, 31,* 819–833.

Nassi, A. J., & Abramowitz, S. I. (1978). Raising consciousness about women's groups: Process and outcome research. *Psychology of Women Quarterly, 3,* 139–156. "The women's consciousness-raising (CR) group has constituted the basic unit of the Women's Liberation Movement" (p. 139).

Orne, M. T. (1959). The nature of hypnosis: Artifact and essence. *Journal of Abnormal and Social Psychology, 58,* 277–299.

Pope, K. S., & Singer, J. L. (Eds.). (1978). *The stream of consciousness: Scientific investigations into the flow of human experiences.* New York: Plenum Press.

Roe, A. (1959). Man's forgotten weapon. *American Psychologist, 14,* 261–266. "You cannot be easily manipulated if you know more about yourself than the would-be manipulator does" (p. 263).

Tart, C. T. (1972). States of consciousness and state-specific sciences. *Science, 176*,
    (No. 4040) 1203–1210. Tart proposes a more intensive application of the scientific
    method to the study of states of consciousness. He discusses various techniques
    that would help to bring this about and he also discusses the refinements in
    knowledge that could result.
Turner, W. J. (1963). Experiences with primary process thinking. *Psychiatric Quarterly*,
    37, 476–488. Turner, a psychiatrist, describes how he was "amazed by the wealth
    of images" that he personally experienced under the influence of drugs (p. 481).

Sources of Additional Information

Collier, R. M. (1964). Selected implications from a dynamic regulatory theory of consciousness. *American Psychologist, 19*, 265–269. The 1955 reference to Collier in the
text was his initial article on this topic. This is the fifth article and in this he notes all
previous ones. Delabarre, E. B., & Popplestone, J. A. (1974). A cross cultural contribution to the cannabis experience. *The Psychological Record, 24*, 67–73. Delabarre died
in 1945, and Popplestone compiled, from archival documents, Delabarre's unpublished
experiments with cannabis between 1893 and 1931. At that time the current social and
legal proscriptions were not in force. Altering states of consciousness is not a new
enterprise. Griffin, D. R. (1984). Animal thinking. *American Scientist, 72*, 456–464.
The author argues that complex and versatile animal behavior implies animal awareness.
Natsoulas, T. (1978). Consciousness. *American Psychologist, 33*, 906–914. The author
reviews seven formulations about consciousness that are prevalent in the current culture.
Tolman, E. C. (1927). A behaviorist's definition of consciousness. *Psychological Review*,
34, 433–439. Tolman strains and struggles to include consciousness in behaviorism.

COPING.   1. The mobilizing of resources in order to manage adversity or
challenges and, in some instances, merely to fulfill a palliative function.

The definition of the concept of coping is not yet solidified, in part because
it has only recently been developed. It did not appear in the *Psychological
Abstracts* until 1967, and the delay seems to be the result of the emphasis in the
study of ADJUSTMENT on people's failures and defeats rather than on their successes: "In applying clinical ways of thinking formulated out of experience with
broken adults, we were slow to see how the language of adequacy to meet life's
challenges could become the subject matter of psychological science. . . . We
know that there are devices for correcting, bypassing, or overcoming threats,
but for the most part these have not been directly studied" (Murphy, 1962,
p. 2).

A second reason for the lag comes from the failure of the few investigators
who did study coping to apply that term, or in fact any other single label, to
their work. Attention was devoted to the handling of difficulties—especially
extreme, life-threatening ones—but the lack of a particular term to describe what
was studied made it easy to fail to relate one particular experiment to others on
the same or allied topics. As a result, investigations were referred to variously
as studies of survival, courage, endurance, or even pluck.

Their diffusion is attested, and dramatically so, in Bettelheim's description (1960) of the strategies some prisoners used to mitigate the effects of being in a Nazi concentration or extermination camp. Shortly after he was imprisoned Bettelheim decided that the probability of his survival would be increased if he practiced what he was most skilled at, that is, if he observed and analyzed the psychological reactions of those around him, both prisoners and guards. This intellectual stance constituted his method of coping, and it allowed him to trace both the disintegration of personalities and efforts to cope. The latter are illustrated in one group of prisoners who predicted that an impending shortage of steel and concrete would create a need for proficiency in brickwork, and so they set about acquiring this skill while at the same time secretively nurturing a hatred of their status. Their know-how made them valuable to their captors and they were allowed to live.

An example of research on coping that is not labeled as such is encountered in experiments conducted by the U.S. Air Force after World War II on how to survive. These investigations were provoked by "the high loss ratio of air crew members in the last war who landed alive and never made it out. . . . It was found that men can starve to death within sight of streams running with fish. . . . Many simply gave up and didn't try because they didn't think that they could do it" (Torrance, 1954, p. 260). In the research program emergencies were simulated and various factors that showed potential for modulating the impact of crises were introduced. The results indicated that coping can be strengthened. Direct tuition in how to survive, for example, was found to augment feelings of personal adequacy, and training in efficiency also increased skills in reacting to vicissitudes (Torrance, 1954, 1958).

The word coping has, of course, always been part of the vocabulary of psychologists, but in the 1940s they began to amend its everyday meaning with some technical qualifications, with the most important centering around the individual's intention to come to terms with, to face up to, or at least to make some attack on a difficulty. In this framework, coping is an orientation, a posture, rather than a particular response. The working out of the details of the concept has followed an uneven course, often hampered both by failures to arrive at clear-cut definitions and by including behavior that resembles coping but is not really a form of it. Probably the most outstanding example of the latter is the confusion between coping and DEFENSE MECHANISMS. The latter are tactics that are used as a means of defusing inner conflicts. They are designed not to resolve difficulties, but to shield a person from an awareness of unpleasant and unacceptable aspects of his or her own personality.

A textbook by Maslow and Mittelmann documents the confusion between coping and self-protection. In a 1941 volume on psychopathology they labeled a section on coping and in this they first identified the topic as qualitatively different from a sense of defeat, from feelings of resignation, and pointed to various strategies that a patient uses when "he takes definite positive measures to strengthen himself" (1941, p. 154). They then describe some assertive reactions, but group them with several of the traditional defense mechanisms. Their use of the phrase "coping mechanisms" is compatible with the fusion that is apparent in the description. The volume mainly deals with emotional problems, but the authors comment that healthy people also cope, and the definition they offer in developing this point is so broad that the singularity of meaning that they initially stated is destroyed: "If we had attempted to make a complete list of coping mechanisms we should eventually have come to realize that *all* behavior, normal or abnormal, copes in one way or another with situational or character difficulties" (Maslow & Mittelmann, 1941, p. 167). A later revision of this text (Maslow & Mittelmann, 1951) retains this diffuseness, but the glossary substitutes "coping reactions" for "coping mechanisms." One of the last volumes written by Maslow (1970) continues to treat coping as a broad spectrum of responses.

Lois Murphy brought several significant aspects of the concept into focus during the course of research on the coping of normal children, ranging in age from infancy to the beginning of adolescence (Heider, 1966; Murphy, 1960, 1962). First, she extends the topic from mere response to adversity to include responses to the more commonplace summons and challenges that are part of growth, for example, entering school, moving to a new house, becoming frightened, being disappointed, failing to accomplish a task, and being ill. Second, she defines the concept so that it includes irregularities that are due both to external environmental pressures and to internal personal problems, but she is explicit about the differences between defense mechanisms and coping. The difference between strategies and outcome is also underlined. She points out that managing is the aim of coping, and that the modus operandi is generally that of organization and planning. There are instances, however, in which she says that behaving in this way will not lead to success. In some situations devising a way to retreat may be prudent. Impulsive running away is defensive behavior, but figuring out the most efficient means of escape is, in some situations, a means of coping.

Coping gradually developed momentum as a research topic, and experiments were conducted with both children and adults (Coelho, Hamburg, & Adams, 1974; Heider, 1966). This work disclosed the influence of a variety of variables, some inherent in the situation and some in personality. To illustrate—studies were carried out on how the probability of being able to manage a challenge increases the probability of endeavoring to do so, on the relationship between the readiness to call up assets and such personality traits as self-esteem, optimism, and self-reliance. A considerable amount of attention was devoted to individual differences in the appraisal of events that are to be managed (Bloom, 1963). Is a flood, for example, taken as a sign that inescapable destruction is under way, and thus resignation is in order, or is it a cue that protective measures, that is, coping, are in order? Is an impending academic or occupational examination seen as a hazard because of the worry that goes with it, or is it seen as an excuse for avoiding a less than intriguing social engagement?

Experimentation added significantly to the knowledge about coping, but when the concept is related to adversity, the definition is often attenuated. *Psychological Stress and the Coping Process*, by Lazarus (1966), illustrates a simultaneous featuring of the concept and a blending of it with others in such a way that much of its uniqueness vanishes. Lazarus states explicitly that his subject matter mainly consists of efforts to meet "threat rather than challenge" (1966, p. 152). The volume details different self-assertive efforts to manage trauma, specifically to be "adaptive and reality-oriented" (p. 162), but it also depicts tactics that are ineffectual, such as loss of control and even death, that is, "regressive solutions" (p. 165). The strivings that are characteristic of coping are commented on, but the failures to confront events are not clearly separated from them.

In 1977 and 1985, Monat and Lazarus edited *Stress and Coping: An Anthology*. In both of these volumes the editors refer to the strategies by which humans deal positively with stress. Again, there is discussion of a spectrum of reactions that range from constructive approaches to specific problems through defense mechanisms and relaxation techniques as well as the use of tranquilizers.

Evans and Fearn (1985) represent a much less restricted definition of coping. They characterize individuals who are believed to represent a TYPE, specifically a "Type A personality," as being masterful at coping because of their "overdeveloped concern with the exercise and maintenance of control over potential threatening events" (p. 98). In one experiment the participants were told to expect a few electric shocks (nondangerous) and were informed that they could watch either a screen that cued the impending shock or one that relayed facts irrelevant to the shock. As predicted, Type A subjects revealed their readiness to cope by spending more time in monitoring the cues, whereas their less tense counterparts, Type B subjects, spent more time attending to factual information. Some readers will be distressed to discover that Evans and Fearn designate the behavior of Type A individuals as "active" coping and that of Type B individuals as "passive" coping.

References

Bettelheim, B. (1960). *The informed heart: Autonomy in a mass age*. Glencoe, IL: Free Press.

Bloom, B. L. (1963). Definitional aspects of the crisis concept. *Journal of Consulting Psychology, 27*, 498–502. A study of how different individuals vary in what they interpret as a crisis. The results indicate that what is threatening and the level of threat vary significantly from one person to another.

Coelho, G. V., Hamburg, D. A., & Adams, J. E. (Eds.). (1974). *Coping and adaptation*. New York: Basic Books. This collection of articles reflects the state of the art at the time of publication.

Evans, P. D., & Fearn, J. M. (1985). Type A behaviour pattern, choice of active coping strategy and cardiovascular activity in relation to threat of shock. *British Journal of Medical Psychology, 58*, 95–99. Evans and Fearn found that Type A in contrast to Type B subjects exhibited an increased number of heartbeats per minute while waiting for the experiment to begin.

Heider, G. M. (1966). Vulnerability in infants and young children: A pilot study. *Genetic Psychology Monographs, 73*, 1–216. There is a Foreword by Lois Murphy. The monograph reports observations of the vulnerability or susceptibility to stress of normal children during infancy (four to thirty-two weeks of age) and also when they are between three and five years of age.

Lazarus, R. S. (1966). *Psychological stress and the coping process.* New York: McGraw-Hill.

Maslow, A. H. (1970). *Motivation and personality.* (2nd ed.). New York: Harper & Row.

Maslow, A. H., & Mittelmann, B. (1941). *Principles of abnormal psychology: The dynamics of psychic illness.* New York: Harper & Bros.

Maslow, A. H., & Mittelmann, B. (1951). *Principles of abnormal psychology: The dynamics of psychic illness* (rev. ed.). New York: Harper & Bros.

Monat, A., & Lazarus, R. S. (Eds.). (1977). *Stress and coping; An anthology.* New York: Columbia University Press.

Monat, A., & Lazarus, R. S. (Eds.). (1985). *Stress and coping: An anthology* (2nd ed.). New York: Columbia University Press.

Murphy, L. B. (1960). Coping devices and defense mechanisms in relation to autonomous ego functions. *Bulletin of the Menninger Clinic, 24*, 144–153. Autonomous ego functions are activities that accrue to growth, and they are not necessarily activated by problems, or challenges, for example, exploring and remembering.

Murphy, L. B. (1962). *The widening world of childhood: Paths toward mastery.* New York: Basic Books. Murphy has published the results of research on coping in various papers and books. This particular work is comprehensive, yet it omits many technical details and appeals to a wide audience.

Torrance, E. P. (1954). The relationship of attitudes and changes in attitudes toward survival adequacy to the achievement of survival knowledge. *Journal of Social Psychology, 40*, 259–265.

Torrance, E. P. (1958). Sensitization versus adaptation in preparation for emergencies: Prior experience with an emergency ration and its acceptability in a simulated survival situation. *Journal of Applied Psychology, 42*, 63–67. The author begins this article with a brief outline of the controversy as to whether encountering fear-inducing stimuli "removes the fear of the unknown" or replaces it with a "fear of the known."

Sources of Additional Information

Goldstein, M. J. (1959). The relationship between coping and avoiding behavior and response to fear-arousing propaganda. *Journal of Abnormal and Social Psychology, 58*, 247–252. This experiment was performed before there was a clear-cut formulation of coping. The researcher divided subjects into "copers" and "avoiders" on the basis of their responses to a personality test. All subjects were exposed to descriptions of severe and mild dental irregularities, and the "copers" were found to be more responsive than the "avoiders" to strong threats. Kobasa, S. C. (1979). Stressful life events, personality and health: An inquiry into hardiness. *Journal of Personality and Social Psychology, 37*, 1–11. Hardiness is the author's term for those who tolerate a high level of stress without becoming ill. These people believe that they can influence events, have deep interests, and see a change as a challenge. Kobasa studied executives under high stress, one group with a low incidence of illness and the other with a high one. Murphy, L. B. (1970).

The problem of defense and the concept of coping. In E. J. Anthony & C. Koupernik (Eds.), *The child in his family* (pp. 65–86). New York: Wiley. The author reviews important aspects of the history in psychoanalysis of the concept of defense mechanisms. She also reports some little-known elaborations of the concept of coping, particularly those discussed by Anna Freud. Roehm, M. E. (1966). An analysis of role behavior, role expectations, role conflict, job satisfaction, and coping patterns of associate degree, diploma, and baccalaureate degree graduates in beginning nursing positions (Doctoral dissertation, Indiana University). *Dissertation Abstracts, 27*(6), 2001-B. This is the inaugural entry under ''coping'' in the *Psychological Abstracts*, 1967, *41*(1), 793.

CURIOSITY. 1. The inspecting of novel, ambiguous, and/or complex stimuli.
EXPLORATION. 1. The inspecting of an area, that is, scouting or reconnoitering and/or the seeking out of the impact capability of stimuli.

Both curiosity and exploration refer to strategies that involve becoming familiar with what is new, and they occur in a variety of contexts, including those that are scientific, artistic, and recreational (Berlyne, 1966; Day, 1981). Some authors combine curiosity and exploration under the label of investigative behavior. Others reserve curiosity for reactions that are principally covert and, when overt, are typically restricted to sensory contacts. In this scheme, exploration is generally applied to reactions that are explicit, ones in which the explorer manipulates and rearranges objects or moves about in order to survey an area. Thus an observant child is said to be curious when apprehending the size, weight, texture, and construction of a new toy, and a bored but resourceful chimpanzee is said to be exploratory when devising different ways of trampling, tossing, and pawing an automobile tire.

There are no responses that are uniquely curiosity or exploration, and there are no stimuli that assure their appearance. This wide diversity is stretched even more by the fact that these responses are prompted by stimuli that are attractive, unfamiliar, novel, complex, and ambiguous—qualities that vary with the experiences of each individual, and thus vary from organism to organism. This heterogeneity makes it necessary to infer the presence of curiosity and exploration. These judgments are not always consistent and, as will be discussed presently, they are not always undertaken.

Humans signal curiosity and exploration by means of a wide variety of reactions, including nodding, smiling, exclaiming, leaning forward, and reaching. At a much more sophisticated level they devise means of extending their powers to observe and explore by building microscopes, perfecting radiological techniques, refining electronic sensors, and constructing spacecraft. All of these achievements are admired and constitute prized components of the human repertoire.

There is also a lengthy and continuing history of not merely recognition of, but also intrigue with, animal prying and searching. The descriptions of such responses were exaggerated in the pre-experimental anecdotal accounts of IN-STINCT, but they remain in restrained form in the laboratory literature. In the latter sector, rats, as early as 1901, were described as prone to "fool" rather than to attend to the business at hand; elephants were reputed to fumble, apparently at will; and kittens were known to pick up objects, apparently because of an intrinsic interest in them (Butler, 1965). Dashiell (1925) observed that food-deprived rats defer eating until they have searched a renovated nest. As recently as 1982, Wellborn, Scudder, Smith, Stimac, and Chiszar made systematic observations of the tongue flicking of snakes reacting to clean, and therefore unfamiliar, cages.

In 1971 Glickman reported observations of how more than 300 zoo animals, constituting more than one hundred species, become familiar with strange objects. He reported, for example, that a giant anteater examined a foot-long rubber tube by inserting its tongue into the tube and extending the tongue to such a length that it protruded at the other end of the tube. One exceptional crocodile removed objects from a rock in the water and then nudged, bit, and shook them. Glickman concludes that investigative behavior may uncover new sources of food, but it also increases vulnerability to attack. He also notes that predators search in ways that are similar to the ones they use to capture and deal with prey, and that animal inquisitiveness tends to peak during youth.

The high level of interest in both curiosity and exploration is not reflected in the professional vocabulary, in that these particular words are used relatively infrequently. Although unusual or atypical manifestations of curiosity and exploration are customarily identified as such, more common reactions are identified as one of several similar responses, probably most frequently as ATTENTION. A twenty-four-year span of failure to apply the terms is documented in the various editions of Carmichael's compendia of child psychology. The first edition (Carmichael, 1946) has no entry in the Index for exploration and only one for curiosity. The second edition (Carmichael, 1954) notes that curiosity was included in early lists of "instincts" or "impulses" but omits any further comments or treatment. The two volumes that make up the third edition (Mussen, 1970) devote only a page and a quarter to "Exploratory Behavior" and there are only a few brief comments about curiosity.

Embedded within these texts, however, are experiments on what is actually curiosity and exploration. For example, Carmichael (1946) briefly reviews a study by Justin (1932) in which the investigator recorded the duration of episodes of smiling and laughter among children, three through six years of age, when they were shown a variety of stimuli. Some were incongruous, for example, a doll with eyes in the back of the head and during a demonstration of how to boil an egg, a watch instead of the egg was dropped, apparently inadvertently, into the water. Some of the children's reactions must have included curiosity, but the results are discussed, both by Carmichael and by Justin, only in reference to laughter.

The same kind of neglect pervades the periodical literature, both early and recent. For example, in an experiment published by McCall and Kennedy in 1980, comparisons were made of the duration of infant eye fixations for stimuli that are new and for those to which the infants are habituated. In the article the authors repeat the word attention and the phrase new stimulus several times, but the words curiosity and exploration are missing even though two references in a list of six include these terms in their titles.

The failures to use the words curiosity and exploration disperse an unknown but probably large amount of relevant experimental data. As a result, much of the information about the concepts is fragmented, and the knowledge that is retrieved when only the two terms are pursued yields information that may be organized on a literal rather than on a conceptual basis.

The reasons for the discrepancy between the high interest in the concepts and the limited labeling of them are perplexing, but they are related to past changes in the importance of the concept of DRIVE. Shortly after research on drives began, curiosity and exploration were included in the network and were promoted by the popularity then accorded the concept of drive. By mid-century the quantity of research was impressive, with much of it suggesting that drives of curiosity and exploration facilitate LEARNING. To illustrate—Montgomery (1954) observed that when an opportunity to search a complex compartment is the only reward, rats will learn a maze that leads them to this area. Myers and Miller (1954) also found that rats learn to press a bar in order to gain an opportunity to rummage.

As experimental sophistication increased, some weakness in the categorizing of curiosity and exploration as drives emerged. Neither response has a specific tissue deficit nor a definite consummatory response. Furthermore, neither shows the relative immunity to extraneous events that is typical of internal motives. Inquisitiveness, for example, diminishes when an organism is fatigued, in pain, or experiences other kinds of distress.

These exceptions provoked psychologists to consider the motivational influence of stimuli other than internal states. One of the charter advocates of this approach was Harry Harlow (1905–1981), who observed rhesus monkeys learning to solve problems. He reported that introducing food interfered with acquisition, and he interpreted the animals' persistence in working on the problems and their mastery of them as due to the gratification that comes from manipulating per se (Harlow, 1950; Harlow, Harlow, & Meyer, 1950).

In 1959 the motive of COMPETENCE was proposed to explain certain complex forms of human behavior, such as creativity and play. This motive was offered as a solution to the impossibility of explaining complicated sequences of response in terms of single needs. It assumes that dealing with selected aspects of the environment or exercising selected interests is satisfying in and of itself. The attention to activity that is intrinsically rewarding gradually increased and did so at the same time as the interest in drive was waning. As the doctrine of drive faded, curiosity and exploration began to be interpreted as responses rather than as motives (Hilgard, 1987). For many psychologists this shift increased the credibility of the concepts, but it has not changed the terminology. Inquisitiveness for example, continues to be studied, but much of the relevant research is still not labeled as such.

References

Berlyne, D. E. (1966). Curiosity and exploration. *Science, 153* (3731), 25–33.

Butler, R. A. (1965). Investigative behavior. In A. M. Schrier, H. F. Harlow, & F. Stollnitz (Eds.), *Behavior of nonhuman primates: Modern research trends* (Vol. 2, pp. 463–493). New York: Academic Press. This article reviews investigative behavior. A review of pre-experimental observations is also included. Butler is among the group who first called attention to curiosity and exploration.

Carmichael, L. (Ed.). (1946). *Manual of child psychology*. New York: John Wiley. Contains nineteen chapters, each written by a specialist in an area of child development. An authoritative reference book for its era.

Carmichael, L. (Ed.). (1954). *Manual of child psychology* (2nd ed.). New York: John Wiley. Many of the chapters are by the same authors as those in the first edition.

Dashiell, J. F. (1925). A quantitative demonstration of animal drive. *Journal of Comparative Psychology, 5*, 205–208.

Day, H. I. (1981). Play: A ludic behavior. In H. I. Day (Ed.), *Advances in intrinsic motivation and aesthetics*. (pp. 225–250). New York: Plenum Press.

Glickman, S. E. (1971, October). Curiosity has killed more mice than cats. *Psychology Today, 5*, 55–56; 86.

Harlow, H. F. (1950). Learning and satiation of response in intrinsically motivated complex puzzle performance by monkeys. *Journal of Comparative and Physiological Psychology, 43*, 289–294.

Harlow, H. F., Harlow, M. K., & Meyer, D. R. (1950). Learning motivated by a manipulation drive. *Journal of Experimental Psychology, 40*, 228–234. The authors begin this report with the following remark: "Psychologists have traditionally utilized the homeostatic drives in learning studies with subhuman animals, and have neglected, if not actually been blind to, the importance of externally elicited drives in learning" (p. 228).

Hilgard, E. R. (1987). *Psychology in America: A historical survey*. San Diego: Harcourt Brace Jovanovich.

Justin, F. (1932). A genetic study of laughter provoking stimuli. *Child Development, 3*, 114–136.

McCall, R. B., & Kennedy, C. B. (1980). Subjective uncertainty, variability of experience, and the infant's response to discrepancies. *Child Development, 51*, 285–287.

Montgomery, K. C. (1954). The role of the exploratory drive in learning. *Journal of Comparative and Physiological Psychology, 47*, 60–64.

Mussen, P. H. (Ed.). (1970). *Carmichael's manual of child psychology* (3rd ed.). New York: John Wiley. In this third edition the contents fill two volumes. The editor asserts that this is not a revision but "a completely new *Manual*" (p. vii). In 1983 the fourth edition, was published. This is a multivolume work and so extensive that comparisons with the original are forced.

Myers, A. K., & Miller, N. E. (1954). Failure to find a learned drive based on hunger; evidence for learning motivated by "exploration." *Journal of Comparative and Physiological Psychology, 47*, 428–436. The authors speculate that sensory variety and freedom of action are the rewarding factors. This explanation is an attempt to "analyze . . . exploratory drive along the same lines as conventional drives" (p. 435).

Wellborn, S., Scudder, K. M., Smith, H. M., Stimac, K., & Chiszar, D. (1982). Investigatory behavior in snakes: 3. Effects of familiar odors on investigation of clean cages. *The Psychological Record, 32*, 169–177. The third in a series of experiments that uses tongue flicking in snakes as an index of exploration. Being placed in clean cages increases the behavior.

Sources of Additional Information

Butler, R. A. (1957). The effect of deprivation of visual incentives on visual exploration motivation in monkeys. *Journal of Comparative and Physiological Psychology, 50*, 177–179. The author, trying to build a case for a predisposing drive, found that monkeys deprived of visual experiences for intervals ranging from zero to eight hours approached the maximal reactivity to visual stimulation after only four hours of deprivation. Nissen, H. W. (1930). A study of exploratory behavior in the white rat by means of the obstruction method. *Journal of Genetic Psychology, 37*, 361–376. Rats increase the number of times they cross an electric grid when that allows them to explore an enclosure that has an interest value, that is, contains wood shavings and bits of cork. Nissen believes that this behavior demonstrates an exploratory drive in rats. Rheingold, H. L., & Eckerman, C. O. (1973). Fear of the stranger: A critical examination. In H. W. Reese (Ed.), *Advances in child development and behavior*, (Vol. 8, pp. 186–222). New York: Academic Press. "*Fear of the stranger* has a nice ring . . . But that nice ring has the pat ring of a slogan, implying absoluteness and universality. To use a term because it is simple and easy does an injustice to the full panoply of the infant's response to an unfamiliar person . . . The term allows no room for the interest, curiosity, and pleasure he often accords new events of all kinds, including people" (pp. 218–219). Wohlwill, J. F. (1968). Amount of stimulus exploration and preference as differential functions of stimulus complexity. *Perception and Psychophysics, 4*, 307–312. A study of the reactions of college students to photographic and nonrepresentational visual stimuli of equal complexity.

D

DEFENSE MECHANISMS. 1. Hypothesized, unconscious psychological maneuvers that fend off, or disguise, unacceptable ideas and/or impulses to act that, if undeflected, would induce anxiety and arouse distressing self-criticism. There are several ways of bringing about this self-deception, and each defense mechanism is given a name that indicates the way the process works.

The aspiration of psychology is to adhere to the precepts of science by restricting its subject matter to the concrete, tangible world and to proceed in such a way that conclusions are based on objective and verifiable evidence. But the defense mechanisms were first described and labeled by psychoanalysts, advocates of a theory that does not meet the criteria of science because it deals with hypothesized intrapsychic forces. These forces were depicted as engaged in an unrelenting struggle to control the individual, and some of them are sinister and ANXIETY-inducing. If unrestrained, they would violate the controls on behavior that society demands.

Although the defense mechanisms are thought to prevent distress because they obscure unacceptable ideas and impulses, they are at the same time self-deceptive, inasmuch as the person is not usually aware that he or she is using them. Repression was the first of these protective strategies that was described, and it was originally characterized as the "pushing down into unconsciousness" of unacceptable motives and/or memories. Such dislodging is not believed to devitalize the ideas, and they continue to struggle to reenter consciousness with the result that repression must be repetitively brought into play.

Most of the information about these unconscious, dynamic events was inferred by psychoanalysts from the recollections and verbal associations of psychiatrically ill patients, a source that makes it difficult to impose objective, scientific controls. Yet from these sources Sigmund Freud began, in the 1890s, to formulate the defense mechanisms, and by 1936 Anna Freud enumerated ten; by 1969 it was possible to list thirty-nine (Siegal). Unfortunately exact criteria for the various defense mechanisms have not been carefully specified, and the reader is cautioned that some with similar characteristics have more than one name. Furthermore, symptoms of merely defensive behavior, such as fighting or turning away, are occasionally erroneously identified as defense mechanisms.

The occasional confusions in the concept as well as its less than credible origins did little to detract from its power to elucidate several kinds of enigmatic behavior. To illustrate—rationalization is said to avert self-censure simply by unwittingly substituting an acceptable for an unacceptable reason for behaving in a particular way. Familiarity with this mechanism allows an individual to interpret personal displays of what others see as cowardice as instances of ir-reproachable caution. It also explains why an individual who predicts impending financial disasters interprets his or her greed as a virtue, as prudence rather than as the cupidity that others perceive. The mechanism of reaction formation, a behavioral emphasis that is the opposite of the impulse, is seen in a perfectionist, an individual who deflects undesirable wishes by magnifying the desirable. Un-like the braggart, the perfectionist is not a hypocrite, in that he or she is not consciously feigning, but is practicing self-protection by looking both firmly and unknowingly at the good in order to fend off the not-so-good.

In brief—the defense mechanisms offered psychologists explanations, and intriguing ones at that, of matters that had previously been perplexing. This clarifying function admitted them to the discipline, not only in clinical work, but in the understanding of how normal personalities function when the going gets rough. In fact, a description of the defense mechanisms is common in contemporary undergraduate textbooks in psychology (Coon, 1980; Fehr, 1983). Hilgard (1949) reports that they appeared in an undergraduate textbook as early as 1923 and were presented in a way that has since become common, specifically defining and comparing the different mechanisms but slighting their origins and omitting systematic discussions of them.

Many psychologists have not been comfortable with the concept of defense mechanisms and have tried to legitimize them both by scrutinizing available research in search of confirming laboratory data and by designing experiments that would throw light on their validity (Hilgard, 1952; Sears, 1943; Sears, 1944). The importance that was assigned to these tasks is attested by the fact that Sears' *Survey of Objective Studies of Psychoanalytic Concepts* (1943) was commissioned by a committee of the Social Science Research Council. Sears' description of a master's thesis, completed in 1940, exemplifies the kind of experiments that he collected and reviewed. In this one study children were given two toys, one that they were known to like and a second that was not particularly attractive. After a period of play each child in the experimental group was told to give one of these toys to another child, but in the control group there was no such direction. All participants were asked which object they thought a friend would have surrendered. A larger number of subjects who had not released the preferred toy, that is, who had made a selfish choice, indicated a similar selection on the part of the other children. They "projected" or saw selfishness in others as a defense against seeing themselves as selfish.

Sears concluded that there was more laboratory support for some maneuvers than for others, but the evidence was not conclusive for any particular defense mechanism. Others took up the burden of proof, and for a period of time the devising of laboratory analogues was popular. Even a few instructional manuals included experiments designed to demonstrate the defense mechanisms (MacKinnon & Henle, 1948). In his Presidential Address to the American Psychological Association, Hilgard (1949) recommended the establishing of laboratories for the study of psychodynamics and making them commensurate with facilities for the investigation of such basic topics in psychology as learning and perception.

Psychoanalysts criticized these attempts to verify their doctrines, largely because many of them involved artificial, experimentally contrived responses that do not simulate the enduring complex, and multidetermined strategies that are the subject matter of psychoanalysis. There was even opinion that the latter may be beyond the grasp of research meticulosity (Pumpian-Mindlin, 1952).

After World War II the field of psychology began to react more enthusiastically than previously to pressures to deal with problems of ADJUSTMENT, and the discipline began to develop its own theories about topics that had previously been the prerogative of psychoanalysis. The defense mechanisms were included in this expansion. The concept of repression, for example, was amended by the research on PERCEPTUAL DEFENSE that disclosed that under certain conditions, unacceptable material was perceived erratically. These perceptual irregularities suggested that there might be a protective excluding as well as the protective forgetting that is classically assigned to repression (MacKinnon & Dukes, 1962).

In summary, the specifications of the defense mechanisms were increased as they were integrated into modern research, but these gains brought with them some reduction in identity. Their psychoanalytic origins were slighted even more than in the past, but descriptions of their relationship to behavior increased. As a result, the concept of defense mechanisms might be labeled as classic rather than as basic, but in both instances it qualifies as an attention commanding explanatory concept.

References

Coon, D. (1980). *Introduction to psychology: Exploration and application* (2nd ed.). St. Paul: West Publishing. This text illustrates the relatively simple, atheoretical discussions of defense mechanisms in current textbooks. The title of the relevant section is "Psychological Defense—Mental Karate" (p. 303).

Fehr, L. A. (1983). *Introduction to personality*. New York: Macmillan. This discussion of the defense mechanisms illustrates one method of explaining psychoanalytic concepts to undergraduates. Freud's theory is generally criticized, but specific parts of it are singled out for praise.

Hilgard, E. R. (1949). Human motives and the concept of the self. *American Psychologist, 4*, 374–382.

Hilgard, E. R. (1952). Experimental approaches to psychoanalysis. In E. Pumpian-Mindlin (Ed.), *Psychoanalysis as science: The Hixon lectures on the scientific status of psychoanalysis* (pp. 3–45). Stanford, CA: Stanford University Press. This section of the book includes two lectures in which Hilgard does a masterful job of assembling and evaluating the research literature relevant to psychoanalytic concepts.

MacKinnon, D. W., & Dukes, W. F. (1962). Repression. In L. Postman (Ed.), *Psychology in the making: Histories of selected research problems* (pp. 662–744). New York: Alfred Knopf. This article reviews the mechanisms of repression from Freud's first formulation of defense mechanisms through modifications of the concept by modern psychologists. The authors' discussion of the changes in American psychology in the mid-twentieth century is informative.

MacKinnon, D. W., & Henle, M. (1948). *Experimental studies in psychodynamics: A laboratory manual.* Cambridge, MA: Harvard University Press. This manual gives directions for conducting several experiments. One is "to attempt experimentally to produce forgetting of material wounding to the ego, that is, to produce repression" (p. 109).

Pumpian-Mindlin, E. (1952). The position of psychoanalysis in relation to the biological and social sciences. In E. Pumpian-Mindlin (Ed.), *Psychoanalysis as science: The Hixon lectures on the scientific status of psychoanalysis* (pp. 125–158). Stanford, CA: Stanford University Press. This volume contains a series of five lectures delivered because of "the controversy over the status of psychoanalysis as a science. . . . There exists no question as to the broad influence which psychoanalysis exerts in our society. Therefore, be it a science or not, it has to be reckoned with as a phenomenon in our present-day world" (p. v).

Sears, R. R. (1943). Survey of objective studies of psychoanalytic concepts: A report prepared for the Committee on Social Adjustment. *Social Science Research Council Bulletin #51.* New York: Social Science Research Council.

Sears, R. R. (1944). Experimental analysis of psychoanalytic phenomena. In J. McV. Hunt (Ed.), *Personality and the behavior disorders: A handbook based on experimental and clinical research* (Vol. 1, pp. 306–332). New York: Ronald Press.

Siegal, R. S. (1969). What are defense mechanisms? *Journal of the American Psychoanalytic Association, 17*, 785–807. This is an unusually lucid explanation of the origin and meaning of the defense mechanisms. The author includes a definition, intended to be comprehensive and authoritative, that was devised by a group of well-known psychoanalysts.

Sources of Additional Information

Freud, A., & Burlingham, D. T. (1943). *War and children.* New York: Medical War Books. This is an account of the reactions of British children to evacuation and the bombing during World War II. Anna Freud refers to the defense mechanisms—particularly regression—in the description of how the children managed the anxiety reactions that were induced by their war experiences. Gilgen, A. R. (1982). *American psychology since World War II: A profile of the discipline.* Westport, CT: Greenwood Press. This volume deals with many of the conspicuous aspects of recent history. The author deals with some highlights of "The Freudian Influence" in a chapter of that title. He indicates that the defense mechanisms were integrated, to some degree, into innovative approaches to personality. Hsu, F. L. K. (1949). Suppression versus repression. *Psychiatry, 12* (3), 223–242. The author, an anthropologist, describes repression and suppression in Chinese, Japanese, German, and American cultures. He defines repression as the unconscious exclusion of ideas from consciousness, and suppression as a conscious tactic of restricting actions but not necessarily thoughts. Kellner, H., Butters, N., & Wiener, M. (1964). Mechanisms of defense: An alternative response. *Journal of Personality, 32*, 601–621. This is an attempt to replace psychoanalytic explanation of defense mechanisms with explanations based on learning. McCall, R. J. (1972). The defense mechanisms re-examined: A logical and phenomenal analysis. In J. O. Whittaker (Ed.), *Recent discoveries in psychology: Readings for the introductory course* (pp. 330–345). Philadelphia: W. B. Saunders. (Original work published 1963). The author explains various defense mechanisms from the point of view of PHENOMENOLOGICAL PSYCHOLOGY—an attempt to align psychoanalytic concepts with a theory other than the one in which it was originated.

DISSONANCE. See COGNITIVE DISSONANCE.

DOGMATISM. 1. Accepting beliefs because selected authorities endorse them and protecting the credence of these beliefs by warding off contradictory or incongruent information. 2. A synonym for a closed mind. **OPEN MIND.** 1. A receptivity to information and the evaluation of it in accord with relevant, objective evidence.

In 1960 Rokeach assembled into a single volume, *The Open and Closed Mind*, the results of a series of experiments that he and colleagues had conducted on the kinds of ideas that individuals favor as well as those that they dislike. The researchers' conclusions are complex, but in bare outline, Rokeach found that people organize ideas into systems that in some instances are logical but in others serve a particular purpose, often that of protecting the believer. This defensive role leads the advocate to place an unduly high value on the belief, but this protection does not eradicate opposition, and the belief system must coexist with disbelief systems, a series of tenets that have been rejected. This combination of the singular and the plural exists because accepting one opinion means excluding others. Such an imbalance is readily apparent in the thinking of a fanatic who, by embracing one set of religious propositions, renounces all others.

Open and closed minds differ in the way the belief-disbelief configurations are patterned (Rokeach, 1954). The latter accept information from sources that they have endowed with infallibility, and they then strive to maintain these convictions. One of their favored tactics is to resist the new. The label closed mind comes from this safeguarding, and in this sense closed-mindedness and dogmatism are synonyms. Open-minded people, in contrast, are less subservient to authority and are amenable to a change of opinion when the evidence warrants. They are called open-minded because they "receive, evaluate, and act on relevant information received from the outside on its own intrinsic merits" (Rokeach, 1960, p. 57).

Both the dogmatist and the AUTHORITARIAN PERSONALITY are sensitized to the power structure. They also cater to and admire the strong, are ethnocentric, and are prone to be intolerant of any outgroup. Rokeach incorporates these facets into the concept of dogmatism but organizes the data around COGNITION rather than around the personality variables that color the concept of the authoritarian personality. This framework was adopted—in part at least—in response to criticisms that the research on authoritarianism neglected the political left. Rokeach suspected that the differences between extremists might be restricted to the *content* of their beliefs and that, paradoxically, their *ways of thinking* might be quite similar. "Persons adhering dogmatically to such diverse viewpoints as capitalism and communism, Catholicism and anti-Catholicism, should all score together at one end of the continuum, and should all score in a direction opposite to others having equally diverse yet undogmatic viewpoints" (Rokeach, 1960, p. 72).

The dogmatists' self-protection contrasts with the commonly expressed preference to continue to learn, to be well informed and knowledgeable. This discrepancy forces the closed mind to follow two divergent paths, that is, convince the self and others that he or she is readily persuasible while actually shunning that which might be out of line with "the truth." The techniques for disguising this duplicity are too complex to be reviewed here, but a few of the more prevalent ones can be mentioned. One way to preserve the credibility of authority is to avoid scrutinizing it, and one means of accomplishing this is to magnify the difference between the belief and the disbelief systems to such a level that it appears unnecessary to pursue the matter further. Following this route allows the dogmatist to arrive at a conviction that "the United States and Russia are completely different." Assessment can also be aborted by dismissing as irrelevant any evidence that suggests a weakness in what is believed. This device leads some people to interpret explicit contradictions as exceptions to a general principle. Such strategists see no problem, for example, in a statement that "democracy must be protected and therefore some people should not be allowed to vote." Limiting the sources of information is another way of insulating one's convictions. Thus a closed mind finds it easy to agree that "reading many books can confuse young people" and that "organizations should not tolerate disagreements."

Open and closed minds are studied by a variety of techniques, but probably the most commonly used one is some form of the D, or Dogmatism, Scale (Hanson, 1975, 1980). Incidentally, the title reflects expediency rather than the originator's preference. "Were it not so clumsy, we would have preferred to call this scale 'The Open-Closed Belief System Scale' " (Rokeach, 1960, p. 19). The test consists of a series of items similar to the paraphrased beliefs reported in a preceding paragraph, and it quantifies individual differences on the level of openness or closedness of the belief system. The test has been revised as experimental data have suggested changes (Troldahl & Powell, 1965).

The research has concentrated more on closed than on open minds, many of the initial results have been supported, but some have not. The overlap between authoritarian personalities and dogmatists has been found to be extensive, but the homogeneity between those at the extreme right and at the extreme left of the political spectrum has been both supported and challenged. Experimenters continue to confirm the initial reports that dogmatic people hold negative images both of themselves and of others, and that they are also prone to protect the inconsistencies in their belief systems. The data also expand the idea that prejudice is not determined solely by ethnicity or race but is also influenced by the belief system. Thus a closed mind has been found to describe a person who exhibits behavior that the bigot approves of as a "good Negro," and describes one who does not exhibit such behavior as an "uppity Negro" (Altemeyer, 1981; Vacchiano, Strauss, & Hochman, 1969).

Investigations of open minds indicate that these people are more tolerant of ambiguity than are dogmatists, and are not as readily influenced by traditional arguments (Vacchiano, 1977). There are also suggestions that a nondogmatic person often, but not always, perceives other people more accurately than a dogmatic one (Sawatzky & Zingle, 1969).

The research questions that have been posed embrace many of the new interests as they appear in the field of psychology. To illustrate—a relationship has been established between dogmatism and alienation, the estrangement from, or rejection of, traditional cultural values (Sexton, 1983). An affinity between these two variables was hypothesized because the closed-minded and the alienated have some common characteristics, including a certainty about the "rightness" of their judgments, the "wrongness" of others, and low confidence in their ability to cope. A second topic that is currently commanding attention is rape. Because observational data about rape are unavailable, researchers often rely on opinion, and this makes them receptive to studies of open and closed minds. Thornton, Ryckman, and Robbins (1982), for example, found that those who scored high on a test of dogmatism are also prone to believe that rape victims contribute to the episode. The authors relate this relationship to various factors, including the dogmatists' reputation for relying on simplistic explanations as well as their failure to seek out supplemental information or to search for extenuating circumstances.

A final example of research that illustrates the wide, even cross-cultural, appeal of the two concepts is a 1980 survey by Reddy, Rao, Padmakar, and Sandeep of "Open and Closed Belief Systems in Students." In this project the D Scale was administered to 1,747 pupils, aged fourteen to twenty years, in Hyderabad, India. No significant age or sex differences were found, but more rural than urban students were found to have closed minds, and more higher than lower socioeconomic students were found to have open minds.

References

Altemeyer, B. (1981). *Right-wing authoritarianism.* Winnipeg: University of Manitoba Press. A review of the literature. The author is critical and alert to methodological flaws.

Hanson, D. J. (1975). Dogmatism and authoritarianism: A bibliography of doctoral dissertations. *Catalog of Selected Documents in Psychology, 5*, 329. (Ms. No. 1100). During the interval 1950 through 1974, 533 dissertations were devoted to these concepts in the United States and Canada.

Hanson, D. J. (1980). Authoritarianism and dogmatism: A bibliography of master's theses. *Catalog of Selected Documents in Psychology, 10*, 87. (Ms. No. 2113). The author located 217 master's theses dealing with these topics and written in the United States and Canada between 1968 and 1978.

Reddy, N. Y., Rao, T. N., Padmakar, V. P., & Sandeep, P. (1980). Open and closed belief systems in students. *Psychological Studies, 25*, 43–47. This brief article describes a survey that required a large amount of work. It is noteworthy more as an illustration of interest in the topic than as authoritative data.

Rokeach, M. (1954). The nature and meaning of dogmatism. *Psychological Review, 61*, 194–204. This article, written for professional psychologists, is technical. Rokeach comments on some dogmatic beliefs about certain aspects of psychology.

Rokeach, M. (1960). *The open and closed mind: Investigations into the nature of belief systems and personality systems.* New York: Basic Books. This is a full-dress presentation of open-and closed-mindedness, and many investigations are reported. The experimental work began in the late 1940s.

Sawatzky, D. D., & Zingle, H. W. (1969). Accurate interpersonal perception and open-mindedness. *Perceptual and Motor Skills, 29*, 395–400. These investigators failed to find the positive relationship between open-mindedness and accuracy of the perception of others that several researchers had previously reported. They discuss problems in methodology that may contribute to the confusion.

Sexton, M. E. (1983). Alienation, dogmatism, and related personality characteristics. *Journal of Clinical Psychology, 39*, 80–86.

Thornton, B., Ryckman, R. M., & Robbins, M. A. (1982). The relationships of observer characteristics to beliefs in the causal responsibility of victims of sexual assault. *Human Relations, 35*, 321–330.

Troldahl, V. C., & Powell, F. A. (1965). A short-form dogmatism scale for use in field studies. *Social Forces, 44*, 211–214. "Short" forms of ten, fifteen, and twenty items (versus forty on the original scale) are described, and both their practicality and limitations are discussed.

Vacchiano, R. B. (1977). Dogmatism. In T. Blass (Ed.), *Personality variables in social behavior* (pp. 281–314). Hillsdale, NJ: Lawrence Erlbaum.

Vacchiano, R. B., Strauss, P. S., & Hochman, L. (1969). The open and closed mind: A review of dogmatism. *Psychological Bulletin, 71*, 261–273.

Sources of Additional Information

Ehrlich, H. J., & Lee, D. (1969). Dogmatism, learning, and resistance to change: A review and a new paradigm. *Psychological Bulletin, 71*, 249–260. This review agrees with the principle that the dogmatic person is less able to learn new beliefs (and to change old beliefs). The authors examine several variables that play a role in acquisition and change. Hoffer, E. (1951). *The true believer: Thoughts on the nature of mass movements.* New York: Harper & Row. A literary consideration of mass movements: "The fanaticism which animates them may be viewed and treated as one" (p. xi). In *The Open and Closed Mind* Rokeach commends Hoffer's "stimulating ideas" (p. 9). Restle, F., Andrews, M., & Rokeach, M. (1964). Differences between open- and closed-minded subjects on learning-set and oddity problems. *Journal of Abnormal and Social Psychology, 68*, 648–654. This study deals with detailed, specific performance on two kinds of learning tasks. Shaffer, D. R., & Case, T. (1982). On the decision to testify in one's own behalf: Effects of withheld evidence, defendent's sexual preferences, and juror dogmatism on juridic decisions. *Journal of Personality and Social Psychology, 42*, 335–346. The behavior of juries is attracting the research attention of psychologists as a situation in which personality may determine judgments. This example looks at the interaction between levels of dogmatism of jurors and three nonevidential variables.

DRIVE. 1. An hypothesized internal force that induces a searching for biological gratification—a primary or basic drive. 2. A synonym for a biological need. 3. An hypothesized activation of an organism by stimuli that are associated with variables that induce an emotional response and, therefore, an acquired, learned, or secondary drive.

The concept of drive was at one time a central topic in psychology, but it is currently out of fashion, although far from obsolete. It was introduced into the field in 1918 by Robert S. Woodworth (1869–1962), who borrowed it from mechanics in order to explain how a sequence of responses is sustained, why there is continuity after the stimulus disappears, why, for example, hunting dogs continue to track after the scent is interrupted. He thought of drive as an internal power, located in the nervous system and responsible for discharging stored energy that in turn activates a mechanism. Different mechanisms serve different purposes, but the gratification of biological needs was considered to be the most important. In this framework, organisms were construed as "driven" by internal forces to eat, to drink, to mate, and so on.

Woodworth's formulation was not entirely new in that it was foreshadowed by laboratory practices that had been in use for approximately two decades, specifically the strategy of withholding food in order to increase activity. Small provided a clear statement of this: "[Hunger] furnishes the best dynamic for mental procedure" (1900, p. 134). He acknowledged the effectiveness of other drives but commented: "Hunger is merely the most fundamental and most surely-to-be-relied-upon" (1900, p. 135).

Researchers welcomed the concept partly because it provided a rationale for what they were already doing and partly because the tangible status of organic conditions, as well as the ease of manipulating them, made them more appropriate research tools than the nonlocalized and elusive motive of *instinct*. Because *need* also denotes insufficiency, the word is sometimes substituted for drive. The two terms are, however, differentiated to the extent that drive is more frequently applied to animals and need, to humans, but the reader is reminded that this distinction is not consistently honored.

Moss' (1924) "Study of Animal Drives" illustrates some of the flavor of the pioneer work. He wanted to measure both drive and "resistance," a "repelling force." He defined drives as "impelling forces," and described what he believed happens when food is withheld: "Certain organic stimulations of the nerve-endings in the stomach provoke in the animal restless and seeking behavior until food is found and the 'drive' for the time being, stopped'' (p. 165). Moss constructed a box in which an electrified grid separated an animal from a goal. The equipment allowed him to determine the strength of a drive (usually quantified in hours of deprivation) that is necessary to overcome a particular resistance (usually a specific level of electric current). He investigated a number of levels of drive and resistance, but the results were awkward, in that they are not behavioral. Moss found, for example, that "when impelled by the sex drive only five of the ten [rats] overcame a resistance of 28v., but when impelled by a 72 hour hunger drive eight of the ten overcame the resistance'' (p. 171). In another part of the experiment Moss studied what he termed "the lesser of two evils'' (p. 176). Specifically, he measured the amount of decrease in the temperature of water in which the animals were standing that prompted them to climb up onto a charged grill.

This research was conducted at a time when the doctrine of evolution was nourishing an interest in the relative strength of drives so that a hierarchy of their contributions to survival could be arranged. Moss, recognizing the complexities in this matter, suggested that a 72 hour food drive may be stronger than the sex drive, and that both may exceed the maternal drive.

Criticisms of Moss' methods were inevitable, and improvements—both in apparatus and procedure—were devised. Probably the most effective of these came in a decision to decrease the amount of shock to a level that did not disturb the animal in any marked way, and to count the number and speed of crossings that an animal makes, a technique that uses behavioral measures (Warden, Jenkins, and Warner, 1935).

As time passed, researchers became less interested in the manipulation of merely biological drives and began instead to explore the activating properties of stimuli that are associated with the arousal of EMOTIONS. One of the first experiments in this extension was conducted by Miller (1948), who demonstrated that stimuli that are associated with fear-inducing events begin to function, in their own right, as motives. The decision to use fear favored obtaining positive results, inasmuch as it was believed to provoke activity and was recognized as "similar to hunger, thirst, sex, temperature deviations, and the many other forms of discomfort that harass living organisms'' (Mowrer, 1939, p. 558).

Miller placed rats in an area of a cage that was painted white with a floor that was an electrified grid. The animals could escape the shock merely by leaving the area and entering an adjoining compartment that was painted black and lacked a grid. After repeated exposures to the current the animals were placed in the lighted area *with no shock turned on*, but with the door to the darkened area closed. The door could be opened at first if the animals rotated a wheel slightly, and later if they pressed a bar. The rats reacted by indulging in random activities, including movements that, in the first problem, fortuitously opened the door and, in the second, moved the lever. On succeeding trials the animals began to make the effective manipulations more and more quickly. This reduction in time provided evidence that the fear the animal had learned constitutes a drive, and fear was labeled as an acquired, learned, or secondary drive. Miller also suggested that the reduction in fear provided REINFORCEMENT for the learning of responses that allow escape. This interpretation was initially resisted, but the ensuing plethora of experimentation on both drive and drive reduction converted many of the doubts into endorsements.

The acme of the concept of drive came in theories of NEOBEHAVIORISM, particularly in one devised by Clark L. Hull. He considered all the drives operative at one time to constitute a drive state, and assigned this a central role in strengthening learning. Waving a banner proclaiming the true scientist, Hull developed a system of theorems, postulates, and proofs. During the 1940s and the early 1950s these emblems of science attracted considerable attention, but the heyday was relatively short-lived, and by the end of the decade of the 1950s criticisms of drive were flourishing.

The luster of the concept was dimmed to some extent by some weaknesses in logic or structure. One of the conceptual limitations is the alleged—rather than the confirmed—status of drives. A second shortcoming involves two closely related assumptions: one that the dynamics of a drive come from depletion, and second that the strength of a drive increases in proportion to the amount of deprivation—the irregular idea that *more* comes from *less*. To illustrate—an eight-hour period of food abstinence is believed to induce a more intense drive than a four-hour interval (Bolles, 1958, 1975). Even learned drives are interpreted in this way. It is said, for example, that the greater the deprivation of parental love, the more intense the drive to retaliate.

A second cause of dissatisfaction came from laboratory data that disclosed some discrepancies between what was actually observed and what drive theory predicted. Miller's (1957) comparison of different ways of measuring drives illustrates a few of these irregularities. He points out the most commonly used measure of the hunger drive is the amount of food consumed, but he demonstrates that these measurements do not always vary in proportion to the amount of food-seeking behavior or with the availability or attractiveness of the reward. Furthermore, these results are altered when certain areas of the brain are stimulated. In other words, the effects of a drive are different, and there is no one-to-one link between the motive and the outcome.

The concept was also eroded as evidence that some phenomena that had been attributed to motivation might be the result of other variables. OPERANT CONDITIONING, for example, produced convincing demonstrations that the consequences of behavior mold or shape behavior. COGNITIVE PSYCHOLOGY called attention to what the organism contributes, and this focus on the properties of the organism disclosed that the decisions and selections, as well as a motive, may guide behavior. Yet another cue that drive may not be the most crucial factor came with the realization that it could not account for some kinds of behavior. EXPLORATION and play, for example, are neither derivatives of particular organic tissue needs nor do they have a specific goal, and they may well be carried on for their own sake. Other kinds of behavior also appeared to be self-supporting, and the motivational concept of COMPETENCE was formulated to account for them.

Many of these criticisms offer alternative explanations, and on the current scene several of these replacements are favored (Brown, 1979). Nonetheless the concept of drive is still in circulation, and some research on this specific topic continues. It is more the importance of the concept than the concept itself that has been diminished.

References

Bolles, R. C. (1958). The usefulness of the drive concept. In M. R. Jones (Ed.), *Nebraska symposium on motivation* (pp. 1–32). Lincoln: University of Nebraska Press. Bolles details various criticisms of the concept of drive.

Bolles, R. C. (1975). *Theory of motivation* (2nd ed.). New York: Harper & Row.

Brown, J. S. (1979). Motivation. In E. Hearst (Ed.), *The first century of experimental psychology* (pp. 231–272). New York: Lawrence Erlbaum.

Miller, N. E. (1948). Studies of fear as an acquirable drive: 1. Fear as motivation and fear-reduction as reinforcement in the learning of new responses. *Journal of Experimental Psychology, 38*, 89–101. This article is seen by many as the reference experiment in the research on learned drives. Miller read an account of an earlier study of anxiety as an acquired drive at the 1941 Annual Convention of the American Psychological Association.

Miller, N. E. (1957). Experiments on motivation: Studies combining psychological, physiological and pharmacological techniques. *Science, 126* (No. 3286), 1271–1278.

Moss, F. A. (1924). Study of animal drives. *Journal of Experimental Psychology, 7*, 165–185.

Mowrer, O. H. (1939). A stimulus-response analysis of anxiety and its role as a reinforcing agent. *Psychological Review, 46*, 553–565. Mowrer uses fear and anxiety as synonyms.

Small, W. S. (1900). An experimental study of the mental processes of the rat. *American Journal of Psychology, 11*, 133–165. A lengthy detailed account that alerts readers to the differences in laboratory procedures then and now.

Warden, C. J., Jenkins, T. N., & Warner, L. H. (1935). *Comparative psychology: A comprehensive treatise. Vol. 1. Principles and methods.* New York: Ronald Press.

Woodworth, R. S. (1918). *Dynamic psychology.* New York: Columbia University Press. Woodworth explains that the continuity among responses cannot be accounted for by either consciousness or behavior. The former discloses only one aspect of mentality, and unconscious processes are elusive. Behavior is merely a series of reactions to external stimuli. He suggests that drive provides coherence.

Sources of Additional Information

Flynn, J. P., & Jerome, E. A. (1952). Learning in an automatic multiple-choice box with light as incentive. *Journal of Comparative and Physiological Psychology, 45*, 336–340. The authors observe rats learning various ways to escape light. The introduction to the article illustrates the undue eagerness, at the time the study was carried out, to infer a drive. Glowa, J. R., & Barrett, J. E. (1983). Drug history modifies the behavioral effects of pentobarbital. *Science, 220* (No. 4594), 333–335. The authors cite research indicating that behavioral effects of drugs are clearly dependent on drug history. Their own results concur that "prior experience with one psychoactive drug can determine the behavioral effects of a different drug" (p. 333). Such data suggest that the dichotomy of primary and secondary drives is artificial, and that, in fact, they influence each other. Miller, N. E. (1951). Learnable drives and rewards. In S. S. Stevens (Ed.), *Handbook of Experimental Psychology* (pp. 435–472). New York: John Wiley. Miller is one of the key figures in establishing the concept of learned drives. "When, as a result of learning, previously neutral cues gain the capacity to play the same functional role in the learning and performance of new responses as do other drives, such as hunger and thirst, these cues may be said to have a learned drive value" (p. 436). Skinner, B. F. (1936). Thirst as an arbitrary drive. *Journal of General Psychology, 15*, 205–210. Skinner wondered if thirst might not be more suitable for experimentation than hunger, primarily because hunger refers to a number of tastes (salt, fat, sugar, etc.), whereas thirst refers to water. Rats, however, performed with less regularity when thirsty than when hungry. This article is a good example of the experimentalists intrigue with drive. Wayner, M. J., & Carey, R. J. (1973). Basic drives. In P. H. Mussen & M. R. Rosenzweig (Eds.), *Annual Review of Psychology*, Vol. 24, pp. 53–80. The authors review recent work and complain about careless procedures in what appears, on the surface, to be meticulous work.

E

ECOLOGICAL PSYCHOLOGY. 1. The study of the frequency and nature of psychological responses in natural settings. ENVIRONMENTAL PSY-CHOLOGY. 1. An approach to, or point of view in, psychology that explores the effects of specific aspects of the environment, often for the purpose of improving the quality of life.

The concepts of ecological and environmental psychology are recent developments, and they are both innovative and similar in that they amend the traditional stress on the importance of the organism with an emphasis on the importance of the environment. This orientation contrasts with a more traditional inclination to interpret the setting as a source of stimulation, a kind of reservoir that can be taken for granted, and to observe and dissect the reactions of organisms to the setting. Most of the concepts in psychology have been formulated within this organism-centered perspective so that PERCEPTION, for example, concentrates on how individuals interpret stimuli, and PERSONALITY targets the consistency of individuality.

Although ecological psychology is considered by some to be a variety of the broader field of environmental psychology, it was the first of the two movements to be organized, and it is sufficiently different in origin and in perspective to merit treatment in its own right. The concept of ecology first emerged in biology as a by-product of the study of the evolutionary principle of the survival of the fittest, and the stress was on the study of the interdependence between both plants and animals and the locations in which they live. During the 1920s and 1930s sociologists began to apply some of the bioecological formulations to humans, with particular attention devoted to the differences among geographic areas in the incidence of disease, crime, and poverty, for example, the "inner city" versus the suburbs (Faris, 1944).

The word ecology has been used by different psychologists in isolated instances, usually to describe some stimulus properties (Wicker, 1979b), but it was not applied to the field as a whole until Roger Barker, beginning in the 1940s, undertook the task of observing what he called the "stream of behavior." His purpose was to ascertain the nature and frequency of responses that psychologists customarily observe under the artificial conditions of the laboratory. In order to become familiar with these noncontrived responses Barker (1963, 1965) and his colleagues observed and recorded the actions of people in their daily routines. The yield from this naturalistic method is overwhelming; for example, 119 children engaged in approximately 100,000 episodes daily, or more than 36 million in a year (Barker, 1968).

This mass pointed to the necessity of organizing the data, and behavior settings were chosen as the foci of this scheme. Barker characterizes these as spatially, temporally, and functionally distinct units, such as an athletic field, a bank, and a medical office. The various roles that are played out in these situations are familiar. Barker construes them as regulating the conduct of the participants, and even suggests that behavior can be more accurately predicted on the basis of behavior settings than on the basis of personality. Personal preferences are expressed in the selection of particular roles in a setting, and the latter also tolerate some individuality. In Barker's own words, "all behavior settings allow some unprogrammed behavior" (Barker, 1968, p. 204), but he pays less attention to this than to the high level of conformity that is displayed on such occasions as weddings, church services, and commencement exercises.

Until the late 1960s Barker and a few colleagues were the principals involved in ecological psychology. Their orientation was resisted in part because it contrasts with the deeply entrenched belief that psychology is a theoretically sophisticated enterprise. Ecological data are often descriptive, lack an elaborate theoretical superstructure, and are static in that they depict sequences of molar activities while neglecting covert components such as feelings and motivation (Marx & Cronan-Hillix, 1987). The proponents' attempts to counter these criticisms often fail to convince, even when they are cogent, as in the case of pointing out the regulating power of a traffic light, or the rapidity with which the label deviant is applied when behavior is inappropriate for a setting—a teacher, for example, who does not control a class and a pupil who does are readily seen as aberrant.

The resistance to tradition was not, however, complete, and some of the formulations of ecological psychology began to attract interest. One illustration of this is the doctrine of manning. Barker, long impressed by the extent to which community residents participated in numerous behavior settings, compared behavior in "undermanned" and optimally manned circumstances. He concluded that in the former, people take up a wider range of tasks and become more involved with functions that are important to the setting. For example, students in a small school, one that is presumably undermanned, are found, in contrast to those in a large school, to be exposed to more pressure to participate and to have more positions of responsibility. This was followed by additional research on "overmanning" or "overstaffing" (Wicker, 1979a; Wicker & Kirmeyer, 1977). A logical extension of this line of inquiry, and one that is being pursued, is a search for ways to improve systems rather than people. Another implication is that of fine tuning or adjusting behavior settings rather than promoting the adaptation of individuals (Willems, 1977, 1987).

Environmental psychologists take a less extreme position than that of the ecologists, in that they do not see the environment largely as a force that fosters conformity, but depict its influence as varying among different people (Wohlwill, 1970). There have been instances throughout the history of psychology in which the weight of circumstances has been featured, but these are largely unrelated. One of the earliest and most influential acknowledgments of the effects of the environment came with the discovery in CLASSICAL CONDITIONING that the repeated presentation of paired *stimuli* results in a conditioned response. Thus a dog, after repeated exposure to the sound of the opening of a refrigerator door just before the presentation of food, comes to react to the previously meaningless noise of the door in a manner similar to the way it reacts to the food. OPERANT CONDITIONING assigned the environment a paramount role when it interpreted conditioning as contingent on consequences. According to this view, a dog learns to sit up and beg for food *as a result of environmental action*.

Although the concept of MOTIVATION is dominated by internal motives, such as drive and need, there are also concepts of external motives, such as GOAL and INCENTIVE. The importance of the setting is also important in the concept of COMPETENCE, in that this motive is believed to be gratified by manipulating or ordering the milieu, as an infant enjoying shaking a rattle and an executive enjoying weighing various arrangements of agenda items.

Interpretations of this nature have reminded psychologists of environmental factors, but they are not antecedents of environmental psychology, in that direct lines of descent cannot be discerned. Some continuity appears to begin with the increased concern about the quality of life that developed during the post-World War II era. At that time at least three groups with divergent purposes began to incorporate psychological variables into their programs. Architects started to pay explicit attention to the human needs that have always been implicit in their designs. A second impetus came from a heightened interest in public welfare and public health, and the third grew out of attempts to protect the limited resources of the earth. These origins fused, and environmental psychology was formed as a multidisciplinary, task-oriented enterprise that embraces "a direct and clearly stated concern with solving environmental problems in order to achieve a better society" (Proshansky & O'Hanlon, 1977, p. 115).

The experimental results that are accumulating from attempts to intervene in a variety of situations indicate that simple, straightforward relationships between specific settings and specific responses are rare, and that indirect, intricate interactions are the rule (Moos, 1976). This complexity is a function of the individuality with which people perceive their surroundings, and these variations make it necessary to ascertain the particulars that individuals expect from settings. In other words, in capturing the effects of circumstances, environmental psychologists attend carefully to the players as well as to the stage. The following examples of research document the interplay.

A network of effects between the size of a building and the satisfaction of its occupants is illustrated in an investigation of the validity of complaints about feelings of social isolation on the part of residents in a modern high-rise dormitory (Holahan, 1978). Two groups of second-semester freshmen—one living in a low-rise facility and the other in a "megadormitory"—were questioned about their satisfaction with living conditions. They also rated their confidence and skill in their own ability to manage social situations, and named other residents whom they would like as companions both in recreational and in discussion groups.

The responses indicate that relationships between endorsement of a housing unit and its size depend on both the capacity of the unit and the adjustment patterns of individuals. Those in the smaller lodging who describe themselves as socially competent tend to report satisfaction with the setting and to be involved in friendship networks within the unit. But, in contrast, megadormitory students who see themselves as socially competent tend not to approve of the residence and to seek companions outside the quarters. The undergraduates in the large unit who see themselves as socially incompetent differ from the mixers in that they find this unit to be satisfactory. The researcher suggests that the extramural contacts of the interpersonally successful residents increase the opportunities for inhouse friendships among those who are less adequate, and the availability of these contacts may be responsible for the approbation.

Some of the experiments are undertaken to clarify unexpected reactions, such as the resistance of some slum residents to moving away from the deprived neighborhoods in which they reside. The evidence of a strong attachment to unhealthy and even dangerous areas prompted Fried and Gleicher (1970) to look for positive benefits of living in such a neighborhood. Interviews disclosed that many of the inhabitants have extensive personal contacts, both kinships and friendships, in the slum, and the stronger these ties, the greater the attraction to the district. Another appeal is found in the way the area immediately adjacent to the home is perceived. For many occupants the barrier between a substandard house and the outside is blurred, in that the surroundings are seen as living space—a place to gather and converse, a playground for children. Thus asking people to change their residence may include a demand to relinquish functionally important territory.

Attitudes toward remote, uninhabited areas indicate that opinions about settings vary from era to era as well as from person to person. Lucas (1970) introduces a study of differences in the assessment of a wilderness region with comments about how the evaluation of the hinterlands has, during the past century, changed from active dislike and avoidance to praise. The pendulum has swung from an appreciation that rested solely on the potential for development to an appreciation of the intrinsic merits of such areas.

Lucas interviewed people while they were visiting an isolated region that is primarily devoted to recreation but also supports some commercial logging. The sense of wildness was found to depend on the number of people whom they encountered, and this number appears to carry more weight than the distance from the access point. Those who share recreational preferences also tend to have some additional common beliefs about the locale, but there are also discrepancies, probably the most marked between canoeists and those who use motorboats. The former frequently remark about the isolated, primeval aspects, are very critical of motorboats, dislike the logging, and judge the area as smaller.

In summary, both ecological and environmental psychology investigate the effects of surroundings on behavior, but they differ in the amount of importance that is assigned to the location. Ecological psychology looks for the control of events in the setting, whereas environmental psychology deals with the interplay between the milieu and the occupants. Ecological psychology stresses the discovery of behavior as it occurs spontaneously, whereas environmental psychology stresses the amelioration of problems.

References

Barker, R. G. (Ed.). (1963). *The stream of behavior: Explorations of its structure and content.* New York: Appleton-Century-Crofts. There are twelve chapters, written by different authors, and the coverage clearly illustrates the methods used in ecological psychology.

Barker, R. G. (1965). Explorations in ecological psychology. *American Psychologist, 20,* 1–14.

Barker, R. G. (1968). *Ecological psychology: Concepts and methods for studying the environment of human behavior.* Stanford, CA: Stanford University Press.

Faris, R. E. L. (1944). Ecological factors in human behavior. In J. McV. Hunt (Ed.), *Personality and the behavior disorders* (Vol. 2, pp. 736–757). New York: Ronald Press. An account of ecology in the field of sociology.

Fried, M., & Gleicher, P. (1970). Some sources of residential satisfaction in an urban slum. In H. M. Proshansky, W. H. Ittelson, & L. G. Rivlin (Eds.), *Environmental psychology: Man and his physical setting* (pp. 333–345). New York: Holt, Rinehart & Winston. This study was first published in 1961. The authors seem to be unusually sensitive to the needs and fears of the people they interview.

Holahan, C. J. (1978). *Environment and behavior: A dynamic perspective.* New York: Plenum Press.

Lucas, R. C. (1970). User concepts of wilderness and their implications for resource management. In H. M. Proshansky, W. H., Ittelson, & L. G. Rivlin (Eds.), *Environmental psychology: Man and his physical setting* (pp. 297–302). New York: Holt, Rinehart & Winston. This article was first published in 1964. This volume in which it is reprinted is edited by the staff of The Environmental Psychology Program established at the City University of New York in 1967.

Marx, M. H. & Cronan-Hillix, W. A. (1987). *Systems and theories in psychology* (4th ed.). New York: McGraw-Hill.

Moos, R. H. (1976). *The human context: Environmental determinants of behavior*. New York: John Wiley. Moos advocates the integration and synthesis of the individual and the environment rather than a focus on either of these two variables. Moos, with the assistance of several colleagues, reviews an extensive amount of relevant literature.

Proshansky, H. M., & O'Hanlon, T. (1977). Environmental psychology: Origins and development. In D. Stokols (Ed.), *Perspectives on environment and behavior: Theory, research, and applications* (pp. 101–130). New York: Plenum Press.

Wicker, A. W. (1979a). Ecological psychology: Some recent and prospective developments. *American Psychologist, 34*, 755–765.

Wicker, A. W. (1979b). *An introduction to ecological psychology*. Monterey, CA: Brooks/Cole. This comprehensive review of the field is written for a general audience. The author comments on uses of the word ecology in relation to a few specialized topics. One illustration of this is also mentioned in this volume in J. J. Gibson's work as described in the discussion on SENSATION

Wicker, A. W., & Kirmeyer, S. (1977). From church to laboratory to national park: A program of research on excess and insufficient populations in behavior settings. In D. Stokols (Ed.), *Perspectives on environment and behavior: Theory, research, and applications* (pp. 69–96). New York: Plenum Press. The authors observe the effects of too few and too many participants in different behavior settings. They amend naturalistic observations with experimental data.

Willems, E. P. (1977). Behavioral ecology. In D. Stokols (Ed.), *Perspectives on environment and behavior: Theory, research, and applications* (pp. 39–68). New York: Plenum Press. Willems stresses the potential contributions of behavioral ecology to human problems.

Willems, E. P. (1987). Strong questions—weak answers. [Review of *Social system accounts: Linking social and economic indicators through tangible behavior settings*]. *Contemporary Psychology, 32*, 561–562. Willems criticizes the research reported in *Social Systems Accounts*, but his remarks provide a perspective on research practices in ecological psychology.

Wohlwill, J. F. (1970). The emerging discipline of environmental psychology. *American Psychologist, 25*, 303–312. Wohlwill's enthusiasm for this new perspective in psychology is typical of many of its proponents: "We can confidently venture a prediction that the near future will see the construction of novel types of environments for living, ranging from individual dwellings . . . to the possible colonization of the moon" (p. 311). He expresses the hope that these plans will be supported by valid psychological data.

Sources of Additional Information

Chein, I. (1954). The environment as a determinant of behavior. *Journal of Social Psychology, 39*, 115–127. This is one of the early arguments that psychologists should attend more carefully to the environment, and Chein offers some guidelines for accomplishing this. This is one of the more explicit discussions—before the formation of ecological and environmental psychology—of the influence of the milieu on behavior.

Craik, K. H. (1973). Environmental psychology. In P. H. Mussen & M. R. Rosenzweig (Eds.), *Annual review of psychology* (Vol. 24, pp. 403–422). Craik's reference list has 280 entries, an impressive number for the date of publication. The author cites both journals and newsletters that are devoted to the topic. Connors, M. M., Harrison, A. A., & Akins, F. R. (1985). *Living aloft: Human requirements for extended space flight.* Washington, DC: National Aeronautics and Space Administration. This is a review of the research on the psychological aspects of space flight—an unusual and demanding environment. O'Neal, E. C., & McDonald, P. J. (1976). The environmental psychology of aggression. In R. G. Geen & E. C. O'Neal (Eds.), *Perspectives on aggression* (pp. 169–192). New York: Academic Press. The authors discuss the relationship between aggression and several other variables, including noise, heat, territoriality, crowding, anonymity, and diffusion of responsibility,

EFFECT. 1. A "law" or observation that the probability that a response will reoccur increases when the response that is being learned is followed by satisfaction and decreases when the response is followed by dissatisfaction. **REINFORCEMENT.** 1. Complementing a response in a way that increases the probability that the response will reoccur.

These concepts are similar in that they assume that environmental reactions determine the responses that are learned. It is this focus on outcome that differentiates them from MOTIVATION, a concept that deals with the instigating and directing of responses. Effect, the older formulation, features the influence of gratification, whereas reinforcement omits references to affective consequences. Reinforcement, a modern concept, has been primarily developed by the proponents of SKINNERIAN OR OPERANT BEHAVIORISM, and it therefore disregards subjective experiences of the learner. Both COGNITIVE PSYCHOLOGY and the HUMAN POTENTIAL MOVEMENT criticize the neglect of the role of the learner, but these attacks are relatively recent and have not obscured the opinion that mastery is a function of its consequences. Rather, they have reactivated prior arguments about the shortcomings of both effect and reinforcement.

The concept of effect grew out of research programs on LEARNING, and Edward L. Thorndike (1874–1949), one of the pathfinders in that enterprise, established an enduring legacy. He first conducted experiments on learning in animals, and stated the results as the law of effect: responses that are accompanied or followed by satisfaction are strengthened and those that are accompanied or followed by discomfort are weakened (1911/1965). Thorndike assumed that learning would be rapid if animals indulged in thinking, but inasmuch as it was found to be gradual he disavowed any mediating processes and referred to the animals' acquisition as "trial and success," and stressed the random basis of the initial solutions. The phenomenon soon came to be called "trial and error" learning, and this label persists.

Thorndike was a prolific experimenter, and he investigated the role of a variety of rewards and punishments in humans as well as in various animal species. As this research continued Thorndike strengthened his initial conclusion that rewards increase the probability of repeating correct responses, and at the same time weakened an earlier impression that annoyance eliminates responses. He finally came to view rewards as much more effective than punishment, and suggested that unpleasantness causes the animal to try something else, but it does not weaken the response per se (Thorndike, 1935). This differential in effectiveness led to an erroneous impression that still persists that punishment is powerless. Marx and Cronan-Hillix single this out for attention by commenting that Thorndike "unwittingly gave rise to one of the most incredible psychological dogmas of the twentieth century: that punishment is ineffective in eliminating responses. . . . Presumably sensible psychologists were heard to say that punishment was really ineffective, because its effects might disappear after the punishment was withdrawn" (1987, p. 58).

Faith in the power of effect became so strong that the conviction developed that effect, in some form at least, is operative in all instances of learning (Postman, 1947). This credence is extreme in that there are instances in which gratifying effects do not lead to repetition. Students, for example, do not repeat academic courses in which they receive high grades. An engineer may well modify a satisfactory product rather than merely reconstruct it.

Many psychologists, reluctant to abandon the concept, tried to accommodate to the exceptions to the law of effect by tinkering with its formulation. To illustrate—Allport (1946) suggested that the law may apply only to the learning of simple, concrete responses on the part of animals and young children, and proposed that acquisition in the case of mature adults is a multidetermined event that involves both motives and intellectual processes—a suggestion that anticipated cognitive psychology. At the same time, Rice (1946) suggested that the responses that are strengthened by their consequences might be covert ones. To illustrate—a successful student's *academic interest* is rewarded when a high grade is earned, and this interest is exercised by enrolling in advanced courses. An engineer's *self-esteem* is enhanced when a highly commended product is devised, and repetition emerges in the making of additional designs. Inflicting harm may gratify a criminal's *wish to harm* and thereby prompt its repetition. This reformulation adds flexibility to the concept but also allows it to be applied without restraint.

During the course of these speculations the vocabulary has been altered and the sequel of a response is now referred to as reinforcement rather than effect. This change came from the dominance of OPERANT CONDITIONING, an enterprise in which reinforcement is central. As early as 1938 its chief advocate, B. F. Skinner, summarized the laboratory data in two conclusions that many assess as inerrant: "Law of conditioning. . . . *If the occurrence of an operant is followed by presentation of a reinforcing stimulus, the strength is increased*;" and "law of extinction. . . . *If the occurrence of an operant already strengthened through conditioning is not followed by the reinforcing stimulus, the strength is decreased*" (p. 21).

A reinforcing stimulus is called a positive reinforcer if its delivery increases the probability that the response will reoccur (food as a consequence of bar pressing). A reinforcing stimulus is called a negative reinforcer if its removal increases the probability that the response will reoccur (stopping electric shock as a consequence of bar pressing). This terminology reflects the insistence of the advocates of SKINNERIAN OR OPERANT BEHAVIORISM that subjective experiences be eliminated from psychology. The vocabulary that results from this demand is a bit unusual. For example, reward is defined as "a colloquial term for a reinforcing stimulus" (Verplanck, 1957, p. 32). Reward is used as a synonym for positive reinforcement by psychologists who are not restrained by behaviorism, but the purists disdain this practice. Furthermore, punishment is clearly not a synonym for a negative reinforcer, but rather it refers to two procedures. In one an aversive stimulus follows a response (reprimand for talking in class), and in the second a positive reinforcer is withheld (denial of recess privileges for talking in class). In the early era, operant behaviorists tended to agree with Thorndike's conclusion that punishment is not effective in suppressing behavior. The issue attracted only limited attention until the 1970s but the research still provokes controversy (Bower & Hilgard, 1981).

Operant conditioning procedures are carried out with precision and caution. For example, when the goal is to train a kindergartner to raise an arm in order to signal the teacher, reinforcement is applied only when the arm and hand are moved. It is withheld when other responses are made, even those that are goal-oriented, such as speaking to or approaching the teacher directly. Because the child may not spontaneously use a signal it may be necessary at first to reinforce any movement of the arm, and after that act is established to reinforce only upward movements, and thus step by step to "shape" the target response.

Critics of both the law of effect and reinforcement encounter a few—but only a few—shortcomings in the data, but there are criticisms of the concepts. There are allegations, for example, that both are contaminated by circular reasoning and by explanations that invoke retroactive phenomena. The usual method of supporting the first of these accusations is to point out that reinforcement is interpreted as strengthening learning, and learning is then interpreted as evidence of reinforcement. Meehl's summary is typical of this kind of censure, both early and recent versions of it: "If we define a reinforcing agent by its effect upon learning, then it seems that whenever learning is effected, we know ('by definition') that we have given a reinforcement" (1950, p. 57).

As early as 1938 Skinner, in line with his well-known preference to rely on data rather than on doctrine, dismissed the indictment: "A reinforcing stimulus is defined as such by its power to produce the resulting change. There is no circularity about this; some stimuli are found to produce the change, others not, and they are classified as reinforcing and non-reinforcing accordingly" (p. 62).

Additional disclaimers from others followed, but there is still no consensus and the argument continues. As recently as 1985 Paniagua repeated the criticism: "Skinner's definition *was circular* (in the earlier days of operant conditioning), *is circular* (in contemporary operant research), *and will always be circular* (in future practices of operant conditioning)" (p. 198).

The charge of retroaction in both the concept of effect and the concept of reinforcement is commonly introduced by calling attention to the temporal sequence: first, a response is made and then it is complemented by a stimulus, and this second event is then reputed to strengthen the prior one. Psychologists, defensive about their qualifications as scientists, reacted to the reproaches for thinking in terms of backward action by searching for explanations in the after-effects of the responses. Several theorists, both pioneers and contemporaries, propose that neural activities connect the response and the consequence (Black, 1971; Landauer, 1969). Others try to deal with psychological events, suggesting, for example, that gratifying results lead to covert rehearsals and these strengthen the response (Bower & Hilgard, 1981).

Skinnerian behaviorists pay little or no heed to the charges of circularity and retroaction, but assiduously continue to refine the technology. Their laboratory results are reported in an objective, atheoretical manner, and they compound the evidence that learning resonates with the environmental reactions to it (Guttman, 1977).

References

Allport, G. W. (1946). Effect: A secondary principle of learning. *Psychological Review, 53*, 335–347. This paper, as well as the one by Rice, was part of a symposium on "The Ego and the Law of Effect."
Black, A. H. (1971). The direct control of neural processes by reward and punishment. *American Scientist, 59*, 236–245.
Bower, G. H., & Hilgard, E. R. (1981). *Theories of learning* (5th ed.). Englewood Cliffs, NJ: Prentice-Hall. The preface to this fifth revision of a highly respected text comments on the fluidity of the field, the large number of players, and the "information overload" (p. v). The authors organize the plethora of facts in a masterful fashion. It is a rich resource for information about learning and relevant theories.
Guttman, N. (1977). On Skinner and Hull: A reminiscence and projection. *American Psychologist, 32*, 321–328. Guttman predicts that Skinner's influence will endure longer in "the active affairs of civilization" (p. 328) than in scientific psychology per se, but no immediate disappearance from the latter domain is predicted.
Landauer, T. K. (1969). Reinforcement as consolidation. *Psychological Review, 76*, 82–96. A fairly typical example of hypothetical neural explanations of psychological events, in this case "the retroactive effect of operant reinforcement." An excerpt from the abstract of the paper: "A hyperexcitable state exists in the nervous system following an experience, such that an ordinarily insufficient stimulus can reexcite all or part of the cells involved in a just prior learning experience" (p. 82).
Marx, M. H. & Cronan-Hillix, W. A. (1987). *Systems and theories in psychology* (4th ed.). New York: McGraw-Hill.
Meehl, P. E. (1950). On the circularity of the law of effect. *Psychological Bulletin, 47*, 52–75. Meehl considered the problem of circularity to be the same in the principle of effect and in reinforcement, and proposed a solution that many accepted. He suggested that the criticism of a closed loop could be dismissed in the case of trans-situational reinforcers, that is, reinforcing stimuli that can be shown to firm up various responses. To illustrate—demonstrating that the phrase "that's right" spoken after correct answers facilitates learning a multiplication table, spelling, and the reading of a ruler.

Paniagua, F. A. (1985). The relational definition of reinforcement: Comments on cir-
    cularity. *The Psychological Record, 35*, 193–202.
Postman, L. (1947). The history and present status of the law of effect. *Psychological
    Bulletin, 44*, 489–563. A "must" for the historian of the concept of effect.
Rice, P. B. (1946). The ego and the law of effect. *Psychological Review, 53*, 307–320.
Skinner, B. F. (1938). *The behavior of organisms: An experimental analysis*. New York:
    Appleton-Century-Crofts. This is one of Skinner's first integrations of his research
    productivity. It is a classic, written when conditioned "reflexes" were still in
    vogue in psychology. Skinner is the outstanding promoter of reinforcement: "The
    study of conditioning is not the study of a kind of reflex but of the operation of
    reinforcement and its effect upon reflex strength" (p. 62).
Thorndike, E. L. (1965). *Animal intelligence: Experimental studies*. New York: Hafner
    Publishing. (Original work published 1911). The 1911 book consists of the 1898
    dissertation supplemented by papers on three species as well as a general discus-
    sion.
Thorndike, E. L. (1935). *The psychology of wants, interests and attitudes*. New York:
    Appleton-Century. Thorndike's interests ran the gamut from simple organisms to
    intricate human learning. In this book he takes on, as the title indicates, complex
    topics and discloses a keen awareness of interpersonal relationships as he relates
    this information to laboratory data.
Verplanck, W. S. (1957). A glossary of some terms used in the objective science of
    behavior. *Psychological Review, 64* (6, Pt. 2).

Sources of Additional Information

Cole, L. E., & Bruce, W. F. (1950). *Educational psychology*. Yonkers-on-Hudson, NY:
World Book. This textbook portrays the resistance that is typical of some educators to
the law of effect because it is an objective, noncognitive account of learning: "When
Thorndike's studies emphasize the blindness of the learner, the random character of his
responses, the failure of imitation to occur, the limited value of guidance, the absence
of anything that looks like reason, we need to recall his basic bias and his preference for
animal subjects, for 'naïve learners' " (p. 459). Dashiell, J. F. (1949). *Fundamentals of
general psychology* (3rd ed.). Boston: Houghton Mifflin. This textbook is from the same
era as the previous entry, Cole and Bruce, but there is a sharp contrast in the assessment
of effect: "Formulated by Thorndike as the *Law of Effect* . . . in its more general formulation is hardly to be challenged" (p. 435). The author then in a manner similar to
that of Allport and Rice, suggests that it "neglects the *relation* of each particular act to
the *total performance* . . . to the *fundamental motivation* of the subject in his learning.
The Law of Effect still holds, but we must broaden our notion of 'effect' " (p. 439).
Higgins, S. T., & Morris, E. K. (1985). A comment on contemporary definitions of
reinforcement of a behavioral process. *The Psychological Record, 35*, 81–88. The authors
point out some instances of carelessness in current uses of the term reinforcement. They
suggest various improvements. Jenkins, W. O., & Rigby, M. K. (1950). Partial (periodic)
versus continuous reinforcement in resistance to extinction. *Journal of Comparative and
Physiological Psychology, 43*, 30–40. There has been a mass of research on the relative
efficacy of a variety of time schedules of reinforcement. This technical paper illustrates
this kind of experiment. Jenkins, W. O., & Stanley, J. C., Jr. (1950). Partial reinforcement: A review and critique. *Psychological Bulletin, 47*, 193–234. This is a scholarly
review of the research concerning the strength of learning when reinforcement is applied

to less than 100 percent of the trials. It places the previous article in perspective and alerts the reader to some of the complexities that reinforcement involves. Rogers, C. R., & Skinner, B. F. (1956). Some issues concerning the control of human behavior. *Science, 124*, 1057–1066 (No. 3231). Skinner values the control of behavior, whereas Rogers values personal freedom and choice. These two psychologists discuss their points of agreement and of disagreement.

EGO DEFENSE MECHANISMS.   See DEFENSE MECHANISMS.

EMOTION(S).   1. A number of responses that range from extreme unpleasantness through extreme pleasantness. They interrupt ongoing behavior and are accompanied by an awareness of certain physiological reactions. 2. A synonym for feeling(s). **FEELING(S).**   1. Responses that are similar to but less intense than emotions.   2. A synonym for emotion(s).

These concepts originated in a philosophical tradition that held that the mind consists of three parts: cognition, conation (volition or striving), and affection. The last of these has been characterized in various ways but frequently subdivided into feeling and emotion. At the time the concepts were adopted by psychology, mentalism was the order of the day, with each considered to be an entity, and thus commonly referred to in the singular. As the field of psychology became more scientific the concepts of response and behavior replaced the idea of an impalpable mind, and a vocabulary change ensued in that feeling often became feelings and emotion became emotions. During this era these terms were used by psychologists almost exclusively in reference to laboratory research, and affection as an aspect of the daily lives of people was not then of much interest to scientists.

Traditionally, affective responses are differentiated from other responses in that they involve various physiological reactions, predominantly involuntary and visceral. Many of these are consciously experienced, such as increases in pulse rate, alterations in rate and amplitude of breathing, and increases in perspiration. This awareness is typically clear, at times so vivid that the descriptions of affective episodes are often dominated by references to them: "My heart was pounding," "I trembled so hard I could not run," "My mouth was so dry I could hardly speak."

A few early theorists defined feeling as a sense of pleasure or displeasure, either brief or extended, and reserved emotion for incidents in which the respondent's ongoing behavior is disorganized. Bentley (1925) comments: "The most obvious thing to be said about the emotion is that it is at once a 'seizure' and a 'predicament.' . . . We confess to being 'seized' by fear, 'overcome' by grief, 'harassed' by uncertainty, 'carried away' by rage and 'beside ourselves' with joy" (p. 295).

This distinction was honored only in restricted circles, and synonymity became, and remains, prevalent: "Feelings and emotions are distinguished with difficulty. One needs but to open any book on psychology to see the confusion which reigns in this subject" (Claparède, 1928, p. 126). "Clearly, one thing we mean if we use the word *emotion* is personal, subjective *feeling*" [italics added] (Strongman, 1973, p. 1).

A second change in vocabulary started to take shape when psychology began to address the concepts of personality and adjustment. Gradually the word emotions rather than feelings came to be used in designating formal laboratory work on affection. The American Psychological Association (1985) recommends using emotions rather than feelings at all times, but both words are applied when the topic is the affective behavior of a person, rather than affective behavior per se. In these instances the referent is frequently a protracted reaction, often one that centers around interpersonal relationships. To illustrate—"Her feelings about her sister are mixed" and "This feeling of regret will not go away."

Ironically the research literature on emotions seldom deals with their motivational properties. Both fear and rage, for example, are recognized by the laity as precipitants of action, but psychologists have generally been quite unconcerned about this attribute. There was a flurry of interest in the 1940s when theorists became interested in how a DRIVE might be learned. But research on the acquisition of drive was popular for only a few years, and when it was removed from the agenda, inquiries about the motivating power of emotion also diminished.

Leeper (1948) was one of the few who made an attempt to integrate emotion and motivation. He suggested that the emphasis on disorganization had distracted from the organizational aspect of emotions—the attention given to being "affected" appears to have obscured the "effective." Leeper pointed out that fright, for example, may interrupt work, but it also mobilizes actions that are designed to deal with the threat. He argued that "emotional responses operate primarily as motives . . . they are processes which arouse, sustain, and direct activity" (p. 17).

Leeper's argument was strong, but as indicated previously, few were convinced. Unfortunately this state of affairs has not changed much. A modern textbook illustrates the confusion that still persists: "Emotions can activate and direct behavior in the same way that basic motives do. . . . Despite their similarities, emotions and motives need to be distinguished. . . . These distinctions are not absolute" (Atkinson, Atkinson, Smith, & Hilgard, 1987, p. 351).

The failures to coordinate these two topics force a person who is seeking information about either of them to survey the literature on both. There is one custom that, in some instances, may shorten this search. This is a tendency to classify long-term, persisting reactions as motivation, and to label immediate reactions, including those aroused during laboratory sessions, as emotions (McTeer, 1972). To illustrate—a desire to gain a prestigious position that is so strong that it sustains effort over a period of time is called a need for achievement, and is considered a motive. A desire to hit an antagonist is called rage, and is considered an emotion.

Now that the reader has been warned of some of the complications and irregularities in the concepts, attention can be directed to the events that did take place. Affection was an important topic in STRUCTURAL PSYCHOLOGY, one of the first theories or systems of psychology, and one that endeavored to discover the elements that constitute the mind, that is, to understand its structure. There was opinion that affection is one of the basic building blocks, and that it consists of both feelings, or weak reactions, and emotions, strong ones, or possibly even combinations of them. These elements were studied by the method of INTROSPECTION, a rigid, artificial way of observing the most minute details of one's own awareness. The technique disclosed that feelings range from pleasant through unpleasant, and suggested that there might be other axes, for example, one extending from calmness through excitement. Both the number and the nature of these dimensions were disputed, and these arguments prompted a considerable amount of research on affection. The controversy was not resolved, however, before it became inconsequential, during the 1920s because structural psychology went out of fashion.

The research agenda during the inaugural period were dominated by matters deemed important to the different schools or viewpoints, each intent on constructing and defending its own doctrine. But neither feelings nor emotions were seen as crucial to the systems that followed structuralism, and much of the experimentation that came to be typical of the study of emotions was initiated by scientists outside the field of psychology. They stressed the physiological basis and the bodily expressions of emotion, and when the psychologists became interested in affection, they picked up on these two topics, more as special interests than as integrated topics.

As a result much of the psychological research consists of an array of artificial, lusterless data that deal with particulars, such as the anatomical location of muscular tension in fear, changes in the blood volume in the arm in anger, and movements of the lips in various emotions. These laboratory measurements are precise and orderly, but they ignore motivation, long-term effects, and UNCONSCIOUS contributors to behavior.

This harvest of tedious tangentials is due in part to the fact that the prescientific culture bequeathed feelings and emotions to psychology in the form of intangibles. Psychologists felt pressured to rectify this status, and Meyer (1933) illustrates the intensity of this threat. He remarked that affection had originated in theology, rather than in naturalistic observations, and he expressed doubt that it would ever meet criteria for scientific subject matter: "The 'will' has virtually passed out of our scientific psychology today; the 'emotion' is bound to do the same. In 1950 American psychologists will smile at both these terms as curiosities of the past" (p. 300). The fate that Meyer predicted was fended off by emphasizing the physical aspects of emotions, by attending, as previously noted, to their biological components and to their facial, gestural, and postural expression.

A key promoter of the organic reactions was William James, one of the more renowned architects of psychology. He was so impressed with the visceral phenomena that he interpreted emotions as their consequences. To illustrate— *we are sad because we weep, we are afraid because our heart beats fast*. James made this proposal in 1884, and in 1885 Carl Lange, a Danish physiologist, decided independently that physiological reactions determine emotions. Although James stressed the awareness of biological activity and Lange stressed activity per se, there was enough similarity that the doctrine became known as the James-Lange theory (Murphy & Kovach, 1972).

Experimental data have failed—even up to the present—to identify particular physiological reactions that are characteristic of different emotions. Blood pressure, for example, increases with fear, with anger, and with other kinds of emotion. The rate of respiration also changes with a variety of affective reactions. Moreover, some of the modifications that are typical of emotional responses also occur in other kinds of behavior. A reflexive catch of the breath comes with the application of cold to the skin, with the inhalation of ammonia, as well as with violence. There are tears in jubilance, in heartbreak, and in polluted air.

Convincing criticisms of the James-Lange theory were expressed by Walter B. Cannon (1927), an American physiologist, who contended that the mechanism for differentiating the emotions is localized in the brain and the visceral changes follow from this neural differentiation. In this frame of reference *we cry because we are sad, our heart beats fast because we are afraid.* Because much of the research in support of this thesis was conducted by Bard (1934), also an American physiologist, a second dual label came into circulation, the Cannon-Bard theory. Once again the experimental data failed to offer definitive evidence, and arguments are still unresolved as to which parts of the brain are involved.

Research on the expression of emotions began in the first part of the nineteenth century when anatomists related facial changes to different emotions in the belief that knowledge of anatomy would help artists to depict various affective responses. At that time the muscular activity of the face was also described as facilitating the reception of some sensory stimuli and impeding others (sniffing and dilating the nostrils, closing the eyes). Darwin brought even more attention to the incipient study of the manifestations of emotions by declaring that such signals serve adaptive purposes for both humans and subhumans.

These pioneers, including Darwin, used line drawings and photographs in observing how emotions are recognized. Beginning in the 1920s the psychologists began to refine these techniques. They included judgments of the voice, of gestures, and of posture, but the concentration has always been on the face (Zajonc, 1985). To illustrate—wooden profiles of the face, patterned after a sketch used by Piderit, a German anatomist, were constructed so that eyes, nose, brows, and mouth can be interchanged and 360 combinations assembled (Boring & Titchener, 1923). Other techniques include the use of pictures, both live and still, taken of actors and actresses emulating different emotions as well as photographs of reactions as they are induced in the laboratory. In these experiments the background was generally neutral, the stimuli not discernible, and subjects were asked to judge the specific emotion portrayed.

The laboratory failed, as it did in the case of the physiological reactions, to uncover reliable indices of different emotions, but it did yield a few guides. For example, Woodworth (1938) using published laboratory data, was able to differentiate six reactions in which there was general agreement between the pose and the judgments. He listed these in an order in which the probability of misidentifying them decreases as the reactions become less similar. For example, the first of these six reactions includes love, happiness, and mirth, and these are frequently confused with one another, but rarely with surprise, the second emotion, and never with disgust and contempt, the fifth and sixth entries on the list.

Experimentation also disclosed that the accuracy of the judgments improves when subjects are provided with information about the stimuli to which a person is reacting. The conclusion that *external* cues are important in the identification of *subjective* reactions was disquieting, but the evidence was impressive: "Our perception of the emotional states in others are in the nature of social meanings dependent more upon the stimulus-situation than anything else" (Fernberger, 1928, p. 567).

The failure to uncover either physiological changes or expressions that are unique to different emotions leaves unanswered both the number and the nature of the basic responses. Suggestions that singularity might not exist began to surface. Dunlap (1932), for example, with extraordinary prescience, asserted that it was impossible to classify emotions into particular varieties because the differentiation was a function of stimulation rather than of response specificity. He also commented that "emotion . . . is a fact quite aside from questions about 'the emotions.' We do get 'stirred up,' 'moved': we *feel*. All introspection agrees on this point" (p. 573).

Many of the questions about emotions were suspended when BEHAVIORISM succeeded in denigrating the study of covert responses. This disavowal was in force until approximately the middle of the current century, when the HUMAN POTENTIAL MOVEMENT moved both feelings and emotions onto the front burner, flaunting them in astonishing contrast to the reserve of prior eras. The proponents of this subjectivism provided, however, displays of and exercises in emotional indulgence rather than restrained, objective information about them. The latter came from COGNITIVE PSYCHOLOGY, a movement that emerged about the same time as the human potential movement and one that also criticized behaviorism for neglecting ideational, internal psychological events. Cognitive psychologists began to revise some of the prior thinking, while at the same time adhering to the customary standards of laboratory research. These restatements are very much a part of the current scene, and thus a valid assessment of or perspective on them is elusive. One of the more influential of these innovations is a "cognitive physiological" formulation, first proposed by Schachter and Singer in 1962. This asserts that the emotion that is experienced is a product of the appreciation of physiological changes and of beliefs about the appropriate reactions under the circumstances. This theory resonates with Dunlap's earlier proposal, in that it suggests that visceral reactions infuse an effective nature into the experiences, but the perception of the situation is what determines which label is assigned.

As might be predicted, Schachter and Singer's critics made their objections known, but the support for this formulation is also strong, and the importance of the cognitive analysis of the emotional context is attracting more and more attention (Reisenzein, 1983). The pendulum may well be swinging in the direction of searches for a common "emotional quality" among affective responses and away from distinct varieties of them.

References

American Psychological Association. (1985). *Thesaurus of psychological index terms* (4th ed.). Washington, DC: Author.

Atkinson, R. L., Atkinson, R. C., Smith, E. E., & Hilgard, E. R. (1987). *Introduction to psychology* (9th ed.). San Diego: Harcourt Brace Jovanovich.

Bard, P. (1934). The neuro-humoral basis of emotional reactions. In C. Murchison (Ed.), *A handbook of general experimental psychology* (pp. 264–311). Worcester, MA: Clark University Press.

Bentley, M. (1925). *The field of psychology: A survey of experience individual, social, and genetic*. New York: Appleton.

Boring, E. G., & Titchener, E. B. (1923). A model for the demonstration of facial expression. *American Journal of Psychology, 34*, 471–485. A description of a device used to judge emotional responses from facial expressions. It was originally devised for classroom demonstrations and was fashioned after a profile drawing used by Piderit, a German anatomist, who wrote on the topic both before and after Darwin. The device was adapted by others for research, for example, the Fernberger entry in this list. There are interchangeable parts for brows, eyes, noses, and mouths, and these allow compilation of 360 different faces.

Cannon, W. B. (1927). The James-Lange theory of emotions: A critical examination and an alternative theory. *American Journal of Psychology, 39*, 106–124. Cannon criticizes the James-Lange theory and details an alternative theory.

Claparède, E. (1928). Feelings and emotions. In M. L. Reymert (Ed.), *Feelings and emotions: The Wittenberg Symposium* (pp. 124–139). Worcester, MA: Clark University Press.

Dunlap, K. (1932). Are emotions teleological constructs? *American Journal of Psychology, 44*, 572–576.

Fernberger, S. W. (1928). False suggestion and the Piderit model. *American Journal of Psychology, 40*, 562–568.

Leeper, R. W. (1948). A motivational theory of emotion to replace "emotion as disorganized response." *Psychological Review, 55*, 5–21. "We are led to the conclusion that emotional processes of all sorts (except perhaps in rarely intense forms) are organizing in their influence and should be studied as an aspect of the motivation of the higher animals" (p. 21).

McTeer, W. (1972). *The scope of motivation*. Belmont, CA: Wadsworth. McTeer notes that some psychologists insist that emotions and motivation are synonymous, but he prefers relating emotions to "keyed-up" short-term goals, and motivation to more enduring ones.

Meyer, M. F. (1933). That whale among the fishes—the theory of emotions. *Psychological Review, 40*, 292–300.

Murphy, G., & Kovach, J. K. (1972). *Historical introduction to modern psychology* (3rd ed.). New York: Harcourt Brace Jovanovich.

Reisenzein, R. (1983). The Schachter theory of emotion: Two decades later. *Psychological Bulletin, 94*, 239–264.

Schachter, S., & Singer, J. E. (1962). Cognitive, social, and physiological determinants of emotional state. *Psychological Review, 69*, 379–399. There were several variables in this experiment, but the more important ones involve receiving either an inactive substance or one that stimulates the organic reactions typical of emotions, and being in the presence of laboratory assistants who behaved in either an angry or an euphoric manner. The subjects who received the active drug tended to reflect the emotion that the assistant portrayed.

Strongman, K. T. (1973). *The psychology of emotion*. New York: John Wiley.

Woodworth, R. S. (1938). *Experimental psychology*. New York: Henry Holt. This is a comprehensive text, accurate and thorough. The presentations of the measurement of the expression of emotions and the psychological changes accompanying them are exemplary.

Zajonc, R. B. (1985). Emotion and facial efference: A theory reclaimed. *Science, 228* (No. 4695), 15–21. Zajonc reviews a theory of the effect of facial muscular activity on cerebral blood flow that was put forth in 1907 by Waynbaum and apparently ignored until Zajonc recently discovered it. Its relevance to the current problems in identifying emotional experiences is discussed.

Sources of Additional Information .

Barrington, B. L. (1963). A list of words descriptive of affective reactions. *Journal of Clinical Psychology 19*, 259–262. A group of psychologists, asked to enumerate the terms they consider to be descriptive of feelings, included words that designate both affective and nonaffective referents. Some describe levels of awareness ("foggy" and "clarity of thinking"), others imply degrees of confidence ("sure" and "doubt"), and still others designate physiological states ("energetic" and "weary"). The respondents also listed different words for similar reactions ("regard" and "respect," "crave" and "desire," "annoyed" and "exasperated"). Even a negation of emotion ("don't know" and "indifferent") was reported to indicate emotionality. Hilgard, E. R. (1980). The trilogy of mind: Cognition, affection, and conation. *Journal of the History of the Behavioral Sciences 16*, 107–117. An account of the influence of these three concepts on psychological thinking from the 17th century to the present. Kleinginna, P. R., Jr., & Kleinginna, A. M. (1981). A categorized list of emotion definitions, with suggestions for a consensual definition. *Motivation and Emotion, 5*, 345–379. Another reminder of the confusion about vocabulary. The authors found a total of ninety-two definitions in the literature. Lund, F. H. (1930). Why do we weep? *Journal of Social Psychology, 1*, 136–151. Lund reports a series of incidents of weeping as it occurs in extralaboratory conditions. The paper covers a variety of situations, including the observation that weeping, as part of grief, is stimulated when a comforting or pleasant reminder of the loss occurs. Wilson, W. (1967). Correlates of avowed happiness. *Psychological Bulletin, 67*, 294–306. The author compiled the results of several studies of self-reports, thence the title "avowed happiness." He concludes that feelings of happiness are reported by a "young, healthy, well-educated, well-paid, extroverted, optimistic, worry-free, religious, married person with high self-esteem, high job morale, modest aspirations, of either sex and of a wide range of intelligence" (p. 294).

ENVIRONMENT.   See HEREDITY and ENVIRONMENT.

ENVIRONMENTAL PSYCHOLOGY.   See ECOLOGICAL PSYCHOLOGY and ENVIRONMENTAL PSYCHOLOGY.

EXISTENTIAL PSYCHOLOGY.   See HUMAN POTENTIAL MOVEMENT.

EXPLORATION.   See CURIOSITY and EXPLORATION.

F

FAILURE. See FEAR OF FAILURE.

FEAR. 1. An emotion or feeling that is dominated by apprehension about a known or readily inferred cause. 2. A drive to escape or to avoid distressors. 3. A synonym for anxiety.

Fear and ANXIETY are often used synonymously, probably because they share a sense of dread and an unpleasant feeling tone, as well as the awareness of physiological reactions that is characteristic of EMOTION. These common features are, however, countered by important differences. The word anxiety, when used accurately, designates distress about events that are vaguely identified and are interpreted as impending rather than as immediate, whereas the precipitants of fear are clearly identified. The two reactions also have different conceptual histories and unequal levels of visibility. Anxiety is a relatively new concept, and is currently in vogue. Fear, in contrast, has been part of the discipline of psychology throughout most of its history, but it has never been a popular topic. It has rarely been studied because of its intrinsic merit, although it has repeatedly been called into service in the promotion of various theories.

A relatively strong surge of interest in the concept, particularly the fright of children, developed shortly before the turn of the current century. This was due, in part at least, to the preoccupation at that time with evolution, a topic that emphasizes survival. It was easy to relate this to fear, inasmuch as energy was believed to be mobilized, and protective impulses to become immobilized, to flee, or to attack were also assumed to be aroused. Childhood was seen as an appropriate stage at which to study apprehension because immaturity avoids the disguising of emotional reactions that comes with maturity (Sully, 1896).

Several of the early researchers used questionnaires, and in the case of children too young to respond on their own, they administered them to parents and teachers (Binet, 1895/1969; Calkins, 1895; Hall, 1897). G. Stanley Hall was a staunch supporter of this method, and he pointed out that it is more suitable than other experimental procedures because "we can neither excite the stronger emotions in the laboratory nor coolly study ourselves while they are on under natural conditions" (1897, p. 147). Hall distributed approximately 2,000 questionnaires, classified the causes of fear that they disclosed, counted the frequencies of different stimuli, and was able to identify both prevalent and rare instigators. He calculated the differences in incidence between boys and girls as well as among age levels. This practice of organizing the information around the cause rather than the experience is still in use (Moracco & Camilleri, 1983).

Hall was certain that the responses to the questionnaires were relevant to the theory of evolution. He interpreted fear as an "instinctive vestige," as having been adaptive at one time. In this frame of reference a dread of water is believed to have assisted organisms, at the time they were becoming terrestrial, to control their previous attraction to water. Hall's own words expose his conviction: "The weather fears and the incessant talk about weather . . . fits a condition of life in trees, caves or tents" (1897, p. 247).

Theory is also a determiner of the research that was conducted by John B. Watson, but in this instance the mission was to promote BEHAVIORISM rather than evolution. Watson, an enthusiastic experimenter, was disdainful of questionnaire data because they are personal reports, not laboratory data. He rejected consciousness and dismissed any need to explore the subjective aspects of fear. However, he was not content with identifying the reaction merely on the basis of the stimuli, and he defined the response in behavioral terms: "Sudden catching of the breath, clutching randomly with the hands . . . blinking of the eye lids, puckering of the lips, then crying" (Watson & Morgan, 1917, p. 166).

Watson studied the reactions of infants in controlled conditions in the laboratory in an attempt to distinguish between the reactions that are innate and those that are acquired. He concluded that only three emotions are present at birth—fear, anger, and love. He also decided that fear in neonates is incited only by a loud noise or by the sudden removal of physical support. This led him to investigate how the reaction is learned, that is, to look for the mechanism by which fear comes to be elicited by different stimuli. Watson believed that this was the result of classical conditioning, and in order to substantiate this, Watson and Rayner (1920) paired a rat and a noise so loud that it induces crying in an infant, and repeated these two stimuli until the subject cried at the mere sight of the animal.

Eliminating fears is a logical sequel to this demonstration, and psychologists pursued this goal, mainly relying on conditioning (Jones, 1924). These enterprises, in many instances, became as much a test of conditioning theory as attempts at treatment. Guthrie, an early behaviorist, represents this kind of involvement. He proposed several techniques, including contriving an arrangement in which "the undesired response is absent and the cue which has been responsible for it is present" (1935, p. 76). He suggested, for example, that "cat fear" in an adult could be eliminated by introducing into the household a kitten so young and helpless that it does not cause any unfavorable reactions, and because growth is imperceptible, alarm should not develop. Successors, using variations of conditioning procedures, also attempted to and on occasion succeeded in eradicating fears.

The effectiveness of this kind of intervention noticeably increased with the advent of behavior modification, a form of OPERANT CONDITIONING. Although the spotlight remained on the method, some limited information about fright per se was brought to light. It was discovered, for example, that reassuring a person who is scared may reward being fearful, and therefore may reinforce rather than weaken the reaction. In order to prevent this advocates of behavior modification take great care not to reinforce any response that is contiguous with the disserviceable one (Brown, Wienckowski, & Stolz, 1975).

The study of fear as a topic in its own right has been hindered by general confusion within psychology about the number and nature of different emotions that humans experience. Investigators were unable to agree with Watson that there are only three different ones at birth, and suggestions were made that this lack of consensus might be valid, that there might not be any real differentiation of infantile fears. Gradually this idea gained ground, and neonatal affective reactions came to be described as diffuse or, at best, distinguished as merely positive or negative (Jersild, 1954), even though this position is divergent from one that is prevalent in both psychiatry and psychoanalysis. In these fields theorists typically assume that emotions are distinct at birth or become so shortly thereafter, and some even propose that affect is differentiated prior to cognition so as to underwrite specific fears in babies, such as dread of rejection, fear of loss of love, and fear of punishment.

The attempts at reconciliation of this controversy are less than satisfactory. One appearance of a resolution comes from the substitution of the word anxiety for fear. Psychologists seem to be more willing to accept anxiety than fear as present at birth, and this change in terms has fostered searches for the specific age at which anxiety emerges. The literature asserts, for example, that "stranger anxiety" appears at eight months (Biehler, 1981; Fein, 1978).

The specification of particular ages does nothing to help identify different emotions, and the belief that they are homogeneous persists (Thompson & Grusec, 1970). This opinion implies that a child's trepidation about snakes, a criminal's panic at the prospect of being caught, and an aged adult's terror of death are similar. Few theorists would argue strongly for this consistency, but surprisingly few counterarguments have been systematically pursued. Despite this slighting some modifications are emerging from research in specialized topics in psychology. One of these is a version of OPERANT CONDITIONING, called systematic desensitization, in which a person is first required to rank stimuli that he or she fears in a hierarchy from the least to the most disturbing (Wolpe &

Lang, 1964). The person is next taught how to relax, and when in that state is instructed to imagine the least frightening stimulus. The person is then encouraged to replace this image with a slightly more threatening one and to move on to even more distressing ones as readily as possible without sacrificing the relaxation. Thus systematic desensitization brings into clear focus the nuances of fears per se.

A second probe of the diversity of fear is encountered in SOCIAL MOTIVATION. This research deals with the motives that are provoked and gratified by the behavior of other people, and it has generated the concepts of FEAR OF FAILURE and FEAR OF SUCCESS. The differences between those reactions exceeds their similarities, and these variations are found in conscious experiences of fear, in the stimuli that arouse them, and in their sequels.

Also, the discovery of the fear of failure and the fear of success may turn out to be an important turning point in the history of the concept, inasmuch as they combine an emotion and a MOTIVE. The reader may have noticed that up to this point, actions that fear is believed to induce have been ignored. Most people believe that not only fears, but all emotions, provoke actions, and many also believe that they are such effective mobilizers that the behavior they incite cannot be controlled. The discipline of psychology has had trouble coming to terms with this activating property. The reasons for this are too complex to be reviewed briefly, but they are dealt with in the discussion of EMOTION.

There have been a few isolated exceptions to the general neglect of the activating potential of emotions, and one of these involved the concept of fear. This is part of an effort, undertaken about the middle of the current century, to ascertain how nonbiological, or secondary, drives might be learned. Miller (1948), in "Studies of Fear as an Acquirable Drive," found that rats that have repetitively received electric shock learn to escape when they are exposed only to the compartment in which the shock was administered. This experiment triggered additional research, and both fear and anxiety were identified, for a time at least, as a drive. This concept of drive was, however, based on psyiological imbalances, and this alignment turned out to be too restrictive to handle many of the intricacies of motivation. As a result the concept lost favor and the interest in its motivating power was suspended.

As previously mentioned, the concern is now returning, especially in attempts to alleviate fear and in social motivation. In both of these frameworks experiments are under way on both activating and differentiated reactions. The concept of fear may now be on a path that leads to more comprehensive research.

References

Biehler, R. F. (1981). *Child development: An introduction* (2nd ed.). Boston: Houghton Mifflin. This textbook covers a spectrum of topics. Biehler discusses some factors that may alter the age at which "stranger anxiety" appears.
Binet, A. (1969). Fear in children. In R. H. Pollack & M. W. Brenner (Eds.), *The experimental psychology of Alfred Binet. Selected Papers.* (F. K. Zetland & C.

Ellis, Trans.) (pp. 179–206). New York: Springer. (Original work published 1895). Binet depended on the questionnaire method. He is one of the few pioneers who tried to describe the experience of fear and also to distinguish between real and imaginary fears.

Brown, B. S., Wienckowski, L. A., & Stolz, S. B. (1975). *Behavior modification: Perspective on a current issue*. Rockville, MD: Department of Health, Education and Welfare. DHEW Publication No. (Adm.) 75–202. An impressive analysis of the state of the art, including the details of various procedures.

Calkins, M. W. (1895). The emotional life of children. *Pedagogical Seminary, 3*, 319–341. Calkins used questionnaires to compare the emotions—with an emphasis on fear—of preschoolers and children who have been in school for six years in order to learn "the effect of training upon imagination and feeling" (p. 319).

Fein, G. G., & the Editorial Staff of Prentice-Hall. (1978). *Child development*. Englewood Cliffs, NJ: Prentice-Hall. This book appears to embrace as many views as possible in child development and this may explain why no questions are raised about "stranger anxiety."

Guthrie, E. R. (1935). *The psychology of learning*. New York: Harper.

Hall, G. S. (1897). A study of fears. *American Journal of Psychology, 8*, 147–249.

Jersild, A T. (1954). Emotional development. In L. Carmichael (Ed.), *Manual of child psychology* (2nd ed., pp. 833–917). New York: John Wiley.

Jones, M. C. (1924). A laboratory study of fear: The case of Peter. *Pedagogical Seminary, 31*, 308–315. This boy, thirty-four months of age when the experiment started, was frightened of both a rat and a rabbit, and in the terminology of the era, "unconditioning" was in order. Among the techniques used was that of placing the animal as close as possible to the child without provoking fear while the boy was eating food that he liked.

Miller, N. E. (1948). Studies of fear as an acquirable drive: I. Fear as motivation and fear-reduction as reinforcement in the learning of new responses. *Journal of Experimental Psychology, 38*, 89–101.

Moracco, J. C., & Camilleri, J. (1983). A study of fears in elementary school children. *Elementary School Guidance and Counseling, 18*, 82–87. The authors list twenty-five possible excitants, and children, aged eight to ten years, indicated which items they actually fear. Sex differences were calculated.

Sully, J. (1896). *Studies of childhood*. New York: Appleton.

Thompson, W. R., & Grusec, J. (1970). Studies of early experience. In P. H. Mussen (Ed.), *Carmichael's manual of child psychology: Vol. 1* (3rd ed., pp. 565–654). New York: John Wiley. This is a well-organized and well thought out appraisal of the effects of early experience. The authors point up the complexities of research in this area, and their questions, appropriately, outnumber their answers.

Watson, J. B., & Morgan, J. J. B. (1917). Emotional reactions and psychological experimentation. *American Journal of Psychology, 28*, 163–174.

Watson, J. B., & Rayner, R. (1920). Conditioned emotional reactions. *Journal of Experimental Psychology, 3*, 1–14.

Wolpe, J., & Lang, P. J. (1964). A fear survey schedule for use in behaviour therapy. *Behaviour Research and Therapy, 2*, 27–30. Wolpe started using desensitization strategy in the late 1950's. He began with the discovery that without intervention, cats would not eat in a room in which they had been shocked, but they would eat in a distant area, and that they could gradually be successfully fed in rooms closer to the original one.

Sources of Additional Information

Blom, G. E. (1982). Psychological reactions of a school population to a skywalk accident. In C. D. Spielberger, I. G. Sarason, & N. A. Milgram (Eds.), *Stress and anxiety* (Vol. 8, pp. 361–370). Washington, DC: Hemisphere Publishing. This is an account of how mental health professionals assisted parents and children in managing their emotions after an accident in which a skywalk was damaged at a time when children were on it. It is an interesting report of an effort at psychological support, and much of the data were obtained by the tried and true questionnaire method. Apparently fear is now an unpopular word. The children were frightened, their parents were frightened, but the article designates "stressful reactions," "stress behavior," "anxiety," "trauma," and "startle." Similar slighting occurs in the Tedder et al. reference (this list). James, W. (1890). *The principles of psychology*. (vol. II.) London: Macmillan. The complaints about the neglect of the subjective aspects of fear started early: "The internal shadings of emotional feeling, moreover, merge endlessly into each other. Language has discriminated some of them ... but in the dictionaries of synonyms we find these feelings distinguished more by their severally appropriate objective stimuli than by their conscious or subjective tone" (p. 448). Messer, S. B., & Winokur, M. (1980). Some limits to the integration of psychoanalytic and behavior therapy. *American Psychologist, 35*, 818–827. Behavior modification on occasion deals with subjective experiences, such as dreams and phobias. These concepts were initially forbidden, and their inclusion in the modern literature on behaviorism suggests some rapprochement between the subjective or covert, the domain of traditional treatment methods, and the objective or overt, the domain of the behaviorists. Tedder, S. L., Scherman, A., & Sheridan, K. M. (1984). Impact of group support on adjustment to divorce by single, custodial fathers. *American Mental Health Counselors Association Journal, 6*, 180–189. This is a report of the effects of attending a support group on fathers who are single custodians of children. The participants have many concerns; adjustment difficulties, feel lonely, and have an impaired self-image. As in the case of the Blom reference (this list), the word fear is avoided. The reader is spared linguistic references to the father's fears but is informed in detail about their problems.

FEAR OF FAILURE. 1. Apprehension about one's ability to accomplish, frequently accompanied by feelings of lowered self-evaluation and expectations of lowered esteem in the eyes of others. 2. Trepidation about being examined, particularly in academic contexts.

Most people are aware of the possibility of defeat, and psychologists are certainly not personally immune to such outcomes, but the concept appears to have escaped them—at least while wearing their laboratory coats—until the middle of the twentieth century. At that time research indicated that people who have a high need and those who have a low NEED FOR ACHIEVEMENT entertain different views about the outcome of their efforts at task mastery. The former, for example, appear to be hopeful and the latter appear defeated. The optimists are believed to have experienced many rewards for successes and the pessimists, to have experienced a great deal of punishment for failures (McClelland, Atkinson, Clark, & Lowell, 1953/1976).

These differences prompted Clark, Teevan, and Ricciuti (1956) to study the hope of success and the fear of failure by means of a standard research design for investigating NEED as a variety of SOCIAL MOTIVATION. This demands segregating subjects into groups of varying levels of intensity of the motive being studied, in this instance, the fear of failure. A second step involves comparing their responses to a request to describe each picture in a series of ambiguously portrayed scenes and to imagine what happened prior to the scene and what will happen next. The assumption is made that what the characters in the story do is directed by their motives, and what the environment does to them—called the press—reveals their apperception, that is, their opinions about the important long-term effects of environmental action. The need-press interactions are called thema, and the procedure is referred to as the thematic apperception method. The lack of clarity of the scenes, produces content that originates within the storyteller, and hence the characters' needs and apperception are those of the narrator.

Guidelines or principles for judging that a particular need is present in the narrator's thoughts are compiled, and applying these to each story—usually called scoring—makes it possible for different experimenters to agree with one another. The criteria also provide an empirically based, detailed definition of the need.

Clark, Teevan, and Ricciuti were under the impression that fear of failure and hope of success are aspects of the need for ACHIEVEMENT, and so they relied on the scoring principles for that concept. The experimental results disclosed, however, that various attempts they made to arouse a fear of failure did not affect the scores. This failure prompted them to conceptualize the need as different from achievement, and they began to search for it in response to a questionnaire concerning LEVEL OF ASPIRATION.

At about the same time, Atkinson (1957) formulated a version of fear of failure, that is structurally similar to other social needs except that there is more than the customary emphasis on anticipations of failure, that is, on reactions that block achievement strivings. In 1958 Moulton published scoring principles for such a fear, one that involves predictions that tasks will not be handled successfully, forecasts punishment for being inept, and depicts avoiding challenges.

The contributions of both Atkinson and Moulton facilitated additional work in the format that is standard for research on social motivation, and some researchers adopted this method but others rely on questionnaires. The two techniques yield different concepts but both are called fear of failure. The thematic apperception method discloses thoughts about numerous aspects of dread, and these are assumed to motivate behavior even though their influence is not always recognized by the individual who experiences the apprehension. Questionnaires, in contrast, elicit self-reports, responses that may or may not disclose motives.

These responses also involve consciously experienced dread that is elicited by clearly recognized, readily identifiable stimuli.

The inventories, commonly called tests of ANXIETY, provide tallies of the frequency of experiences of apprehension—in some instances fear and in others anxiety. These instruments inquire about a variety of provocative situations, but classroom examinations are by far the most common (Alpert & Haber, 1960). In fact, so much emphasis has been placed on this that some psychologists include only this kind of assessment in their definition. Feij, for example, states that "the construct 'fear of failure' refers to a person's fear of situations in which he is evaluated, such as examinations and tests" (1975, p. 1147).

The fear of failure as studied by the thematic apperception method has been found to color various segments of the behavioral repertoire, and in some instances it appears to do so in a way opposite to that of a high need for achievement. Time perspective, for example, is well developed in those who are preoccupied with excellence, but it is relatively brief in the stories devised by subjects with high fear-of-failure scores (Heckhausen, 1967).

Learning rate may also be disrupted. This kind of interference is illustrated in a study by Karebenick and Youssef (1974) in which motivation was measured both by the thematic apperception method and by responses to a questionnaire concerning anxiety. Combining these scores allowed segregation of the subjects into different groups, including one that can be characterized as having an investment in achievement but relatively free of fear, and a second that is not involved with accomplishment but is aware of many fears. Each of these samples memorized pairs of words that were rated as easy, average, or hard to learn. The efficiency varied, as expected, only for words of moderate difficulty and the students who anticipated failure learned a fewer number of these words.

The *Fear of Failure*, by Birney, Burdick, and Teevan (1969), offers an enlightening and interesting account of the concept. These investigators synthesized results obtained by various methods, including those they and others obtained by the use of a Hostile Press score, one originally conceptualized by McClelland et al. as part of the research on need for achievement. In its amended form, Hostile Press highlights an expectation of censure that features the personal and social consequences of defeat; that is, it depicts fear of failure as based more on social than on task considerations.

The discussion of the ingredients that are requisite for an experience of failure is intriguing, not only in its own right, but also because failure to arouse all these variables may account for the experimental difficulties in arousing the motive. Birney et al. conclude that a sense of defeat occurs when the failed task was deemed manageable at the time it was undertaken and when effort was expanded on its completion. A job that is obviously very easy but botched is merely laughed off, and one that is obviously far too complex to be mastered is not even attempted. But a person who undertakes a challenge and fails to meet it is confronted with evidence of having incorrectly assessed his or her capabilities and of having been inadequately involved. The researchers suggest that the loss of personal esteem that comes from not performing as well as one thought one could is probably the most critical factor. They also indicate that the sense of failure is intensified as the level of self-evaluation declines. The experience becomes even more distressing when others learn of the defeat because private wounds are then supplemented by threats or by actual loss of status. In other words, failure is a sequential reaction in which the deprivation of rewards that success would have brought are supplemented by decrements both in feelings of worth and in an impairment in reputation.

Competition is accepted, even aggrandized, in modern Western cultures, and disquieting misgivings about failure allow one neither to decry nor to escape rivalry. Birney et al. address this dilemma and point out that a person with a fear of failure may resort to interpersonal maneuvers that offer protection but also appear to be assertive and independent. There are various ways of accomplishing this, one of which is to take cover in situations in which evaluations are dispersed, that is, to seek circumstances in which group rather than individual effort is accentuated. The pursuit of popularity rather than excellence may also help to fend off failure. Dixon talks about this duality in some military personnel: "Those who have plodded up the hard but safe way—the 'good' boys who never speak out of turn, who make up in tact and conformity for what they lack in enterprise and initiative" (1976, p. 245).

These masquerades make the researcher's task much more difficult because they disguise the existence of the fear and interfere with its measurement. The belief that a large number of people are uncomfortable about their skills is probably valid, but unfortunately there is currently no thoroughgoing definition of the fear, nor is there a trustworthy census of it for either men or women (Karebenick, 1977).

References

Alpert, R., & Haber, R. N. (1960). Anxiety in academic achievement situations. *Journal of Abnormal and Social Psychology, 61*, 207–215. This article refers to several of the anxiety questionnaires that are in common use.

Atkinson, J. W. (1957). Motivational determinants of risk-taking behavior. *Psychological Review, 64*, 359–372. This is a theoretical formulation of both the fear of failure and the hope of success. The phrase "risk-taking" in the title highlights the fact that these motives have a strong anticipatory component, that fear and hope refer to expectations rather than events.

Birney, R. C., Burdick, H., & Teevan, R. C. (1969). *Fear of failure*. New York: Van Nostrand. This volume offers an extensive coverage of the literature.

Clark, R. A., Teevan, R., & Ricciuti, H. N. (1956). Hope of success and fear of failure as aspects of need for achievement. *Journal of Abnormal and Social Psychology, 53*, 182–186.

Dixon, N. (1976). *On the psychology of military incompetence*. New York: Basic Books.

Feij, J. A. (1975). Construct validation of a fear-of-failure measure using an operant type of behavior. *Psychological Reports, 37*, 1147–1151.

Heckhausen, H. (1967). *The anatomy of achievement motivation*. (K. F. Butler, R. C. Birney, & D. C. McClelland, Trans.). New York: Academic Press.

Karabenick, S. A. (1977). Fear of success, achievement and affiliation dispositions, and the performance of men and women under individual and competitive conditions. *Journal of Personality, 45*, 117–149. This article reports an experiment but one that is introduced with an extensive review of the literature, including some comments about the research on sex differences in fear of failure. Studies of this type are few in number and inconsistent in results.

Karabenick, S. A., & Youssef, Z. I. (1974). Performance as a function of achievement motive level and perceived difficulty. In J. W. Atkinson & J. O. Raynor (Eds.), *Motivation and achievement* (pp. 83–90). Washington, DC: V. H. Winston. One of the main issues in this chapter is the comparing and contrasting of fear of success and fear of failure.

McClelland, D. C., Atkinson, J. W., Clark, R. A., & Lowell, E. L. (1976). *The achievement motive.* New York: Irvington. (Original work published 1953)

Moulton, R. W. (1958). Notes for a projective measure of fear of failure. In J. W. Atkinson (Ed.), *Motives in fantasy, action, and society: A method of assessment and study* (pp. 563–571). Princeton, NJ: Van Nostrand.

Sources of Additional Information

Nygård, R. (1981). Toward an interactional psychology: Models from achievement motivation research. *Journal of Personality, 49*, 363–387. This lengthy article deals with both the need for achievement and the motive to avoid failure. Nygård argues that accurate prediction of the effects of each of these motives can increase only when both the personality and the situation in which the person is functioning are taken into consideration. Saltoun, J. (1980). Fear of failure in career development. *Vocational Guidance Quarterly, 29*, 35–41. The subjects in this experiment are white male students in a community college in New York City. Those with a high fear of failure, as indicated by a Hostile Press score, appear to have only a limited desire either to make vocational plans or to acquire vocational information. Sarason, I. G. (1975). Test anxiety and the self-disclosing coping model. *Journal of Consulting and Clinical Psychology, 43*, 148–153. This research deals with anxiety about examinations, and the differential effects on a learning task when anxiety is ignored, when it is recognized, and when it is merely tolerated. Teevan, R. C., & Greenfeld, N. (1985). Note on fear of failure in golfers. *Perceptual and Motor Skills, 60*, 910. These investigators found that golfers who play regularly in a foursome, a public achievement situation, have a low Hostile Press score. They relate this to the broader conclusion that subjects with high Hostile Press scores refrain from volunteering in contexts in which skills will be exposed.

FEAR OF SUCCESS.   1. A dread of success because of the penalties that are assumed to come with it.

Fears that victory invites misfortune have been acknowledged for a long time, but only rarely studied systematically. In 1966 Haimowitz and Haimowitz published an experiment they had conducted in 1958 in which they found that words that connote accomplishment (for example, "promotion," "best in class") elicit unusual or erratic associations much more frequently than words that do not connote success (for example, "wood," "crayon"). The authors explain these irregularities as due to the superstition, prevalent in many cultures, that one cost of success is adversity.

Some of the early research on the NEED FOR ACHIEVEMENT indicated that some people may be disturbed by the prospects of achievement and self-protectively retreat from victory, generally without being aware that they do not want to succeed. There were also confusing, not clear-cut, indications that this reaction might be more prevalent among women than among men. At first neither the concept of fear of success nor the possibility of a discrepancy between the sexes attracted much notice, but a turning point in this pattern came in Matina Horner's doctoral dissertation (1968/1969). This was a study of the hypothesis that the expectation of negative consequences that accompanies success thwarts achievement in women and that this fear is the factor responsible for the previously reported inconsistent findings of sex differences.

Horner made a few modifications in the typical design for research in the study of NEED as a form of SOCIAL MOTIVATION. Ordinarily this involves comparing stories imagined by subjects who are believed to vary in the strength of the need being studied. They are asked to describe each picture in a series of ambiguously portrayed scenes as well as to imagine what happened before the scene and what will happen next. The assumption is made that what the characters in the stories do is directed by their needs and that the press, what the environment does to them, discloses their apperception, this is, their beliefs about the long-term effects of events. The need-press interactions are called thema, and the procedure is referred to as the thematic apperception method. The lack of clarity of the pictures and the lack of information about the sequence of events elicit content that comes from within the narrator and thus discloses his or her needs and apperceptions. Clear-cut criteria are devised for judging—or what is usually called scoring—the presence of the need in the storyteller's thinking. These principles make it possible for different examiners to agree with one another and they also furnish an empirically based, detailed definition of the motive.

Horner replaced the commonly used pictures with a series of "verbal leads," brief descriptions of various situations. The subjects were male and female undergraduates, and the sex of the main character in each lead was the same as that of the respondent. In order to arouse the need for achievement, the subjects were asked to work on tasks such as arithmetic and anagrams, some alone and others in a competitive atmosphere. Some believed that the problems were of intermediate level of difficulty, and others were under the impression that the assignment was so formidable that they had only an even chance of doing better than a competitor.

The experimental results for the men agreed with findings in previous experiments, but the women's achievement scores were inconsistent and inconclusive. As a means of pursuing the reasons for this irregularity Horner presented her subjects with a "lead" that would gain renown: "After first-term finals, John (Anne) finds himself (herself) at the top of his (her) medical school class."

The system Horner devised for judging the presence of the fear of success consists of scoring references to conflicts about success, predictions of unfortunate outcomes of achievement, descriptions of activities that would defeat such accomplishments, and direct expressions of conflict about being number one.

The distribution of scores in one sample disclosed that fewer than 10 percent of the men, but more than 65 percent of the women, made these kinds of negative comments. Further, those female subjects who fear success were also found to perform more efficiently when working alone than when in competition. Evidence of this nature convinced Horner that ambivalence about success slows down a few men and the majority of women. Horner points out that this motive is not a lack of interest in achievement; that is, it is not a "will to fail," but a fear that blocks or inhibits achievement strivings. Social rejection appears to be one of the most frequently anticipated penalties. A second prevalent one involves personal doubts about the compatibility of feminity and success.

The fear of success was examined in a number of laboratories and related to numerous demographic variables such as chronological age (Monahan, Kuhn, & Shaver, 1974) and both social class and race (Weston & Mednick, 1970). Variations in methodology were also developed (Zuckerman & Allison, 1976). Discussions abound about the reasons women retreat from contests (Hoffman, 1972; Horner, 1972, 1974).

There is a continuing flow of information, criticism, modification in experimental design, and refutation, and at this stage confusion outweighs consensus: "In fact, FOS [fear of success] stands out more for what it doesn't relate to than for what it does" (Condry & Dyer, 1976, p. 68); "The concept of fear of success has been unmercifully assailed because it did not consistently predict impaired competitive performance against males, because it did not show the expected relationship to academic performance, and because the level and content of fear-of-success imagery did not show reliable trends over time" (Fleming, 1982, pp. 63–64).

Despite the severity of the censure, critics generally do not suggest abandoning the concept, but they do indict many of the research methods. Shaver, for example, suggests that a "fear of beauty" might have been discovered if the subjects had been asked to react to "Anne is by all accounts the most beautiful coed" (1976, p. 307). This prediction is based, of course, on the anticipation of the arousal of concomitant negatives such as stupidity and envy.

Many of the arguments revolve around just *what* is feared. In these discussions success is often indicted as merely a general term for a variety of more specific factors that could elicit fear. Winners, for example, are said to run the risk of having to change occupation, residence, and the like. There may be timidity about separating from friends and colleagues, and trepidation about having to meet the demands of complex and unfamiliar responsibilities. Jackaway and Teevan (1976) comment that fear of success and fear of failure may both elicit in women a fear of social rejection.

Initially men's fear of success was neglected, a paradoxical omission, in that ambivalence on the part of a man could be seen as a more serious violation of the success ethic than it would be in the case of a woman. Gradually, however, this slighting was rectified, and fear of success began to be investigated. One example of this kind of research is *The Success-Fearing Personality* by Canavan-Gumpert, Garner, and Gumpert (1978). The procedures used by these investigators included measuring task proficiency following both success and failure, as well as administering questionnaires about reactions that are believed to be concomitants of fear of success, such as anxiety, indecisiveness, and censure of boasting. These topics were singled out for inquiry because many people are not aware that they fear success, and direct inquiries are thus nonproductive.

The results supported this innocence, in that fearful subjects, after an episode of success, for example, displayed a tendency to lower efficiency on a similar task, but after an episode of failure, they tended to perform more effectively. Following both successes and failures these same subjects tended to improve their efforts on unrelated tasks. The authors suggest that this variation helps both to sabotage success and to minimize failure.

As implied by the title, the study is more an investigation of personality than of sex differences. In fact, the researchers found no appreciable sex differences. This contrasts with many, but not all, prior results, and the discrepancies may be a function of method rather than of behavioral differences. Whatever the cause, this reporting of gender similarity serves as a reminder that the question merits more exploration.

The research on the fear of success that is currently available cannot be considered conclusive, but it demonstrates the staying power of the concept. Any specification of the attributes that will endure would, at the date of this writing, have more of an oracular than a factual tinge.

References

Canavan-Gumpert, D., Garner, K., Gumpert, P. (1978). *The success-fearing personality*. Lexington, MA: Heath.

Condry, J., & Dyer, S. (1976). Fear of success: Attribution of cause to the victim. *Journal of Social Issues, 32*, 63–83. A thoughtful, comprehensive review of the literature, and one that adds perspective to this emotionally laden debate.

Fleming, J. (1982). Projective and psychometric approaches to measurement: The case of fear of success. In A. J. Stewart (Ed.), *Motivation and society: A volume in honor of David C. McClelland* (pp. 63–93). San Francisco: Jossey-Bass.

Haimowitz, M. L., & Haimowitz, N. R. (1966). The evil eye: Fear of success. In M. L. Haimowitz and N. R. Haimowitz (Eds.), *Human development: Selected readings* (pp. 677–685). New York: Thomas Y. Crowell. The authors' abstract highlights widespread and strong reservations about accomplishment. "There has been much discussion of the fear of failure, but very little of the fear of success. The general prevalence of failure throughout the world may, however, indicate that more people fear success than fear failure" (p. 677). This research was first reported in an education journal in 1958.

Hoffman, L. W. (1972). Early childhood experiences and women's achievement motives. *Journal of Social Issues, 28,* 129–155. This article is comprehensive and much more objective than many that deal with this topic.

Horner, M. S. (1969). Sex differences in achievement motivation and performance in competitive and non-competitive situations (Doctoral dissertation, University of Michigan, 1968). *Dissertation Abstracts International, 30,* 407B.

Horner, M. S. (1972). Toward an understanding of achievement-related conflicts in women. *Journal of Social Issues, 28,* 157–175.

Horner, M. S. (1974). The measurement and behavioral implications of fear of success in women. In J. W. Atkinson & J. O. Raynor (Eds.), *Motivation and achievement* (pp. 91–120). New York: John Wiley.

Jackaway, R., & Teevan, R. (1976). Fear of failure and fear of success: Two dimensions of the same motive. *Sex Roles, 2,* 283–293.

Monahan, L., Kuhn, D., & Shaver, P. (1974). Intrapsychic versus cultural explanations of the "fear of success" motive. *Journal of Personality and Social Psychology, 29,* 60–64. The investigators report data for subjects aged ten to sixteen years of age. They used the medical school "lead," but in one group of both boys and girls they used the "Anne" cue and in a second the "John" cue. There was a higher proportion of fear of success imagery in response to the feminine name. The authors interpret this as evidence of a cultural rather than a gender reaction to achievement.

Shaver, P. (1976). Questions concerning fear of success and its conceptual relatives. *Sex Roles, 2,* 305–320.

Weston, P. J., & Mednick, M. T. (1970). Race, social class and the motive to avoid success in women. *Journal of Cross-Cultural Psychology, 1,* 283–291.

Zuckerman, M., & Allison, S. N. (1976). An objective measure of fear of success: Construction and validation. *Journal of Personality Assessment, 40,* 422–430. As the title implies, this article contains a questionnaire that was designed to assess aversion to achievement. The authors present this technique as more valid than the one Horner used. They suggest that the "Anne" and "John" cues might elicit stereotypes about male and female achievement rather than fear of success.

Sources of Additional Information

Adler, A. (1927). *Understanding human nature* (W. B. Wolfe, Trans.). Garden City, NY: Garden City. Much of Adler's famous theory of psychoanalysis revolves around struggles with feelings of inferiority. He deals at some length with the sexual inequality that emerges from society's earlier convictions that competitiveness is requisite for achievement but inappropriate for women. Bryson, J. B., & Bryson, R. (Eds.). (1978). *Dual-career couples: A special issue of* Psychology of Women Quarterly. New York: Human Sciences. This book contains reports of different investigations of dual-career couples. Fear of success as a variable is not dealt with explicitly, but the majority of the wives who are described in this volume would probably obtain low fear of success scores. Horner, M. S. (1969, November). Fail: Bright women. *Psychology Today,* pp. 36–38, 62. Horner's account of her dissertaton is written for this popular magazine in a style in which excitement and attention compete with objectivity. Sutherland, E. (1978). Fear of success and the need for power. *Psychological Reports, 43,* 763–766. Studies of the relationship among the various social motives are popular, and this article exemplifies an interrelationship of topics. Winter, D. G., Stewart, A. J., & McClelland, D. C.

(1977). Husband's motives and wife's career level. *Journal of Personality and Social Psychology, 35*, 159–166. This study spans fifteen years and deals with the influence that husbands with a high need for power have on the encouragement/discouragement of wives' careers.

FEELING(S).   See EMOTION(S) and FEELING(S).

FEMININITY.   See MASCULINITY, FEMININITY, and ANDROGYNY.

FIELD DEPENDENCE.   1. Sensitivity to external cues and to the organization of one's surroundings. **FIELD INDEPENDENCE.**   1. Sensitivity to internal cues and to elements rather than to the organization of one's surroundings.

The concept of field dependence, and its reciprocal, field independence, grew out of research on how a person recognizes the upright position, both of their own body and of objects. Ordinarily, maintaining orientation is a relatively effortless, essentially automatic process, but when either a horizontal or a vertical axis, or both, are distorted, perplexity and distress are apt to ensue. This disorientation has caught the attention of people with diverse interests. The unpleasant experiences of sea voyagers when they are repetitively confronted with an unstable horizon are all too well known. J. E. Purkinjě (1787–1869), a Czechoslovakian physiologist, noted that when riding on a carrousel, the floor appears to be tilted (Brožek, 1971). Amusement park personnel are alert to such distortions, and they replicate, and even intensify, them. Aircraft pilots may become confused when the visual field is obscured by fog or clouds, and space exploration has spawned a lengthy list of questions about orientation (Lackner & Graybiel, 1983).

From time to time scientists have investigated different variables that are involved in the perception of the upright. They devised apparatus that distorted the cues of what is seen and what is felt. There was consensus that both visual and postural information play a role, but there was disagreement about the relative importance of each factor and only limited information about the ways in which the different kinds of sensory data interact (Gibson & Mowrer, 1938).

The study of the topic was episodic and not integrated until Herman A. Witkin (1916–1979) began to conduct a series of related experiments in the 1940s. The initial work concentrated on the influence of visual and postural cues, and complex laboratory equipment was used. A brief account of some of the experiments illustrates the designs. In one investigation research participants, looking through a tube at a mirrored scene that is tilted 30 degrees, are required to adjust a rod until it appears to be upright. In another design, a subject, in a completely darkened room and with head and body at times in an erect position and at other times in an inclined position, is required to adjust a luminous rod—that is in itself in a slanted luminous frame—until it appears to be upright. There is one room that can be inclined to either the right or the left. It contains a chair that can also be tipped in both the same or the opposite direction of the room. There is a second room that can be both tilted and rotated on a circular track (Witkin, Lewis, Hertzman, Machover, Meissner, & Wapner, 1954/1972).

The data obtained by the use of this equipment indicate that some individuals rely more on visual than on postural signs, whereas others depend more on bodily sensations. The two groups appear to be comparable in accuracy, and each tends to maintain its preference in different surroundings. Witkin labeled individuals who are more alert to the visual field, that is, those who depend on a visual framework, as field dependent, and those who are more alert to internal cues, to their posture, as field independent. This nomenclature does not indicate a TYPE because people do not react to only one kind of lead, but rather depend more on one source than another.

The preference for particular cues suggested that PERSONALITY contributes significantly to spatial perception, and this interpretation coincided with an emerging curiosity about the interplay between perception and numerous aspects of individuality. Witkin et al. (1954/1972) began the task of finding out if the source that is favored in making spatial judgments is also the one that is relied on in responses that do not involve orientation. This was first explored by means of what is called the Embedded Figures Test, but this name is misleading because it suggests the puzzles in which children try to find toys or objects that are concealed in a large scene. Witkin's test consists of a series of demanding problems. The subject is first allowed to look at a complex design, next at merely a single component of it, and then is required—while viewing only the complex design—to locate the component. This is difficult because the segment is integrated into a larger design in such a way that it is not readily segregated or extracted (Witkin, 1950).

Field independent individuals as a group, were found to discern embedded figures quickly, whereas field dependents tended to require more time, probably because they were influenced more by the structure of the visual patterns. This difference prompted a move away from investigations of judgments of immediately current stimuli in favor of assessments of more abstract factors. The results indicated that field dependent individuals share some personality traits, as well as perceptual preferences. They are apt to be guided, for example, by the social context, and their self-awareness is apt to be less dominant. Field independent people also tend toward a shared pattern, one that is consonant with a relative freedom from the surroundings. One component of this is an awareness that one's body is a source of pride. Others include a tendency to be assertive, to be influenced by internal standards, and to act in a targeted fashion.

This expanding program was reported in a comprehensive volume, *Psychological Differentiation: Studies of Development*, by Witkin, Dyk, Faterson, Goodenough, and Karp (1962/1974). This details a sequence of modifications that started shortly after field dependence-independence was first related to the broader concept of personality. In this extension, attention was focused on "disembedding ability" in perception, and the research stressed a possible congruence between intellectual and perceptual behavior. The experimental results disclosed that subjects who quickly locate an obscured figure are apt to be intellectually innovative and flexible. When the need arises they are quick, for example, to use items in unusual ways, such as adapting a pair of pliers to support a shelf. They are able to devise a way of procuring exact amounts of liquid, without access to graduated measuring containers, such as obtaining twelve quarts of liquid when all there is at hand is a single four-quart and two five-quart bottles.

These as well as several other differences in performance were construed as a tendency either to leave the field "as is" or to rearrange it. This choice acquired a series of names that include global versus analytical or articulated approach, a cognitive structuring versus a restructuring, and, as a general term, cognitive style. Again, it would be an error to assume a typology because the label reflects only a bias, not an exclusive way of responding.

Witkin, ever alert to possible relationships between field dependence-independence and other psychological concepts, then connected cognitive style to psychological differentiation. The latter idea is analogous to the biological phenomena of the transformation of homogeneous cells into specialized ones. In psychology, differentiation deals with the changing of behavior from the global reactivity of the infant to the integrated, specialized functioning of the adult (Werner, 1940/1957). Witkin related levels of differentiation to such phenomena of growth as the gradual segregation of the self from the environment, the developing of information about its boundaries, and the forming of impressions about the functions of different anatomical parts (Witkin, Goodenough, & Oltman, 1979).

The research on field dependence-independence mushroomed, particularly after the introduction of the Embedded Figures Test. Much of the expansion seems to be due to the fact that the Embedded Figures Test allows bypassing the complex paraphernalia of the first Witkin laboratory in favor of simple pencil-and-paper procedures, even ones that can be administered to groups (Witkin, Oltman, Raskin, & Karp, 1971). Goodenough (1978) reports that in thirty years, a bibliography of almost 2,000 items has accumulated.

The reader is reminded that the literature contains both confirmation and contradiction of Witkin's findings. To illustrate the latter—Kurtz (1969) accuses Witkin of failing to explain and merely connecting "unrelated events by grammatical assimilation" (1969, p. 530). Wachtel (1972) points to the proclivity of the investigators to read more concurrence among the variables than the evidence warrants. He also accuses them of ignoring some of the relevant factors. Wachtel and Kurtz both point out that the laboratory data on which the concepts are based are actually tallies of accuracy and are not displays of a style or particular manner of responding.

Only a fortune teller would attempt to describe the resolution of these arguments. A bit of looking back is, however, appropriate. The study of the judgment of the upright appears to be adequately designed, and field dependence and field independence appear both to be clearly defined and to have convincing support.

The modifications of these concepts seem to be less adequately examined, and it is this difference that led to the choice for *this* discussion of field dependence and field independence as the pivotal concepts.

References

Brožek, J. (1971). Purkyně and psychology in a historical research perspective. In V. Krata (Ed.), *J. E. Purkyně (1787–1869) Centanary Symposium, Prague* (pp. 105–118). Brno: J. E. Purkyně University. Purkyně was an unusually productive and creative physiologist. He devoted a great deal of attention to sensory processes and has had more influence on psychology than is generally recognized.

Gibson, J. J., & Mowrer, O. H. (1938). Determinants of the perceived vertical and horizontal. *Psychological Review, 45*, 300–323. The authors review the prior research in a concise, informative way. Various kinds of equipment that are used are identified.

Goodenough, D. R. (1978). Field dependence. In H. London & J. E. Exner, Jr. (Eds.), *Dimensions of personality* (pp. 165–216). New York: John Wiley.

Kurtz, R. M. (1969). A conceptual investigation of Witkin's notion of perceptual style. *Mind, 78*, 522–533. A critique of Witkin's use of the words perception, style, experience, and field.

Lackner, J. R., & Graybiel, A. (1983). Perceived orientation in free-fall depends on visual, postural, and architectural factors. *Aviation, Space, and Environmental Medicine, 54*(1), 47–51. This article points to the complexities that determine the perception of the position of the body during space flights.

Wachtel, P. L. (1972). Field dependence and psychological differentiation: Reexamination. *Perceptual and Motor Skills, 35*, 179–189.

Werner, H. (1957). *Comparative psychology of mental development* (rev. ed.). New York: International Universities Press. (Original work published 1940). Werner traces the course of an individual's discrimination of the world in which one lives. Differentiation, articulation, and organization are included, and the success of each of these processes demands overcoming a preoccupation with the global and the obvious.

Witkin, H. A. (1950). Individual differences in ease of perception of embedded figures. *Journal of Personality, 19*, 1–15. This article traces the history of the procedure, illustrates the figures that are used in the test, describes the scoring method, and provides both qualitative and quantitative results.

Witkin, H. A., Dyk, R. B., Faterson, H. F., Goodenough, D. R., & Karp, S. A. (1974). *Psychological differentiation: Studies of development*. Potomac, MD: Lawrence Erlbaum. (Original work published 1962). This is the second comprehensive volume. The first is Witkin, Lewis, Hertzman, Machover, Meissner, & Wapner, 1954/1972.

Witkin, H. A., Goodenough, D. R., & Oltman, P. K. (1979). Psychological differentiation: Current status. *Journal of Personality and Social Psychology, 37*, 1127–1145.

Witkin, H. A., Lewis, H. B., Hertzman, M., Machover, K., Meissner, P. B., & Wapner, S. (1972). *Personality through perception: An experimental and clinical study*. Westport, CT: Greenwood Press. (Original work published 1954). A comprehensive report of the work of the Witkin group from its inception.

Witkin, H. A., Oltman, P. K., Raskin, E., & Karp, S. A. (1971). *A manual for the Embedded Figures Test*. Palo Alto, CA: Consulting Psychologists Press.

Sources of Additional Information

Gardner, R. W., Holzman, P. S., Klein, G. S., Linton, H. B., & Spence, D. P. (1959). Cognitive control: A study of individual consistencies in cognitive behavior. *Psychological Issues, 1*, Monograph No. 4. This monograph gives the details of some of the earlier work. The authors demonstrate the way cognitive control varies with different cognitive styles. Goldstein, K. M., & Blackman, S. (1978). Assessment of cognitive style. In P. McReynolds (Ed.), *Advances in psychological assessment* (Vol. 4, pp. 462–525). San Francisco: Jossey-Bass. The authors discuss the details of five approaches to cognitive style. Goodenough, D. R. (1976). The role of individual differences in field dependence as a factor in learning and memory. *Psychological Bulletin, 83*, 675–694. Reviews the literature on the differences in learning and memory between field dependent and field independent people. Karp, S. A. (1977). Psychological differentiation. In T. Blass (Ed.), *Personality variables in social behavior* (pp. 135–177). Hillsdale, NJ: Lawrence Erlbaum. Karp reviews research with an emphasis on the social behavior of field dependent and field independent people and reminds readers that subjects do not always interpret experimental situations as investigators believe they do. He suggests that this lack of control has contaminated some research in social behavior. Wapner, S. (1976). Commentary: Process and context in the conception of cognitive style. In S. Messick and Associates (Eds.), *Individuality in learning* (pp. 73–78). San Francisco: Jossey-Bass. Wapner defends Witkin's contributions but suggests some amendments, with an emphasis on problems in education. Witkin, H. A. & Goodenough, D. R. (1977). Field dependence and interpersonal behavior. *Psychological Bulletin, 84*, 661–689. The authors mobilize support for the premise: "People with field dependent or field-independent cognitive styles are different in their interpersonal behavior in ways predicted by the theory of psychological differentiation" (p. 661).

FRUSTRATION. 1. Interference with ongoing behavior. 2. Feelings of being thwarted.

The word frustration is used to designate both the blocking of behavior, a stimulus, and a baffled organism, a response. In both instances there is a theme of disruption, an emphasis on negatives with little or no acknowledgment of the common wisdom that holds that being blocked and feeling defeated can, under some circumstances at least, spur creativity and sharpen the acuity of problem solving. Psychologists do not dispute these opinions, but with few exceptions they ignore them, and in the psychological literature frustration connotes obstruction, prohibition, being defeated, ineffectual, and the like.

Two misleading linguistic practices pervade discussions of frustration, and they are paradoxical in that one makes the concept more conspicuous than its substance merits and the second makes it less conspicuous than the substantive information warrants. The inflated visibility comes from the custom of using paired terms that begin with the word frustration to designate research that is more concerned with sequels or reactions to frustration than with the nature of frustration per se. Among the more common of these are frustration-AGGRESSION, frustration-regression, and frustration-fixation.

The reduced visibility comes from the custom of referring to frustration in specialized terms. For example, the phrase LEARNED HELPLESSNESS, rather than frustration, is applied to the feeling of being unable to exert any influence on an outcome. COGNITIVE DISSONANCE, rather than frustration, is used to indicate the obtaining of information that is distressing because it conflicts either with behavior or with a belief. The word HOSTILITY is commonly used to describe the reaction when frustration is experienced as damage to self-esteem. The choice of either the word frustration or the word failure appears at times to be mainly due to chance, and suggestions about the appropriate use of these words are still being made. For example, as recently as 1978 Van Der Keilen suggests reserving failure for contexts in which nonattainment is due to personal inability, and frustration for those in which nonattainment is due to external obstacles.

The scattering of information that results from these practices is further increased by some biases in the selection of research topics. There is, for example, a dearth of laboratory work on the generally acknowledged relationship between frustration experienced during infancy and early childhood and adult traits (Hilgard, 1952). This slighting is due, in good measure, to the fact that research on this matter demands longitudinal studies, and these are not only expensive, but they are also not feasible for a variety of reasons. Psychologists have, however, assiduously studied the short-term aftereffects of frustration, and these experiments typically fit into one of four aspects of the topic.

The first of these began when Rosenzweig (1934), while experimenting with psychoanalytic concepts, noted that some people appear to react minimally to experiences of failure, whereas others are prone to ascribe blame, some to other people and some to themselves. He began to study these differences and, after trying various techniques, decided that one of the more practical and appropriate methods is to use responses to a series of cartoon-like drawings. Each of these depicts people in a defeating situation and provides some remarks about the difficulty, and subjects are asked to supply additional remarks. A man returning a torn newspaper, a customer complaining to a clerk, and a man accusing another of being a liar typify the content.

This particular procedure has an extended history of use, and one that is still continuing, both as a research tool and as a measure of personality (Rosenzweig, 1978). It is generally called "The Rosenzweig Picture Frustration Study," even though the focus is on various *reactions to* frustration. One of these reactions is called extrapunitive because the thwarted person infers that the fault comes from some external source. An accused liar who is extrapunitive would evidence anger toward the antagonist: "You are wrong. I never stretch the truth." A second is called intropunitive because the respondent is self-accusatory: "I guess I did overstate what happened." The third is labeled impunitive because the subject neutralizes or plays down the problem: "There is a misunderstanding here—we can straighten it out."

Many psychologists accept the word frustration in this frame of reference at face value and fail to realize that the responses are actually forms of aggression, rather than frustration. The pervasiveness of this misalignment is indicated by the practice in the *Psychological Abstracts* of indexing studies of "The Rosenzweig Picture Frustration Study" under the topic of frustration, rather than under a more appropriate category.

Rosenzweig stands apart in several ways from many of those who use his method. He is aware that aggression is the central topic, and he also points out that it is not the only behavior that is elicited by frustration. He laments the neglect of other reactions, particularly the positive ones, and in this connection takes care to point out that impunitiveness may on occasion be constructive. Rosenzweig has also refined the topic of frustration by contributing the exceptionally useful idea of frustration tolerance, that is, the ability to handle being thwarted in a calm, composed rather than a self-defeating manner.

Additional investigations of reactions that are provoked by frustration emerged shortly after Rosenzweig's inaugural work. They are similar in that each elicited both support and criticism, generally during the 1940s and 1950s. This attention was followed first by a blending of the studies into the psychological literature and then by a suspension of significant numbers of attempts to refine and elaborate them.

In 1939 Dollard, Doob, Miller, Mowrer, and Sears published *Frustration and Aggression*. This landmark treatise stated that "*aggression is always a consequence of frustration*" (p. 1). The authors proposed various relationships between these two concepts, such as an equality between the amount of frustration experienced and the amount of aggression that follows, as well as a modulation of the intensity of aggression by virtue of the amount of retaliation that is anticipated.

The postulated inevitability of frustration-aggression soon came under fire, and less binding relationships were proposed (Miller, 1941). Many of these endeavors represent a move away from the study of frustration toward the study of aggression, but again, the vocabulary is misleading. Yates, for example, entitled a book *Frustration and Conflict* (1962), and devoted a chapter to "Frustration and Aggression." He reviews the research that was provoked by Dollard et al. and organizes criticisms of it under seven headings. The word aggression appears in six of these, and the seventh also ignores frustration in that it is entitled "Methodological Criticisms" (p. 109).

Research on a second reaction to frustration started with an experiment conducted by Barker, Dembo, and Lewin (1941) on the relationship between frustration and regression, that is, the reverting under duress to behavior that is characteristic of an earlier age. In this study the researchers first allowed young children to play freely with a set of toys and then introduced them to much more attractive play equipment and permitted them to enjoy it for a period of time. In order to frustrate the children the investigators moved these appealing items to an area behind a wire screen so that they were visible but not accessible. The children were then offered the opportunity to amuse themselves with the original materials. In the majority of the children the frustration of seeing but not being able to use the desired toys brought with it less constructive play, more attempts to leave the situation, and increased efforts to manipulate the barrier. This behavior was interpreted as regressive.

As in the case of the frustration-aggression hypothesis of Dollard et al., this experiment triggered controversy about the inevitability of regression. The arguments also included speculations about the mechanics of the interference and attempts to determine the kinds of behavior in which the aggression is more pronounced (Child & Waterhouse, 1952, 1953).

Information about another kind of response to frustration was published in *Frustration*, a 1949 report of a decade of research conducted by N. R. F. Maier. In this research program, fixation is identified as the culminating reaction in a sequence of frustrating conditions. This begins with rats learning that pushing one of two panels allows them access to food. Whenever the animal jumps toward a locked panel, it is forced to land on the floor from a height above the animal's jumping tolerance. Once the discrimination between the rewarded and the unrewarded section is mastered *both* are locked. An animal typically reacts to this by trying to move the previously fastened panel. After several failures it simply sits on the jumping stand, attempting to avoid a forced landing on the floor. The rat is then exposed to a blast of air. This provokes it to leap to the side or above the apparatus, but barriers that prohibit escape are then erected. The animal is now in a situation in which it cannot obtain a reward, cannot leave the field, and yet is under pressure to respond. Rats react to this by indulging in stereotyped behavior. The particular configuration varies from animal to animal but generally remains the same in any one rat. The ritual is repeated whenever the animal is put in the situation, and reintroducing food—even making it visible—does not alter the stereotype, and the animal, when placed in the frustrating setting, continues to indulge in its characteristic stereotype. This rigidity led Maier to designate the response as fixation and to characterize it as nonmotivated behavior.

Maier worked mainly with animals, but he was alert to the relevance of his work to humans, and in this connection pointed to similarities between fixation and resignation, the giving in to loss by renouncing goals and ceasing to strive. Maier's research was carried out at a time when LEARNING THEORY was in vogue, and because fixation appeared not to respond to REINFORCEMENT the work was, until the recent past, disdained and even ignored. When it was addressed, fixation was often not treated as an independent topic, but was evaluated in relation to learning theory (Lawson, 1965; Yates, 1962).

By the 1970s learning theory had lost much of its appeal, and this brought with it some interest in reactivating Maier's design. The return is illustrated by Winefield (1979), who outlines both the similarities and differences between learned helplessness and frustration. He notes that in both concepts the organism has no effect on outcome. A difference—and one that may be crucial—is Maier's opinion that fixation is specific to the context in which it is instigated, and the belief that learned helplessness is generalized to other contexts. The resolution of the equivalence, or the nonequivalence, of these two concepts is probably not as important as the fact that they are being compared, a step that can contribute to the integration of the information about frustration that has been obtained under various names and various concepts.

References

Barker, R. G., Dembo, T., & Lewin, K. (1941). Frustration and regression: An experiment with young children. *University of Iowa Studies in Child Welfare, 18*, 1–314. Much of the content of this lengthy monograph is included in *Frustration: The Development of a Scientific Concept* (pp. 77–99) by R. Lawson (see this reference list).

Child, I. L., & Waterhouse, I. K. (1952). Frustration and the quality of performance: I. A critique of the Barker, Dembo, and Lewin experiment. *Psychological Review, 59*, 351–362.

Child, I. L., & Waterhouse, I. K. (1953). Frustration and the quality of performance: II. A theoretical statement. *Psychological Review, 60*, 127–139. The authors contend that frustration produces both interfering responses and changes in motivation, and that these variables are responsible for various changes in behavior. In other words, there is no unique, distinct mode of reacting to frustration.

Dollard, J., Doob, L. W., Miller, N. E., Mowrer, O. H., & Sears, R. R. (1939). *Frustration and aggression*. New Haven, CT: Yale University Press.

Hilgard, E. R. (1952). Experimental approaches to psychoanalysis. In E. Pumpian-Mindlin (Ed.), *Psychoanalysis as science* (pp. 3–45). Stanford, CA: Stanford University Press. Hilgard deals briefly but effectively with the problems of demonstrating experimentally the long-term effects of early experiences. His review of the outcome of infantile frustration is dated, but more recent history had added little new information.

Lawson, R. (1965). *Frustration: The development of a scientific concept*. New York: Macmillan. This volume amends the author's review of theories about and research on frustration with reprints of eight of the most frequently cited papers on the concept.

Maier, N. R. F. (1949). *Frustration: The study of behavior without a goal*. New York: McGraw-Hill. This research was first presented at the 1938 annual meeting of the American Association for the Advancement of Science, and the association awarded Maier a $1,000 prize. This favorable initial reception soon faded, but more recent endorsement is gaining momentum.

Miller, N. E. (1941). The frustration-aggression hypothesis. *Psychological Review, 48*, 337–342.

Rosenzweig, S. (1934). Types of reaction to frustration. *Journal of Abnormal and Social Psychology, 29*, 298–300. In this initial presentation Rosenzweig indicates that anger and indignation constitute the emotional basis of extrapunitiveness, that humiliation and guilt support intropunitiveness, and that embarrassment and shame give rise to impunitiveness. Specific emotional reactions were soon omitted, and the basic units became the three punitive reactions.

Rosenzweig, S. (1978). *Aggressive behavior and the Rosenzweig Picture-Frustration Study*. New York: Praeger. Rosenzweig reviews his research as well as that of others during a forty-year span. The technique has been widely adopted, and translations of the procedural manuals have been published in eight foreign languages.

Van Der Keilen, M. (1978). Critical note on use of the terms "failure" and "frustration" in defining experimental situations. *Psychological Reports, 43*, 1269–1270. An illustration of a recent complaint about the disarray of the vocabulary in relation to frustration.

Winefield, A. H. (1979). Frustration-instigated behavior and learned helplessness. *Journal of Psychology, 102*, 267–274.

Yates, A. J. (1962). *Frustration and conflict*. London: Methuen. An accurate and thorough review of the major theories of frustration.

Sources of Additional Information

Barker, R. G. (1938). The effect of frustration upon cognitive ability. *Character and Personality, 7*, 145–150. One of the few proposals in the psychological literature that frustration may, on occasion, increase efficiency. Lawrence, D. H., & Festinger, L. (1962). *Deterrents and reinforcement: The psychology of insufficient reward*. Stanford, CA: Stanford University Press. An account of research on learning that includes some notable efforts to explain some of the effects of deprivation. The subject matter meets several of the criteria for frustration, but it is treated as COGNITIVE DISSONANCE. Marquis, D. P. (1943). A study of frustration in newborn infants. *Journal of Experimental Psychology, 32*, 123–138. The author describes the reactions of infants to a withdrawal of the bottle after each fourth of its contents were consumed. Maslow, A. (1941). Deprivation, threat and frustration. *Psychological Review, 48*, 364–366. Maslow is one of several psychologists who is explicit that frustration is applicable only when the interference is important, when it threatens security, self-esteem, or crucial goals. He uses the word deprivation to describe failures to obtain unimportant items—ones that have ready substitutes. Sargent, S. S. (1948). Reaction to frustration—a critique and hypothesis. *Psychological Review, 55*, 108–114. This paper represents the kind of criticism that followed the linking of frustration and aggression. It is also atypical in that Sargent argues that the covert, implicit aspects of frustration should be given more attention. Sears, R. R. (1941). 2. Non-aggressive reactions to frustration. *Psychological Review, 48*, 343–346. One of the five proponents of the frustration-aggression hypothesis backs away from the rigid relationship proposed in the original hypothesis. Sears is a productive contributor to the research on frustration in childhood.

FUNCTIONAL PSYCHOLOGY. 1. A viewpoint in psychology that stresses the utility of numerous psychological processes, including learning, remembering, thinking, and perceiving.

The word function has various meanings, but the most common one in the psychological literature designates role or purpose, frequently categorized as either serviceable or disserviceable to the organism. The idea of utilitarian activity is much older than experimental psychology, and the integration of this concept was neither novel nor startling. What was unusual is that it was initially promoted in the field of psychology in attempts to devise psychological examinations by two very different groups: students of evolution and practitioners of phrenology.

Darwin stressed both biological and psychological adaptation, and various scientists began to pursue these interests in a diversity of contexts. The most direct effect on psychology came through the work of Darwin's advocate Francis Galton. Galton (1883) wanted to improve the human stock, and he believed that this goal would be fostered by the identification of superior individuals. So he devised techniques for measuring individual differences in physical attributes and in such simple psychological responses as reaction time and memory for form. Galton did not measure complex responses, but his sponsorship helped to promote mental testing, an enterprise that many see as a basic tool in efforts to foster adjustment.

A second impetus for psychological examinations came from phrenology. Phrenological diagnoses are predicated on the assumption of conformity between the size and contour of the brain and of the skull, and until the inaccuracy of this premise was discovered, phrenologists used the proportions among various parts of the skull as indicators of the nature of psychological variables, such as intelligence, aptitude for various occupations, and personality traits (Bakan, 1966; Walsh, 1970). There is even evidence that the phrenologists were the first to apply the term function to the mind (Dallenbach, 1915). The renunciation of the theory did not erase the interest of psychologists in diagnoses, and they were pursued by other means (Bakan, 1966). In fact, the practice of psychology and phrenology overlapped, since the *American Phrenological Journal* did not cease publication until 1911 and the American Institute of Phrenology existed until 1925, at least two decades after the emergence of functional psychology (Dallenbach, 1955).

The precursors of functional psychology within psychology itself constitute more of a series of separate events than an all encompassing formulation of how to organize the subject matter. One of the most conspicuous background figures is William James, a theorist who advocated pragmatism, a proposal that value is best judged in terms of practical consequences. James' (1890) thinking moved freely from this idea to demonstrations of how consciousness allows humans to choose courses of action and the way such variables as habit and instinct facilitate adjusting to the environment. He dealt with a variety of additional factors as well and developed an approach to psychology that stresses function.

The functional stance in one of James' arguments was strengthened by John Dewey (1896) in a landmark article on the reflex arc. In this Dewey suggested that the custom of subdividing events into elements produces artificial abstractions. In developing this point he reinterpreted James' breakdown of the sequence of events that occurs when a child first sees a flame, reaches for it, and then withdraws. James perceived this as a sensation preceding each response, but Dewey commented that the chain does not begin with a sensation, but with a function, specifically the act of looking. He then pointed out that this was followed by coordination, by a reciprocity of sensory and motor responses, that vision, for example, guides the hand and the changes in the position of the hand modifies what is seen. Dewey suggested that psychologists had singled out stimulus and response for attention because they serve different purposes, but there was more significance in the relationship between them.

A second article that also called attention to the idea of function in psychology came in 1898, when E. B. Titchener participated in a controversy concerning the validity of reaction time data that are procured from trained as opposed to untrained research participants. Much of the argument centered around the fact that the repertoire of the unpracticed group is not modified before the experimental observations, but that the repertoire of the second group is altered by practice, that is, by adaptive exercise. Developing his case, Titchener, an eminent theorist of the era, contrasted the system of STRUCTURAL PSYCHOLOGY with what he called functionalism or functional psychology. The word functional had not been previously paired with the word psychology: "What Titchener was attacking was in fact nameless until he named it; hence he thrust the movement into high relief and did more than anyone else to get the term *functionalism* into psychological currency" (Harrison, 1963, p. 395).

In 1903 J. R. Angell, responding to Titchener's challenge, elaborated the concept of functional psychology. He published a book (1904/1908) in which the word function was included in the subtitle. His 1906 presidential address to the American Psychological Association, published in 1907, was entitled "The Province of Functional Psychology." In these presentations Angell offered some specifications for a psychology of adaptation, but he did not combine them into a comprehensive, unified theory. For Angell, the subject matter of psychology consists of mental operations, including consideration of what consciousness does and the effectiveness of such processes as selective attention and problem solving.

Dewey and Angell were both on the faculty of the University of Chicago, and the functionalist character of that department was further strengthened when they were joined in 1908 by Harvey A. Carr, a student of Angell's who became head of the department of psychology in 1926. Carr's writings (1925, 1930), like those of his colleagues, were more clarifications than rejoinders. Carr's main interest was in research on learning, but he did not suggest restricting psychology to any one area.

The functionalists' concern about utility and purpose coalesced with the American preference for the practical. Inquiries about just what mental operations accomplished were more acceptable than abstruse inquiries into the nature of the mind. A wide acceptance of functional psychology was inevitable, and it soon developed.

One of the more influential settings in which it emerged was Columbia University, where research on individual differences and on educational procedures were promoted by two faculty members. In the 1890s James McKeen Cattell began devising mental tests, and Edward L. Thorndike, both a student and an admirer of James and a doctoral student of Cattell, investigated trial and error

LEARNING. Thorndike's dedicated pursuit of this topic made him both one of the foremost learning theorists as well as one of the leading authorities on instructional techniques and the measurement of their effects (Marx & Cronan-Hillix, 1987).

In the course of his professional development Thorndike came to be identified more with the *field* of learning than with the *viewpoint* of functional psychology, but this alignment is merely a single example of the widespread disappearance of the *label* of functional psychology. The concern with adaptation and its mechanisms became characteristic of the discipline as a whole, and this acceptance, paradoxically, obscured the identification of its origin (Harrison, 1963). Researchers began to be identified with the topic they worked on, such as specialists in the field of memory, concept formation, creativity, emotion, and so forth. But this was merely a change in name, not a rejection of the idea of functional psychology. The viewpoint had been presented more in an open, receptive fashion than in a defensive one. This tactic did not set the stage for an "either for or against" conflict, but fostered a ready, unselfconscious integration: "Many, if not most, American psychologists have simply continued on their quiet ways, following something resembling a functionalist program without thinking much about it" (Marx & Cronan-Hillix, 1987, p. 139).

References

Angell, J. R. (1903). The relations of structural and functional psychology to philosophy. *Philosophical Review, 12*, 243–271. This lengthy presentation depicts the influence of philosophy on psychology as it was perceived at the date of publication.

Angell, J. R. (1907). The province of functional psychology. *Psychological Review, 14*, 61–91. This is a frequently cited address. It is clear, straightforward, but not doctrinaire.

Angell, J. R. (1908). *Psychology: An introductory study of the structure and function of human consciousness* (4th ed., rev.). New York: Holt. (Original work published 1904).

Bakan, D. (1966). The influence of phrenology on American psychology. *Journal of the History of the Behavioral Sciences, 2*, 200–220.

Carr, H. A. (1925). *Psychology: A study of mental activity*. New York: Longmans Green. An introduction to the field that is clearly functional, in that psychology is conceived as "mental activity . . . concerned with the acquisition, fixation, retention, organization, and evaluation of experiences, and their subsequent utilization in the guidance of conduct" (p. 1).

Carr, H. A. (1930). Functionalism. In C. Murchison (Ed.), *Psychologies of 1930*, (59-78) Worcester, MA: Clark University Press.

Dallenbach, K. M. (1915). The history and derivation of the word "function" as a systematic term in psychology. *American Journal of Psychology, 26*, 473–484. The author includes some discussion of the use of "function" by nonpsychologists.

Dallenbach, K. M. (1955) Phrenology versus psychoanalysis. *American Journal of Psychology, 68*, 511–525.

Dewey, J. (1896). The reflex arc concept in psychology. *Psychological Review, 3*, 357–370. Dewey saw the reflex arc as important because it conveys "divisions of labor, functioning factors, within the single concrete whole" (p. 358).

Galton, F. (1883). *Inquiries into human faculty and its development*. New York: Macmillan.

Harrison, R. (1963). Functionalism and its historical significance. *Genetic Psychology Monographs, 68*, 387–423. The author emphasizes the integration into modern psychology: "Functionalism in its painless and gradual passing has not failed in achieving its purposes because its principles in some form are recognized by almost all psychologists and have been incorporated into the general body of present doctrine and method" (p. 419).

James, W. (1890). *The principles of psychology* (Vols. 1 & 2). New York: Holt.

Marx, M. H., & Cronan-Hillix, W. A. (1987). *Systems and theories in psychology* (4th ed.). New York: McGraw-Hill. An authoritative account, with a strong emphasis on experimental psychology.

Titchener, E. B. (1898). The postulates of a structural psychology. *Philosophical Review, 7*, 449–465.

Walsh, A. A. (1970). Is phrenology foolish? A rejoinder. *Journal of the History of the Behavioral Sciences, 6*, 358–361. The author has compiled a large collection of phrenological materials and literature, and is a scholar of the movement.

Sources of Additional Information

Galton, F. (1978). *Hereditary genius: An inquiry into its laws and consequences*. New York: St. Martin's Press. (Original work published 1869). Galton believed that the pattern of inheritance of mental traits is the same as that of physical traits. Heidbreder, E. (1969). Functionalism. In D. L. Krantz (Ed.), *Schools of psychology: A symposium* (pp. 35–50). New York: Appleton-Century-Crofts. The discussion includes consideration of the implications of functionalism for more recent developments in psychology. Ruckmich, C. A. (1913). The use of the term *function* in English textbooks of psychology. *American Journal of Psychology, 24*, 99–123. This is a review of the use of function in fifteen textbooks. Ruckmich found that the referents are various psychological activities (dreaming, thinking) as well as their benefits. He is critical of this confusion, but Carr (*Psychologies of 1930*) argues that the two meanings are congruent. Sokal, M. M. (Ed.). (1981). *An education in psychology: James McKeen Cattell's journal and letter from Germany and England, 1880–1888*. Cambridge, MA: Massachusetts Institute of Technology Press. The title identifies the bulk of the text, but there is also information about Cattell's later career. The book constitutes an interesting account of student experiences in Germany and, in this instance, the development of a functional point of view.

G

GESTALT PSYCHOLOGY. 1. A system of psychology that interprets psychological events as indivisible and organized.

Gestalt psychology originated in Germany. The word Gestalt does not have a precise English equivalent, but is translated with a variety of terms, commonly as a pattern, a configuration, or a segregated whole. One of the clearest illustrations of a Gestalt is a melody, a phenomenon that retains its identity when played on different instruments and at different tempos. The stress on configuration stands in opposition to the reductionism of most scientific theories, but this is Gestalt psychology's main thrust. The system is primarily concerned with theoretical aspects of psychology and is only seldom used in applied areas. This insularity combines with the unusual perspective of the viewpoint to make it generally unfamiliar. Probably it can be most readily understood by learning about some of the specifics that come with dealing with a totality rather than with parts or components.

The movement has three principals, German citizens, mature and distinguished scholars who migrated to the United States: Max Wertheimer (1880–1943), Kurt Koffka (1886–1941), and Wolfgang Köhler (1887–1967). The formal beginning of the school is customarily dated as 1912, the publication date of Wertheimer's "Experimental Studies on the Seeing of Motion" (Wertheimer, 1912/1965). Koffka and Köhler served as subjects in this initial research, and the trio, working cooperatively and maintaining consensus, became known informally as "The Three G's." They attracted a group of followers, relatively small in number but prolific (Heidbreder, 1933; Henle, 1977).

The inaugural article deals with the perception of motion when separate stimuli are successively exposed. An illustration, common on the current scene, is the practice of successively lighting a series of bulbs so that the immediate experience is one of movement, that is, of fluidity, rather than a sequence of sensations. Wertheimer called this stroboscopic effect the phi phenomenon, and asserted that it is not an illusion, but it is apparent motion that is perceived.

Other perceptual experiences were studied, and important among these, and illustrative of the work, is the attention given to the relationship between foreground and background. In the visual field this is exemplified by the distinct contours of buildings against a formless sky, and in the field of audition, by sounds against intervals of silence. The research disclosed that Gestalten vary in stability, and an impressive amount of research was devoted to learning the principles of the organization of the perceptual field. These include studies of the limits within which grouping is facilitated by proximity (...... or .. .. ..) and the pervasiveness of closure, a perceptual completing of imperfect wholes. For example, Γ, is apt to be seen as T. Perceptual principles of this nature explain some of the everyday experiences outside the laboratory—why patterns are discerned in proximate stars and why "comin' " is heard as "coming."

Gestalt psychologists favor the method of PHENOMENOLOGY, a technique of observing immediate experience, just as it occurs and unanalyzed. The suitability of this technique was apparent as early as the discovery of the phi phenomenon, and it has turned out to be productive in a number of problems. One topic in which its value is obvious is the study of object constancy, the retaining of a similar appearance under different conditions. Snow, for example, is seen as white at night, and there are only insignificant changes in the perceived size and shape of familiar objects when the view of them changes from near to far range (Katz, 1950).

The perception of animals as well as of humans was also studied. A significant pioneer experiment involved the training of hens to peck food from the lighter of two papers. When the training paper was replaced with one lighter than either of the original two, the hens displayed an appreciation of the relative brightness by pecking from the recently added rather than the previously rewarded one (Köhler, 1918/1967).

The principles of organization were investigated in various responses in addition to perception. One of the more noteworthy extensions began in research on the concept of THINKING, or, more precisely, problem solving. The initial work in this domain was Köhler's observations of chimpanzees, first published in English in 1925 in *The Mentality of Apes* (1951). Köhler placed the animals in situations in which a reward, fruit, could be procured only when the relationships among various elements in the situation are comprehended. All of these involve a detour, that is, in order to secure the food the animal is first forced to turn away from it. Thus a chimpanzee, watching an attendant who throws fruit out a window and then immediately closes it, must leave the window where the food can be seen to go outside in order to retrieve it. In another situation the lure is suspended at a height that exceeds the animal's reach, but there is a box in the pen, placed at some distance from the lure, but of adequate height if placed under the reward. An even more difficult problem is one in which three or four boxes, located in different parts of the enclosure, must be stacked in order to reach the fruit.

Köhler reported that chimpanzees initially attempt to obtain the reward directly, that is, they extend a forepaw as far as possible or shake the fence that is closest to the goal. After a series of inept responses the animal appears suddenly to realize the relationships within the configuration, and this leads to constructive behavior. To illustrate—after a period of time in the multiple-box puzzle the chimpanzees give up the pacing and reaching, and once started on the correct sequence of responses, quickly complete them, for example, collect and stack the requisite number of boxes and then climb this new construction and procure the food.

Köhler used the word "insight" to designate the grasping of the situation, the understanding of the relationships among the components of the problem. His conclusion that apes made intelligent analyses contrasted with the preoccupation of psychologists at that time with the lack of comprehension, with the "trial and error" method that they thought was characteristic of animals. Controversy arose as to whether the change in behavior resulted from acquisition or reorganization, and in these debates insight was related more to learning than to problem solving. The topic soon came to be categorized as LEARNING rather than thinking. The insight of children and adults was investigated, and the subject became a prominent one in learning research. The label insight even acquired a colloquialism—the "aha" or "ah-ah" experience, a sudden realization of relationships—"I see it, I understand" (Bower & Hilgard, 1981).

Although the Gestaltists concentrated their research on perception and on problem solving, there were significant probes into various additional topics. Kurt Lewin (1890–1947) began his career in Germany in a Gestalt milieu, and during the early part of his professional life he drew from Gestalt theory (Hartmann, 1935). One of these contributions that mirrors the interest in cohesion is a postulated sequence that develops when activity is interrupted or blocked. He assumed that interfering with activity arouses tension, and he invokes this to explain such instances of persistence as the pleadings of a child to be allowed to continue play and the pressures felt by adults to complete a project once it is started. A landmark experiment was conducted by Zeigarnik (1927/1967) in which subjects were given simple tasks, such as counting backwards and completing jigsaw puzzles. There was sufficient time to finish only half of these projects, and at the end of the session the subjects were asked to recall what they had done during the laboratory period. The majority named more interrupted than uninterrupted tasks. This higher recollection is called the Zeigarnik effect, and in Lewin's frame of reference, the tension induced by the instructions was not dissipated because the task was not completed, and thus more interrupted assignments were recalled.

The influence of Gestalt theory on modern psychology seems to be uneven. There are segments of it that appear to be primarily of historic interest, but there are also segments that are now assessed as basic or fundamental in the discipline, particularly the principles of perceptual organization and insight. Recent changes in the study of learning have also increased the relevance of Gestalt investigations of "meaningful learning" (Henle, 1987). COGNITIVE PSYCHOLOGY is emphasizing the processing of information, and the research on problem solving and meaning seems more in line with this than the research on the learning and remembering of nonsense syllables.

The proponents of Gestalt psychology are gratified by the impact they have made, but they also find some recent references to the theory to be most unfortunate. At issue here is a misrepresentation, and one that appears to be spreading, that "gestalt therapy" is an extension of Gestalt psychology. The former is an invention of Fritz Perls, who extracted some of the terminology of Gestalt theory and transposed it inappropriately to variables related to psychiatric disturbances. Henle, an exceptionally sophisticated scholar of Gestalt psychology, reviews Perls' writings in the 1960s and 1970s and concludes: "His work has *no* substantive relation to scientific Gestalt psychology" (1978, p. 31).

Arnheim, a second Gestalt expert, also reacted in a strongly negative manner to a discussion of "gestalt therapy" in a publication of the American Psychological Association: "It took me a moment to realize that the term *gestalt* in its precise historical and theoretical sense is losing its sanctuary even in professional journals" (1974, p. 570). Let the reader be warned: Gestalt psychology is a recondite, and thus often unfamiliar, viewpoint in psychology, and references to it—even in learned circles—may deviate markedly from the actual concept.

References

Arnheim, R. (1974). "Gestalt" misapplied. *Contemporary Psychology, 19*, 570. Arnheim disavows any identification of Fritz Perls with Gestalt psychology.
Bower, G. H., & Hilgard, E. R. (1981). *Theories of learning* (5th ed.). Englewood Cliffs, NJ: Prentice-Hall
Hartmann, G. W. (1935). *Gestalt psychology: A survey of facts and principles.* New York: Ronald Press. The text is supplemented by a glossary and brief biographies of "The Three G's."
Heidbreder, E. (1933). *Seven psychologies.* New York: Appleton-Century.
Henle, M. (1977). The influence of Gestalt psychology in America. In R. W. Rieber, K. Salzinger, & T. Verhave (Eds.), The roots of American psychology: Historical influences and implications for the future. *Annals of the New York Academy of Sciences, 291*, 3–12. A synopsis of the role of Gestalt psychology in America. Henle believes that the theory has been denied adequate opportunities for development, and discusses the reason for this.
Henle, M. (1978). Gestalt psychology and gestalt therapy. *Journal of the History of the Behavioral Sciences, 14*, 23–32.
Henle, M. (1987). Koffka's *Principles* after fifty years. *Journal of the History of the Behavioral Sciences, 23*, 14–21. Kurt Koffka published *Principles of Gestalt Psychology* in 1935. In 1985 the historians of psychology invited Mary Henle to speak at the Annual Convention of the American Psychological Association on the reception and legacy of this work. This paper is a revised version of that address.

Katz, D. (1950). *Gestalt psychology: Its nature and significance* (R. Tyson, Trans.). New York: Ronald Press. More readily intelligible than many of the books dealing with Gestalt psychology. The coverage is extensive.

Köhler, W. (1967). Simple structural functions in the chimpanzee and in the chicken. In W. D. Ellis (Ed. & Trans.), *A source book of Gestalt psychology* (pp. 217–227). London: Routledge & Kegan Paul. (Original work published 1918). This volume contains summaries of German publications of the Gestaltists.

Köhler, W. (1951). *The mentality of apes* (2nd rev. ed.). (E. Winter, Trans.). London: Routledge & Kegan Paul. This book was first published in English in 1925. It is both informative and delightful to read. Köhler appreciates the individual personalities as well as both the insight and the lack of insight of each of the chimpanzees he observed. The factual material is presented in an understanding, sympathetic writing style.

Wertheimer, Max. (1965). Experimental studies on the seeing of motion (D. Cantor, Trans.). In R. J. Herrnstein & E. G. Boring (Eds.), *A source book in the history of psychology* (pp. 163–168). Cambridge, MA: Harvard University Press. (Original work published 1912)

Zeigarnik, B. (1967). On finished and unfinished tasks. In W. D. Ellis (Ed. & Trans.), *A source book of Gestalt psychology* (pp. 300–314). London: Routledge & Kegan. (Original work published 1927). The differences between the recall of interrupted and uninterrupted tasks were striking, and the author includes various tallies to document this.

Sources of Additional Information

Ash, M. G. (1983). The emergence of Gestalt theory: Experimental psychology in Germany, 1890–1920 (Doctoral dissertation, Harvard University, 1982). *Dissertation Abstracts International*, Order No. DA8303408. This is a comprehensive account of the rise of Gestalt psychology in Germany. Freeman, F. S. (1977). The beginnings of Gestalt psychology in the United States. *Journal of the History of the Behavioral Sciences, 13*, 352–353. Freeman was on the faculty of Cornell University when successful efforts were made on that campus to introduce Gestalt psychology to America. Helson, H. (1933). The fundamental propositions of Gestalt psychology. *Psychological Review, 40*, 13–32. Helson presents 114 propositions, "the initial assumptions, definitions, and chief findings of the *Gestalt* psychologists" (p. 13). Koffka, K. (1928). *The growth of the mind: An introduction to child psychology* (2nd ed. rev.). (R. M. Ogden, Trans.). New York: Harcourt Brace. The application of Gestalt psychology to development. Wertheimer, Max. (1959). *Productive thinking* (enlarged ed.). (M[ichael] Wertheimer, Ed.). New York: Harper & Row. (Original work published 1945). This book is a classic, and one that helps to elucidate problem solving and insight. Wertheimer was a personal friend of Albert Einstein, and studied Einstein's thinking patterns in detail.

GOAL. 1. An attraction, often an object or a status, that prompts striving. 2. A synonym for incentive. **INCENTIVE.** 1. An attraction, often varying in intensity or amount, that prompts striving. 2. A synonym for goal.

The concepts of goal and incentive have been selected for discussion in this volume because they are the residuals of a group of older psychological terms with similar meanings, such as aim, end, lure, and purpose (American Psychological Association, 1985). Each of these refers to factors that are external to the organism, and MOTIVATION theory demands that each must be perceived as a probable source of gratification. This necessitates relating desire and desired, and two approaches to this problem have been adopted. One proposes various mechanisms that link anticipation and a target, but these explanations are often awkward and forced. The second approach is more pragmatic in that attempts are made merely to acquire predictive power, that is, to learn enough to predict changes in behavior that can be expected when goals and incentives change.

The proponents of both procedures are prone to casual, imprecise terminology, and a few comments about these linguistic practices are in order. On the one hand the words goal and incentive are frequently used interchangeably because each involves reaching for something extraneous to the organism: a luncheon, a new garment, an admission ticket to a concert, a high score on an examination today, tomorrow, or four years hence. But on the other hand the terms are on occasion differentiated, in that goal is recommended for objects (a yacht) or status (yachtsman) and incentive for activities (sailing). In this scheme, goals frequently designate what is sought, whereas the word incentive refers to gradations in the potential to satisfy. For example, the goal might be to become a stage performer with the incentive being the level of applause, the amount of deference with which one is treated, and/or the dollar value of the income that is expected.

In precise terminology the words goal and incentive refer to variables that precede action, and reward and punishment or REINFORCEMENT are variables that follow action (Logan, 1960). Thus, in strict parlance, *after* a child meets the *goal* of pleasing a teacher, a *reward* of praise ensues. A desire for a new home is aligned with expectation and achieving it with a result.

Although the distinction between motive and consequence appears to be straightforward in actual practice, the two are often confused. A well-known 1925 study by Hurlock illustrates this, and at the same time documents the longevity of the practice of failing to separate measurements of anticipation and outcome. In this experiment Hurlock calculated the accuracy of children's addition during successive practice periods, each of which was followed by criticism of some children, praise of others, and the ignoring of still others. The sequence was clearly one of performance supplemented by praise, reproof, or no attention. Even though the children's expectations were not assessed, the study is entitled "An Evaluation of Certain Incentives Used in School Work."

A second illustration of the confusion about temporal order is contained in a widely circulated text by McGeoch, *The Psychology of Human Learning: An Introduction* (1942). The author first defines incentive as "*an object or condition which is perceived as potentially satisfying to a motive*" (p. 27). Later, in reviewing an experiment, McGeoch describes "the introduction of an effective incentive (a penny) *after* [italics added] each trial" (p. 268).

There are similar failures in the more recent literature. For example, Kenny and Blass (1977) use the word incentive in the title of an experiment on spatial orientation in neonatal rats, but during the experiment they allowed pups to suck *after* they made a particular directional choice.

Despite this laxity, an impressive amount of information about external motives has been accumulated, and the study of tropisms marks one starting point. The word tropism comes from the Greek and it means "to turn." As early as 1835 it was applied to the orienting, or growth, of plants toward a light source. In 1890 Loeb, a physiologist, began to apply this phenomenon of plant physiology to animal behavior because he saw it as more satisfactory than the then prevalent custom of invoking free volition, divine wisdom, and other supernatural forces. He reasoned that because organisms are bilaterally symmetrical, any differential in lateral stimulation would prompt turning in order to reestablish equal stimulation. The objectivity of this theory impressed Loeb so much that he predicted that it would eventually be developed into a mathematical theory of human conduct (Gussin, 1963). A few psychologists were attracted to Loeb's idea, but it turned out to be too simplistic to explain the mechanism of psychological responses and the concept was relegated to the appropriate domain—the reactions of uncomplicated organisms in a relatively constant environment (Warden, Jenkins, & Warner, 1935).

The fade out of tropism was also the fade out of relatively simple explanations. From then on theorists took on the problem of characterizing the bonds between the lure and the organism, but the connections that were hypothesized tended to be cumbersome. William McDougall, an early systematist, illustrates the awkwardness in a proposal that a *purposive* tendency "pulls" the organism toward goals. He assumed that movements are "made for the sake of attaining their natural end" (1923, p. 47). McDougall came to assign so much weight to striving that his doctrine acquired the label of purposive or hormic psychology.

Although its importance is more historic than contemporary, purposive psychology did have a significant influence on the attempts of the proponents of NEOBEHAVIORISM to demonstrate that learning relates external motives to internal variables. One of the main theorists in this enterprise was Edward C. Tolman, who drew ideas from various sources, including McDougall. He gives McDougall credit for the phrase "purposive behavior," part of the title of a volume he published in 1932 *Purposive Behavior in Animals and Men*. This is an account of an unusually complicated attempt to relate overt responses to implicit processes, and it fell under its own weight. It did, however, have a heyday, and during that interval the concepts of goal and incentive were in the foreground.

The general public, ignorant of the riddles that theorists face and confronted with practical matters, has long been aware of the effectiveness of goals and incentives, and has relied on them to achieve desired aims. Parents have used educational, financial, and recreational goals and incentives to spur children. In fact, educational and occupational progress is often charted as a sequence of subgoals. Psychologists, on the other hand, have been somewhat slow to begin explaining the empirical effects of externals. An early exception was William Lowe Bryan, an academician who wanted to broaden the scope of psychology beyond theory by including everyday problems and strategies for handling them. In his presidential address in 1903 to the American Psychological Association he referred to the wisdom of striking a balance between doctrine and application, "between abstract aspects or fragments of truth and the requirements of practice" (1904, p. 79). He recommended giving more attention to "concrete psychology" (1904, p. 80).

A few investigators acted in the spirit of this endorsement by compiling various kinds of empirical information relevant to industry, including advertising, an enterprise that may be defined as the manipulation of incentives (Hollingworth, 1913; Scott, 1903/1913). Research was carried out on many other problems, and by the end of World War I the specialty of industrial psychology was under way. Since that era the field has developed a technology that exceeds the scope of this discussion both in volume of output and in the diversity of subject matter (Dunnette, 1976; Muchinsky, 1983). The research includes both goals and incentives, but in the literature in this field they are referred to not only in these terms, but also by means of innovative and sometimes occupationally oriented ones, such as inequity and job enrichment. An analysis of the referents suggests that incentives are probably more frequently studied than goals. There is, for example, a credible literature on the influence on productivity of the amount of reimbursement, the schedule on which it is delivered, as well as the basis on which it is determined. The influence of working conditions has also attracted attention, and in recent years these conditions have been extended to include the social climate in which the work is accomplished as well as the attitudes and beliefs that the employees bring to, and modify in, the occupational arena. Much of this research is similar to prior work in that it does not partition anticipation and consequence. Nonetheless there remains an accumulation of data that documents changes in behavior when goals and incentives are varied.

References

American Psychological Association. (1985). *Thesaurus of psychological index terms* (4th ed.). Washington, DC: Author.

Bryan, W. L. (1904). Theory and practice. *Psychological Review, 11*, 71–82. "It is believed that there is a philosophy, which gives a finally valid account of all reality and which lays down the law for action in every field . . . it is not philosophy, but empirical science which, as it develops, is to free us from all the rules of thumb . . . and which is to show us with certainty and on rational grounds exactly what to do in every field" (p. 71).

Dunnette, M. D. (Ed.). (1976). *Handbook of industrial and organizational psychology*. Chicago: Rand McNally. A multiauthored account of the state of the art.

Gussin, A. E. S. (1963). Jacques Loeb: The man and his tropism theory of animal conduct. *Journal of the History of Medicine, 18*, 321–335.

Hollingworth, H. L. (1913). *Advertising and selling: Principles of appeal and response*. New York: Appleton. This volume consists of a series of lectures "Published for the Advertising Men's League of New York City, Inc." (front cover). Hollingworth, a professional psychologist, gives advice on motivation.

Hurlock, E. B. (1925). An evaluation of certain incentives used in school work. *Journal of Educational Psychology, 16*, 145–159. A frequently cited pioneer study—the second of two by Hurlock—on the relative effectiveness of praise and punishment in modifying children's behavior.

Kenny, J. T., & Blass, E. M. (1977). Suckling as incentive to instrumental learning in preweanling rats. *Science, 196*, (No.4292) 898–899.

Logan, F. A. (1960). *Incentive: How the conditions of reinforcement affect the performance of rats*. New Haven,: Yale University Press. Logan is explicit about the differences between incentive and rewards.

McDougall, W. (1923). *Outline of psychology*. New York: Charles Scribner's Sons.

McGeoch, J. A. (1942). *The psychology of human learning: An introduction*. New York: Longmans, Green.

Muchinsky, P. M. (1983). *Psychology applied to work: An introduction to industrial and organizational psychology*. Homewood, IL: Dorsey Press. A reasonably comprehensive introduction to the technology psychologists bring to commercial endeavors.

Scott, W. D. (1913). *The theory and practice of advertising: A simple exposition of the principles of psychology in their relation to successful advertising*. Boston: Small, Maynard. (Original work published is 1903). Scott is a practical, problem-oriented pioneer, but he is also tied to a tradition of theory: "There should be a theoretical basis for every important practical undertaking" (p. 229). The last statement in the book caters to both the academic and the applied camps in the hope that the volume will add "its mite to the spread of science and to the advancement of industry" (p. 233).

Tolman, E. C. (1932). *Purposive behavior in animals and men*. New York: Century.

Warden, C. J., Jenkins, T. N., & Warner, L. H. (1935). *Comparative psychology: A comprehensive treatise: Vol. I Principles and methods*. New York: Ronald Press.

Sources of Additional Information

Baron, P., & Watters, R. G. (1982). Effects of goal-setting and of goal levels on weight loss induced by self-monitoring. *International Review of Applied Psychology, 31*, 369–382. This research illustrates relatively recent efforts in the use of self-regulation to control various personal difficulties. Goals are often used in these enterprises. Blue, J. H. & Ross, S. (1982). Spatial discrimination learning by young rats. *Bulletin of the Psychonomic Society, 19*, 35–36. Another illustration of the failure to distinguish between incentives and rewards: "Both suckling and homing are effective incentives" (p. 36). Condry, J. (1977). Enemies of exploration: Self-initiated versus other-initiated learning. *Journal of Personality and Social Psychology, 35*, 459–477. There is a historical section in this paper that begins with the introduction in the 1820s of tokens as rewards in grade school classes. Ryan, T. A. (1970). *Intentional behavior: An approach to human motivation*. New York: Ronald Press. Ryan uses intention to designate task, purpose, or goal. He laments the relative neglect of this topic and attributes it to "a mistaken belief that it is philosophically unsound to use explanatory concepts which refer to conscious experiences" (p. 21). He deals at considerable length with this matter. Viteles, M. S. (1932). *Industrial psychology*. New York: W. W. Norton. One of the early treatises. It includes reports about the effects of incentives.

H

HABITUATION. 1. Becoming accustomed to repetitious stimulation. 2. A synonym for accommodation, adaptation, and adjustment. **ADAPTATION.** 1. Changes in a species that enhance compatibility with the environment. 2. Flexibility of an individual that facilitates functioning. 3. A synonym for accommodation, adjustment, and habituation.

Equilibrium between living matter and the environment is seldom achieved spontaneously or maintained automatically, and in response to this elusiveness, both biologists and psychologists have searched for variables that do foster alignments between the organism and the surroundings. This work has brought into service a number of terms that overlap in meaning. Among the more familiar are acclimation, accommodation, adaptation (qualified as sensory, dark, light, negative, and positive), ADJUSTMENT, and habituation. A common theme among these words is a change in responding that promotes the ease and economy of functioning. This modification frequently, but not always, takes the form of a decrement or a consolidation in responding, such as becoming accustomed to the sound of the surf or arriving at the product of 3 × 7 by associating rather than by calculating. The similarities among these numerous terms are complemented by differences, and many of these are so specialized that a review of them resembles a glossary more than an explanation. In order to avoid beginning with a "tail wagging the dog" format, the authors have deferred enumerating the antonyms, synonyms, and other collaterals until after a general discussion of both concepts.

Habituation and adaptation were used interchangeably by the proponents of STRUCTURAL PSYCHOLOGY, an early theory that had several aims, including that of ascertaining how the mind distorts the physical world. The probability that abridged reactivity induces discrepancies between being aware of something and the objective nature of the thing provoked a considerable amount of research. This was cut off, however, during the first quarter of the current century when BEHAVIORISM succeeded in establishing the appropriate task of psychology as that of studying behavior.

The behaviorists' renunciation of the mind did not, however, abolish either of the concepts, but it did lead to the application of the terms habituation and adaptation in different contexts. Research that is labeled habituation has been carried out on a variety of animal species, as well as on humans, and in an array of responses (Harris, 1943). The credibility that made this scope possible was largely established by shifting the topic from "mental habituation" to "behavioral habituation." Some of the observations are made in natural habitats, including, for example, the seasoning of free-roaming animals to traffic on a nearby highway and subhuman primates coming to accept the gradual intrusion of a human into their territory (Goodall, 1986). There has also been an impressive amount of formal research, and this has produced techniques that minimize extraneous reactions. Many of these are now standard laboratory procedures, and they typically involve routines that accustom animals to new cages and to unfamiliar apparatus (Denny & Ratner, 1970).

Research on adaptation began during the last half of the nineteenth century at a time when the study of evolution was gaining ground, and it brought with it a stress on the adaptation of the species to the environment. Darwin, and his immediate successors, assumed that adaptive modifications were transmitted from generation to generation, and thus many of the benefits that came from evolution were believed to be due to changes that occurred in ancestors rather than in the current generation (Sohn, 1976).

The notion of evolutionary mutability caught the attention of psychologists, and exploring its relevance to psychological responses, they began to assess the changes that occur within the life history of individual organisms. Most of this early effort was undertaken by supporters of FUNCTIONAL PSYCHOLOGY, a theory well under way by the turn of the century. These theorists were concerned with the functions of the mind, that is, how it works, and especially its contributions to well-being. This point of view directed attention to additions to the behavioral repertoire as well as to deletions from it. These extensions altered the meaning of the concept, and the word began to be replaced, typically with labels that specify the behavior in which the adaptive changes were originally studied. To illustrate—the acquisition of skills and knowledge is obviously adaptive, but research in this area is, almost without exception, referred to as learning. The task of selecting individuals who are best suited, or adaptable, to particular occupations is known as vocational guidance, not as adaptation.

These changes in terms did not eliminate the concept, and in some contexts there is an uninterrupted history of the use of the word. One of these occurs in references to the diminution in both reflexes and sensory reactions that occurs under repetitious stimulation. In some of these the phrase negative adaptation is used as a way of underlining the decrements, but in others the adjective is not stated, but merely implied.

There is also an unbroken tradition of using adaptation to designate the variations in vision that came from variations in the level of illumination. Under these changes there is an initial reduction in efficiency, but the outcome is beneficial inasmuch as sensory effectiveness is soon restored, and in view of this the label "positive adaptation" is applied. There are two varieties: light and dark adaptation (Riggs, 1971). When illumination changes from strong to weak there is initial decrease in sensitivity, but this reverses as the exposure to the reduced illumination is continued. This process of dark adaptation is a familiar experience. Theater patrons, for example, are aware that after a period of time in the reduced light of the theater, the details within the auditorium will become discernible. Naval and military personnel assigned to a night watch and pilots on night flights are also aware of this initial reduction in vision, realize that it seriously interferes with visual sensitivity, and use techniques that minimize or compensate for it.

Light adaptation, the second variety of positive adaptation, occurs when the illumination changes from low to high. At first there is a decrement in visual acuity, but recovery comes with sustained exposure to the increased light. This particular sequence is familiar to those who have moved from a dimly lighted room into bright daylight, as when a patron leaves a theater and experiences the daylight glare of the street.

There are other instances of sensory adaptation that are also referred to by means of highly specialized terms. Both adaptation and accomodation are used to label changes in the visual apparatus but adaptation refers to pupillary and retinal reactions, whereas accommodation refers to changes in the muscles that modify the shape of the lens. In a strict sense, these are physiological phenomena, but they increase visual clarity and thereby facilitate psychological behavior (Alpern, 1971).

During the very recent past the word adaptation seems to be more popular than it was during the previous thirty to forty years. Further, as in the period when evolution was introduced, it is used in connection with responses that are much more complicated than reflexes and sensory reactions. The modern concern about caring for the environment has also reactivated an interest in the benefits, both for animals and humans, that can be extracted from the environment. In the case of animals this has provoked both field observations and formal experiments on behavior that fosters survival, such as food seeking, territoriality, aggression, and defense (Hinde, 1970; Maple, 1979).

The concern about the quality of human life has also prompted researchers to feature adaptation. Glass and Singer, in *Urban Stress: Experiments on Noise and Social Stressors* (1972), for example, assign the highest priority to becoming accustomed to distractors: "Hurried meals, hectic traffic, brusque and even hostile interpersonal exchanges, also lose their apparent power to disrupt. It is this fascinating loss of reactivity to stimuli generally regarded as aversive that makes the general issue of adaptation not only pertinent to our studies but a *sine qua non* for understanding urban stressors'' (p. 9).

Another area in which the concept of adaptation is being revived is in relation to interpersonal problems. White (1985), for example, entitled a chapter "Strategies of Adaptation," and in this he characterizes the concept as a "striving toward acceptable compromise" (p. 126). This is in line with curtailed reactivity in that White develops the argument that in some situations retreat and relinquishing may be the best strategy for fostering equilibrium.

Psychologists use words freely, and as indicated at the beginning of the discussion, they apply a series of terms in addition to habituation and adaptation to designate smooth, friction-free responses. Accommodation, adaptation, and adjustment, for example, are all found in discussions of the management of disagreements. Adjustment is the more common term, but accommodation is applied to conflicts in industry (Stagner, 1956), in marriage (Stagner, 1974), as well as in other situations in which the individual benefits more by accepting than by countering (Eitzen, 1978).

The psychologists' propensity to be more casual than careful in word choice makes it necessary to include acclimation in this group of terms. Initially the word designated the specialized adaptation that is implied by its root, that is, becoming accustomed to the climate, but English and English (1958) point out that this has been extended so much that the word is now unrestricted.

There are numerous additional shades of meaning that refer to the ease and economy of reacting, but enough illustrations have been given to apprise the reader that the concepts of habituation and adaptation cover a diversity of situations. They also provide authors and lecturers with a wide selection of terms!

References

Alpern, M. (1971). Effector mechanisms in vision. In J. W. Kling & L. A. Riggs (Eds.), *Woodworth and Schlosberg's experimental psychology* (3rd ed., pp. 369–394). This chapter offers a technical account of eye movements and a discussion of sensory adaptation.

Denny, M. R., & Ratner, S. C. (1970). *Comparative psychology: Research in animal behavior* (rev. ed.). Homewood, IL: Dorsey. A spectrum of topics is covered, including reports of animal habituation to research procedures.

Eitzen, D. S. (1978). *In conflict and order: Understanding society*. Boston: Allyn & Bacon.

English, H. B., & English, A. C. (1958). *A comprehensive dictionary of psychological and psychoanalytical terms: A guide to usage*. New York: Longmans, Green.

Glass, D. C., & Singer, J. E. (1972). *Urban stress: Experiments on noise and social stressors*. New York: Academic Press. The authors comment: "We have been struck by the discrepancy between repeatedly stated condemnations of the quality of life in the city and the fact that many people not only survive in these circumstances, but actually thrive and enjoy them. We speculated on the reasons for this disparate state of affairs" (p. 1).

Goodall, J. (1986). *The chimpanzees of Gombe: Patterns of behavior*. Cambridge, MA: Harvard University Press. The habituation of chimpanzees to humans requires a

long time. In fact, Goodall reports that months passed before the apes would carry
on normal activities when she was thirty to fifty feet away. Eventually some would
eat from her hand.

Harris, J. D. (1943). Habituatory response decrement in the intact organism. *Psychological Bulletin, 40*, 385–422. The author introduces this review with a discussion of the profusion of terms, and the reasons for his preference for habituation.

Hinde, R. A. (1970). *Animal behaviour: A synthesis of ethology and comparative psychology* (2nd ed.). New York: McGraw-Hill. The text includes a recital of many of the important events in the history of the study of animals.

Maple, T. L. (1979). Primate psychology in historical perspective. In J. Erwin, T. L. Maple, & G. Mitchell (Eds.), *Captivity and behavior: Primates in breeding colonies, laboratories, and zoos* (pp. 29–58). New York: Van Nostrand Reinhold.

Riggs, L. A. (1971). Vision. In J. W. Kling & L. A. Riggs (Eds.), *Woodworth and Schlosberg's experimental psychology* (3rd ed., pp. 273–314). New York: Holt, Rinehart & Winston. This comprehensive, scholarly treatment includes details of the physics of light and the anatomy and physiology of the eye.

Sohn, D. (1976). Two concepts of adaptation: Darwin's and psychology's. *Journal of the History of the Behavioral Sciences, 12*, 367–375.

Stagner, R. (1956). *Psychology of industrial conflict*. New York: John Wiley.

Stagner, R. (1974). *Psychology of personality* (4th ed.). New York: McGraw-Hill. This was first published in 1937 and is a widely used undergraduate text.

White, R. W. (1985). Strategies of adaptation: An attempt at systematic description. In A. Monat & R. S. Lazarus (Eds.), *Stress and coping: an anthology* (2nd ed., pp. 121–143). New York: Columbia University Press.

Sources of Additional Information

Bower, G. H., & Hilgard, E. R. (1981). *Theories of learning* (5th ed.). Englewood Cliffs, NJ: Prentice-Hall. This comprehensive treatise includes a discussion of the distinctions between habituation and learning. The authors suggest that in the case of simple responses, only sensory changes may be involved, but in the case of complicated responses, learning occurs. Flavell, J. H. (1963). *The developmental psychology of Jean Piaget*. New York: Van Nostrand Reinhold. Piaget's theory and methods are complicated, and he writes in a less than clear style. Flavell has done a masterful job of explaining Piaget's theory about how a child organizes the world in which he or she lives. This is a theory of cognitive development that preceded the popularity of that topic. It involves numerous technical terms, including accommodation and adaptation. Piaget gives each of them a specialized meaning that is quite removed from the concepts described in this discussion. Lindley, E. H. (1897). A study of puzzles with special reference to the psychology of mental adaptation. *American Journal of Psychology, 8*, 431–493. A treatise on the importance of play. An interesting example of the intrigue of the era with adaptive benefits. Martin, I. (1964). Adaptation. *Psychological Bulletin, 61*, 35–44. Martin comments on the spectrum of events that adaptation embraces: "Used loosely, adaptation refers to an enormous array of phenomena, ranging across a time span of millions of evolutionary years to a few minutes in the case of 'adaptation' of sensory processes" (p. 35).

HELPLESSNESS. See LEARNED HELPLESSNESS.

HEREDITY. 1. An hypothesized force believed to be responsible for the similarities and dissimilarities between generations in both biological and psychological characteristics. 2. Biochemical processes that mediate biological characteristics from parent to offspring. 3. In the jargon, a synonym for nature. **ENVIRONMENT.**1. An hypothesized force believed to be responsible for the similarities and dissimilarities between generations in both biological and psychological characteristics. 2. The conditions in which organisms live. 3. In the jargon, a synonym for nurture.

Both heredity and environment have been conceptualized in two quite different ways. The first formulation emerged during an era when it was impossible to observe hereditary processes directly, and scientists had to be content with inferences based on comparisons of the traits of parents and offspring. The early geneticists concluded that some kind of an entity controlled inheritance. This came to be called a gene, but empirical information was not available until near the middle of the current century when molecular biology and molecular genetics were able to identify genes and began to master techniques of manipulating them experimentally.

Because this is such a recent accomplishment a large portion of the history of heredity is a chronicle of speculation and during this period in which conjecture outweighed facts, heredity was erroneously endowed with certain properties. One depicted the genes as immune to the surroundings, that is, the bearer was said to pass them on without any significant change in them. A second elaboration extended the domain of inheritance from biological structures so as to include psychological phenomena. A third embellishment came in an interpretation of heredity as a power or agent rather than as a sequence of events.

The environment *also* came to be considered as a force rather than as a source of nourishment and stimulation, and these two powers were then assumed to be competitive. Arguments as to which of them was the more influential were common. Many of these disputes were heated, with much of the feeling stemming from the difference in the suggestions about intervention that were intrinsic to each point of view. Because the environment could be manipulated there was the possibility of rectifying defects that are caused by nurture, but inasmuch as heredity was seen as immutable, there was no possibility of correcting the faults of nature. This contrast of optimism and pessimism gained added emotional strength from the implications as to where—or perhaps more accurately on whom—to place the blame for any deficits. Different conclusions were advocated, but heredity appears to have been the stronger force, in that biological structures and psychological reactions were generally assumed to have a genetically determined upper limit that could not be exceeded. There was pervasive opinion that a ''poor'' environment debilitates an organism, and that a ''good'' environment fosters functioning near the limit of the potential. No amount of nurturing would, however, allow functioning above that point. One result of these arguments is a fusion of evidence with value judgments so that in much of the literature—even scientific publications—it is difficult to distinguish fact from contention.

Decisions about the relative strength of heredity and environment preceded scientific evidence. Shakespeare has been identified as the first to contrast the words nature and nurture, and he included them in *The Tempest*, asserting that nature is more influential than nurture (Conley, 1984). There is, however, a second opinion that Mulcaster, writing nearly thirty years before *The Tempest*, is the originator (Teigen, 1984). Francis Galton, a British gentleman scientist, is generally credited with introducing the terms into the scientific literature (Fancher, 1979). In *Hereditary Genius* (1869/1978) Galton dealt at length with the inheritance of INTELLIGENCE, and because this attracted so much agreement, and disagreement, intelligence is used in *this* discussion to exemplify arguments about the source of numerous psychological responses.

Terman's remarks about the families of the superior children whom he studied in *Genetic Studies of Genius* exemplify a dominance of credence over facts in the inheritance of intelligence: "The data . . . are very incomplete, but fragmentary as they are, they give considerable support to Galton's theory as to the hereditary nature of genius. Unfortunately, it has thus far not been possible to carry out any studies of a kind which would give exact data on family resemblances in the group or reveal the laws by which superior mental ability is transmitted" (Terman, 1925/1926, p. 111).

A year after Terman declared his faith, John B. Watson, the founder of BEHAVIORISM, took the opposite position in regard to the inheritance of psychological traits, also with more conviction than corroboration:

> There is no such thing as an inheritance of *capacity, talent, temperament, mental constitution and characteristics*. These things again depend on training that goes on mainly in the cradle. The behaviorist would *not* say: 'He inherits his father's capacity or talent for being a fine swordsman.' He would say: 'This child certainly has his father's slender build of body, the same type of eyes. His build is wonderfully like his father's.' And he would go on to say: '—and his father is very fond of him. He put a tiny sword into his hand when he was a year of age, and in all their walks he talks sword play, attack and defense, the code of duelling and the like' (1926, p. 2).

These quotations also demonstrate the common practice of invoking familial patterns as evidence to support either nature or nurture. There is little dispute about the biological and psychological similarities within a family, and in order to strengthen arguments, researchers began to look at the amount of resemblance in kinship patterns. These investigators typically assume that a genetic basis is demonstrated when the level of agreement for both psychological and biological attributes is higher in the case of children and natural parents than in the case of children and foster parents. They also postulate that the similarity is highest among identical twins and that it decreases successively from fraternal twins and siblings to unrelated individuals. The fact that the similarity in living conditions is apt to vary the most among the unrelated and the least among identical twins is neglected.

The measurements of both similarity and dissimilarity are typically expressed in coefficients of correlation. These are numerical indices of merely the degree to which variables co-relate, that is, they quantify the extent to which changes in one variable equal those in a second. These coefficients are not statements of cause. A simple illustration brings this to the forefront: height and weight are correlated, but weight does not cause height and height does not cause weight. Most researchers are aware that coefficients do not indicate why there is a correlation, but they often overlook this, in part because more satisfactory procedures are not available (Kenny, 1979).

A pioneer study of the psychological similarities of twins, *Inquiries into the Human Faculty and Its Development*, was published by Galton in 1883, and similar investigations were made in America, particularly during the middle to late 1930s. One of the earlier and more impressive of these is *Twins: A Study of Heredity and Environment*, by Newman, Freeman, and Holzinger (1937). These investigators took care to confirm the identical or fraternal status of each pair of subjects. Their design is also more elaborate than many experiments in that the data about identical twins reared together were supplemented by information about identical twins reared separately. The authors measured numerous variables, including, but not limited to, the number of ridges in finger prints, height, weight, IQ, academic levels of proficiency, and temperament. They reported that the coefficients of correlation varied among these different measurements, and concluded that unraveling the effects of heredity and environment is very complicated.

Many researchers who study twins conclude that inheritance is the critical antecedent, but in 1979 assurance about this matter was weakened by the disclosure that the statistics that Cyril Burt, a British psychologist, had reported were fraudulent (Hearnshaw, 1979). This was demoralizing because Burt's figures, reputed to be based on the largest number of twins, disclosed more resemblance than other reports. In fact, the coefficients were so consistent with a hereditarian interpretation that researchers became suspicious and questioned the "facts." The unmasking has unsettled, but not defeated the conviction that nature is the cause of intelligence (Eysenck & Kamin, 1981; Kamin, 1974).

The comparisons of parent-child data seem to conclude more often than twin studies that nurture is the stronger of the two forces (Stoddard, 1945). After an initial spurt of interest in the 1930s and 1940s this design was rarely used, but it has been recently reactivated, and in 1985 Plomin and DeFries published the results of observations both of children (at ages twelve and twenty-four months) and of their parents, both biological and adoptive. The study is an ongoing one, and at this early stage the authors appear to be more cautious than many of their predecessors. They join Newman, Freeman, and Holzinger in concluding that they are dealing with a very complicated matter: "This distillation of . . . results yields one last general principle: Much remains to be learned about the origins of individual differences in infancy" (Plomin & DeFries, 1985, p. 343).

The attention that has been devoted to the relative potency of heredity or environment is concomitant with an experimental neglect of other factors that influence intelligence. There is, for example, a scarcity of knowledge about the effects of age and duration of the separation of family members (Kamin, 1974). This interval is only rarely controlled, even though the variations in it may be extreme. A splitting up that begins, for example, at six months and continues to adulthood is markedly discrepant from one of twelve months' duration that begins at the age of fifteen. A second neglected area is the psychological nature of the environment (Bijou, 1971). Researchers are prone to quantify the milieu by means of variables that are selected more on the basis of feasibility than of known relevance, for example, the number of rooms in the home, or the number of books. "Living conditions" embrace a mass of stimulation, and psychologically, the phenomenological aspects may be the most effective, but these have not been brought under experimental control.

One of the methods of investigating the relative contributions of heredity and environment is the selective breeding of animals. During the 1950s and 1960s the popularity of this method increased, and this kind of research became identified as behavior genetics (Hirsch, 1971). Animals that react in similar and in dissimilar ways are bred and the responses of the offspring of various combinations are investigated. Behavior geneticists would like to reduce the number of inferences that have to be made, and to do this they try to incorporate the genes, principal variables, into the design. This leads to the study of simple reactions, often ones in which biological components outweigh psychological ones, as, for example, the speed with which animals travel over runways and the mating speed of fruit flies. This simplification dilutes the information: "An honest summary must admit that there are few valid generalizations or even hopeful speculations to be made about the genetic basis of behavioural units" (Manning, 1976, p. 335).

Fundamental changes in the concept of heredity have been accumulating since the late 1940s, a result of impressive and dramatic gains in molecular biology and molecular genetics. The details of both the theories and these laboratory manipulations are understood only by professionals in specialized disciplines, but the broad outlines of their accomplishments are being made known to the culture at large (Hawkins, 1985; Hoagland, 1981). The properties of genes have been identified as chemical, and observations are being made of the effects of the surrounding tissue on the genes as well as the effects of the genes on the tissue. In other words, the concept of the gene as an inert agent has been replaced by a concept of influenced and influencing biochemical processes.

Much of this information has been gleaned from the study of simple organisms, and the phenomena occurring in more complicated forms of life have yet to be traced. The search, however, is in full swing, but the ideas of mutable genes and mutuality between genetic and environmental events oppose tradition, and attention is currently paid to both the views of molecular genetics and the conventional dichotomy. The latter is, of course, the more pervasive but the former is gaining ground, not as a product of objective evaluation of scientific information but as a product of fears- sometimes transformed into opinions or predictions—that environmental contamination will induce genetic damage.

Psychologists, reacting to these refinements in the biochemistry of genetics, are updating formulations about the environment, frequently by looking much more carefully than they did in the past at particulars. "Environment" as a whole is being replaced by analyses of its components. An article by Lipsitt (1984) represents this shift. This paper, "Mental Retardation: A View from the Infant Learning Laboratory," is primarily concerned with individuals who are diagnosed as mentally retarded. These people are typically only mildly retarded, have no known biological deficits, and, until the recent past, have been assumed to have a genetic defect. Research has demonstrated repeatedly that the IQs of children who grow up in unfavorable circumstances decrease as their age increases. Lipsitt reviews various individual experiments, particularly those dealing with the learning of infants and young children, and uncovers a number of instances in which poverty fails to provide the support that is requisite for healthy development. The shortcomings in which he notes retarded development include such misfortunes as inadequate nourishment before birth, difficulties during birth, unhygienic living conditions, and a lack of sufficient stimulation to learn. He suggests that the variety of mental retardation he is discussing may come from the compounding of these adversities: "The human product of this cumulative and spiraling conspiracy of events is a child who does not learn well, has difficulty reading, and becomes disinterested in the schooling process . . . one of the major milestones in the life itineraries of children who travel this developmental route is the point at which the child becomes regarded as retarded, and then is so labeled" (p. 255).

Other researchers may agree or disagree with the entries in this sequence, but more pertinent to this discussion is the breaking away from the idea of a "global" environment in favor of probing its effective vectors. This practice, as in the concept of heredity, allows replacing inferences with actual details. As a result the previously assumed competition between hypothetical forces is being dislodged by descriptions of reciprocity. Investigations of when to intervene and in what way are becoming the order of the day.

References

Bijou, S. W. (1971). Environment and intelligence: A behavioral analysis. In R. Cancro (Ed.), *Intelligence: Genetic and environmental influences* (pp. 221–239). New York: Grune & Stratton.

Conley, J. J. (1984). Not Galton, but Shakespeare: A note on the origin of the term "nature and nurture." *Journal of the History of the Behavioral Sciences, 20,* 184–185. Conley points out that Shakespeare made frequent references to the control of nurture by nature. He cites the juxtaposition of the two terms in *The Tempest*, Act 4, Scene 1: "A devil, a born devil, on whose nature/Nurture can never stick" (p. 184).

Eysenck, H. J., & Kamin, L. (1981). *Intelligence: The battle for the mind*. London: Macmillan. Eysenck mobilizes evidence that intelligence is inherited, and Kamin counters with evidence that it is nurtured. The evidence is subjected to much more penetrating criticism than is the concept of intelligence.

Fancher, R. E. (1979). A note on the origin of the term "nature and nurture." *Journal of the History of the Behavioral Sciences, 15*, 321–322.

Galton, F. (1883). *Inquiries into human faculty and its development*. New York: Macmillan. Galton covers a diversity of topics in this volume, including a review of information he obtained on numerous traits in thirty-five pairs of twins who were reported to be "extremely similar," and twenty pairs who were reported to be "extremely dissimilar." Galton's interpretation of both samples is strictly hereditarian: "The impression that all this evidence leaves on the mind is one of some wonder whether nurture can do anything at all, beyond giving instruction and professional training" (p. 240).

Galton, F. (1978). *Hereditary genius: An inquiry into its laws and consequences*. New York: St. Martin's Press. (Original work published 1869)

Hawkins, J. D. (1985). *Gene structure and expression*. Cambridge, UK: Cambridge University Press.

Hearnshaw, L. S. (1979). *Cyril Burt: Psychologist*. Ithaca, NY: Cornell University Press. A forthright recital of the flaws in Burt's data. Burt was, throughout most of his career, a highly respected and eminent figure in British psychology.

Hirsch, J. (1971). Behavior-genetic analysis and its biosocial consequences. In R. Cancro (Ed.), *Intelligence: Genetic and environmental influences* (pp. 88–106). New York: Grune & Stratton.

Hoagland, M. (1981). *Discovery: The search for DNA's secrets*. Boston: Houghton Mifflin.

Kamin, L. J. (1974). *The science and politics of I.Q.* Potomac, MD: Lawrence Erlbaum.

Kenny, D. A. (1979). *Correlation and causality*. New York: John Wiley. A commendable appraisal of the topic, but it demands sophistication about statistics.

Lipsitt, L. P. (1984). Mental retardation: A view from the infant learning laboratory. In J. A. Mulick & B. L. Mallory (Eds.), *Transitions in mental retardation: Vol. 1. Advocacy, technology, and science* (pp. 249–260). Norwood, NJ: Albex.

Manning, A. (1976). The place of genetics in the study of behaviour. In P. P. G. Bateson & R. A. Hinde (Eds.), *Growing points in ethology* (pp. 327–343). Cambridge, UK: Cambridge University Press.

Newman, H. H., Freeman, F. N., & Holzinger, K. J. (1937). *Twins: A study of heredity and environment*. Chicago: University of Chicago Press. A landmark study. The authors are a psychologist, a statistician, and "a specialist in the biology of twins" (p. v).

Plomin, R., & DeFries, J. C. (1985). *Origins of individual differences in infancy: The Colorado adoption project*. Orlando, FL: Academic Press.

Stoddard, G. D. (1945). *The meaning of intelligence*. New York: Macmillan. Stoddard is a staunch advocate of the importance of the environment.

Teigen, K. H. (1984). A note on the origin of the term "nature and nurture": Not Shakespeare and Galton, but Mulcaster. *Journal of the History of the Behavioral Sciences, 20*, 363–364.

Terman, L. M. (Ed.). (1926). *Genetic studies of genius: Vol. 1 Mental and physical traits of a thousand gifted children* (2nd ed.). Stanford CA: Stanford University Press. (Original work published 1925)
Watson, J. B. (1926). What the nursery has to say about instincts. In C. Murchison (Ed.), *Psychologies of 1925* (pp. 1–36). Worcester, MA: Clark University Press.

Sources of Additional Information

Beloff, H. (Ed.). (1980). A balance sheet on Burt. *Bulletin of the British Psychological Society, 33* (Supp., November), 1–38. This publication consists of a lecture and symposium held at the 1980 Annual Conference of the British Psychological Society. The participants include Oliver Gillie, the British journalist who publicized the fraud, L. S. Hearnshaw, Burt's biographer, as well as six of Burt's contemporaries. Dugdale, R. L. (1910). *The Jukes: A study in crime, pauperism, disease, and heredity* (4th ed.). New York: G.P. Putnam's Sons (Original work published 1877). One of the very early studies of intellectual patterns in families. McClearn, G. E. (1962). The inheritance of behavior. In L. Postman (Ed.), *Psychology in the making: Histories of selected research problems* (pp. 144–252). New York: Alfred Knopf. This article includes an account of the research that Tryon started that involved breeding strains of rats markedly different in their ability to learn a maze, one described as "bright" and the other as "dull." McClearn reviews the experiments that the original study provoked, ones in which the learning of each of these two strains was examined in a variety of situations. The results disclosed that the "bright" are not consistently superior and that they rely on spatial cues, whereas the "dulls" rely on visual cues. Smith, N. W. (1976). Twin studies and heritability. *Human Development, 19*, 65–68. The author, the father of identical twins, is a psychologist with a theoretical preference for the analysis and interpretation of behavioral events rather than "factitious constructs" (p. 67). He reviews a few highlights of children's development and points to biological similarities and psychological dissimilarities. Whipple, G. M. (Ed.). (1940). *The thirty-ninth yearbook of the National Society for the Study of Education: Intelligence its nature and nurture: Pt. 1. Comparative and critical exposition.* Bloomington, IL: Public School Publishing. Included in this multi-authored volume are George Stoddard and Beth Wellman, of the Iowa Child Welfare Research Station, and Lewis M. Terman, of Stanford University. These psychologists were involved in acrimonious controversy in which Stanford University personnel defended the inheritance of intelligence, and the University of Iowa personnel defended an environmental interpretation.

HOSTILITY. 1. Animosity that leads to retaliation by indirect means. 2. A synonym for aggression.

Although hostility is a familiar concept, there is no consensus as to its definition, and a review of its history is more a recital of recommendations and opinions than of conclusive, authoritative decisions. Much of the confusion arises from the similarity among a group of responses that consists of AGGRESSION, ANGER, FRUSTRATION, and prejudice. Anger stands apart in that it is briefer and more volatile than the other reactions. A sense of negativism pervades both hostility and prejudice, but some theorists distinguish these two reactions by identifying prejudice as emerging from vicarious experiences, and hostility from actual ones (Allport, 1954/1979). Frustration and hostility are also differentiated by some authors by reference to the kind of behavior that is blocked. In this scheme frustration is applied when there is an interference with goal-directed behavior, and hostility when there are threats to self-esteem.

Even though hostility and aggression are frequently used synonymously, in precise terminology they have quite different referents. Direct, open attacks are categorized as aggressive, and figurative or masked ones as hostile. The latter involves responses that may be either lively and exertive or passive. These tactics include, but are certainly not limited to, treating others in a condescending manner, withdrawing from or refusing to participate in enterprises, withholding information, teasing, and joking at the expense of others. The distinction between an obvious and a disguised assault is important in that hostility may be obscured but aggression is in full view.

The amount of attention that researchers devote to the ideation that is concomitant with hostility and aggression varies. In experiments on the former what is imagined is often featured, but in investigations of aggression there is a tendency to minimize the role of fantasy. There are no clear differences between the daydreaming that is characteristic of the two reactions. In both cases measurement is elusive and the content is diverse such as mulling over an offense, nurturing a grudge, imagining a ''putdown'' of the offender, and devising various means of defeating an opponent—some violent and abusive and some indirect and even ingenious. Because fantasies are private they are not restrained by the controls that society imposes on overt attacks. Yet, fantasy has the same power as action to generate guilt feelings. This combination of autonomy and negative self-appraisal can compound the self-condemnation to a level that is more unfavorable than public disapproval.

Hostility intrigues researchers, but its complexities make it awkward to manage in the laboratory. As a result, the concept remains fluid. Much of the information that has been acquired about it has come not from the formal laboratory, but from projective tests of PERSONALITY and from interviews, especially those designed to expose the subtleties of mentation. In fact, aggression, in an era in which it was a synonym for hostility, was first studied in detail in psychoanalysis, a therapeutic technique that is designed to probe the inner life in great depth (Freud, 1920/1938).

The concept came to more general attention in psychology when Dollard included some of Freud's formulations as interpretive guides in a study of *Caste and Class in a Southern Town* (1937). This is a report of the interpersonal relations between ''Negroes'' and whites in the late 1930s in a southern community, a culture that prohibited ''Negroes'' from behaving aggressively against whites and thereby fostered their hostility toward the whites. Although Dollard uses aggression and hostility interchangeably, his descriptions allow one to single out behavior that would later be labeled hostile, for example, working slowly, leaving employment without notice, and spreading gossip. Dollard reminds readers that while the suppression of aggression reduces the incidence of violent acts, it makes retaliation furtive and nonpredictable, and this pseudocompliance is hostile to the extent that it keeps the oppressor on the alert.

Just two years after this study, Dollard, Doob, Miller, Mowrer, and Sears published *Frustration and Aggression* (1939). In this they presented formal hypotheses about the relationship between the two reactions. These hypotheses appeared, at first glance, to be admirably suitable for experimentation, but attempts to develop actual research designs indicated several obscurities, and unraveling them produced refinements in the concept of hostility.

One of the amendments came in a paper written in 1941 by Levy, "The Hostile Act." In this Levy offered experimental evidence that frustration does not consistently elicit aggression, but that what is now identified as hostility also occurs. This conclusion grew out of a study of sibling rivalry, one in which children, aged two to thirteen years, were confronted with a play situation in which a doll representing an older sibling observed a doll representing a mother nursing a newborn, a sight that is believed to frustrate the older sibling. Each child was requested to demonstrate, by moving and playing with the dolls, what the older child does. This procedure bypasses the barrier of the immature speech of young children and allows the child's play to speak for the child.

Levy described several responses that he interpreted as substitutes for attacks on the baby, that is, displays of hostility rather than of aggression. He believed that these resulted from a self-imposed inhibition of impulses to strike out physically. The methods that the children used to avoid combativeness illustrate how readily and variously hostility is diffused. They included pretending not to understand what is required, trying to leave the room, and stopping short of hitting the infant and merely touching it.

Other investigators took on the task of eliciting both hostility and aggression in the laboratory. These efforts produced informative data, but they made little or no progress in straightening out the vocabulary. The disorder is clearly exemplified in the following quotation, which acknowledges and then disregards differences between the two concepts: "The literature reflects increasingly that a differentiation is being made between 'aggression' and 'hostility.' . . . In the course of this study, for convenience of reporting, the words 'hostility' and 'aggression' will be used interchangeably, even though 'aggression' is considered to be a broader term" (Korner, 1949, p. 3).

A surge of interest in terminology began in the late 1950s and early 1960s, and a number of discussions about the meaning of both hostility and aggression appeared in print (Berkowitz, 1958; Feshbach, 1964; Kaufmann, 1965; Worchel, 1960). These papers provoked recognition that intention is as important as the nature of the attack in distinguishing between aggression and hostility. Including maliciousness removes the hostility from the downgrading of others that is sometimes unavoidable, as in the case of being able to promote only one employee or having to vote for one candidate.

At least one definition of hostility would make it dependent on language: "*An implicit verbal response involving negative feelings (ill will) and negative eval-*

uations of people and events" (Buss, 1961, p. 12). A formulation of this nature denies hostility to children before the development of language, and thus isolates it from the familiar infantile reactions that occur when pleasure is denied or distress develops.

These suggestions have been introduced in order to call attention to a few of the complexities that are involved in defining hostility, and there is currently no basis on which to build a strong support for them because none of the numerous recommendations has gained widespread acceptance. The persisting disorder is illustrated in a modern definition that states that "*Aggression* is defined as 'overt destruction, fighting . . . [and] covert hostile attitudes' " (Price, 1982, p. 97).

These inconsistencies remind the reader that in considering the concept of hostility, one is confronted with two tasks: first, to try to discover the referent that each author has in mind, and second, to exercise caution in comparing and contrasting the conclusions arrived at by different psychologists. They may be using the same words, but they may not be relaying information about the same concepts!

References

Allport, G. W. (1979). *The nature of prejudice* (25th anniv. ed.). Reading, MA: Addison-Wesley. (Original work published 1954)

Berkowitz, L. (1958). The expression and reduction of hostility. *Psychological Bulletin, 55*, 257–283. Berkowitz discusses the incompleteness of and the confusion about the concept of hostility.

Buss, A. H. (1961). *The psychology of aggression.* New York: John Wiley.

Dollard, J. (1937). *Caste and class in a southern town.* New Haven, CT: Yale University Press. The author is a sociologist who is also familiar with psychoanalysis. This volume is not only a pioneering effort, but also a masterful adaptation of the insights of psychoanalysis to a hostility-fermenting culture.

Dollard, J., Doob, L. W., Miller, N. E., Mowrer, O. H., & Sears, R. R. (1939). *Frustration and aggression.* New Haven, CT: Yale University Press.

Feshbach, S. (1964). The function of aggression and the regulation of aggressive drive. *Psychological Review, 71*, 257–272. An astute, comprehensive review of the variables that arouse aggression as well as a thoughtful discussion of the meaning of various related words.

Freud, S. (1938). *A general introduction to psychoanalysis* (J. Riviere, Trans.). New York: Garden City Publishing. (Original work published 1920). Freud modified his theory throughout his lifetime. This account is accurate at the date of writing, but it does not reflect the later revisions.

Kaufmann, H. (1965). Definitions and methodology in the study of aggression. *Psychological Bulletin, 64*, 351–364.

Korner, A. F. (1949). *Some aspects of hostility in young children.* New York: Grune & Stratton. This is a report of an experiment on how preschool children deal with hostility in play and in fantasy. In order to study the latter the author asked the children to complete incomplete stories. Because the child is free to finish the story in any way he or she wishes, each conclusion reveals the child's own affect.

Levy, D. M. (1941). The hostile act. *Psychological Review, 48*, 356–361.

Price, V. A. (1982). *Type A behavior pattern: A model for research and practice*. New
    York: Academic Press. The author offers evidence that both hostility and aggres-
    sion may be linked to coronary heart disease.
Worchel, P. (1960). Hostility: Theory and experimental investigation. In D. Willner
    (Ed.), *Decisions, values and groups* (pp. 254–266). London: Pergamon Press.
    Worchel takes note of various differences between hostility and aggression: "Hos-
    tile behavior has many characteristics which seem quite different from those of
    aggressive behavior. There are changes in the perception of the field, widespread
    physiological involvements, interference with complex learning, and an affectual
    component of hate" (p. 257).

Sources of Additional Information

Bok, S. (1978). *Lying: Moral choice in public and private life*. New York: Pantheon
Books. Lying is hostile in some contexts, protective in others. The author discusses many
nuances of the behavior and also refers to the writings of philosophers on the topic.
Hokanson, J. E., & Gordon, J. E. (1958). The expression and inhibition of hostility in
imaginative and overt behavior. *Journal of Abnormal and Social Psychology, 57*, 327–
333. This is a comparison between the hostility expressed in a projective task (a measure
of fantasy) and statements about the intensity of punishment (aggression) that a delinquent
should receive. Newcomb, T. M. (1947). Autistic hostility and social reality. *Human
Relations, 1*(1), 69–86. This is a plea to reduce hostility, to keep it from becoming a
"persistent attitude." Newcomb suggests that talking about hostility, discussing it, and
evaluating it with others can help to bring it under control. He relates hostility to prejudice
and to discrimination. Pepitone, A. (1964). *Attraction and hostility: An experimental
analysis of interpersonal and self-evaluation*. New York: Atherton Press. Pepitone extends
the traditional focus of hostility on the individual to groups. He is also concerned with
both the similarities and the differences between attraction and hostility. There is an
informative review of the literature and a presentation of research data.

HUMANISTIC PSYCHOLOGY.   See HUMAN POTENTIAL MOVEMENT.

HUMAN POTENTIAL MOVEMENT   this roster embraces four concepts in
psychology that were formed in the decade 1960–1970. They vary one from
another, but they also have a common goal, the maximizing of human functioning, and many of their views are shared. They all stress the study of the
person as a whole, put more weight on understanding than on explaining, attend
more to the expression than to the constraint of the self, are eager to adapt
innovative methods, and are casual about exerting experimental controls. The
advocates write with an attitude of revolt and with an unrestrained individuality
that yields so much more diversity than consensus that at times the concepts
overlap and the differences among them are blurred. Each view is offered as
either an alternative or an amendment to mainstream psychology and is said to
be justified because of shortcomings in traditional viewpoints. For example,
behaviorism is seen as oversimplified, artificial, and dehumanizing in that it
treats the person as an object, and psychoanalysis is criticized because it features
pathology and emphasizes analysis rather than wholeness.

Each of these innovations has at least one journal devoted to the dissemination of its point of view, and the four concepts are presented here in the chronological order in which these publications appeared. This calendar arrangement obscures the priority of some of the antecedent events, but it registers their introduction into the literature of psychology.

Existential Psychology. 1. An approach to psychology that seeks to understand how individuals experience various facets of existence, with the emphasis clearly on the person's own interpretations.

Humanistic Psychology. 1. An orientation that is committed to the enhancement of human experience, and guided by a belief that this is to be achieved by playing down the supremacy of rationality and playing up the subjective and intuitive.

Transpersonal Psychology. 1. A search for the optimal, the ultimate in the human capacity to experience.

Phenomenological Psychology. 1. The view that behavior is guided by the way an individual personally comprehends the self, and the environment in which he or she functions.

The goal of existential psychology is not so much that of displacing prior schools or systems of psychology, but of complementing them by correcting for their neglect of the intact, integrated person that came from an overattention to such sticks and stones as processes, functions, and particular kinds of responses. A search for ways to correct this error led to a consideration of each person as a target topic. Existential psychology assumes that the reality that each individual knows is yoked to the human condition, to existence. The facets of existence that are the most frequently studied are awareness of the self, of others, and of the natural world.

The most valued information about existential psychology is believed to come by means of the method of PHENOMENOLOGY, that is, by the study of experience, unanalyzed, and accepted just as it appears to be. Existential psychology disavows unconscious forces and holds naive experience in such high regard that it maintains that it is one criterion of truth. This opinion, when combined with the focus on the individual, results in the assertion that the person is able to decide what personal experience should be, and is also able to take steps that may be necessary to align behavior and experience (Binswanger & Boss, 1985).

The existentialist movement arose out of a philosophical movement in Europe, and its impact, when introduced into the American scene, was initially more pronounced in psychiatry than in general psychology. Two periodicals are devoted to the viewpoint: *Journal of Existentialism* (formerly the *Journal of Existential Psychiatry*, Volume 1, 1960), and *Review of Existential Psychology and Psychiatry*, Volume 1, 1961.

The reader is reminded that this modern concept is quite different from a much earlier movement in psychology that was also called existential. The latter was a logical construction that was applied to STRUCTURAL PSYCHOLOGY in order to indicate that the content of the mind represents existent data. This meaning is now obsolete and is mentioned here more for completeness than for relevance.

Humanistic psychology crystallized at approximately the same time as modern existential psychology, with the *Journal of Humanistic Psychology* first appearing in 1961. The concept is broader, and also more widely dispersed, than is existential psychology (Bugental, 1963). It strives for the celebration of life, and embraces efforts to enlarge and enrich the subjective domain so that the person is guided by what he or she understands rather than by the manipulations of others. One of the recurrent themes is the pursuit of psychiatric integrity, which is conceived as more than the absence of disease. There is an emphasis on so-called peak experience, conceptualized by Abraham Maslow (1908–1970), one of the foremost advocates of humanistic psychology, and described by him and various other psychologists as intense feeling, exalted being, enriched awareness, even as the "hilt," and "illumination." Also featured on the agenda is self-actualization, a concept Maslow (1967) borrowed from Goldstein (1939), and one that involves strivings to fulfill personal potential by such means as nurturing interests that are intrinsically gratifying, maintaining a deep commitment to causes extrinsic to the self, establishing freedom from debilitating self-criticism, and giving reign to spontaneity.

Maslow (1954) labeled humanistic psychology the "third force" in psychology, apparently as a way of underscoring its break with tradition. He dubbed behaviorism as the "first force" and psychoanalysis as the "second force." In 1968 Sutich announced the emergence of the "fourth force," transpersonal psychology. This version of the human potential movement is also dedicated to maximizing human development. It is differentiated from other, similar enterprises by virtue of the interest "in those *ultimate* human capacities and potentialities that have no systematic place" in any of the first three forces (Sutich, 1968, pp. 77–78). An inventory of the topics of interest includes "maximal sensory awareness," ecstasy, "mystical experience," "ultimate meaning," and "cosmic awareness." Some of the articles in the *Journal of Transpersonal Psychology*, which began publication in 1969, develop nonconforming subject matter, whereas others combine deviance with conventional psychology. The latter is illustrated in a 1981 article by Earle, "Cerebral Laterality and Meditation." In this the author surveys relationships between highly technical electrical measurements of cortical activity and meditation, a means of "abandoning the intellect" (p. 156).

The fourth variety of the human potential movement is called phenomenological psychology. This embraces many of the views of the preceding three concepts, and it also advocates extending the method of PHENOMENOLOGY in a way that organizes the entire field of psychology around phenomenological data. Some seeds for this approach were sown in 1941 when Snygg came close to suggesting that phenomenology constitutes a theoretical frame but stopped short of actually doing so. A few aspects of his thinking on this matter are offered, both to clarify the method and to illustrate its significance. Snygg called attention to the confusion that researchers create when they combine subjective, phenomenological reports with objective measurements, such as those read from instruments. He suggested reducing this variety in the study of personality by utilizing only phenomenological material, and indicated that this simplification would increase the accuracy of predictions of behavior. He did not give phenomenology the sole billing, but proposed the more orthodox course of developing "Gestalt psychology along purely phenomenological lines" (1941, p. 423).

This change in role from that of a technique to that of a cardinal principle was marked in 1970 when the *Journal of Phenomenological Psychology: Studies in the Science of Human Experience and Behavior* came into existence. The nine-year delay between the publication of this periodical and the *Review of Existential Psychology and Psychiatry* suggests that it may have been the promotion of phenomenology by the existentialists rather than any changes within phenomenology that prompted the expansion.

The editorial in the first issue of the *Journal of Phenomenological Psychology* states that the challenge for the movement "is to *invent* [italics added] methods and other types of analyses that *will unveil* [italics added] significant aspects of man's relatedness to himself, others and the world" (Giorgi, 1970, p. 5). This futuristic orientation facilitates bypassing the checks and balances of the here and now and opens the door to "original moments" and "the life-world" (Corriveau, 1972, pp. 32–33). Discussions that detail the modifications that phenomenological psychology exerts on various topics in psychology are available (McCall, 1983; Spiegelberg, 1972).

The existential, humanistic, transpersonal, and phenomenological views overlap in substance as well as in methodology. In fact, the labels are on occasion interchangeable. One volume, for example, is entitled *Existential Humanistic Psychology* (Greening, 1971). The relationships between the existential and phenomenological views are particularly intimate, and Pollio (1982) is one of several who refers to "existential phenomenology." A leader of one system may also be a leader in a second. Rollo May, for example, is referred to, in a single article, both as "Mr. Humanist" and "*the* spokesman for the existential approach" (Hall, 1967, p. 25).

The third and fourth "forces" are anathema to many of the psychologists who are striving for precision and scientific stature (Smith, 1973). But this censure competes with attraction to these viewpoints, particularly the more restrained varieties. Abraham Maslow, for example, was elected president of the American Psychological Association in 1968, and in 1978 M. Brewster Smith, a friend of humanistic psychology, albeit one who is also critical, was elected to the same office.

One measure of acceptance is the growth of encounter and support groups. They have nurtured all forms of the human potential movement, and the latter, in turn, has subsidized many, but not all, of them. The notion is pervasive that benefits—palliative, curative, preventive, and restorative—come from participating in assemblies. These are labeled in a variety of ways, such as T-group, lab-group, basic encounter group, and sensitivity training.

Some bear the names of particular topics or skills, such as "Practice Forgiving," "Exploring the Meaning of Love and Death," and "Learning Parenting Skills." The programs were initiated to sharpen the interpersonal skills of upper and middle management, but the technique soon spread to other achievement-oriented populations, such as nurses, college students, and educators (Bradford, Gibb, & Benne, 1964). The method was also applied to common problems that confront otherwise healthy people, for example, stopping smoking, being a single parent, and managing various postsurgical conditions. There was also an extension to personality disorders, to the psychiatrically disabled, to substance abusers, and to criminals.

Meetings devoted to personal growth are polymorphic, but they tend to involve only a small number of people at any one session, and the leader—or in the ingroup language, the facilitator—strives to provoke expressions, sometimes of emotion and sometimes of reason. The intention, in some instances, is to elicit advice as to how to modify specific behavioral patterns and alleviate personal discomfort. In others, the goal is to revise personal perspective, and this is often pursued by confronting the participants with the manner, particularly the disserviceable ways, in which they handle themselves. The candor with which the behavior is mirrored varies, as does the duration of the group experience. For example, a gathering may consist of factory foremen, meeting for two hours once a week to monitor appropriate assertiveness when dealing with subordinates. Quite different is a so-called synanon—a group composed of individuals who are overly dependent on chemicals—that is assembled for a marathon weekend, a period of two or three days of contacts interrupted only by minimal periods of sleep. These groups, using explicit language and gestures often call attention to the parasitical quality of the members' interpersonal relationships. Groups in which the customary amenities are suspended and the confrontations are uncensored have been criticized by some and even described as dangerous, but proponents maintain that encounter groups can facilitate self-understanding and growth (Rogers, 1967; Tomkins, 1976).

References

Binswanger, L., & Boss, M. (1985). Existential psychology. In C. S. Hall, G. Lindzey, J. C. Loehlin, & M. Manosevitz (Eds.), *Introduction to theories of personality* (pp. 243–264). New York: John Wiley. Two psychiatrists review existential psychology. They discuss the full realization of one's potentials as well as techniques for managing choice, guilt, and dread.

Bradford, L. P., Gibb, J. R., & Benne, K. D. (Eds.). (1964). *T-group theory and laboratory method: Innovation in re-education.* New York: John Wiley. This volume contains articles by various authors. Different aspects of T-groups are described in detail.

Bugental, J. F. T. (1963). Humanistic psychology: A new break-through. *American Psychologist, 18*, 563–567.

Corriveau, M. (1972). Phenomenology, psychology, and radical behaviorism: Skinner and Merleau-Ponty on behavior. *Journal of Phenomenological Psychology, 3*, 7–34. The author points out that behaviorism and phenomenology are similar in that neither is interested in reducing the organism to physiology and both are concerned with behavior as it occurs. He then, in an unrestrained manner, elaborates on the differences.

Earle, J. B. B. (1981). Cerebral laterality and meditation: A review of the literature. *Journal of Transpersonal Psychology, 13*, 155–173.

Giorgi, A. (1970). Journal aims and policies [Editorial]. *Journal of Phenomenological Psychology: Studies in the Science of Human Experience and Behavior, 1*, 5.

Goldstein, K. (1939). *The organism: A holistic approach to biology*. New York: American Book. A classic treatise on the psychological sequelae of neurological damage. The author is sensitized to the discomforting and perplexing episodes that these patients often experience.

Greening, T. C. (Ed.). (1971). *Existential humanistic psychology*. Belmont, CA: Brooks/Cole.

Hall, M. H. (1967, September). An interview with "Mr. Humanist" Rollo May. *Psychology Today*, pp. 25–29; 72–73.

Maslow, A. H. (1954). *Motivation and personality*. New York: Harper & Row. A second edition was published in 1970, and in 1987 Harper & Row also issued a third, posthumous edition.

Maslow, A. H. (1967). Self-actualization and beyond. In J. F. T. Bugenthal (Ed.), *Challenges of humanistic psychology* (pp. 279–286). New York: McGraw-Hill.

McCall, R. J. (1983). *Phenomenological psychology: An introduction with a glossary of some key Heideggerian terms*. Madison: University of Wisconsin Press. This presentation emphasizes the historical, European roots more than the current American scene.

Pollio, H. R. (1982). Let it happen [Review of *An Introduction to Phenomenological Psychology*]. *Contemporary Psychology, 27*, 221.

Rogers, C. R. (1967). The process of the basic encounter group. In J. F. T. Bugental (Ed.), *Challenges of humanistic psychology* (pp. 261–276). New York: McGraw-Hill. The author describes the group approach and makes a serious attempt to evaluate the results. The research base for this is less than adequate.

Smith, M. B. (1973). On self-actualization: A transambivalent examination of a focal theme in Maslow's psychology. *Journal of Humanistic Psychology, 13* (2), 17–33. This author has two contrasting opinions about the "third force." "There is much in his [Maslow's] writings that appeals to me strongly. There is much else that sets my intellectual teeth on edge and makes me squirm in discomfort or withdraw in impatience or disagreement" (p. 17).

Snygg, D. (1941). The need for a phenomenological system of psychology. *Psychological Review, 48*, 404–424.

Spiegelberg, H. (1972). *Phenomenology in psychology and psychiatry: A historical introduction*. Evanston, IL: Northwestern University Press.

Sutich, A. J. (1968). Transpersonal psychology: An emerging force. *Journal of Humanistic Psychology, 8* (1), 77–78.

Tomkins, C. (1976, January 5). Profiles (Michael Murphy). *The New Yorker*, pp. 30–51. An informal account of the human potential movement, centering around the

Esalen Institute and its cofounder Michael Murphy, but also describing the activities of many of the leaders in the human potential movement.

Sources of Additional Information

Bugental, J. F. T. (1965). *The search for authenticity: An existential-analytic approach to psychotherapy*. New York: Holt, Rinehart, & Winston. An account by a psychologist of his methods and goals in psychotherapy with well-educated, successful people who feel that their lives have more potential meaning and vitality than they have achieved. Bühler, C. (1971). Basic theoretical concepts of humanistic psychology. *American Psychologist, 26*, 378–386. This is a carefully thought through speech, the Presidential Address at The First International Invitational Conference on Humanistic Psychology in Amsterdam, Netherlands, 1970. Hall, M. H. (1967, December). A conversation with the father of Rogerian therapy: Carl Rogers. *Psychology Today*, pp. 19–21, 62–66. Rogers is acclaimed for his respect for the person, his refusal to impose judgments on others, and his skill in helping an individual to clarify his or her own thinking. James, M., & Jongeward, D. (1975). *The people book: Transactional analysis for students*. Menlo Park, CA: Addison-Wesley. A set of instructions for a variety of "games" or encounters. MacLeod, R. B. (1964). Phenomenology: A challenge to experimental psychology. In T. W. Wann (Ed.), *Behaviorism and phenomenology: Contrasting bases for modern psychology*. (pp. 47–78). Chicago: University of Chicago Press. This is a scholarly, objective evaluation of the two movements.

I

IMAGE. 1. Subjective representations of experience(s). **IMAGINATION.** 1. The combining of images. 2. A synonym for fantasy and daydreaming.

Imagery is a generic term for image and imagination, both in wakefulness and in dreaming. Image generally refers to subjective replicas of experiences, while imagination refers to the ideational elaboration of these images into a sequence or theme. The two responses blend into each other, and because there are no sharp lines of demarcation the choice of either of the two terms is somewhat arbitrary. All varieties of image and imagination are, by definition, recognized as phantoms. An image that is believed to be real is referred to as an hallucination or false perception, and imagination that is accepted as actual is called a delusion or false belief. Except in rare circumstances hallucinations and delusions are pathological, and thus beyond the limits of this discussion.

There have been two periods in which the study of imagery has been important. One occurred during the formative era of psychology and the second began in the recent past and is still continuing. In the former the stress was on the cognitive aspects of both concepts, but in the latter there is much more emphasis on the emotional aspects. Francis Galton, a British "gentleman scientist," was one of the first to conduct research on images. He was led more by personal curiosity than by investigative rigor, and he delved into an unusually wide variety of topics. One of these was "the mind's eye." He instructed subjects to "picture" their breakfast table and then asked about such details as the vividness, size, and location of various components of the image. He was impressed by "the great variety of natural powers of visual representation" (Galton, 1880, p. 306).

In 1909 Betts, an American researcher, devised a 150-item questionnaire concerning the clarity of visual imagery in various modalities as represented, for example, in images of the sun sinking, a pinprick, cabbage boiling, running upstairs, eating an orange, and drowsiness. The results supported Galton's observation of marked individual differences, and the longevity of Betts' questionnaire is exceptional. In 1967 Sheehan identified it as "the most comprehensive test of imagery available" (p. 386). He reduced it to thirty-five items in order to have a more feasible experimental tool, and reported that the results of this abbreviated scale do not vary significantly from those of Betts. This version is still in use (Johnson 1980, 1981).

The first golden age in the laboratory study of imagery started when Titchener, one of the principal advocates of STRUCTURAL PSYCHOLOGY, decided that images constitute one of three basic components of the "mind." He identified them as "the characteristic elements of ideas, of the mental pictures that memory furnishes of past and imagination of future experience" (1909, p. 48). INTROSPECTION, a highly specialized technique for observing consciousness, generated masses of particulars about this fundamental element, and this laborious scrutiny disclosed four varieties that, albeit with a bit of arbitrariness, can be arranged in the order of their fidelity to the original experience; afterimages, eidetic images, memory images, and imagination images. This arrangement is based on the composition of images, and it is unrelated to either their purpose or any emotions that are aroused or accompany them.

The first entry in this scheme is the aftersensation or, more commonly, the afterimage, the involuntary sensing of a stimulus after its removal. Afterimages occur in all senses with the possible exception of audition (Rosenblith, Miller, Egan, Hirsch, & Thomas, 1947). Most experiments have concentrated on vision, but aftersensations have been described for pressure, temperature, taste, and balance. The casual observer is aware that a flash of light may be "seen" after it has disappeared, but the introspectionists discovered that the interval between the sensation and the image is typically two to three seconds, and then it is followed by a sequence of three additional afterimages. Travelers are familiar with the sensations of movement that persist at the end of a long journey, but the introspectionists know: "If you turn round rapidly upon the heels several times in succession, and then come to rest with closed eyes, you have a sensation which can only be described as a swimming in the head. Its apparent direction is opposed to the direction of the actual movement, so that it wears the appearance of a negative afterimage" (Titchener, 1909, p. 174).

A second kind of image is called eidetic. This comes from the Greek *eidolon*, which means idol or image, and was brought into use by the German psychologist E. R. Jaensch (1925/1930) in order to convey the unusual clarity of the likeness. Eidetic imagery occurs in different senses, but it has been studied so much more thoroughly in vision than in other modalities that it connotes visual images, and people who experience eidetic imagery are described as having a photographic memory. The phenomenon is much more common in children than in adults (Allport, 1928), but there are exceptions. Titchener's subjective representations were unusually clear. He explains how they influence his performance in the classroom: "I am able . . . to lecture from any one of the three main cues. I can read off what I have to say from a memory transcript; or I can follow the lead of my voice, or I can trust to the guidance of kinaesthesis, the anticipatory feel of the movements of articulation. . . . I draw up in mind's eye a table of contents, written or printed, and refer to it as the hour proceeds. . . . I hear my own voice speaking just ahead of me. . . . I let my throat take care of itself; so that I am able to give full attention to blackboard drawing" (1909/1973, p. 8).

A third variety is a memory image. The simulation of a previous experience is recognized as personal, and introspective data indicate that the fidelity between the original and the recalled varies from person to person, from time to time, and from topic to topic.

The fourth variety of likeness is called the imagination image. These representations are on occasion unusual and even startling. They are probably basically memory images inasmuch as there is evidence that the imaginative component is in the combination rather than in the ingredients. Picturing an "18th-century coach coated with multicolored psychodelic tiles" may be described as imaginative, but it consists of an unusual combination of familiar items.

The pursuit of the information about images was curtailed during the early part of the twentieth century, when BEHAVIORISM succeeded in repudiating subjective concepts and restricted the subject matter of psychology to behavior. This changed opinion that imagery is important into opinion that it is not a suitable subject matter for scientific research. There was a suspension of work on the concept, and no significant amount of experimentation was resumed until the 1950s. During this interval only a few textbooks mentioned fantasy or daydreaming, and when these topics were discussed, their consequences were apt to be depicted as unfortunate. For example, Shaffer, in *The Psychology of Adjustment* (1936), a landmark volume in ADJUSTMENT, devoted only eleven pages to the topic, and he identifies daydreaming as reactive rather than creative. He evaluated it as benign but unfortunate in that the activity is a substitute and consumes time that could be spent more profitably.

This abeyance, ascribed to events within psychology, was also consonant with a reticence throughout society. One kept one's private representations to one's self. Holt suggests that this reserve may have diminished the recognition of even nonemotionally toned, faint, but ubiquitous sensory irregularities, such as double images and blind spots. He is much more certain about the dampening effect on images: "In a factually oriented, skeptical, anti-intraceptive, [anti-imaginative, anti-subjective] brass-tacks culture like ours . . . the capacity for vivid imagery has little survival value and less social acceptability" (1964, p. 262).

One of the first returns of the study of imagery grew out of research on sleep. This started in 1952, when a graduate student of physiology, Eugene Aserinsky, observed rapid eye movements in sleeping subjects, and found, on direct inquiry, that these were concomitant with dreaming. This disclosure demonstrated that imagery involves muscle activity, and that tangible status licensed additional research (Trillin, 1965). Night dreams had not previously been investigated in detail because they were not considered important. They were also looked on with suspicion because of a belief that they are not the product of real events, but are manifestations of prophetic voices or directives by divine figures. This unfortunate reputation was not significantly improved when psychoanalysts began to interpret dreams as the product of an impalpable, but turbulent UNCONSCIOUS.

Once the resistance to studying dreams was dissipated, individuals were brought into the laboratory to sleep, with some aroused and asked to describe an interrupted dream, and others allowed to recall the dreams after self-awakening. Subjects are stimulated in various ways before falling asleep and with a variety of stimuli while slumbering. Numerous measurements are made, including the electrical activity of the brain, general motility, and chemical analyses of body fluids. A host of records of the imagery of the dreams, as well as their sequences and emotional tone, has been assembled (Cohen, 1979).

Beginning in the 1950s psychologists undertook experimental work on various kinds of imagery. Much of the initial work was concerned with rational responses, and in this connection, for example, imagery in the thinking of scientists was explored (Roe, 1951). Images of objects and events that are feared were incorporated into a learning strategy that is designed to reduce FEAR. Organized research programs grew out of COGNITIVE PSYCHOLOGY, a view that makes both images and imagination important by virtue of a stress on implicit behavior that includes discovering how humans seek and handle information. An endorsement that is typical of cognitive psychology is illustrated in the observation that "seeing" lightning makes thoughts about an electrical storm more vivid, and this enhancement increases the number of associations that are made. These increments then expand the meaning or significance of stimuli, and as a result other responses, such as learning, memory, and language comprehension, are promoted. An illustration of this compounding is found in an experiment by Pate and Newsom (1983), in which both stimuli and responses that readily evoke imagery were found to be associated more rapidly than those that provoke less imagery. It is interesting to note that this investigation is relevant to an argument that began in the 1910s as to whether or not imagery increases learning. The attempts to resolve this matter have been few and episodic, but now that imagery has credibility, the matter may be studied with some continuity (Paivio, 1970). One of the cumulative effects of these changes in attitude is a favorable overall perception of both images and imagination. They are described as constructive for both emotion and cognition, offering, for example, a means of directing thought and of trying out various plans (Singer, 1975).

A second modern promoter of imagery is the human potential movement, a composite of EXISTENTIAL, HUMANISTIC, TRANSPERSONAL, and PHENOMENO-LOGICAL PSYCHOLOGY. Proponents of these schools play down cognition and play up emotions. They recommend converting the culture that Holt characterized in the previously cited quotation as "factually oriented, skeptical, anti-intraceptive," into one that is "affectively oriented, believing, extraceptive." The advocates entertain an exuberant eagerness to flaunt imagery and to endow both images and imagination with creative powers. These emancipated versions of psychology attract people with a diversity of interests and skills—artists, authors, and educators, in addition to psychologists. An interdisciplinary periodical, *Journal of Mental Imagery*, was established in 1977, and in 1983 a news-letter, *Imagery Today*, appeared. These outlets promote a faith that to many is incredible, as, for example: "Mental imagery really can perform miracles. It can cure physical ailments, emotional problems, accident traumas, learning disability, problems like depression, and even a cold" (Dolan 1983, p. 2).

Such optimism has yet to be substantiated. Evidence abounds, however, that image and imagination are *au courant*, both in the laboratory and in less restrained segments of society.

References

Allport, G. W. (1928). The eidetic image and the after-image. *American Journal of Psychology, 40,* 418–425. The descriptions of the two images in the title are amended with an account of memory images, and comparisons are made among these three types.

Cohen, D. B. (1979). *Sleep and dreaming: Origins, nature and functions.* Oxford, England: Pergamon Press. This is a comprehensive report of the status of dream research. The author deals explicitly with the variables that intervene between dreaming and reality: "In a sense, a dream report is twice removed from the dream; it is a report of a memory of an experience" (p. 157).

Dolan, A. T. (1983). Image & mind. *Imagery Today, 1 (1),* 2.

Galton, F. (1880). Statistics of mental imagery. *Mind, 5,* 301–318.

Holt, R. R. (1964). Imagery: The return of the ostracized. *American Psychologist, 19,* 254–264. This paper represents one of the turning points in the reactivation of the concept of imagery.

Jaensch, E. R. (1930). *Eidetic imagery and typological methods of investigation* (2nd ed.). (O. Oeser, Trans.). New York: Harcourt Brace. (Original work published 1925)

Johnson, R. A. (1980). Sensory images in the absence of sight: Blind versus sighted adolescents. *Perceptual and Motor Skills, 51,* 177–178. The research tool was Sheehan's form of Betts' questionnaire. The results disclosed visual imagery among adolescents blinded before the age of one year. The reasons for this are far from clear.

Johnson, R. A. (1981). Sensory images among deaf adolescents. *Journal of General Psychology, 105,* 167–168. Essentially the same methology as the previous study. And, again, a surprising result: Deaf subjects have 95 percent as many auditory images as hearing subjects.

Paivio, A. (1970). On the functional significance of imagery. *Psychological Bulletin, 73,* 385–392. This paper reviews much of the history of imagery, with the emphasis on the relationship between imagery and children's learning.

Pate, J. L. & Newsom, M. W. (1983). Imagery effects with mixed and unmixed lists. *The Psychological Record, 33,* 379–389.

Roe, A. (1951). A study of imagery in research scientists. *Journal of Personality, 19,* 459–470.

Rosenblith, W. A., Miller, G. A., Egan, J. P., Hirsch, I. J. & Thomas, G. J. (1947). An auditory afterimage? *Science, 106* (No. 2754), 333–334. The authors remark on the reputed absence of auditory afterimages and report an "aftereffect" of stimulation by a loud buzzing sound. This is experienced as a metallic quality imposed on familiar sounds. The authors suggest that this is an afterimage.

Shaffer, L. F. (1936). *The psychology of adjustment: An objective approach to mental hygiene*. Cambridge, MA: Houghton Mifflin.

Sheehan, P. W. (1967). A shortened form of Bett's questionnaire upon mental imagery. *Journal of Clinical Psychology, 23*, 386–389.

Singer, J. L. (1975). *The inner world of daydreaming*. New York: Harper & Row. This book reports formal research, but it is also a clearly written discussion of normal people and everyday fantasy.

Titchener, E. B. (1909). *A text-book of psychology* (Pt. 1). New York: Macmillan.

Titchener, E. B. (1973). *Lectures on the experimental psychology of the thought-processes*. New York: Arno Press. (Original work published 1909). Titchener, the prototypical formal scholar, drops a bit of his intellectual reserve and talks about his own imagery.

Trillin, C. (1965, September 18). A third state of existence. *The New Yorker*, pp. 58–125. This article in a popular magazine describes accurately and in highly readable fashion the history of the discovery of different kinds of eye movements during sleep and their relationship to dream imagery. The results are discussed in reference to various personality theories.

Sources of Additional Information

Barron, F. (1958). The psychology of imagination. *Scientific American, 199* (3), 150–166 This is one of the systematic studies of the relationship between creativity and imagination. Haber, R. N. (1980, November). Eidetic images are not just imaginary. *Psychology Today*, pp. 72–82. An attractively illustrated, clearly written popular review of the concept of eidetic imagery, both the history and current status. Perky, C. W. (1910). An experimental study of imagination. *American Journal of Psychology, 21*, 422–452. This is a report of several experiments, including one that is frequently cited. In this design subjects were asked to image an object (such as a banana, tomato, lemon) on a screen while the experimenter projected, at increasing levels of discernibility, the actual object. The observers unwittingly incorporated these visible forms into their "images." This failure to detect the difference suggested that an imagination image is similar to ordinary perceptions and to memory images. White, H. E., & Levatin, P. (1962). "Floaters" in the eye. *Scientific American, 206* (6), 119–127. This article deals in a highly technical way with common, but unobtrusive visual phenomena, an example of the phenomenon that Holt says the culture teaches us to ignore.

IMAGE, BODY. See BODY IMAGE.

IMPERCEPTION. is referred to by various terms, including unconscious and unconsciousness, and these words, like CONSCIOUS and CONSCIOUSNESS, in some contexts have equivalent meanings and in others they have different ones. Historically, conscious and unconscious were used as adjectives to refer to a level of awareness, with unconscious designating reduced sensibility, lapses in memory, failures to perceive and/or failures to apprehend one's basic wishes. The referent of consciousness was a noun, a hypothesized entity, "the mind," a register of experiences, and a director of activity. Unconsciousness was also believed to be an entity, but the functioning of these two parts was seen as distinctive. Consciousness functions in a straightforward manner, but unconsciousness is devious and cunning. To illustrate—consciousness or the conscious mind makes a person "throw the dish on the floor," but unconsciousness or the unconscious mind might provoke one to "accidentally drop the dish." Under the influence of psychoanalysis the adjective unconscious began to be used as a synonym for unconsciousness, so that in modern parlance unconscious may refer either to a reduced level of awareness or to mental activity.

Unconscious. 1. A diminution of awareness that ranges from slight to profound. 2. A hypothesized, impalpable apparatus that is a composite of different parts, some of which act antagonistically, persistently, deviously, and surreptitiously.

Unconsciousness. 1. A hypothesized, impalpable apparatus that is a composite of different parts, some of which act antagonistically, persistently, deviously, and surreptitiously.

A Comprehensive Dictionary of Psychological and Psychoanalytical Terms takes note of the confused terminology, and warns the reader that "there are no less than 39 distinct meanings of unconscious; it is certain that no author limits himself consistently to one" (English & English, 1958, p. 569). This capriciousness makes it necessary to try to impose at least some order before considering the history of the concepts. The word unconscious is applied to the insensibility, even the coma, that comes with certain illnesses and drug intake, but in a psychological context the preferred referents are perceptions, memories and wishes that are not sensed. The words unconscious and subliminal both designate imperception, but subliminal refers traditionally only to failure to appreciate minute amounts of sensory stimulation. The words habit and unconscious are also sometimes treated as equivalents. Habit indicates a familiar and facile reaction, and although unconscious is also used in this way, the word automatic is a better choice. Habit does not connote a lack of responsiveness, but rather a lack of a need to attend because the reaction is mechanical and consistent, an outgrowth of many repetitions.

Additional linguistic disorder is found in a series of technical and proximate terms (Miller, 1942). One of the oldest of these is coconsciousness, a word devised in the study of multiple personalities to indicate that a subpersonality may be aware of but may not share the desires of the "true" personality (Prince, 1921). The words foreconscious and preconscious are generally more familiar, and they often refer to experiences that are unnoticed but may be brought to attention readily and without emotional resistance (Moore & Fine, 1968). A familiar example is the ignoring of background music until a favored piece is played. Some authors treat subconscious as equivalent of foreconscious and preconscious, but others use it as a synonym for any designation of the nonconscious. A bit of restraint of this practice comes from the opinion that the word subconscious is a popular term, and hence to be avoided in professional literature.

From almost the earliest experimental work the discipline of psychology has acknowledged both varieties of imperception but has not stressed either of them. In fact, the treatment of lowered sensitivity was often incidental, in that it was largely acknowledged as an adjunct of other reactions, for example, involuntary fluctuations in ATTENTION, memory lapses, and the effects of drug intake. When information about weak sensibility was organized, it was considered important for reasons other than the diluted awareness. One of the topics in which this subordinate status is apparent is concerned with THRESHOLD measurements, that is, with the determination of both the minimal amount and the minimal differences in physical energy that are appreciated. The research in this area began even before the inaugural era of experimental psychology, and gradually various laboratory procedures for determining a threshold were developed. Each of these constitutes an orderly way of handling data about imperception, but this concept is played down in that the work is usually identified as the study of the relationship between sensation and physical energy.

A second, similar situation is found in early research on THINKING. Some evidence, uncovered in the founding laboratories, indicated that thinking might not always be accompanied by an IMAGE. This possibility violated a basic assumption of STRUCTURAL PSYCHOLOGY, a dominant school of the era that held that mental content is always supported by so-called mental elements, such as images. This was a serious problem, and it was examined by means of INTRO- SPECTION, a formal procedure in which trained individuals observe their own awareness. The introspectionists searched scrupulously for the missing elements, but their failures to discover them, that is, their probes of imperception, were, as in the case of thresholds, played down, in this instance in favor of devising ways of accommodating to the theory.

The history of the concept of the unconscious, as a compartment within the mind, predates the founding of experimental psychology in that it was a rec- ognized topic in philosophy. The German philosopher J. F. Herbart (1776–1841) was one of the pioneer advocates of the idea that the mind consists of active ideas, varying in strength, with some compatible and others incompatible. The former strive to coalesce, and they also exclude the latter from consciousness. This displacement made it necessary for Herbart to posit a location, and he handled this by assuming an unconscious compartment of the mind. Herbart depicted this as a region in which ideas are not destroyed, but one in which they remain viable and struggle to become conscious once again (Murphy & Kovach, 1972).

Psychology made limited use of Herbart's formulations, but they were influ- ential in the field of education in that they suggested relating new ideas to ones already familiar to the learner. The affinity between psychoanalysis and Herbart's dynamics is even more striking, and the main modification that psychoanalysis made was to depict the contestants as impulses and wishes rather than as ideas.

The most important single event in the history of imperception is the emergence of psychoanalysis, a viewpoint that emphasizes both attenuated experiences and dynamic psychic forces. Psychoanalysis began to gain an audience in the United States toward the end of the first decade of the twentieth century. There are so many versions of psychoanalytic theory that the proponents have acquired a reputation for internal dissent and for defections from "orthodoxy." Sigmund Freud (1856–1939), the foremost advocate, modified his own system throughout his life. It is not within the scope of this discussion to review these doctrines, and the writing is restricted to issues that illustrate the concept of the unconscious (Munroe, 1955).

Many psychologists consider contentious homunculi that can be discerned only in concealed forms, such as slips of the tongue, dreams, and psychiatric symptoms, to be an affront to science. They anathematize any combination of diminished responsiveness and conscious intentions, as, for example, unrecognized wishes, disguised impulses, and rationalized rather than rational reasons (Klein, 1933). Other psychologists endeavor to reconcile these unacceptable formulations with scientifically acceptable ones (Hilgard, 1962).

The differences between psychoanalytic and psychological formulations are striking, and some of their flavor can be illustrated in two explanations of how therapeutic sessions transform unconscious material into conscious material. Practically all interpretations of this change invoke association, a process in which the analysand pursues ideas and thoughts as they are provoked by his or her own mentation. Psychoanalytic doctrine commonly assumes that experiences have been forced out of consciousness because they are painful and that association releases a bit of the emotional charge so that the episodes of association cumulatively defuse the distressing material, with the result that it is no longer necessary to block reentry into awareness.

Psychological explanations, in contrast, assert that the conversion from the nonsensed to the sensed is not a restructuring of affect and psychic forces, but rather is a matter of MEMORY, an exercise of the psychological principle that more intense stimulation elicits more responses. Specifically, association is believed to increase the number and organization of stimuli, and these changes improve recall (Bradburn, Rips, & Shevell, 1987).

Let us assume that a request to recall clothing that was worn during the first year in grade school failed initially to elicit any recollection. A psychoanalyst would probably initiate a search for emotional barriers, whereas an experimental psychologist would probably initiate reminiscing about home or school. This should lead to remembering companions and games, and these associations, in their own right should nourish further recall. To illustrate—a recollection of finding a baseball *glove* might well revive a feeling of disappointment that ensued when this glove was found to be only about half as large as the finder's *red mitten*. Ruminating about this could evoke remembering that the color matched a *red scarf* Mother purchased in order to brighten a *dark school jacket*. Thus, in a simple stimulus-response framework, the inventory of the wardrobe is under way.

There are some signs that rapprochement between psychology and psychoanalysis may be emerging, and one of the more convincing of these comes in the research on feedback. This phenomenon, originally studied in the physical sciences, deals with the modification of a mechanism that is induced by the way the mechanism operates. In the behavioral sciences the word feedback is changed to biofeedback and subjects are presented with visual, auditory, or kinesthetic signals of body functions that are customarily neither under voluntary control nor clearly discerned, such as blood pressure and pulse rate. This biofeedback helps subjects to learn to recognize faint sensations, and this information helps them to modulate the function. Developing this skill demands considerable practice, but autoregulation can be achieved, and it is now in use for therapeutic purposes (Simkins, 1982).

This technique is seen as a modern way of manipulating the unconscious because is is intended "to train people to observe minutely their own slight changes of feeling tone as simultaneous information is obtained on bodily changes" (Murphy, 1964, p. 106). The psychologists who initiated the research on biofeedback might well resist this interpretation because they see themselves as hard-core scientists. They are experts in the area of learning, and they rigidly adhere to scientific protocol and are resolutely committed to maintaining experimental controls. Their vocabulary is selective, and they avoid such terms as unconscious in favor of such labels as "physiological information processing" and "informational biofeedback." Their early successes authorized extending the technique to disorders in which behavioral components are as conspicuous as the physiological ones, for example, anxiety, asthma, insomnia, and sexual dysfunctioning. The effectiveness of the procedures with these problems has recently caught the attention of psychoanalysts, and as a result theoretical antagonists are now carrying out similar procedures (Burish, 1985).

Because of the rejection of psychoanalysis by many psychologists much of the study of the unconscious has taken place outside of universities, often in therapeutic facilities, settings in which the treatment functions dominate the theoretical ones. However, psychoanalysis became popular with various non-academic, nonscientific groups, and the doctrines were flaunted in fiction, in cartoons, and in the press. But the publicity exceeded the amount of firsthand contact with either the technique or the theory, and by the late 1960s the movement had lost much of its force, both in the popular intellectual culture and in professional circles. With the exception of a few stalwarts it is currently conceded that its past is more impressive than its future (Burnham, 1978).

There is, however, a legacy and in fact psychoanalytic sequels abound, particularly in topics that were initially clarified by psychoanalytic theories. These topics were brought into psychological laboratories, sometimes redefined, and investigated with as much control and precision as possible. As a result, several phenomena that were initially disdained are now accepted. These include a prevailing consensus that there are recognizable consequences from unrecognized motives (Shakow & Rapaport, 1964). PERCEPTUAL DEFENSE and SUBCEPTION now have endorsers. The persistence of childhood into adulthood has been converted from an inference into a "given" (Rapaport, 1960).

References

Bradburn, N. M., Rips, L. J., & Shevell, S. K. (1987). Answering autobiographical questions: The impact of memory and inference on surveys. *Science, 236,* (No. 4798), 157–161.

Burish, T. G., (1985). A psychotherapist's primer of clinical biofeedback [Review of *Symptom reduction through clinical biofeedback*]. *Contemporary Psychology, 30,* 26–27. The author of the book that is reviewed is a psychologist who uses biofeedback as one of several therapeutic strategies. The reviewer comments on the increasing recognition of the relationship between psychoanalysis and biofeedback.

Burnham, J. C. (1978). The influence of psychoanalysis upon American culture. In J. M. Quen & E. T. Carlson (Eds.), *American psychoanalysis: Origins and development* (pp. 52–72). New York: Brenner/Mazel.

English, H. B., & English, A. C. (1958). *A comprehensive dictionary of psychological and psychoanalytical terms: A guide to usage.* New York: Longmans, Green.

Hilgard, E. R. (1962). Impulsive versus realistic thinking: An examination of the distinction between primary and secondary processes in thought. *Psychological Bulletin, 59,* 477–488. Hilgard reviews Freud's theory that orderly, logical thought is a "secondary process," a derivative of a more basic, earlier form of thinking or "primary process," the illogical thinking that disregards space and time and is most commonly experienced by adults in dreams. The article relates this dichotomy to general psychology.

Klein, D. B. (1933). Psychology and Freud: An historico-critical appraisal. *Psychological Review, 40,* 440–456. This paper describes the rejection of psychoanalysis by academic and experimental psychologists, and discusses some of the sources of the theory.

Miller, J. G. (1942). *Unconsciousness.* New York: John Wiley. This is a book-length treatment of the many meanings and interpretations of unconscious. One of its purposes is to foster understanding among academic psychologists, psychoanalysts, and psychiatrists.

Moore, B. E., & Fine, B. D. (Eds.). (1968). *A glossary of psychoanalytic terms and concepts* (2nd ed.). New York: American Psychoanalytic Association.

Munroe, R. L. (1955). *Schools of psychoanalytic thought: An exposition, critique, and attempt at integration.* New York: Dryden Press. An accurate presentation of different psychoanalytic theories.

Murphy, G. (1964). Communication and mental health. *Psychiatry, 27* (2), 100–106. The author, a well-known psychologist, describes a demonstration of a visual display of his own muscular reactions: "He . . . attached electrodes to my left little finger and left ear lobe and asked me to watch an oscilloscope as I carried out small directed movements with my left little finger. Whenever I extended my finger to the left, this produced, in the midst of a shower of 'noise,' a well-defined peak on the oscilloscope which, as I practiced, became more and more clear" (p. 105).

Murphy, G., & Kovach, J. K. (1972). *Historical introduction to modern psychology* (3rd ed.). New York: Harcourt Brace Jovanovich.

Prince, M. (1921). *The unconscious: The fundamentals of human personality normal and abnormal* (2nd ed. rev.). New York: Macmillan. Prince depicts the coconscious at least as early as 1908, but this volume has been selected for reference here because it includes a comprehensive discussion. In this book Prince deals with normality as well as abnormality.

Rapaport, D. (1960). Psychoanalysis as a developmental psychology. In B. Kaplan & S. Wapner (Eds.), *Perspectives in psychological theory* (pp. 209–255). New York: International Universities Press. The author traces the implications of Freudian doctrines for normal growth and development.

Shakow, D. & Rapaport, D. (1964). The influence of Freud on American psychology. *Psychological Issues, 4* (Monog. 13). The authors discuss the influence of Freud's explications of the unconscious and motivation on the psychological scene.

Simkins, L. (1982). Biofeedback: Clinically valid or oversold? *The Psychological Record, 32,* 3–17. The author indicates that biofeedback is on occasion successful, but that in some areas it has been evaluated too positively. He discusses several of the difficulties that interfere with valid assessments.

Sources of Additional Information

Aarons, L. (1976). Sleep-assisted instruction. *Psychological Bulletin, 83,* 1–40. The author details evidence that both supports and denies learning during sleep. The relevant variables are numerous and confusing, and there is a dearth of practical applications of the available information. Adler, A. (1927). *Understanding human nature* (W. B. Wolfe, Trans.). Garden City, NY: Garden City Publishing. Adler, an analyst who disagreed with Freud, was especially concerned with a drive for power and authority. For him the unconscious and the conscious have compatible goals. Freud, S. (1938). *The basic writings of Sigmund Freud* (A. A. Brill, Trans. & Ed.). New York: Random House (Modern Library). Freud was prolific, and his work has appeared in numerous outlets. This volume reprints several of his articles. Jung, C. G. (1958). *Psyche and symbol: A selection from the writings of C. G. Jung* (V. S. de Laszlo, Ed.). Garden City, NY: Doubleday. Jung was initially in agreement with Freud, but the two became antagonists, and Jung developed his own analytical psychology. Miller, N. E. (1982). Some directions for clinical and experimental research on biofeedback. In L. White & B. Tursky (Eds.), *Clinical biofeedback: Efficacy and mechanisms* (pp. 1–20). New York: Guilford Press. The title is self-explanatory. The author is one of the most distinguished authorities in this area. Watson, J. B. (1927). The myth of the unconscious: A behavioristic explanation. *Harper's, 155,* 502–508. In this article Watson reviews his criticisms as a behaviorist of the unconscious. He substitutes the word unverbalized for unconscious (p. 503).

INCENTIVE. See GOAL and INCENTIVE.

INSTINCT. 1. A force hypothesized as innate and manifest in behavioral patterns that are executed in a smooth manner and in a fixed sequence by all members of a species.

Instinct, one of the oldest and most durable motives, has been invoked to explain a remarkable diversity of events: the cat's pursuit of the dog, the dog's pursuit of the cat, a child's fear of water, an animal's ability to swim, a bird's incubation of eggs, a human father's purchase of a home, the need for solitude, the need for companionship, a capitalist's acquisition and hoarding of resources, a squirrel's harvesting of nuts, and a lion's choice of a lioness as a mate. Instincts have also been so harshly condemned that the level of censure may well exceed the level of approval. Yet, for reasons that are far from clear, the concept appears invincible (Beach, 1955; Joffe, 1973).

The modern history of the concept of instinct gained momentum when the doctrine of evolution called attention to similarities among species. Naturalists began to search for corroborative evidence, and they were so eager that much of the information they procured was merely anecdotal, often hearsay, and so lacking in restraint that a backlash in the form of a demand for objectivity developed. In this restructuring, would-be scientists began to observe animals both in their natural living conditions and in the laboratory, and they also began to reject the supernatural as an explanatory source. The transition to naturalism was, however, labored, and reasoning, both in theory and in the laboratory, combined realistic ideas with notions of various first causes or ultimate principles including instincts.

Hodge (1894), a physiologist, clearly illustrates a fusion of the palpable and the impalpable. He was eager to dislodge the belief that organisms can find their nests because a divinely implanted occult power guides them. Lubbock had demonstrated that the paths that ants follow vary as the light patterns change, and Hodge, perceiving this as an impressive intellectual gain, set about procuring information about the cues that birds use. From his own research he concluded that they rely on familiar landmarks as visual guides. These discoveries of environmental cues explained the behavior in a naturalistic frame, but they did not remove the concept of instinct from Hodge's thinking. Rather, they prompted him to expand it so as to explain a wider range of behavior. He asked, for example: "May there not be a fundamental logic of search as universal as the search itself?" (p. 768). After comparing the paths that people follow when looking for a lost object, he decided that there is "instinctive logic" (p. 770).

William James, one of the pioneer elucidators of psychology, also illustrates the struggle to conceptualize instincts as material. He denounced the theological aura of the concept: "The older writings on instincts . . . smothered everything in vague wonder at the clairvoyant and prophetic power of animals—so superior to anything in man—and at the beneficence of God in endowing them with such a gift" (1892/1908, p. 392). The method that he used to transform the "vague wonder" into substance was merely to assume that the power is localized in the nervous system.

James deviated from a prevalent perception of instincts as predetermined and invariant by postulating some effects of both memory and experience on them. For James, this modifiability explained why people make responses that are more appropriate than raw impulsive ones. It also suggested to him that humans have more instincts than animals.

William McDougall, one of the founders of social psychology, concurred that instincts are localized in the nervous system but disagreed with James in that he saw them as immutable: "The behaviour of some of the lower animals seems to be almost completely determined throughout their lives by instincts modified but very little by experience; they perceive, feel, and act in a perfectly definite and invariable manner whenever a given instinct is excited" (1908/1912, p. 30). McDougall's ledger of instincts is lengthy, including, for example, flight, repulsion, curiosity, pugnacity, self-assertion, gregariousness, acquisitiveness, and the like. He questioned some of James' entries, for example, emulation and rivalry.

Bernard (1924), a sociologist, called attention to the indiscriminant applications of the concept. In 495 books written by 412 authors he encountered 2,539 references to general instincts, 5,684 to specific ones, and 2,238 to indefinite or aberrant ones. There are also 3,585 uses of the word instinctive.

Such high tallies are due in part to the circularity of the explanation, in Bernard's phrase, 'useless redundancies.' To illustrate—a bird is observed to gather grass for a nest, and this behavior is taken as evidence of a grass gathering instinct. Because of this instinct the prediction is made that grass will incvitably be gathered. A species that uses twigs discloses an additional instinct, in this instance a twig-gathering one. Such verbiage can be, and apparently was, applied to nearly any response.

By the 1920s psychologists were beginning to expose some of the weaknesses of instincts, but again, some facets of the concept were retained. One of the more highly cited of these arguments was written in 1919 by Knight Dunlap, who pointed out that instincts are identified by reference to their outcome rather than to behavior, and thus they constitute a classification of effects, not of events. Dunlap's proposed solution was to replace the concept of instinct with instinctive activity.

An experiment that had a strong impact on the topic was conducted by Kuo in 1931 under the title "The Genesis of the Cat's Responses to the Rat." Kuo raised kittens under such varying conditions as being in the same cage with rats, isolated, exposed to cats that destroy rats, being trained to fear a rat, and allowed only a vegetarian diet. These variables were found to have different effects; for example, 85 percent of those raised with rat killers also annihilated, whereas only 45 percent of those raised in isolation killed.

Kuo writes: "The more proof or disproof of an instinct . . . will not lead us anywhere. We need to know the potential range or repertory of activities of a given species . . . kittens can be made to kill a rat, to love it, to hate it, to fear it or to play with it . . . researches in the past have been in the wrong direction, because *instead of finding how we could build nature into the animal, we have tried to find nature in the animal*" (1931, pp. 34–35).

Experimental psychologists did become deeply involved in the problem of "how we could build nature into the animal," but they mainly pursued this by investigating LEARNING and DRIVE. This research, however, undermined the concept of instinct in that it indicated that many of the responses that were originally believed to be innate are actually gradually acquired and that the rate of this acquisition varies with the intensity of the motivation. This kind of information dampened much of the interest in instinct, and by the mid-1930s some psychologists believed that instincts had been drummed out of the laboratory.

About the same time as this fade out was under way, European ethologists began to promote the concept as central to their viewpoint. Ethology, a division of zoology, is broadly defined as the study of the relationship between organisms and their natural habitats. The details of this topic are interpreted somewhat differently, but the advocates stress instincts, or, in ethological terms, "species-specific" behavior, and seek to observe organisms throughout their life cycle. This last goal favors field rather than laboratory research, but since obtaining data on free-roaming animals is arduous, and sometimes impossible, substitute methods have to be devised. One of the more popular compromises is the rearing of animals in domestic situations while allowing them as much freedom as possible. An excerpt from a description of some of these procedures indicates that this autonomy could strain one's tolerance: "A tame rat to run free around the house, gnawing neat little circular pieces out of sheets to furnish her nests, which she built in even more awkward places than men's Sunday hats...a cockatoo who bit off all the buttons from the washing hung up to dry in the garden" (Lorenz, 1952, p. 1).

Ethologists modified the concept of instinct by characterizing it as a kind of reservoir of nervous impulses that is unblocked when a specialized stimulus pattern triggers an internal releasing mechanism. This is an improvement over prior formulations in that it accounts, at least logically, for a sequence of responses, and it also might explain why practice is not requisite for smooth, skilled action. It also underwrites the chance that instincts will be aroused only in appropriate circumstances. Probably the most important of all the features is the idea that an instinct involves a series of events because a succession of activities would allow opportunities for learning to modify instincts.

Ethologists became deeply involved in discovering the particular stimulus pattern for each instinct. Some of these searches—for what is called both a releaser and "sign stimuli"—are empirically based and others not. Tinbergen (1951), for example, describes the "sign stimuli" for the parental instinct in humans as a combination of characteristics of human infants as well as pets in a schematic figure that the film industry, "intending to meet man on the instinctive level," considers to be alluring (p. 209). The product is a sketch that depicts a short face, a high forehead, full cheeks, and "maladjusted limb movements" (p. 209).

Although much of their work has been with animals, the ethologists consider instincts to be influential in human affairs. There were even attempts to accommodate the doctrine to political ideology (Kalikow, 1978). Instinct is also injected into discussions of population density: "*Our individual and social need for space has been laid down by our phylogenetic history and is therefore a basic characteristic of the genus,* i.e., within certain limits it is an *immutable natural right''* (Lorenz & Leyhausen, 1973, p. 109).

Many psychologists are severely critical of ethology (Piel, 1970). Others, despite some reservations, are attracted by the doctrine because it appears natural, noncontrived. People of this persuasion have undertaken research on problems that ethologists favor, particularly those in which both learning and instinct might be involved (Hinde, 1970). One of these topics is imprinting, the attachment of the young to the first moving object they encounter. This is generally the mother, but imprinting on less appropriate targets also occurs, and some animals under hand-rearing have imprinted humans as well as objects. The study of this phenomenon includes bonding, the solidifying of a mutual attraction between mother and offspring. DeCasper and Fifer (1980) found, for example, that babies as young as three days learn to suckle a nonnutritive nipple in a temporal pattern that allows them to hear their own mother's headset-delivered voice rather than that of a stranger. The authors suggest that learning to discriminate the mother's voice at this very young age facilitates bonding.

The battles over instinct continue, and not only is there no resolution in sight, but there is a persistence of the overworked pattern of casting the arguments in an either-or frame, such as instinct versus no instinct, instinct versus learning, or instinct versus process. Attending to the antithesis strengthens the supporting evidence, but it also deflects attention away from what is transpiring, that is, away from analyses of behavior (Brown, 1979). Diamond (1974) concludes a review of "Four Hundred Years of Instinct Controversy" with an observation of what-should-be: "The enormous energies which have been expended in fighting about '*if*' could be directed toward the only real question, which is '*how*' " (p. 250).

References

Beach, F. A. (1955). The descent of instinct. *Psychological Review, 62,* 401–410. This history of the concept includes searching for "the reasons for the remarkable vitality of a concept which has stood without objective test for at least two millennia" (p. 401).

Bernard, L. L. (1924). *Instinct: A study in social psychology.* New York: Henry Holt.

Brown, J. S. (1979). Motivation. In E. Hearst (Ed.), *The first century of experimental psychology* (pp. 231–272). New York: Lawrence Erlbaum.

DeCasper, A. J., & Fifer, W. P. (1980). Of human bonding: Newborns prefer their mothers' voices. *Science, 208* (No. 4448), 1174–1176.

Diamond, S. (1974). Four hundred years of instinct controversy. *Behavior Genetics, 4* (3), 237–252. An insightful review of the appearances and reappearances of both pro- and anti-instinct arguments.

Dunlap, K. (1919). Are there any instincts? *Journal of Abnormal Psychology 14,* 307–311.

Hinde, R. A. (1970). *Animal behaviour: A synthesis of ethology and comparative psychology.* (2nd ed.). New York: McGraw-Hill.

Hodge, C. F. (1894). The method of homing pigeons. *The Popular Science Monthly,*
    44, 758–775. One sketch that was used in this investigation remains on the current
    scene as a single item on an intelligence test. A modification of Hodge's diagram
    is printed and the examinee is requested to trace the path that would be followed
    in order to locate a lost item.

James, W. (1908). *Psychology: Briefer course.* New York: Henry Holt. (Original work
    published 1892)

Joffe, J. M. (1973). The Peromyscus papers. *American Psychologist, 28*, 527–529. In-
    stincts and vitalism versus learning and mechanism are treated as a loyalist-
    insurgency conflict in an authoritarian state. The author is one of many who suggest
    that extremism has interfered with understanding.

Kalikow, T. J. (1978). Konrad Lorenz's "Brown Past": A reply to Alec Nisbitt [Review
    of *Konrad Lorenz: A biography*]. *Journal of the History of the Behavioral Sciences,*
    14, 173–179. Kalikow documents more interest in Nazism on Lorenz's part than
    his biographer discloses. Nisbitt's reply appears at the conclusion of Kalikow's
    review.

Kuo, Z. Y. (1931). The genesis of the cat's responses to the rat. *Journal of Comparative*
    Psychology, 11, 1–35.

Lorenz, K. (1952). *King Solomon's ring: New light on animal ways.* New York: Thomas
    Y. Crowell. A fascinating account of Lorenz's study of animals, written for a
    general audience.

Lorenz, K., & Leyhausen, P. (1973). *Motivation of human and animal behavior: An*
    ethological view (B. A. Tonkin, Trans.). New York: Van Nostrand Reinhold.

McDougall, W. (1912). *An introduction to social psychology* (6th ed.). Boston: John W.
    Luce. The first edition was published in 1908.

Piel, G. (1970). The comparative psychology of T. C. Schneirla. In L. R. Aronson, E.
    Tobach, D. S. Lehrman, & J. S. Rosenblatt (Eds.), *Development and evolution*
    of behavior: Essays in memory of T. C. Schneirla (pp. 1–13). San Francisco:
    W. H. Freeman. Schneirla was an articulate, sophisticated critic of ethology. This
    chapter capsules the reasons for his censure.

Tinbergen, N. (1951). *The study of instinct.* London: Oxford University Press.

Sources of Additional Information

Cardno, J. A. (1958). Instinct: Some pre-experimental landmarks. *Australian Journal of*
Psychology, 10 (3), 329–340. Cardno relates the definitions of instincts of some nine-
teenth-century scholars to popular definitions. Kalikow, T. J. (1975). History of Konrad
Lorenz's ethological theory, 1927–1939: The role of meta-theory, theory, anomaly and
new discoveries in a scientific "evolution." *Studies in History and Philosophy of Science,*
6 (4), 331–341. Kalikow, T. J. (1976). Konrad Lorenz's ethological theory, 1939–1943:
"Explanations" of human thinking, feeling, and behaviour. *Philosophy of the Social*
Sciences, 6, 15–34. Kantor, J. R. (1920). A functional interpretation of human instincts.
Psychological Review, 27, 50–72. A penetrating criticism of instincts, with attention to
their immaterial status. Keverne, E. B., Levy, F., Poindron, P., & Lindsay, D. R. (1983).
Vaginal stimulation: An important determinant of material bonding in sheep. *Science,*
219 (No. 4580), 81–83. This paper reports that stimulation induces "a state of plasticity
in maternal behavior" (p. 81). This is a departure from the traditional idea of immutable
instincts. Yerkes, R. M., & Bloomfield, D. (1910). Do kittens instinctively kill mice?
Psychological Bulletin, 7, 253–263. The authors conclude that there is an inborn force

to kill, but they also studied the environmental cues that elicit this instinct—an interesting combination of the innate and the learned.

INSTRUMENTAL CONDITIONING.   See CONDITIONING.

INTELLIGENCE.   1. General awareness, comprehension, understanding, and/ or cognizance. 2. A hypothetical mental force that is characterized as genetically transmitted, immune to experience, and limiting the maximum level of achievement. 3. Behavior that is said to be a product both of experience and of various postulated internal variables. 4. An attribute of behavior rather than of the person.

The concept of intelligence has acquired a surfeit of interpretations, but its unique characteristics have not been captured and much more has been said about the *way* in which intelligence functions than *what* it is. There have been at least four versions of the concept, and describing them is a lengthy process, but it is shortened a bit by the relative simplicity of the initial formulation.

This is amorphous in that intelligence is depicted as consciousness, as synonymous with apprehension, awareness, or, in some instances, the mind. The nuances of this cognizance are seldom elaborated, but one exception to this did occur during the incipience of comparative (animal) psychology. Darwin's then revolutionary proposal that animals and humans form a single continuum prompted searches, during the last half of the nineteenth century, for "animal intelligence," that is, for responses that are analogous to those humans make. Many were reported, but they were frequently described by anecdotes and in anthropomorphic terms with the facts unduly embellished. Insects, for example, were said to show affection. The lack of objectivity prompted more realistic descriptions, and as a part of this compliance the phrase "animal intelligence" was frequently replaced with the names of the actual tasks that the animals performed, such as "box stacking" and "maze learning" (Warden, Jenkins, & Warner, 1935).

Even though the second variety of the concept of intelligence is, scientifically, the least adequate of the four, it is by far the best known and is still defended by some psychologists. Its deficit is the interpretation of intelligence as an internal, impalpable power. Little is known about the nature of this power but paradoxically, some of its attributes are believed to be known. Intelligence is reputed, for example, to be inborn, to predetermine both the maximum level at which each person is able to perform and the intellectual efficiency that is typical of each individual throughout life. These and other specifications were used as guides in the construction of intelligence tests. The situation was most unusual in that researchers thought they understood the way an agent functioned even though they understood the agent only vaguely. This conceptual idiosyncrasy deflected attention away from intelligence in the direction of tests and this chronology makes it necessary to describe some of the details of the examinations before discussing the meaning of intelligence.

The first widely used method for measuring intelligence was devised by Alfred Binet, a French psychologist. With the assistance of a colleague, Théodore Simon, they constructed examinations, from 1905 through 1911, to use in identifying those children in the Paris schools who could not be expected to profit from education. Binet was interested in the relationships among various "psychical processes," and he also believed that intelligence could be most readily discerned in complex psychological responses. Thus he combined into single scales a number of different problems. This structure contrasted with the few tests that were then available in that it consists of heterogeneous items many of which resemble tasks that are encountered outside the testing situation, such as interpreting scenes that depict different interpersonal relationships, defining words, and enumerating the differences between a king and a president. Binet administered these items to each child individually, scoring each response as either right or wrong. He arranged the tests in order of difficulty and indicated the age level at which success was expected. These procedures came to be called age scaling (Wolf, 1973).

At the same time that Binet was working, Henry H. Goddard, an American, was looking for a means of ascertaining the level of development of hospitalized mentally retarded patients. Goddard (1908) traveled to Europe in search of help, discovered Binet's methods, perceived them as highly suitable for his own clinical needs, and introduced the scales into this country. His enthusiasm was picked up by Edmund B. Huey, Fred Kuhlmann, and Lewis M. Terman, and these four psychologists became the dominant figures in the compilation of age scales, both for adults and for children (Popplestone & McPherson, 1984).

These leaders had been fellow graduate students at Clark University, where G. Stanley Hall, the president and stellar professor, taught the theory of recapitulation, a doctrine that emphasized a predetermined progression in development (Ross, 1972). Hall was only incidentally interested in the nature of intelligence, and his students appear to have followed this pattern in that they attended much more to the structure than to the content of the examinations. They worked assiduously at improving the Binet scales, and in doing so they searched for individual test items that can be passed without any specialized training as well as for ones that regularly increase in difficulty from age level to age level. The concern with the placement of tests made it necessary to examine individually a large number of subjects and to select them so that they represent the population at large and thus provide a norm or standard level of performance. In other words, the emphasis was on population sampling rather than on behavioral sampling. The extent of the slighting of intellectual behavior is illustrated in the method Terman used to locate words for use on a vocabulary test. The words that he chose were obtained not from observations of the spontaneous speech of individuals, but by taking a sample of entries from a dictionary and arranging them in the order of accuracy with which the subjects defined them (Terman & Childs, 1912).

Shortly after Binet devised age scaling Stern (1912/1914), a German psychologist, advocated relating the examinee's level of intelligence to his or her age, specifically dividing the mental age, a quantification of responses to test items, by the chronological age, a quantification of time. This index, or intelligence quotient (IQ), was intended to quantify the "degree" of intelligence. Its potential for predicting the development at maturity was so appealing that Goddard and his co-workers endorsed it and overlooked the invalidity of using a fraction in which the denominator and numerator are qualitatively different.

A second approach to testing started at about the same time as age scaling and is generally credited to Carl Spearman (1904), a British psychologist, whose contributions mainly consist of devising statistical procedures that identify tests in which the scores tend to agree with one another as well as those that tend to stand alone. He assumed that the former measured a "fundamental function," that is, general intelligence, or simply g, and that it is an innate power that is responsible for the intellectual rank of any particular individual within a group. Spearman characterized the unrelated scores as measures of specific functions, or simply s, and assumed that these are modified by experience. Spearman's procedures were elaborated by various successors, and the statistical technique of factor analysis became an accepted procedure in research on intelligence.

It was not until age scaling and factor analysis were both well under way that psychologists seriously undertook the task of conceptualizing just what they were measuring. Unfortunately neither the heterogeneous tests nor their statistical manipulations were of assistance in clarifying the nature of intelligence. The definitions were linguistically extravagant and very limited in meaning. The deficits are illustrated in excerpts from the responses of a group of psychologists who responded in 1921 to a request to define intelligence. Peterson proposed: "A biological mechanism by which the effects of a complexity of stimuli are brought together and given a somewhat unified effect in behavior" (1921, p. 198). Thurstone stated: "Intelligence is the capacity to inhibit instinctive behavior in an unfinished stage of its formation and to modify it at that stage by means of an imaginal stimulus which is relatively remote from that which is immediately and perceptually present" (1921, p. 204). Woodrow saw intelligence as more constrained, and his nomination of "an acquiring-capacity" gained more approval than many others (1921, p. 207).

The third concept of intelligence represents a transition between the traditional one and the most modern version in that it combines an internalized force with more scientifically acceptable ingredients. An example is a concept devised by Anastasi. First, she notes that the word intelligence actually represents behavior, criticizes the prevalent ignoring of this fact, and allocates a formative role to the history of the individual. She disdains the "strange notion of 'innate intelligence,' " but at the same time retains a mechanism of internal control: "What the individual inherits is not intelligence . . . but certain chemical substances which . . . lead eventually to different degrees of intelligent behavior" (1967, p. 301).

A transitional definition is also advocated by David Wechsler, a proficient and prodigious psychometrist, who, from 1939 through 1981, compiled and revised the most commonly used scales of intelligence (Matarazzo, 1972; Wechsler, 1981). Components from two sources are clearly apparent in Wechsler's concept. In a 1975 address entitled "Intelligence Defined and Undefined" he stated: "Actually, intelligence is *an aspect of behavior* [italics added]; it has to do primarily with the appropriateness, effectiveness, and worthwhileness of what human beings do or want to do" (1975, p. 135). He concluded with a statement of what intelligence tests measure, and in this he reverts to the traditional idea of predetermination: "The *capacity* [italics added] of an individual to understand the world about him and his resourcefulness to cope with its challenges" (1975, p. 139).

Wechsler's method of test construction is called point scaling and it is different in several respects from age scaling. IQs are computed by means of a formula in which the numerator and denominator are homogeneous in that the subject's score is divided by the mean score for the subject's age group. The IQs are, however, treated statistically in a manner that is consonant with the innate capacity component of the definition, specifically in a way that increases the probability of obtaining an equivalent score on reexamination. Each scale consists of ten or eleven different sections of similar tasks, with the individual items scored not as either correct or incorrect, but in terms of the level of accuracy. The different kinds of tasks include a series of arithmetic problems, requests to deal with analogies, and inquiries that tap general information. The content is diverse, and as a result, point scales are no more effective than age scales in bringing the properties of intelligence to light.

The fourth and last concept depicts intelligence as an attribute of behavior rather than of the individual. In this orientation, intelligence is seen as a qualification, an endorsement of what a person does. Descriptions of this kind of concept frequently start with a reminder that the prior formulations are based on artifacts. J. R. Kantor, the protagonist of INTERBEHAVIORAL PSYCHOLOGY, is an advocate of intelligence as behavior, and as early as the academic year 1916–1917, in a seminar at the University of Minnesota, he asserted: "Now when we study intelligence as an observed fact we never find any absolute essence or faculty performing unique kinds of activities" (1920, p. 261).

Chein writes in a similar view: "No psychologist has ever observed *intelligence*; many have observed intelligent behavior. This observation should be the starting point of any theory of intelligence, but such has, unfortunately, not been the case" (1945, p. 111). He continues: "No amount of abstracting from behavior will, however, bring us to a capacity or an ability" (1945, p. 114). Wesman concurs: "We have all too often behaved as though intelligence is a physical substance . . . we might better remember that it is no more to be reified than attributes like beauty, or speed, or honesty" (1968, p. 267).

The innovative component in these last formulations is the featuring of a behavioral repertoire, unrestrained by any internal agent. Biological adequacy is considered a requisite for intelligent behavior, and when it is within normal limits it is believed to contribute much less to individual differences than do variations in experience. Wesman states: ''We start with an organism which is subject to modification by interaction with the environment; as a product of that interaction, the organism has been modified. Further interaction involves a changed organism—one which is ready to interact with its environment in a new way'' (1968, p. 267).

Definitions of this genre do not have to contend with the problems of identifying the basic function or functions of intelligence for the obvious reason that intelligence is dismissed as nonsubstantive. In this frame of reference the psychologist has the task of specifying serviceable responses. These tangible phenomena are both scientifically creditable and amenable to education, to manipulation. The concept of intelligence as an evaluation of behavior also obviates questions about overall racial, cultural, and sexual superiority and inferiority. Answering a question of this nature demands comparing specific skills or efficiency on different tasks, with a rearrangement of the rankings of various samples of the population expected for each comparison.

References

Anastasi, A. (1967). Psychology, psychologists, and psychological testing. *American Psychologist, 22*, 297–306. This is Anastasi's presidential address to the Division and Evaluation and Measurement of the American Psychological Association. She notes that test constructors have become so involved in refining their techniques that they are slighting the behavior they purport to measure.

Chein, I. (1945). On the nature of intelligence. *Journal of General Psychology, 32*, 111–126.

Goddard, H. H. (1908). The Binet and Simon tests of intellectual capacity. *Training School, 5*, 3–9.

Kantor, J. R. (1920). Intelligence and mental tests. *The Journal of Philosophy Psychology and Scientific Methods, 17*, 260–268.

Matarazzo, J. D. (1972). *Wechsler's measurement and appraisal of adult intelligence* (5th ed). Baltimore: Williams & Wilkins. This is a revision of Wechsler's 4th or 1958 revision of the volume first published in 1939. Matarazzo includes a chapter, ''The Definition of Intelligence: An Unending Search.''

Peterson, J. (1921). Intelligence and its measurement: A symposium. *Journal of Educational Psychology, 12*, 198–201.

Popplestone, J. A., & McPherson, M. W. (1984). Pioneer psychological laboratories in clinical settings. In J. Brozek (Ed.), *Explorations in the history of psychology in the United States* (pp. 196–272). Lewisburg, PA: Bucknell University Press.

Ross, D. (1972) *G. Stanley Hall: The psychologist as prophet.* Chicago: University of Chicago Press. Hall was very active in psychology, both in the organization and in the substance of the discipline. He was a transitional figure in that his theories were linked both to outmoded concepts as well as to prescient ideas about growth.

Spearman, C. (1904). ''General intelligence'' objectively determined and measured. *American Journal of Psychology, 15*, 201–293. Spearman holds the unusual belief that the influence of ''general intelligence'' is deferred until the ninth year.

Stern, W. (1914). *The psychological methods of testing intelligence* (G. M. Whipple, Trans.). Baltimore: Warwick & York. (Original work published 1912)

Terman, L. M., & Childs, H. G. (1912). A tentative revision and extension of the Binet-Simon measuring scale of intelligence, Part II. Supplementary tests continued. *Journal of Educational Psychology, 3,* 198–208.

Thurstone, L. L. (1921). Intelligence and its measurement: A symposium. *Journal of Educational Psychology, 12,* 201–207.

Warden, C. J., Jenkins, T. N. & Warner, L. H. (1935). *Comparative psychology: A comprehensive treatise. Principles and methods* (Vol. 1). New York: Ronald Press.

Wechsler, D. (1975). Intelligence defined and undefined: A relativistic appraisal. *American Psychologist, 30,* 135–139.

Wechsler, D. (1981). *The Wechsler Adult Intelligence Scale—Revised.* New York: Psychological Corporation. This revision of the adult test was printed in the year of Wechsler's death.

Wesman, A. G. (1968). Intelligent testing. *American Psychologist, 23,* 267–274. Wesman places much of the responsibility for the traditional concept of intelligence on factor analysis. His terminology is novel and strong. For example, factor analysis is described "not so much as mathematicodeductive as mathematico*se*ductive." In reference to the statistical sophistication he comments: "We need not believe that the power of the tool assures the validity of the product" (p. 272).

Wolf, T. H. (1973). *Alfred Binet.* Chicago: University of Chicago Press. This is a comprehensive, intellectual biography of Alfred Binet.

Woodrow, H. (1921). Intelligence and its measurement: A symposium. *Journal of Educational Psychology, 12,* 207–210.

Sources of Additional Information

Boring, E. G. (1923). Intelligence as the tests test it. *The New Republic, 34,* 35–36. This brief article is famous for the statement "Intelligence is what the tests test" (p. 35). This is interpreted by some as an example of valid operationism and by others as a statement of insoluble confusion. Cattell, J. McK. (1890). Mental tests and measurements. *Mind, 15,* 373–381. This is a classic paper. Its author coined the phrase "mental tests," and in the early days of tests, Cattell's label was used more often than 'intelligence tests.' Kamin, L. J. (1974). *The science and politics of I.Q.* New York: John Wiley. This book explores the reasons why the genetic viewpoint is so widely held. Kamin's criticisms are penetrating and involve careful assessment of the research literature. Kurzweil, R. (1985). What is artificial intelligence anyway? *American Scientist, 13,* 258–264. An objective discussion written for the educated layman of the similarities and differences between intelligent behavior and computers. Piaget, J. (1952). *The origins of intelligence in children.* (M. Cook, Trans.). New York: International Universities Press. This is an interpretation by a famous child psychologist of the nature of intelligence. The theory is based on meticulous observations and astute insight into how a child develops an intellectual repertoire, but for Piaget, the role of experience is limited by a programmed biology. The vocabulary is complex and at points idiosyncratic.

INTERBEHAVIORAL PSYCHOLOGY. See STIMULUS FUNCTION, RESPONSE FUNCTION, and INTERBEHAVIORAL PSYCHOLOGY.

INTROSPECTION. 1. Self-examination, the ordinary procedures of looking inward, contemplating any or all aspects of consciousness, including thoughts, moods, and emotions. 2. An intricate, formal research procedure for observing in meticulous detail the minutiae of awareness. 3. Self-observation during an experiment for the purpose of augmenting information relevant to the topic under investigation.

Introspection is an ancient and familiar activity as well as an important component of various formal intellectual enterprises. Numerous philosophers have acknowledged the importance of self-knowledge and in doing so have defined it in various ways. "Know thyself" and "I think, therefore I am" attest to the attention that the activity commands.

In the latter part of the nineteenth century psychologists adopted introspection as an appropriate laboratory procedure. It was used at the University of Leipzig in Germany, the location of one of the pioneer research laboratories, and its founder, Wilhelm Wundt (1832–1920), was among the first experimental psychologists to apply the method. There is some evidence that he doubted its usefulness (Blumenthal, 1977), but what is certain is the endorsement of the technique by Edward B. Titchener, one of Wundt's students and a figure who dominated psychology at Cornell University, one of the larger American centers of graduate education in psychology from 1892 to 1927. Titchener elaborated the theory of STRUCTURAL PSYCHOLOGY, a system that sought to identify the fundamental elements or units that make up the mind and to learn the ways in which they are connected. Because this information is accessible only to the experiencing individual, introspection was ipso facto the most suitable investigative procedure. The phenomena of experience or awareness were analyzed by trained laboratory personnel, and in this role they were called observers. The limitation on who could procure data was believed to be compensated, to some degree at least, by the direct accessibility of consciousness to observers. Titchener realized that if introspection were to meet the laboratory requirements of consistency and thoroughness, it had to be systematic. He undertook the task of refining procedures, and he tuned the method to a level that made it highly artificial and esoteric. As a result of this honing, the term introspection acquired a new and specific meaning (Titchener, 1912a, 1912b, 1912c).

Observers were taught to focus on their ongoing conscious experiences, to exclude attention to stimuli, and even to ignore the meaning of the experiences to which they were attending. They were forbidden to use words that refer to external objects or events, and were ordered to describe their awareness in terms of certain specified attributes. The technique is very different from the familiar process of self-examination, and it acquired such qualifiers as "trained," "classical," "systematic," "experimental," and even "systematic experimental."

Becoming a skilled introspectionist demands intensive and protracted practice. One recurring mistake is called the stimulus error, a reporting of what causes the experience rather than describing it. To say, for example, that illumination disappears when an incandescent bulb is turned off is an account of what is known, not of what is sensed. The introspectionists would correctly indicate that the brightness moves back from a focal point while decreasing both in intensity and in size. To describe exploding fireworks as "vivid" is also erroneous inasmuch as the sensation is dim and the clarity is merely an impression that is derived from the surrounding darkness. An observer who admits being "puzzled" signals the existence of a predicament but neglects "the observer's individual experience . . . the particular 'feels' that constituted the perplexity" (Titchener, 1912a, pp. 167–168). Laboratory notebooks were filled with accounts of such matters as the duration of a state of unpleasantness; the intensity of a sensation of pressure; the fusion or separation of experiences of touch; the size, brightness, and duration of visual afterimages; the changes in the volume of a tone of ascending pitch; and the presence of musical overtones.

In some experiments awareness was systematically stimulated by means of instruments. Observers, for example, might use an olfactometer, an instrument that delivers odors directly into the nostrils. In research on color, papers of different hues were placed on a color wheel and rotated so rapidly that only a single color is seen. Pure tones of different frequencies were produced by lamellae, strips of steel that vibrate slowly, and by tuning forks—electrical, mechanical, hand-held, mounted on wooden bases of various sizes.

Titchener was convinced that psychologists could, by means of introspection, obtain unobstructed views of the human mind, and those who concurred were prone to use the words introspectionist and psychologist synonymously. This identity was, however, far from universal, and many psychologists began to see these probes of the units of experience as artificial, devoid of meaning, ignoring unconsciousness, and, on occasion, yielding inconsistent results (Boring, 1953). They began to bend the rules of introspection, primarily at first by soliciting retrospective observations and attending to stimuli. A quotation from a research report on the changes in blood circulation during sleep illustrates the extent of the heresy: "A careful introspective report was taken from the subject after every experiment, and usually whenever he awoke during an experiment. He was asked to tell how he *seemed to have slept* [italics added], whether he remembered anything of disturbances, *stimuli* [italics added] or any previous awakenings, and what he could *recall* [italics added] of dreams" (Shepard, 1914, p. 9).

Psychologists not only failed to practice what Titchener prescribed, but a few also impugned the notion of "systematic experimental" introspection. Ruckmich, for example, suggested that the reliance on introspection might contribute to the low status of psychology as a science (1912). Dunlap was more explicit: "There is, as a matter of fact, not the slightest evidence for the reality of 'introspection' as the observation of 'consciousness' " (1912, p. 412).

Titchener's staunchest and most articulate defender conceded that introspection went "out of style" after 1927, the year of Titchener's death (Boring, 1953, p. 174). Boring's choice of words is apt because the censure of introspection was not fatal in that self-observations did not disappear from the research scene, but survived even the condemnation that came early in the 19th century, when BEHAVIORISM proclaimed that behavior is the only suitable research topic. Watson (1913), the most vocal and unrestrained advocate of this system, announced that he failed to discern any merit in introspection, but merely one year later he wrote that research participants might "state in words whether a given stimulus is present or absent" (Watson, 1914, p. 14). He denied that this was a form of introspection, and identified it as "the *language method* in behavior" (1914, p. 15). In 1919 he included "the verbal report method" in an inventory of research methods in psychology.

The label verbal report has endured, but these descriptions are those of *subjects* rather than of *observers*, and they vary from formal introspection in that they are more often accounts of a conclusion or an impression than descriptions of awareness. The segments of consciousness that are described are varied. Some are the same as those in the early days of PSYCHOPHYSICS in that observers report brief episodes, such as indicating that a weight is heavier or lighter than a standard or that a skin sensation is felt as one or two points of stimulation. In more recent experiments subjects announce the presence or absence of visual stimuli in VIGILANCE research, advise when brief visual exposures are sensed as a number of stored units (Sperling, 1960), or discriminate between gastric motility and hunger pangs (Stunkard & Koch, 1964).

Many verbal reports contrast with these announcements in that they cover larger segments of experience. To illustrate—Festinger (1958) used subjects' verbal assessments of the laboratory procedures as one factor in interpreting the strength of their motivation. Blindfolded individuals learning how the sightless avoid obstacles inform experimenters that they tried to follow the practice of the blind by learning to listen for reflected sounds (Supa, Cotzin, & Dallenbach, 1944). These accounts are not solicited under the rigid rules of trained intro-spection, and they are not servants of theory, but they are designed to promote the goals of particular investigations, to increase the information obtained in experiments.

During the 1950s a significant number of psychologists began to express concern that their predecessors had too summarily dismissed implicit behavior. Both COGNITIVE PSYCHOLOGY and the HUMAN POTENTIAL MOVEMENT began to devote attention to subjective experiences, and even assigned private events paramount importance. The word introspection reappeared, but its use was un-accompanied by the Titchenerian ritual. The modified method is now being endorsed by an increasing number of researchers, but the prior condemnation of introspection has not entirely disappeared. Current writers often display what may be called a wary appreciation. They no longer argue merely for or against introspection, but point out both strengths and weaknesses. The assets that are mentioned include the importance and uniqueness of conscious experiences as well as their potential to bring to light information that would otherwise be missed. The deficits that are discussed include the probability that formulating verbal reports or introspections may distort cognitive processes, complaints that it is difficult to confirm or substantiate verbal data, and observations that giving verbal reports may detract from efforts to attend to experience per se. Many of the problems of the structural laboratory are again on stage (Ericsson & Simon, 1980; Nisbett & Wilson, 1977; Radford, 1974).

References

Blumenthal, A. L. (1977). Wilhelm Wundt and early American psychology: A clash of two cultures. In R. W. Rieber & K. Salzinger (Eds.), The roots of American psychology: Historical influences and implications for the future. *Annals of the New York Academy of Sciences, 291* (pp. 13–20.)

Boring, E. G. (1953). A history of introspection. *Psychological Bulletin, 50*, 169–189. Boring's loyalty to Titchener may color his interpretation of the importance of the Cornell University laboratory.

Dunlap, K. (1912). The case against introspection. *Psychological Review, 19*, 404–412. Dunlap's role in the evolution of behaviorism and his influence on Watson are equivocal, and no convincing documentation of their relationship has been located. This paper antedates the first Watson proclamation (1913) and suggests that Dunlap's thinking was syntonic with that of Watson.

Ericsson, K. A. & Simon, H. A. (1980). Verbal reports as data. *Psychological Review, 87*, 215–251. A prolonged, and at times labored, discussion of an information-processing model for cognition. There are specific suggestions concerning uniform procedures for obtaining verbal reports.

Festinger, L. (1958). The motivating effect of cognitive dissonance. In G. Lindzey (Ed.), *Assessment of human motives* (pp. 65–86). New York: Grove Press.

Nisbett, R. E., & Wilson, T. D. (1977). Telling more than we can know: Verbal reports on mental processes. *Psychological Review, 84*, 231–259. A discussion of cognitive events that includes introspection. The paper suggests that accurate reports are contingent on the salience and plausibility of the thought content.

Radford, J. (1974). Reflections on introspection. *American Psychologist, 29*, 245–250. Reviews the history and current status of both the criticisms and endorsements of introspection and calls for a truce.

Ruckmich, C. A. (1912). The history and status of psychology in the United States. *American Journal of Psychology, 23*, 517–531. An example of the criticisms of classical introspection that occurred even during its heyday.

Shepard, J. F. (1914). *The circulation and sleep: Experimental investigations accompanied by an atlas.* New York: Macmillan.

Sperling, G. (1960). The information available in brief visual presentations. *Psychological Monographs, 74* (Whole No. 498).

Stunkard, A., & Koch, C. (1964). The interpretation of gastric motility: 1. Apparent bias in the reports of hunger by obese persons. *Archives of General Psychiatry, 11*, 74–82. The scrutiny and analysis of inner states are now components of behavioral medicine.

Supa, M., Cotzin, M., & Dallenbach, K. M. (1944). "Facial vision"; the perception of obstacles by the blind. *American Journal of Psychology, 57*, 133–183. This is a report of a research program carried out at Cornell. Pure introspection was not practiced, but alertness to consciousness served admirably in the analysis of how obstacles are avoided.

Titchener, E. B. (1912a). Description vs. statement of meaning. *American Journal of Psychology, 23*, 165–182.

Titchener, E. B. (1912b). Prolegomena to a study of introspection. *American Journal of Psychology, 23*, 427–448.

Titchener, E. B. (1912c). The schema of introspection. *American Journal of Psychology, 23*, 485–508.

Watson, J. B. (1913). Psychology as the behaviorist views it. *Psychological Review, 20*, 158–177. A classic paper. Introspection and a variety of other topics are repudiated.

Watson, J. B. (1914). *Behavior: An introduction to comparative psychology.* New York: Holt.

Watson, J. B. (1919). *Psychology from the standpoint of a behaviorist.* Philadelphia: J. B. Lippincott. Watson includes a defense of the "verbal report method" in this book.

Sources of Additional Information

Bakan, D. (1954). A reconsideration of the problem of introspection. *Psychological Bulletin, 51*, 105–118. A humanistic psychologist advocates conceding that introspection has "considerable value" for modern psychology. This is one of the early briefs in the revival of the method. DeSilva, H. R. (1930). The common sense of introspection. *Psychological Review, 37*, 71–87. The date of this article coincides with the triumphant era of behaviorism, but the content is more closely aligned with writings in the 1970s. The author elaborates on the yield from introspection when it is not encumbered with ritual. Henle, M. (1971). Did Titchener commit the stimulus error: The problem of meaning in structural psychology. *Journal of the History of the Behavioral Sciences, 7*, 279–282. A sophisticated article suggesting that the master may not have personally met the rigors of classical introspection. Moore, J. (1980). On behaviorism and private events. *The Psychological Record, 30*, 459–476. The author relates introspection and operant behaviorism.

L

LEARNED HELPLESSNESS. 1. The giving in to discouragement, the withholding of effort because of the expectation of being unable to influence the outcome of events.

Learned helplessness is a recently formulated concept, and the phenomenon is believed to be the result of exposures to distressing stimuli under conditions that do not allow either deflecting or stopping them. The adversity is generally thought to result from failure, from being victimized, or from a combination of the two. These two kinds of misfortune are experientially similar but they vary in the way in which they are interpreted. Frequently the responsibility for failure is ascribed to the failing person, whereas a victim is generally considered not to contribute significantly to the difficulty, as in the case, for example, of bereavement, being a hostage, and being unable to obtain employment in a depressed job market.

For quite some time psychologists have been aware of the maleffects of enervation in both animals and humans, but systematic study was neglected until the mid-1960s. Bettelheim, for example, reported that COPING characterized the reactions of only a few inmates in Nazi concentration camps, and he observed a high incidence of inertia. He pointed out that this resignation indicated that the guards did accomplish their aim *"to break the prisoners as individuals* and to change them into docile masses from which no individual or group act of resistance could arise" (1943, p. 418).

Students of CLASSICAL CONDITIONING have known for a long time that using shock as an unconditioned stimulus in animal research retards, or even prevents, conditioning. In a study of reactions to FRUSTRATION N. R. F. Maier (1949) found that rats cease trying to solve a problem when the circumstances do not allow them to make satisfactory response but they are nonetheless forced to respond. Richter (1959) reported that under life-threatening situations, contrived in the laboratory, rats simply give up struggling and succumb.

A research program on learned helplessness began in 1967 (Overmier & Seligman; Seligman & Maier). In the initial experiments observations were made of dogs' reactions to aversive stimuli, both when irritants could and could not be avoided. In one design, for example, exposures to unpleasant, but not harmful, electric shock were followed by putting the animals in apparatus so constructed that they could escape the current if they learned to jump over a barrier immediately on perceiving a signal that preceded the onset of the electricity. The dogs that in the first part of the experiment had been able to get away from the shock learned quite readily to jump out of the charged area. In contrast, animals that had not been able to avoid the shock initially made little effort to find ways to prevent it, and they merely passively waited. Their resignation is described as "learned" because the crucial factor in determining whether or not an animal behaves in a helpless manner appears to be personal experiences of vulnerability.

A relinquishing of effort similar to that observed in dogs was established experimentally in other species, including cats, birds, and primates. Learned helplessness was first reported in humans by Thornton and Jacobs (1971), but the design was criticized because it is not comparable to the prior animal work. By 1974 this had been rectified, and more satisfactory analogues between the learned helplessness of animals and humans were in use (Abramson, Seligman, & Teasdale, 1978). The interest in the phenomenon in people is high, but the experiments on humans do not involve the extreme duress that is found in some animal research, and, the indices of helplessness are typically a reduction in the speed of response or a diminution of effort. The experimental manipulations also fail to replicate the insurmountable barriers that characterize some living situations. These differences make it impossible to demonstrate experimentally that learned helplessness is responsible for such social and psychiatric problems as insufficient initiative, work shyness, and failure to plan. But this lack of evidence does not obviate the features that are common to socioeconomic deprivation and the laboratory conditions in which a sense of uselessness is experienced.

Much of the research on learned helplessness in humans includes the concept of locus of control. This concept deals with an individual's ideas about the source of power over both negative and positive events, ranging from those with very mild consequences through those that produce momentous results. Two contrasting convictions are described: opinion that power is external in the sense that it is in the hands of individuals other than the self, and opinion that it is internal in that the self is believed to be able to influence the outcome of events. In the professional jargon an individual who holds the former belief is referred to as "external" and one who holds the latter is called an "internal" (Lefcourt, 1966).

Hiroto (1974) illustrates one method of incorporating locus of control into an experiment. He classified each of the undergraduate subjects whom he observed as either "external" or "internal." He then exposed all participants to episodes of a very loud noise, and allowed some subjects to terminate the sound, but denied others relief from this unpleasant, inescapable stimulation. After these experiences all subjects were confronted with a tone that could be silenced. Some were told that learning how to do this was essentially a guessing game, whereas others were told that it was possible to shut off the noise, but that each participant must independently learn how to do this. The results disclosed that the speed and efficiency of learning to terminate the sound was impaired under each of the following conditions: having no control over the noise in the first situation, believing that terminating the tone was a chance event, and believing that power is externally controlled.

Hiroto and Seligman (1975) demonstrated that learned helplessness is not the result of a particular kind of experience. They exposed one group of participants to a loud noise, allowing some to shut it off but not permitting others to do so. They also asked subjects to solve a series of visual discrimination problems, some solvable and others insolvable. These manageable-unmanageable experiences were then followed by measures of efficiency in two additional tasks. The results disclosed that learned helplessness followed exposures to both inescapable noise and unworkable problems.

Experiments also disclose that decrements in performance are not inevitable and a belief in an internal locus of control often is often used as an explanatory factor in these conclusions. To illustrate, Cohen, Rothbart, and Phillips (1976) informed some undergraduate subjects who were under an impression that they were taking a test of spatial reasoning ability, that they were accurate each time they made a correct response, whereas others were informed that they were correct only on a random basis. The effects of this difference in praise were measured by comparing the performance of these two groups in two tasks. One measured efficiency in dealing with discrepancies between color names and colors, for example, identifying instances in which the name of color that the printed word specifies is different from the color of the print. The second task was a problem in reasoning in which subjects were requested to trace a series of line diagrams without going over any line more than once or without lifting the pencil. In some diagrams this was possible and in others it was not. The subjects who were informed of their accuracy only on a chance basis were, as predicted, less adequate in managing the problems, but only those who believed that the control of events was outside themselves were impaired on the efficiency tests. Belief in efficacy of the self apparently wards off a sense of futility, at least to some extent.

Additional variables that are aligned with learned helplessness continue to be investigated. In 1978 Abramson et al. reviewed the relevant literature, and also pursued the implications of different personal explanations of why inertia develops. They enumerate some of the consequences for both internal and external subjects, separated into those who believe that the causative agent is stable or unstable as well as global or specific. These decisions appears to determine whether a sense of debilitation is episodic or chronic and whether it extends over a broad or a narrow range of tasks. There are numerous disserviceable ramifications of these explanations and they color responses in at least three areas. One example in each follows. One sphere is motivation where the ineffectiveness leads to a reduction in initiative. The second is cognition where the vulnerability underwrites increased difficulty in realizing that one's efforts can, under favorable circumstances, turn the tide. The third domain is emotion where the lack of force nourishes depression.

In order to understand the incomplete, inclusive nature of the information about the concept, the reader is advised of recently acquired information about a previously unrecognized, but nonetheless effective factor. This surfaced in animal research that is designed to elucidate variables related to drug abuse. In one experiment Siegel, Hinson, Krank, and McCully (1982) compared rats that had no history of drug consumption with ones that had been injected with gradually increasing amounts of heroin. Some of these animals were given lethal doses in the same room in which smaller portions had been administered, but others received the very strong doses in an area not associated with the drug intake. The drug-inexperienced rats had a higher mortality rate than the drug-experienced animals, and there were more survivals among those that received the life-threatening amounts in the same area in which weaker doses were administered. The authors suggest that a familiarity with the assaultive agent and with the environment in which the insurmountable is encountered strengthens the organisms' resistance. The spectrum of variables that alter resignation is yet to be detailed.

References

Abramson, L. Y., Seligman, M. E. P., & Teasdale, J. D. (1978). Learned helplessness in humans: Critique and reformulation. *Journal of Abnormal Psychology, 87*, 49–74.

Bettelheim, B. (1943). Individual and mass behavior in extreme situations. *Journal of Abnormal and Social Psychology, 38*, 417–452. The author was a political prisoner in both Dachau and Buchenwald. He defended himself against disintegration by maintaining an intellectual approach—by concentrating on understanding what was happening to the prisoners, by trying to play the role of an observer rather than merely that of a victim.

Cohen, S., Rothbart, M., & Phillips, S. (1976). Locus of control and the generality of learned helplessness in humans. *Journal of Personality and Social Psychology, 34*, 1049–1056.

Hiroto, D. S. (1974). Locus of control and learned helplessness. *Journal of Experimental Psychology, 102*, 187–193.

Hiroto, D. S., & Seligman, M. E. P. (1975). Generality of learned helplessness in man. *Journal of Personality and Social Psychology, 31*, 311–327.

Lefcourt, H. M. (1966). Internal versus external control of reinforcement: A review. *Psychological Bulletin, 65*, 206–220. The author traces the continuity between Alfred Adler's concept of "striving for superiority" and the theory of locus of control. His account of the development of this concept is authoritative and thorough.

Maier, N. R. F. (1949). *Frustration: The study of behavior without a goal.* New York: McGraw-Hill.

Overmier, J. B., & Seligman, M. E. P. (1967). Effects of inescapable shock upon subsequent escape and avoidance responding. *Journal of Comparative and Physiological Psychology, 63,* 28–33.

Richter, C. P. (1959). The phenomenon of unexplained sudden death in animals and man. In H. Feifel (Ed.), *The meaning of death* (pp. 302–313). New York: McGraw-Hill. The editor's introduction to this volume emphasizes the importance of time in psychological phenomena: "In chemistry and physics, a 'fact' is always determined by events which have preceded it; in human beings, present behavior is dependent not only on the past but even more potently, perhaps, by orientation toward *future* events" (p. xiv).

Seligman, M. E. P., & Maier, S. F. (1967). Failure to escape traumatic shock. *Journal of Experimental Psychology, 74,* 1–9.

Siegel, S., Hinson, R. E., Krank, M. D., & McCully, J. (1982). Heroin "overdose" death: Contribution of drug-associated environmental cues. *Science, 216* (No. 4544), 436–437. The researchers describe their design as one of conditioning. Some would argue this point. What is important is the attempt to understand the failures of tolerance. These appear to involve nonpharmacological factors. "Many experienced drug users die after a dose that should not be fatal in view of their tolerance" (p. 436).

Thornton, J. W., & Jacobs, P. D. (1971). Learned helplessness in human subjects. *Journal of Experimental Psychology, 87,* 367–372. This first experiment in which humans were observed has a complex design. It involves shocking subjects at varying levels of intensity and relating these variations to shock avoidance behavior.

Sources of Additional Information

Adler, A. (1927). *Understanding human nature* (W. B. Wolfe, Trans.). Garden City, NY: Garden City Publishing. The concept of learned helplessness resonates with Adler's well-known views about human ineptness: "Man, seen from the standpoint of nature, is an inferior organism. This feeling of his inferiority and insecurity is constantly present in his consciousness . . . forces him to seek situations in which the disadvantages of the human status in the scheme of life will be obviated and minimized" (p. 29). Cole, C. S., & Coyne, J. C. (1977). Situational specificity of laboratory-induced learned helplessness. *Journal of Abnormal Psychology, 86,* 615–623. This study reports the effects of escapable-inescapable noise on later anagram performance, both in the original and in a different situation. Cole and Coyne found less debilitation than other researchers do. Dweck, C. S., & Reppucci, N. D. (1973). Learned helplessness and reinforcement responsibility in children. *Journal of Personality and Social Psychology, 25,* 109–116. The subjects are fifth-grade children. Initially they were allowed to succeed in the presence of one experimenter and to fail in the presence of a second. Later, when the problems were solvable, a number of children tended not to pursue those administered by the previously failing experimenter. The decrements were most marked in children who were prone not to take personal responsibility and, if they did, to attribute more importance to ability than to effort. Glass, D. C., & Singer, J. E. (1972). *Urban stress: Experiments on noise and social stressors.* New York: Academic Press. This volume reports research on the effects of noise on behavior, an important variable in urban living. The results indicated that the most deleterious impairments in both cognitive tests and tolerance for frustration came from aperiodic and unsignaled sound. Seligman, M. E. P. (1975). *Helplessness: On depression, development, and death*. San Francisco: W. H. Freeman. A book-length account of the concept by one of the pioneer researchers.

LEARNING. 1. Acquiring knowledge and skills as the result of experience.

All species learn, often by similar methods, but what is learned ranges from the simplicity of a single-cell organism learning to avoid light to the complexity of a sophisticated human becoming familiar with the technology of the Middle Ages by drawing abstract inferences from a bank of relevant, but incomplete and clouded facts. The experimental evidence indicates that an infant learns to stand and maintain balance in essentially the same way that an adult acrobat learns to stand and maintain balance on a tightrope. The means of acquiring knowledge of what is honest seems to be virtually the same as the means of acquiring knowledge of what is dishonest.

Learning is such a complex matter that psychologists have tended to slight concise definitions in favor of enumerating specifications about it. One of these identifies learning as persistent, and the assigning of this property differentiates it from short-term changes in behavior that come from boredom, fatigue or illness.

A second qualification affirms the dependence of learning on experience. This connotes practice, and this exercise calls attention to the integration of learning and MEMORY. Behavior changes only if modifications are remembered, and remembering also provides evidence that acquisition has occurred. Practice is not, however, indispensable in that organisms do learn in a single episode—"In that accident he learned to be terrified of traffic." Such a statement both underlines the necessity of personal encounters and corrects any assumption that biological or genetic antecedents are the significant determiners.

During the first half of the twentieth century learning and LEARNING THEORY came to dominate psychology. For some psychologists the topic became synonymous with the field of psychology, and for many others the study of the changes in behavior that come with experience was claimed as the sphere of knowledge that is uniquely psychological. To illustrate—the differences between an adult who speaks only English and one who is fluent in French, German, Spanish, and English depend on experience, practice, learning. The subject matter of a wide variety of sciences is involved in this acquisition. The physicist, for example, understands the transmission of sound that is necessary for the development of language skills. The physiologist understands the physiological events that transpire, but it is the psychologist who captures the information about the amount and kinds of practice that underwrite learning.

The significance of learning was, however, obscured in the early days of psychology, primarily because of the power that was ascribed to various internal mechanisms. One of these was maturation, a process that connects the orderly growth of anatomical structures with a hereditary mechanisn. Psychologists drew an analogy between this internally controlled progression and psychological development from infancy to adulthood. The environment was believed to support the maturation of organisms, but it was assumed not to have the capability of modifying this. The impact of opportunities to learn was severely restricted in that they were believed to be effective only if they occurred during an appropriate maturational phase (Stone, 1934).

The doctrine of INSTINCT also deferred the appreciation of the weight of learning. Instincts were seen as the cause of intricate reactions, even in lower forms of animal life, but most of the evidence for these responses was anecdotal, often exaggerated, or even legendary. The efforts to discover a more objective reality led to carefully controlled observations of changes in behavior, and these turned into experiments on learning (Warden, Jenkins, & Warner, 1935).

By the turn of the current century, research of this nature began to burgeon, and the laboratory started to generate what developed into a massive factual base. At least five distinctive varieties or kinds of learning were identified. In the temporal order in which they were acknowledged, they are trial and error learning, conditioning, insight, incidental or latent learning, and imitation. Most of this sophistication is a product of the laboratory, and it is therefore colored by experimental practices. Conspicuous among these is a deeply entrenched assumption that all learning is motivated. This hypothesis was accepted very early, and led to the long-standing custom of manipulating motives in order to increase the probability that learning will occur. As a result, much of the information is derived from observations of animals that are hungry, thirsty, cold, or in some biologically uncomfortable condition. These practices have been used in part at least because it is easier to manipulate and to measure the biological status of animals than the social needs of humans. Humans, however, have not been excluded, and they do participate in experiments, generally under conditions of physical normality, and, uniquely, in investigations in which language and responsiveness to nuances are required. The tasks that are to be learned are frequently chosen more for their feasibility for laboratory work than for their relevance to extralaboratory problems. Typically they are assignments in which improvement can be readily quantified, and are of such a level of difficulty that subjects are initially inept in handling them but, with practice, soon begin to improve, usually succeeding in a matter of hours, days, or weeks. For animals the discovery of maze pathways or learning to press a lever so as to procure a reward is popular. Representative tasks for humans include the memorizing of nonsense syllables and the acquiring of skill in hitting and/or tracing a target. The learning is generally reported in an abridged manner, often in terms of the number of correct responses or number of errors, and only seldom are qualitative accounts of behavioral changes included (McGeoch & Irion, 1952).

Trial and error was first described by Edward L. Thorndike (1874–1949), who began research as early as 1896 (Joncich, 1968). His initial experiments involved putting cats and dogs individually in a cage, and in order to obtain food each had to learn to manipulate a simple mechanism that opened a door and thereby allowed access to food. An animal generally tries various means of getting out and eventually *accidentally* releases the latch. On successive trials the animal confines its activity to the area in which the lever is located, and this restriction increases the *probability* of additional fortuitous successes. Gradually the time required to obtain the food decreases, and this temporal change is taken as evidence of learning.

Thorndike believed that this reduction resulted not from the animal's thinking about or understanding the problem, but from the association of components of the experience. The relationship is "stamped in" as a result of the satisfying state of affairs that follows the response, that is, because of the EFFECT. At a later date LEARNING THEORY took on the challenge of trying to explain how the EFFECT, which actually comes after the response, could strengthen the response that preceded it. But Thorndike and his immediate successors were satisfied with their own explanations, and they concluded that humans and subhumans react, in a diversity of contexts, to perplexity not with cognitive analyses, but simply by trying one solution, then a second, a third, and so on until a successful tactic is found (Bower & Hilgard, 1981).

Conditioning, a second variety of learning, was discovered shortly after the turn of the century, and three varieties were found. The research on these is too sophisticated and complicated to review briefly. The reader is referred to the sections on CONDITIONING, on REINFORCEMENT, and on SKINNERIAN BEHAV-IORISM in this book.

Insight, a third kind of mastery, came to the forefront in the 1920s when Köhler (1917/1927), a protagonist of GESTALT PSYCHOLOGY, observed chimpanzees' reactions to a problem in which food is placed at such a distance, or height, that it can be obtained only if the animal rearranges some of the parts, that is, combines sticks to provide a tool of adequate length or piles boxes to form a ladder. A chimpanzee, baffled by such a setup, is apt to stretch as far as possible to reach the bait, to shake the cage forcefully, to wander about aimlessly, and to display frustration in various ways. At some point the animal ceases this disorganized behavior and quickly sets about assembling available objects in a way that will allow procurement of the food. This sequence of task-irrelevant behavior followed by an unhesitating assembly of the materials necessary for a solution suggested to Köhler that the animal gains insight into the problem; that is, it perceives the relationship among various key elements. Other investigators, using both the same and somewhat different problems and observing both humans and animals, also reported insightful behavior, and the phenomenon was added to the list of varieties of learning. This entry is significant in that insight is the result of activity on the part of the learner and thus qualitatively different from the learning that is believed to result from outcomes provided by the enviroment.

The remaining varieties of acquisition, incidental or latent learning and imitation, were reluctantly accepted by psychologists, in part because their motivational basis was elusive. In 1929 Blodgett noted that reports of learning in the absence of rewards were accumulating. These induced him to pursue the matter, and he allowed rats a few runs in a maze but did not give them any food. He found that as soon as the bait was introduced, the decline in their errors was unusually sharp. Blodgett applied the label "latent learning" to the acquisition that took place when the food was withheld.

In 1933 Jenkins, using human subjects, investigated what he called "incidental learning," that "which occurs in the absence of a specific intent to remember" (p. 471). He noted that this phenomenon was reported in more than 150 references at the time of his research, but despite this prior activity Jenkins' work is often cited as the landmark experiment. In this he asked undergraduates to read a list of twenty nonsense syllables to a fellow student until the latter could recite them accurately. A day later both subjects and "experimenters" were asked to recall the list. Those who intended to memorize remembered an average of 15.9 syllables, whereas those who were directed only to read defied theory by recalling an average of 10.8 syllables.

Gradually information of this nature became so extensive that it could not be ignored, and efforts were made to discover if the laboratory controls are ineffective or if motivation is not essential. It is easier for psychologists to decide in favor of the former alternative, and in order to develop this they began to consider the implications of the probability that human research participants do not divest themselves of their own preferences while serving as subjects and that they learn what personally interests them. Animals are not accorded as much latitude, but they are also not seen as controlled exclusively by the research design. HABITUATION, for example, is invoked as one factor that may alter the clarity of the stimuli (Mackintosh, 1974). During the course of these deliberations it became a common but far from universal practice to call the learning *incidental* when it is manifest by humans and *latent* when manifest by animals (American Psychological Association, 1985).

There was also a delay in the recognition by psychologists of the importance of imitation a lag that contrasts with the widespread conviction among the laity that it is the basis of a great deal of learning. Children, for example, are assumed to copy the behavior of their parents. Simulating is also used to account for a wide variety of responses in different species, and for behavior that ranges from the learning of specifics, such as the vocalization of the mockingbird, to abstractions, such as the religious values of one's culture. The reasons for the reluctance within psychology to accept imitation are more numerous and different in the case of animals than in the case of people. Emulating implies an intention to do so as well as a perception and anticipation of outcome, and such cognitive reactions in subhumans have yet to be established (Putney, 1985).

Techniques were devised to avoid anthropomorphism, and one of these consists of replacing studies of the genesis of responses with investigations of how innovative reactions spread throughout a group. Miyadi (1964) describes how monkeys adopted the practice, novel to them, of washing sweet potatoes in salt water before eating them. This was initiated by a young female and then adopted by her mother, followed by a playmate, and then by sisters and brothers, after which the practice displaced a general disdain and was taken up by all members of the troop except for a few elderly, conservative males.

A second way of pulling back from anthropomorphism is to tease out details of the effects of the presence of other animals. In these investigations the group is seen both as orienting the learner to certain particulars and as increasing the members' reactivity. That is, witnessing an animal performing a certain activity is not interpreted as exposure to a pattern to be mimicked, but is believed to highlight cues as to what is to be learned (Zentall & Hogan, 1976).

Although the study of imitation in humans bypasses these problems of attributing abstract responses, it draws other kinds of cross fire, particularly questions about motivation. This was such a perplexing problem that until the 1950s, only episodic attempts were made to handle it. One of these efforts is illustrated in Allport's (1924) explanation of how a baby learns the "bye-bye" gesture. He proposed that an adult attracts the infant's attention when mimicking the baby's arm movements, and that this reinforces the child's action. A second and more general solution suggested that imitation is a learned motive or NEED. Miller and Dollard (1941), noting that children are frequently rewarded for trying to respond as an adult, suggested that these "natural" episodes promote so much association between approbation and emulation that the latter acquires the activating power of the former.

Imitation did not, on its own merits, attract a significant amount of research, and the provocation for studying it in depth came from COGNITIVE PSYCHOLOGY, a viewpoint that emerged during the 1950s and one that disavows the learner as the passive reactor that is perceived by adherents of trial and error learning, conditioning, and incidental learning. Cognitive psychology views learning as an active process, similar to the constructive reactivity in insightful learning, but more versatile in that numerous variables in the learning context are manipulated, both explicitly and implicitly. The role of motivation is played down, but at the same time reinforcement is seen as an informative source or guide. This role, paradoxically, promotes the motivational credibility of imitation inasmuch as perceiving the reinforcement of others is said to induce individuals to anticipate similar personal gains (Bandura, 1971).

The impetus for the study of imitation that came from cognitive psychology has been augmented by concern about two specific problems. One of these is the fear, pervasive among the public at large, that the violence depicted on television is contagious, particularly among children. This provoked an initial concentration on the effects of witnessing varying amounts and kinds of antisocial behavior. It is interesting to note that these experiments are referred to as studies of learning, even though they typically assess the results of only one exposure, a single trial, and they seldom measure the acquisition of new responses, but merely tally the frequency of violent responses (Fehr, 1983).

The second topic that fostered the study of simulating is the development of socialization in children, and investigations of this matter feature explorations of role identity, particularly gender identity. Most of this research is based on the premise that socialization is facilitated by exposure to a "model," and assessments are made of the learner's success in copying a model during a sequence of trials. Systematic investigations are made of the effects of the number of opportunities to observe, of the nature and amount of guidance, of role playing, and of similarities between the mimicked and the mimicker (Bandura, 1965).

The most recent innovations in the study of learning are products of the assumption that it is analogous with information processing. This orientation points to the assessment of how people screen, encode, symbolize, store, and retrieve material that is to be learned. At first glance this approach appears to enlarge the concept of learning, but this potential is blocked by the impossibility of directly observing the component responses. This barrier appears in fact to have constrained the measurements of learning more than those used in the past in that it is most feasible to measure the differences between the original stimuli and their recall. In other words, the spotlight has been focused on memory with such an intensity that in some circles the two concepts are identified with each other: "Thus information-processing models view verbal learning as a storage-retrieval problem" (Kausler, 1974, p. 21).

The future of the concept of learning is elusive, but the superabundant stock of laboratory data discloses that in some instances it is a function of such peripherals as accidental success, contiguous experiences, and most significantly, REINFORCEMENT. In other instances it is interpreted as a function of more enlightenment, such as insight and the appreciation of the cognitive reactions of other people. As the research continues the importance assigned to both effect and reinforcement is being weakened, and attention is being directed toward the mastery of abstractions. Nonetheless investigations of discrete tasks that can be mastered in relatively brief periods of time are still in favor.

References

Allport, F. H. (1924). *Social psychology*. Boston: Houghton Mifflin. Allport dismisses an imitative basis for human learning and proposes that any apparent imitation is really a pursuit of the model's goal: "One boy follows another over the fence in order to get his share of the farmer's apples" (p. 241).

American Psychological Association. (1985). *Thesaurus of psychological index terms* (4th ed.). Washington, DC: Author.

Bandura, A. (1965). Vicarious process: A case of no-trial learning. In L. Berkowitz (Ed.), *Advances in experimental social psychology* (vol. 2, pp. 3–55). New York: Academic Press. The author reviews the history of the modern study of human imitation.

Bandura, A. (1971). Vicarious and self-reinforcement processes. In R. Glaser (Ed.), *The nature of reinforcement* (pp. 228–278). New York: Academic Press.

Blodgett, H. C. (1929). The effect of the introduction of reward upon the maze performance of rats. *University of California Publications in Psychology, 4* (8), 113–134.

Bower, G. H., & Hilgard, E. R. (1981). *Theories of learning* (5th ed.). Englewood Cliffs, NJ: Prentice-Hall.

Fehr, L. A. (1983). *Introduction to personality*. New York: Macmillan. Presents a concise, readily comprehended review of modern observational learning theory.

Jenkins, J. G. (1933). Instruction as a factor in "incidental" learning. *American Journal of Psychology, 45*, 471–477.

Joncich, G. (1968). *The sane positivist: A biography of Edward L. Thorndike*. Middletown, CT: Wesleyan University Press. An authoritative biography. It is unusually comprehensive and portrays the specifics of the long and prolific career of this pioneer in learning, an architect both of research methods and of theoretical interpretations.

Kausler, D. H. (1974). *Psychology of verbal learning and memory*. New York: Academic Press.

Köhler, W. (1927). *The mentality of apes* (2nd rev. ed.) (E. Winter, Trans.). New York: Harcourt, Brace. (Original work published 1917)

Mackintosh, N. J. (1974). *The psychology of animal learning*. London: Academic Press. This comprehensive text includes a review of numerous variables that accompany observational learning in animals.

McGeoch, J. A., & Irion, A. L. (1952). *The psychology of human learning* (2nd rev. ed.). New York: Longmans, Green. This widely used book offers an overview of the psychology of learning and includes readily understood accounts of many phenomena that could not be included in the current discussion. It depicts many research procedures and the reasons they are followed.

Miller, N. E., & Dollard, J. (1941). *Social learning and imitation*. New Haven, CT: Yale University Press. This volume represents a ground-breaking attempt to fit social behavior into the motivational frame of biological or primary drives.

Miyadi, D. (1964). Social life of Japanese monkeys. *Science, 143* (No. 3608), 783–786.

Putney, R. T. (1985). Do willful apes know what they are aiming at? *The Psychological Record, 35*, 49–62. A brief review of the labored history of intention and volition in psychology. The author describes recent changes in attitude toward the topic.

Stone, C. P. (1934). Learning: 1: The factor of maturation. In C. Murchison (Ed.), *A handbook of general experimental psychology* (pp. 352–381). Worcester, MA: Clark University Press.

Warden, C. J., Jenkins, T. N., & Warner, L. H. (1935). *Comparative psychology: A comprehensive treatise* (vol. 1). *Principles and Methods* New York: Ronald Press.

Zentall, T. R., & Hogan, D. E. (1976). Imitation and social facilitation in the pigeon. *Animal Learning and Behavior, 4*, 427–430. This article deals with pigeons observing pecking. The authors conclude that some birds probably learn the pecking of illuminated stimuli from observing. Other birds, however, evidenced merely social facilitation, that is, the mere presence of other pigeons prompted them to peck.

Sources of Additional Information

Hall, K. R. L. (1963) Observational learning in monkeys and apes. *British Journal of Psychology, 54*, 201–226. An assessment of imitative learning, but the author is reluctant to ascribe psychological sophistication to anthropoids. Irion, A. L. (1966). A brief history of research on the acquisition of skill. In E. A. Bilodeau (Ed.), *Acquisition of skill* (pp. 1–46). New York: Academic Press. Irion reviews the humans' learning of motor skills. The military needs of World War II intensified research on motor skills, but the field has generally been more concerned with promoting the study of verbal learning than of skills.

Watson, J. B. (1903). *Animal education: An experimental study on the psychical development of the white rat, correlated with the growth of its nervous system.* Chicago: University of Chicago Press. One of Watson's studies, completed during the formative period of behaviorism. In this work Watson deals with "the gradual unfolding of the associative processes in the rat" (p. 5). Zajonc, R. B. (1965). Social facilitation. *Science, 149* (No. 3681), 269–274. The author reviews the influence of others on the learning efficiency of both humans and animals. He would "advise the student to study all alone, preferably in an isolated cubicle, and to arrange to take his examinations in the company of many other students, on stage, and in the presence of a large audience" (p. 274).

LEARNING THEORY. 1. The ordering of information about learning. 2. A synonym for behavior theory. **BEHAVIOR THEORY.** 1. The systematizing of the "facts" of behavior. 2. A synonym for learning theory.

The research on LEARNING has generated a mass of information that is so large that it invites efforts to organize it into comprehensive systems or principles. For some the lure is compelling. To illustrate—Tolman, one of the protagonists of NEOBEHAVIORISM, a view of psychology that stresses theory construction, discloses the depth of commitment: "Even if we had all the million and one concrete facts, we would still want theories to, as we would say, 'explain' those facts. Theories just seem to be necessary to some of us to relieve our inner tensions" (1938, p. 9). A few details of Tolman's proposals are reported in the discussion of neobehaviorism, and it is not feasible to review these complex formulations, but theory compilation by systematists of various viewpoints is so popular that some remarks about it are in order.

One of the precursors was the observation made early in the current century that the graphs of human and animal learning are similar in shape. This suggested that acquisition might be the same among different species, and this possible homogeneity nourished ideas that it might be feasible to reduce complex data to a few fundamentals. Typically theorists tried to identify the underlying processes of learning, generally assuming them to be few in number, and then organized them into internally consistent relationships. Originally these explanations covered relatively specific phenomena, usually factors known to alter the rate and amount of learning, but in the 1930s this restraint began to be displaced by attempts to incorporate all variables relevant to learning into a single system. The goal was to express these principles and, whenever possible, to symbolize them in formulae (Boring, 1953).

The belief that all behavior is learned made it easy to extend the scope covered by these generalizations from learning to behavior, and psychologists began to try to formulate the "laws of behavior" and even the basics of "human nature" (Schwartz, 1984). The easy flow in this transition is illustrated in Spence's statement of his aims for neobehaviorism. He starts with the relatively clearly differentiated topic of conditioning but becomes vague as he comments on the limits of the theory: "The major purpose of the theoretical concepts proposed here is not only to provide for the integration of the specific laws found in conditioning experiments but also to attempt to extend in a preliminary way the theoretical structure so developed to more complex behavior situations'' (1956/ 1978, p. 200).

It is noteworthy that the ''facts'' on which the theories, about both learning and behavior, are based are primarily animal learning data. The extent of this dependence is illustrated in Beach's disclosure (1950) that during the 1930s and 1940s more than half of the articles on learning and conditioning in the mainstream journals of comparative psychology used the Norway rat.

There is no indication that the popularity of rodents has declined in any significant amount since Beach's paper. Their use is convenient, but it is misleading to ascribe their popularity merely to this factor, and substantive arguments in favor of animal data have been developed. Theorists point out that it is advantageous to study simple organisms; their past experiences can be held constant, and their responses are easier to observe than those of humans. They defend the assumption that the ''difference in complexity between human and nonhuman is only quantitative, not qualitative'' (Schwartz, 1984, p. 39). The view that valid generalities about people can be derived from analogies from animals is not, however, without challenge, and researchers are accused of failing to probe the matter in depth (Jenkins, 1979).

By the 1950s the sweeping abstractions began to lose their appeal, and the organizing of experimental data about more limited problems came back into fashion (Bower & Hilgard, 1981). Some of the explanations of decrements in memory are used here to illustrate these abridged formulations. This topic is typical of many in the field of learning in that it has an extended history, and a tracing of it portrays the gradual and stepwise evolution that is characteristic of many theories. In this instance the starting point came in the prescientific doctrine of faculty psychology, which held that the mind is composed of different powers (memory, will, reason, etc.) and that exercising them strengthens them. Unfortunately the laboratory failed to uncover any mental faculties, let alone any development of them, but it did disclose that remembering is influenced, both favorably and unfavorably, by other activities that the learner undertakes. This erraticism suggested that forgetting might be a function of the interference of other responses rather than merely disuse, the commonly assumed reason.

In light of this possibility Münsterberg and Bigham (1894) compared the retention of both visual and auditory material when the periods between learning and memory were ''vacant'' in some trials but enriched in others by an opportunity to read or to listen to someone reading a newspaper aloud. These researchers reported that ''the filling of the intervals hinders the memory'' (p. 459).

The apparent relevance of this discovery to forgetting elicited additional research. The results supported the original conclusion and demonstrated that the amount that is forgotten increases as the similarity between the original and the intervening task increases. Unfortunately this phenomenon, as early as 1900, acquired the name ''retroactive inhibition.'' The label was intended to be metaphorical, indicating merely that the interpolated activity acted *as if* it worked backward in time. The point was made repeatedly that a reversal of this nature is impossible (McGeoch, 1942), but these disclaimers were not always effective, and erroneous suggestions that retroaction may actually occur are discernible in the literature.

The importance of a second temporal pattern came to the forefront in 1927 when Whitely found that memory scores may be impaired by carrying on certain kinds of activity *prior* to memorizing. This sequential effect was soon substantiated by other investigators, and it came to be known as "proactive inhibition." As in the case of retroactive inhibition, the amount that is forgotten increases as the similarity between the tasks increases.

Theories about the mechanisms for inhibition came into fashion (Britt, 1936). Some of these ascribed the phenomena to the nervous system, commonly in the form of hypothesized memory traces or engrams, that is, mechanisms in which memory is "engraved" or recorded in neural tissue. Psychological variables were also used as explanatory agents, and two factors that are frequently linked with forgetting are the amount and nature of the stimulation as well as the personal history of the learner. Underwood (1957) was curious as to why only about 25 percent of the rote learning in formal experiments is recalled the next day. He found it difficult to believe the then commonly held assumption that this was due to retroactive inhibition: "It seems to me to be an incredible stretch of an interference hypothesis to hold that this 75 percent forgetting was caused by something which the subjects learned outside the laboratory during the 24-hour interval" (p. 50). He speculated that "a 20-year-old college student will more likely have learned something during his 20 years prior to coming to the laboratory that will interfere with his retention than he will during the 24 hours between the learning and retention test" (p. 55).

Underwood assembled recall data from several sources and plotted these against the total number of lists that subjects had previously memorized when participating in various investigations. The graphs indicated that the greater the amount of prior practice, the greater the decrement in memory score. Furthermore, subjects just beginning to contribute to this kind of research recall approximately 75 percent of the material they memorize.

Observations that the amount forgotten also varies with the nature of the stimulation to remember have been made episodically. While pursuing the role of interference, McGeoch (1932, 1942; McGeoch & Irion, 1952), for example, became aware of the importance of the cues that elicit recall, and he reminded psychologists that remembering, like all responses, demands stimulation. He observed that remembering in some unusual circumstances, such as an intense emotional disturbance or deliruim, is so accurate that it suggests that irretrievable decrements may not exist. In these instances, "had disuse brought decay there would have been no memory to heighten" (1932, p. 365). He also indicated that many apparent failures to remember may be due to inappropriate stimulation, as in the case of a student who does not react constructively to an examination question because it is phrased in an unfamiliar way.

The modern research that is conducted in a format that makes memory analogous to electronic information processing has generated some additional data about the effect of provocation to recall. To illustrate—Tulving and Thomson (1973) report that what is remembered is due not only to the strength of memory traces, but also to the similarity between the meaning at the time of learning and at the time of retrieval. For example, including the word violet in a list of colors to be memorized increases the probability of its recall when the subject is asked to remember the names of colors but decreases the probability of its recall when the subject is asked to remember the names of flowers. In their words, "the target item must be encoded in some sort of reference to the cue for the cue to be effective" (1973, p. 359). This statement is essentially the same as McGeoch's assertion made thirty years earlier that "recall . . . depends upon the presence of some stimulating situation with which the learned act is directly or indirectly associated. . . . Alteration or removal of these stimuli at the time of recall will be correlated with a failure of recall" (1942, p. 501). In this one instance at least, modern theory appears to be reaching toward the past.

References

Beach, F A. (1950). The snark was a boojum. *American Psychologist, 5*, 115–124. Beach laments the psychologists' "preoccupation with a few species and a few types of behavior" (p. 121).

Boring, E. G. (1953). The role of theory in experimental psychology. *American Journal of Psychology, 66*, 169–184. Boring gives an account of the role of theory and comments: "At the present time you can find laboratories where concern with theory and systems is so great that the divorce from philosophical heritage seems little greater than it was fifty years ago" (p. 171). In evaluating the gains and liabilities in this state of affairs he views the impact of theories with and theories without evidence, those that are testable and not testable, as well as those that are conceptual, those that rectify, etc.

Bower, G. H., & Hilgard, E. R. (1981). *Theories of learning* (5th ed.). Englewood, NJ: Prentice-Hall. The authors estimate that "several thousand psychologists and scientists in related fields are doing research that can be roughly classified as investigations of learning" (p. 253).

Britt, S. H. (1936). Theories of retroactive inhibition. *Psychological Review, 43*, 207–216.

Jenkins, H. M. (1979). Animal learning and behavior theory. In E. Hearst (Ed.), *The first century of experimental psychology* (pp. 177–228). Hillsdale, NJ: Lawrence Erlbaum.

McGeoch, J. A. (1932). Forgetting and the law of disuse. *Psychological Review, 39*, 352–370. The author believes that the principle of disuse has been overworked, and he advocates other explanations of forgetting. He emphasizes both the nature of the activity between learning and recollection and the similarity between the stimulating conditions when memorizing and when recalling.

McGeoch, J. A. (1942). *The psychology of human learning: An introduction*. New York: Longmans, Green.

McGeoch, J. A., & Irion, A. L. (1952). *The psychology of human learning* (2nd ed rev.) New York: Longmans, Green.

Münsterberg, H., & Bigham, J. (1894). Studies from the Harvard Psychological Laboratory: Memory (II) *Psychological Review, 1,* 453–461.

Schwartz, B. (1984). *Psychology of learning and behavior* (2nd ed.). New York: W. W. Norton. In the first edition of this book, 1978, the author comments that "learning, learning theory, behavior theory, and behavior analysis . . . [are] explicitly committed to the view that *human nature* [italics added] can be revealed and understood" (p. 2). He also notes that "our evaluation of experiments will also be an evaluation of the conception of human nature" (p. 2). The scope of theory in the revised edition is reduced. "Human nature," for example, is replaced by "laws of behavior."

Spence, K. W. (1978). *Behavior theory and conditioning.* Westport, CT: Greenwood Press. (Original work published in 1956.)

Tolman, E. C. (1938). The determiners of behavior at a choice point. *Psychological Review, 45,* 1–41. This article exemplifies Tolman's writing style—a combination of the matter of fact, the mundane, and symbolism. For example, the question of " 'why rats turn the way they do, at a given choice-point in a give maze at a given stage of learning' " is answered in two ways: by means of complex formulae and by the simple statement that this is what the animal has done on previous trials.

Tulving, E., & Thomson, D. M. (1973). Encoding specificity and retrieval processes in episodic memory. *Psychological Review, 80,* 352–373.

Underwod, B. J. (1957). Interference and forgetting. *Psychological Review, 64,* 49–60. A frequently cited experiment and one that led psychologists to reinterpret Ebbinghaus' 1885 calculations of the amount of forgetting.

Whitely, P. L. (1927). The dependence of learning and recall upon prior intellectual activities. *Journal of Experimental Psychology, 10,* 489–508. This article describes three aligned experiments and exposes the naiveté of the era about both the facts of learning and the respect that was accorded new data.

Sources of Additional Information

Gomulicki, B. R. (1953). *The development and present status of the trace theory of memory.* Cambridge: Cambridge University Press. A chronicle of trace theory, covering 2,500 years, but the emphasis is on the scientific era. Hefferline, R. F. (1962). Learning theory and clinical psychology—an eventual symbiosis? In A. J. Bachrach (Ed.), *Experimental foundations of clinical psychology* (pp. 97–138). New York: Basic Books. This chapter conveys many of the difficulties encountered in trying to bridge the gap between theory and application. Hicks, V. C. (1911). The relative values of the different curves of learning. *Journal of Animal Behavior, 1,* 138–156. Attempts to find indices of learning started almost as soon as the experimentation began, and learning curves or graphs soon became the prevalent index. On these, successive practice periods are marked at regular intervals on the abscissa, and a single measure of learning, such as errors, correct responses, or time per trial, on the ordinate. These plots are useful even though they are artificial in that they summarize merely one variable, and the first and last trials coincide merely with the beginning and end of the experiment on learning, not with learning per se. Lockard, R. B. (1971). Reflections on the fall of comparative psychology: Is there a message for us all? *American Psychologist, 26,* 168–179. A plea for increasing the number of species in order to make laboratory data more meaningful. "We have no animal-based science of human behavior despite the assemblage of suspect analogies. If anything, we have had a human-based methodology of animal behavior'' (p. 177). Underwood, B. J. (1982). *Studies in learning and memory: Selected papers.* New York: Praeger. This volume contains original articles by one of the leading investigators of learning. They are supplemented by the author's account of his professional experiences, written in a personal manner and one that adds perspective to the field.

LEVEL OF ASPIRATION. 1. The level of performance that an individual says he or she can attain on tasks that demand effort but can be mastered. 2. An assigned goal.

The concept of level of aspiration first came to attention as a by-product of an experiment on a quite different topic, and its later formulation was guided by the results of additional formal investigations. Because of these close ties to experimental work the concept was initially defined quite consistently. In the prototypical experiment each subject is observed individually and is asked to perform a task on which proficiency can be quantified—typically a series of problems of increasing difficulty (puzzles to be assembled) or repetitive exercises (dart throwing or solving arithmetic problems). In order to become familiar with the assignment each subject is allowed a few practice trials and is then requested to predict the score he or she expects to achieve on each succeeding trial. Each forecast is considered to be a measure of the level of aspiration, and the subject is apprised of the discrepancy between the anticipated and the obtained score. It is assumed that a sense of failure is experienced when the actual performance is below the predicted one and a sense of success when it is exceeded. In other words, expectation, success, and failure are quantified. This threefold assessment makes the label ''level of aspiration'' somewhat arbitrary, but after some early slighting, it became the dominant one (Frank, 1941; Rotter, 1942). When psychologists refer to aspirations that are measured or assessed in other ways, they tend, with one notable exception, to avoid the phrase ''level of aspiration'' and to use the word ambition or to modify aspiration, for example, ''educational aspiration'' or ''occupational aspiration.''

The distinguishing features of the original concept of level of aspiration are the subject's, rather than the experimenter's, specification of the level that will be reached and the objective measurement of the accomplishment. Approximately twenty-five years after this concept was formulated, Siegel (1957), studying the ways decisions are made, on occasion designated a specific profit that must be negotiated or bargained in order to acquire the maximum reward. He called this goal the level of aspiration even though it is an assigned rather than a personally predicted one, and attaining it demands skill in interpersonal maneuvering rather than task proficiency (Siegel & Fouraker, 1960). This sleight of nomenclature persists even though it produces two different concepts with the same name (Pruitt, 1976).

The inception of the basic concept occurred about 1930 at the University of Berlin, when it became part of the research being conducted by students of Kurt

Lewin (1890–1947), a German theorist who would soon migrate to the United States and achieve eminence for a variety of contributions to psychology (Marrow, 1969). One of these students, Tamara Dembo, was conducting an experimental investigation of frustration-induced anger, and she noticed that subjects, when faced with a goal that they do not expect to attain, may substitute another one that is easier than the original but still of sufficient difficulty to demand at least some striving. She referred to this replacement as the "momentary level of aspiration." Ferdinand Hoppe, also a student and the first to conduct a major study on this topic, was aware that tasks that are either unduly easy or unduly difficult do not elicit effort, and he explored the range of difficulty in which success and failure are experienced. He was more interested in stable, long-term subjective hopes, in what was then identified as the "ideal goal," than in the "momentary level of aspiration," and he supplemented the quantified data with inferences about the "ideal" level as disclosed in spontaneous remarks and by the attitude with which the task was undertaken. He believed that "real aspiration" is related to certain personality characteristics, and commented that some people keep their expectations very low, whereas others are prone to maintain very high goals, sometimes so lofty that their efforts are futile (Gardner, 1940).

These inaugural investigations gained wide circulation in America after 1935 when they were described in an English language volume, *A Dynamic Theory of Personality* by Lewin. North American research workers were intrigued with the possibility of investigating ambition, winning, and losing in the laboratory. They abandoned Hoppe's complicated data and began to investigate selected aspects of level of aspiration. They studied how it is affected by different kinds of tasks, by particular personality traits, and by the effects of knowing one's own efficiency as well as that of other individuals and of various groups. Rotter's review (1942) of the research literature led him to conclude that the methods are generally adequate. This commendation was followed shortly by a second by Lewin, Dembo, Festinger, and Sears (1944).

Despite these assurances doubts arose about the meaning of some aspects of level of aspiration. For example, researchers are aware that different social pressures come into the picture when experimental subjects are required to reveal the score they hope to achieve. A participant who believes that the experimenter wants an accurate forecast may replace a statement of hope with an estimate of the most probable performance. An individual who is sensitive to failure may predict a cautious rather than a desired level. These personalized interpretations inject unmeasured, uncontrolled modifications into the degree of success or failure that the participant experiences.

The probability of such distortions prompted researchers to try to ascertain the similarity between the conclusions that are reached in an artificial context and those that are characteristic of real life. One of the early participants in this effort was Sears (1940), who chose to experiment with tasks that are similar to extralaboratory ones and for which there is also a preexperimental history of success or failure. Her subjects were nine- to twelve-year-old children whose school grades fell into three patterns: high grades in all academic subjects; low grades in all classes; and proficient in reading but deficient in arithmetic. The children were required to read passages and to solve arithmetic problems, in some instances praised for previous performances and in others criticized. Sears found that the academic achievers generally predict scores slightly above the level of their previous performance; that is, they most frequently say that they expect to improve slightly over the immediately past performance. This realistic optimism contrasts with the subjects who have records of failure in that the predictions made by these children are erratic. Some anticipate a score lower than the one they have just achieved, whereas others have an eye on one much too high to be reached. In summary, the experimentally measured level of aspiration appears to be similar to educational aspiration in those who are successful, but discrepant in those who are academically frustrated. This suggests that the laboratory yield is relevant for some subjects but irrelevant for others.

Later researchers also assessed the match between laboratory and extralaboratory patterns, and generally they agree with the early conclusions. To illustrate— in an introduction to an experiment conducted forty-five years after Sears' work, Halpin, Halpin, and Whiddon summarize prior findings: "While success tends to lead to realistic or probably higher goals, the effects of failure on aspirations may be hard to predict . . . some individuals seem to set goals below what they have already achieved. Others with repeated failures—and a low sense of efficacy—may set goals so far above their actual performance level as to be unreachable" (1985, p. 204).

There has been a progressive refinement of specific details, and these frequently involve the identification of aspects of the concept of the level of aspiration that need additional investigation. An example of this is encountered in a study of the behavioral effects of sex role stereotypes (Ryan and Pryor, 1976). College students were asked to use a large plastic disc to flip as many smaller discs as possible across a goal line. Some were informed that the average score for men on this assignment is 25; others were told that 25 is the average score for women; and others were merely informed that the average is 25. The results disclosed that both male and female students who were aware of a masculine norm predicted and achieved lower scores than those informed of the women's norm. The investigators have only a tentative explanation for this unexpected discrepancy, but they point without hesitation to the importance of sex role. This variable has been neglected in the past, and its emergence in this experiment points up the need for continuing research.

References

Frank, J. D. (1941). Recent studies of the level of aspiration. *Psychological Bulletin,* *38*, 218–226. Frank was one of the early investigators of the level of aspiration. This article was written a decade after the concept appeared in the literature, and Frank was able to collect twenty-one experimental reports, including one doctoral dissertation. This rate of productivity during that era points to a viable concept.

Gardner, J. W. (1940). The use of the term "level of aspiration." *Psychological Review,* *47,* 59–68. The Dembo and Hoppe experiments were first published in German. Gardner provides a description of each of them.

Halpin, G., Halpin, G., & Whiddon, T. (1985). Factors related to adolescents' level of aspiration. *Psychological Reports, 56,* 203–209.

Lewin, K. (1935). *A dynamic theory of personality: Selected papers* (D. K. Adams & K. E. Zener, Trans.). New York: McGraw-Hill. These articles cover a diversity of topics, and two of them are different from the major content of this volume in that they were originally published in English.

Lewin, K., Dembo, T., Festinger, L., & Sears, P. S. (1944). Level of aspiration. In J. McV. Hunt (Ed.), *Personality and the behavior disorders: A handbook based on experimental and clinical research* (Vol. 1, pp. 333–378). New York: Ronald Press. The concept is clearly elaborated in this chapter. It is also integrated into Lewin's general theoretical framework.

Marrow, A. J. (1969). *The practical theorist: The life and work of Kurt Lewin.* New York: Basic Books. This biography of Lewin also includes summaries of the research of Lewin's students and colleagues.

Pruitt, D. G. (1976). Power and bargaining. In B. Seidenberg & A. Snadowsky (Eds.), *Social psychology: An introduction* (pp. 343–375). New York: Free Press. This chapter describes some of the so-called level of aspiration research in bargaining situations and does so in a straightforward, relatively jargon-free manner.

Rotter, J. B. (1942). Level of aspiration as a method of studying personality: 1. A critical review of methodology. *Psychological Review, 49,* 463–474.

Ryan T. T., & Pryor, F. A. (1976). Sex cues in estimating and performing a simple motor task. *Perceptual and Motor Skills, 43,* 547–552.

Sears, P. S. (1940). Levels of aspiration in academically successful and unsuccessful children. *Journal of Abnormal and Social Psychology, 35,* 498–536.

Siegel, S. (1957). Level of aspiration and decision making. *Psychological Review, 64,* 253–262. Siegel is frank about the linguistic maneuvering in which he indulged: "It is a remarkable fact that *by a simple change in nomenclature* [italics added] the theoretical model used by Lewin et al. in the prediction of the choices (decisions) of individuals in a goal-striving situation . . . may be rendered fundamentally equivalent to the theoretical model employed by decision and game theorists" (p. 253).

Siegel S., & Fouraker, L. E. (1960). *Bargaining and group decision making: Experiments in bilateral monopoly.* New York: McGraw-Hill.

Sources of Additional Information

Chapman, D. W., & Volkmann, J. (1939). A social determinant of the level of aspiration. *Journal of Abnormal and Social Psychology, 34,* 225–238. One of the earliest papers on the effects of social norms. The authors report that being told about the proficiency of others changes level of aspiration if the subjects have not had an opportunity to perform the task. Hilgard, E. R. (1942). Success in relation to level of aspiration. *School and Society, 55,* 423–428. Hilgard emphasizes the relationship between laboratory procedures and extralaboratory contexts, particularly academic success. Kahan, J. P. (1968). Effects of level of aspiration in an experimental bargaining situation. *Journal of Personality and Social Psychology, 8,* 154–159. The title of the article refers to "level of aspiration," but the abstract refers only to "goals." Pairs of subjects played "a bargaining game" and "as the joint level of goals increased to and above the total rewards available, the mood of the bargaining changed from cooperative to competitive" (p. 154). Rotter, J. B. (1942). Level of aspiration as a method of studying personality. *Journal of Experimental Psychology, 31*, 410–422. Rotter devised the Aspiration Board for use in research on level of aspiration. It is a test of motor control, of an appropriate range of difficulty, and it offers the subject a novel task. Wiederanders, M. R. (1975). Effects of failure experiences on configural properties of the aspiration level concept. *Psychological Reports, 37*, 371–377. This experiment deals with changes in level of aspiration as a function of cumulative failures. The effects of hope of achievement are discussed.

M

MASCULINITY. 1. Personality characteristics that society traditionally associates with males. **FEMININITY.** 1. Personality characteristics that society traditionally associates with females. **ANDROGYNY.** 1. The presence in one person of masculinity and femininity.

The attribute of either masculinity or femininity is assigned to a diversity of responses such as aggression, aspiration, attitudes, compassion, intellectual skills, emotions, and vocational aptitude. Until the recent past there was a firm conviction that these qualities are biologically determined and that they are different in men and women, both in the quality and frequency of the reactions and in the manner in which they are displayed. Among the better known examples are competitiveness, ascribed to males, and tenderness, ascribed to females. The behavior that was prescribed for one's biological sex was considered requisite for psychological health, and sex-inappropriate behavior was treated as psychologically unhealthy and frequently explained as the result of hormonal imbalance.

The scientific study of sex has been marked by a series of corrections or modifications of these stereotypes, and in the course of this there has been a shift away from an emphasis on diversity between the sexes to an emphasis on their similarity. One of the first of these departures from established doctrine emerged from the evidence that masculine and feminine behavioral patterns are molded by learning and experience as well as by biology. Another source came from the discovery in the field of biology that organisms possess both male and female properties. The normality of such combinations paved the way for a proposal that human beings, both those who are psychologically healthy and those who are not, display both masculine and feminine behavior.

Confidence that the variations in the psychological repertoires of men and women are physiologically determined was as strong in experimental psychology as it was in other segments of society. Jastrow, speaking clearly to this point, represents the voice of many of his colleagues: "There is but one supreme natural differentiation—that of sex . . . .For men and women are organically different; which means that the physiological differentiation in the reproductive system involves a contrasted psychology" (1915, pp. 366–367).

Questions about the validity of such statements were asked by experts in various disciplines and among the more influential were the anthropologists who found that masculinity and femininity in non-Western, nonindustrialized societies are quite different from the patterns with which they are familiar. Even a brief excerpt from the descriptions of field observations of the Tchambuli highlights the contrast: "A genuine reversal of the sex-attitudes of our own culture, with the woman the dominant, impersonal, managing partner, the man the less responsible and the emotionally dependent person" (Mead, 1935, p. 279).

Psychologists also began to explore the matter. Some domestic cultural changes prompted Catharine Cox Miles and Lewis M. Terman to explore the reality and extent of sex differences that had been reported in the experimental literature. They commented: "The problem is peculiarly complex because social conditions, the weight of tradition and the pillars of custom, maintain an equilibrium now that is not necessarily according to Nature's original construction plan" (1929, p. 166). They surveyed the research on the association of ideas, with this topic selected because of their belief that the association of ideas plays a central role in the formation of interests. They concluded that associations do vary in frequency between the sexes, but they also concluded that these differences decrease in amount as the experimental similarity between the sexes increases. The associations of educated men and educated women, for example, are more alike than are the associations of uneducated men and uneducated women.

In 1935 Miles published a second article in which she reviewed experiments on numerous variables that have been related to sex. The nature and size of the variations were found to be erratic and, in some instances, to fall into unpredicted configurations. In an early investigation, for example, no unevenness was found in the number of calculation problems that children in grades three to eight solved correctly. This homogeneity, however, disappeared when the problems were arranged in the order of their difficulty. An analysis of accuracy under this arrangement disclosed that more girls than boys solved the easy problems, but more boys than girls solved the hard ones. It is noteworthy that the relationships between level of skill and sex have not yet been settled, and, as will be reported later in this discussion, they are included in the research agenda in the latter half of the 1980s.

Psychologists are fond of devising tests to measure each topic they investigate. These instruments often constitute the detailed responses that are studied, and in that sense they serve as definitions. Terman and Miles were in the vanguard of the testing of sex differences, and in 1936 they published "The Attitude-Interest Analysis Test." This scale covers a variety of topics, including procuring

the examinee's associations to words and to ink blots, their vocational, avoca-
tional, and literature preferences, and assessing their general information. Each
item that is included in the test was found to elicit differences in male and female
responses. For example, a woman's association to "baby" is apt to be "infant"
or "darling," whereas a man's is apt to be "cry." If an artist, a man would
like to draw horses, tigers, or ships, whereas a woman would prefer to sketch
children, flowers, or clouds. Men are more apt than women to know that the
tide is influenced by the moon, but women are more apt than men to know that
the color of sapphires is blue.

In order to understand the test definition of masculinity and femininity it is
necessary to pay attention to a few details of the scoring procedures. Each
response on the Attitude-Interest Analysis Test is scored as either + (masculine),
or − (feminine), or zero (neutral). The final score, the algebraic sum of these
marks, indicates a point on a range that at one extreme is labeled masculine, at
the other feminine; the mid-range is not weighted in either dimension. Thus the
multifaceted concept of masculinity-femininity is, on this test, scored as a unidimensional variable.

The Terman-Miles test was the first of similar ones that were devised by other
psychologists (Constantinople, 1973). What is labeled masculine and feminine
is a social product and therefore varies with time. A comparison between the
content of the first test and a modern one brings these changes into clear relief.
In 1936 Terman and Miles inquired about Punch and Judy, asked for the value
in cents of a shilling, asked if examinees liked or did not like Congressman
Volstead, and solicited opinion as to whether or not "married women ought not
to be permitted to teach school" (1936, p. 528). A 1978 test (Spence & Helmriech) solicits reactions to statements about the merit of equal opportunity for
men and women to enter various trades and the sharing of entertainment costs.

The idea that male and female attributes are not mutually exclusive has long
been part of mythology and of literature, but it has not been a significant viewpoint
in psychology until the past twenty-five years. Bakan (1966), one of the first to
suggest a way of breaking away from the dichotomy, proposes that "agency"
and "communion" are "fundamental modalities" or tendencies. He defines
agency as a masculine characteristic and describes it as an orientation toward
mastery, a concern with individuality, and an interest in self-enhancement and
self-protection. The feminine counterpart, communion, is depicted as orientation
toward others, selflessness, and cooperation. Bakan suggests that mature people
balance these two, that purposeful reactions, for example, can be mitigated by
interpersonal sensitivity and fellowship can be complemented by enterprise.

The replacing of tradition with a concept of androgyny began to gain momentum, and as part of this expansion, test construction was revised. The Bem
Sex-Role Inventory (1974) was one of the first revisions to appear. It requires
the respondent to rate how well each trait in a list of sixty reflects the examinee's
personality, and the responses are scored for masculinity, for femininity, and
for androgyny, with the latter reflecting the amount of endorsement of both

masculinity and femininity. Other tests have been devised, and they vary in details but are similar to the Bem Scale in that they assess each of the concepts as separate dimensions of personality.

These conceptual changes have brought with them some additions to the vocabulary, and included among these is an expanded meaning of the word gender. Originally this referred to grammatical distinctions, but it is now used as the equivalent of the word sex. The recent emergence of this terminology means that currently there are more trends than established practices in vocabulary. "Gender role" and "sex role" generally refer to the attitudes, interests, and actions that society sees as characteristic of one sex but not of the other. "Gender identity" and "sex identity" refer to the masculine and feminine patterns that an individual personally accepts and displays (Block, 1973; Cook, 1985; Franklin, 1984).

Research has included an extensive assessment of the age at which gender identity is established, and what experiences are most salient in determining the choice. The studies are so numerous, the laboratory results so complex, and the conclusions so much in dispute that the reader should consult the reviews of the investigations (Block, 1973; Kohlberg, 1966; Samuel, 1981; Sears, 1965).

The issue of differential cognitive skills has also been pursued in depth, but once again, the conclusions are far from convincing. A review of relevant research between 1966 and 1973 by Maccoby and Jacklin (1974) documents the perplexity. Many of the experiments included adults, but there was a much stronger emphasis on stages of growth and development. The authors exercised considerable caution in tracking down inconsistencies and identifying irregularities that come from differences in measurement techniques that children of different ages require. They categorized the validity of each of their conclusions about sex differences as those that are believed to exist but are actually unfounded, those for which the documentation is too limited to warrant definitive judgments, and those that are "fairly well established" (p. 351). One striking aspect of this article is the presence of only four entries in the last category: greater verbal skills among girls, male superiority in both visual-spatial analysis and mathematics, and more aggression on the part of boys.

Maccoby and Jacklin's conclusion is, however, far from final. The question of dissimilarity in cognition is still unanswered, as evidenced by a 1987 meeting of the American Educational Research Association in which twenty-five sessions were devoted to the lack of uniformity in merely two areas, science and mathematics. Some changes in trends were noted; apparently the frequency of "math anxiety," for example, has been reduced among girls. One set of data that points up the complexity of the problem is the disclosure that diversity is larger at the extreme ends of the achievement spectrum than in the middle. Among the thirteen-year-olds who obtain the highest mathematics scores on the Scholastic Aptitude Test there are 12.9 males to every female, but at the mean score for males the ratio is 1.5:1 (Holden, 1987). Many lay people and too many professionals are certain that there are sex differences, and many claim to know what they are, but the participants in this conference stress that there is a need for accurate appraisals of variations in competency. Opinion about this issue appears to be stronger than knowledge.

References

Bakan, D. (1966). *The duality of human existence: An essay on psychology and religion.* Chicago: Rand McNally. The argument is at times difficult to follow, but often rewarding.

Bem, S. L. (1974). The measurement of psychological androgyny. *Journal of Consulting and Clinical Psychology, 42*, 155–162.

Block, J. H. (1973). Conceptions of sex role: Some cross-cultural and longitudinal perspectives. *American Psychologist, 28*, 512–526.

Constantinople, A. (1973). Masculinity-femininity: An exception to a famous dictum. *Psychological Bulletin, 80*, 389–407. A comprehensive and insightful review of the details of the concepts of masculinity and femininity and various ways of measuring them.

Cook, E. P. (1985). *Psychological Androgyny.* New York: Pergamon Press.

Franklin, C. W. (1984). *The changing definition of masculinity.* New York: Plenum Press.

Holden, C. (1987). Female math anxiety on the wane. *Science, 236* (No. 4802), 660–661. This is an informal account of the sessions on male and female achievement and interest in mathematics and science at the 1987 meeting of the American Educational Research Association.

Jastrow, J. (1915). *Character and temperament.* New York: Appleton.

Kohlberg, L. (1966). A cognitive-developmental analysis of children's sex-role concepts and attitudes. In E. E. Maccoby (Ed.), *The development of sex differences* (pp. 82–172). Stanford, CA: Stanford University Press. This contains an extensive annotated bibliography.

Maccoby, E. E., & Jacklin, C. N. (1974). *The psychology of sex differences.* Stanford, CA: Stanford University Press. This volume also includes a lengthy annotated bibliography.

Mead, M. (1935). *Sex and temperament in three primitive societies.* New York: William Morrow. Both Mead's field data and her arguments make a strong case for the social malleability of the personality of both sexes.

Miles, C. C. (1935). Sex in social psychology. In C. Murchison (Ed.), *A handbook of social psychology* (pp. 683–797). Worcester, MA: Clark University Press. This is an unusually comprehensive commentary on sex differences. It brings into clear focus both the history of the topic and the social sophistication of the 1930s.

Miles, C. C. & Terman, L. M. (1929). Sex difference in the association of ideas. *American Journal of Psychology, 41*, 165–206.

Samuel, W. (1981). *Personality: Searching for the sources of human behavior.* New York: McGraw-Hill. This is a textbook, but the chapter "Sex Differences in Personality and Behavior" is unusually thorough.

Sears, R. R. (1965). Development of gender role. In F. A. Beach (Ed.), *Sex and behavior.* (pp. 133–163), New York: John Wiley.

Spence, J. T., & Helmriech, R. L. (1978). *Masculinity and femininity: Their psychological dimensions, correlates, and antecedents.* Austin, TX: University of Texas Press.

Terman, L. M. & Miles, C. C. (1936). *Sex and personality: Studies in masculinity and femininity*. New York: McGraw-Hill. This landmark publication reported an extensive amount of data. The changes in gender preference that come with increasing amounts of education are highlighted. A successful male author, for example, may have many feminine interests, whereas a male day laborer has few. A beauty operator is typically feminine, but a female physician or attorney is apt to have many masculine interests.

Sources of Additional Information

Buss, A. R. (1976). Galton and sex differences: An historical note. *Journal of the History of the Behavioral Sciences, 12*, 283–285. This is a short article, but it does identify Francis Galton as a progenitor of the study of sex differences. David, D. S., & Brannon, R. (Eds.). (1976). *The forty-nine percent majority: The male sex role*. Reading, MA: Addison-Wesley. A collection of papers, the majority by men, discussing the role of males in modern society. Heilbrun, C. G. (1973). *Toward a recognition of androgyny*. New York: Alfred Knopf. A demonstration of the literary treatment of androgyny in myth and fiction. Iazzo, A. N. (1983). The construction and validation of Attitudes Toward Men Scale. *The Psychological Record, 33*, 371–378. This is a technically adequate instrument, but its appeal may be stronger in the popular culture than in professional circles.

MEMORY. 1. The recall of past experiences that are assumed to be stored in unidentified biological structures, most probably neural. 2. Remembering, that is, behavioral sequences in which ongoing, prior, and later experiences are synthesized. 3. The treatment of past experiences in a manner analogous to electronic information processing.

Relatively few of the "facts" about memory are in dispute, but theories about it are actively contested. Memory is an intricate, multidetermined, poorly understood phenomenon, overloaded with doctrine and often discussed in confusing terminology. The topic has attracted notice for a long period of time, and the accuracy of recall, before the advent of writing, was of fundamental importance (Yates, 1966). This significance developed when the intellectual culture was dominated by supernaturalism and memory was interpreted as an entity or inner power. Because science rejects intangibles, theorists were faced with the task of transforming this impalpable concept into a palpable one. Their solutions did not modify the original formulation in any fundamental way, but they appeared to improve the credibility, primarily by declaring that memory is a manifestation of neurological activity and that experiences are recorded in neural traces or engrams.

When psychology became a science, internal forces were replaced with the concept of behavior, and as a result, the entity of memory was discarded and organisms were said *to remember* but *not to have a memory*. Unfortunately linguistic habits prevail over accurate terminology, and the word memory continues in common use. In most instances the authors intend the referent to be remembering, but a few still retain the idea of a reified and enlivened entity.

Additional confusion in terminology comes from a second linguistic practice, specifically using the word memory to designate both evidence of remembering per se and the presence of learning. Thus the referent for the phrase "I remember the poem" may be "I can recite the poem" or "I learned the poem." The second interpretation reflects a relationship between LEARNING and memory that is seen as infrangible inasmuch as learned behavior is assumed to be possible only if the changes in behavior are remembered and to become increasingly complex only if the fundamentals are remembered.

The vocabulary is further clouded by the lack of particular specifications for the several collaterals of the word memory that begin with "re." These terms are often used synonymously, but some are also differentiated on occasion (but only on occasion) (English & English, 1958). Following are a few remarks that are intended to remind the reader both of the large choice of words and the lack of precision in their meaning. *Remembering* lacks the connotation of effort that *recollecting* frequently conveys. *Recall* is applied when remembering is stimulated both by a general instruction to remember and by a request to remember specific details.

There are three terms for which there is both a common and a technical meaning. *Reminiscence* designates the familiar mulling over of the past, and in professional literature it also designates the recall, in the absence of practice, of material that was not previously recollected, an improvement that is not common, but one that does occur. *Reconstruction* refers to an experimental procedure in which subjects arrange the items that were initially displayed in the same order in which they were originally presented. *Recognition* also designates a particular procedure, specifically having subjects select from a group of items those that were included in an initial presentation.

Some of the research on memory includes observations of the period between the experience and its recall. Traditionally this interval was construed as merely *retention*, most often a static phase but sometimes interrupted by episodes of *rehearsing*. This traditional notion of "memories on deposit" is currently being displaced by credence in a more active process of *retrieving*, that is, one that locates target items in storage, possibly organizing them before recalling them.

The word forgetting, a corollary of memory, adds even more disorder to the vocabulary in that it designates interruptions in memory, but none of these are unique to forgetting. Rather, they constitute a wide range of actions that replace remembering: "I was *paying so much attention to the game* that I forgot the time"; "During the test I *tried so hard to think of the right answer* that I just forgot everything." Many of the entries in this vast array of ad hoc responses have important consequences, but these are more often academic, economic, occupational, or social than psychological.

The initiation of experimentation on memory is generally credited to Hermann Ebbinghaus (1850–1909), a German psychologist who established numerous research customs for the study of memory. Ebbinghaus was determined to incorporate experimental controls, including quantification, in the then new science of the mind. He was unusually innovative, and several of his research procedures are still in use. He was aware that the amount that is remembered may be a function of how well it is understood, and that recall is not simply accurate or inaccurate, but often partial or fragmented. He decided to use nonsense syllables as a means of homogenizing the meaning of what is memorized, and he devised more than two thousand, each consisting of a combination of two consonants and a vowel in a pattern that is relatively equal in novelty, for example, *vos, diw, dop*. Using only himself as a subject Ebbinghaus repeated lists of nonsense syllables aloud and at a constant rate until he could recite them in order without error. He then relearned these lists after various intervals and used the reduction in the number of trials needed for the second learning as a measure of the amount remembered. Ebbinghaus found that the amount that is forgotten is most marked immediately after acquisition and then drops more slowly, with the curve gradually flattening (Ebbinghaus, 1885/1913).

These results have been repeatedly confirmed and, with only a few exceptions, are still accepted as valid. A significant modification in them was delayed until 1957, when Underwood demonstrated that the steepness of the initial forgetting increases in proportion to the subject's prior experiences in memorizing. LEARN-ING THEORY now suggests that Ebbinghaus' history of memorizing reduced his efficiency and that the amount that is immediately forgotten is not as extensive as had the early data indicated.

Most of the alterations that were made in the Ebbinghaus model are more in the nature of amendments than of basic changes. One of the first of these variations is called the paired associates method, devised in 1894 by Calkins. It involves displaying a series of paired items and then requiring subjects to respond with the second member of the dyad as soon as the first is presented. This task resembles learning the vocabulary of a foreign language, and it has the merit of allowing the identification of correct responses within a series.

A second innovation, the method of recognition, requires subjects to identify material that has been previously presented. In one of the early applications (Baldwin & Shaw, 1895) a square was drawn on the blackboard, removed, and then replaced either by a display of a number of squares of different sizes or by a display of only one square. In both conditions subjects were asked to identify the item of the same size as the original. The participants were also asked to draw, that is, to reproduce, the square. Accuracy was higher when it was measured by recognition rather than by reproduction. Analogous discrepancies have been found in the recall of verbal content, thus providing laboratory support for students' convictions that objective examinations are generally easier than the essay variety as well as support for the psychologists' convictions that more intense stimulation increases recall.

The enthusiastic endorsement of Ebbinghaus fostered constraining much of the information about memory to recollections of the past rather than to projections of the future. Experiments relevant to "I remember what happened yesterday" overwhelm those relevant to "I will remember to do that tomorrow."

The procedures also insulated memory from psychological responses other than learning, including a neglect of the interplay between memory and EMOTION, a relationship of deep concern outside the laboratory. A considerable amount of data are recorded about recall and affect in clinical reports, but these often describe unusual, even idiosyncratic, events that are difficult to quantify, and thus researchers find them unattractive. As a result, experimental psychology has little systematic knowledge about either long-range remembering or the mutuality of emotion and memory (Murphy, 1956; Rapaport, 1943).

One of the few exceptions to the Ebbinghaus tradition consists of observations of what is remembered rather than simply how much. This approach is encountered in an early investigation conducted by Kuhlmann (1906) in which he asked subjects on repeated occasions, during a three-month interval, both to describe and to sketch unusual visual designs that they had seen only once. The data indicated that the reproductions were influenced by the previous drawing. Many of the errors that appeared in the first sketch tended to remain, but changes that were made were in the direction of the commonplace, such as the straightening of slanted lines and the equalizing of uneven lengths. Later investigators, particularly advocates of GESTALT PSYCHOLOGY, also found that errors are not random and that they progress toward a familiar or standard stimulus (Wulf, 1922/1938). Bartlett (1932), a renowned British experimenter, was so impressed with changes of various kinds in the recall of numerous visual and auditory stimuli that he referred to memory as "productive" rather than "reproductive." These modifications in what is recalled have, however, attracted much less attention than the reports of the amount that is remembered.

The second concept of memory was formulated in the theory of INTERBE-HAVIORAL PSYCHOLOGY, and it contrasts sharply with the Ebbinghaus model. Interbehaviorism rejects the concept of memory as a warehouse and conceptualizes the phenomenon as a response, specifically as remembering, and this is construed both as recalling the past and as relating previous events to the immediate present and to the future. These reactions occur only in the presence of relevant stimuli, and these may be either explicit or implicit. To illustrate— yesterday's promise to return a telephone call today comes to fruition when an incoming call triggers the recall of the promise; reminiscing about childhood provokes thinking about a playmate and that reaction stimulates speculation about the person's current whereabouts and that association in turn elicits others.

Interbehavioral psychology also relates remembering to perspective. Each person views the world in unique ways. There is little doubt, for example, that a surgeon and an accountant perceive a surgical suite differently. The traditional concept of memory ascribes this variation to the storage of different personal experiences. Interbehaviorism, in contrast, proposes that personal contacts modify both STIMULUS FUNCTIONS and RESPONSE FUNCTIONS. Once a person learns, for example, to use a suture needle it is psychologically a different stimulus than it was before this practice; that is, the object has acquired a new function. In this frame of reference, remembering is not a process of tapping into storage, but a process of eliciting responses and ones that vary with both the intensity of provocation and its meaning for each individual. In other words, differences in perspective are not the result of a record, but of the quality and quantity of the arousal (Verplanck, 1983).

The third and most recent concept of memory grew out of the currently popular practice in COGNITIVE PSYCHOLOGY of drawing analogies between information processing and psychological phenomenon. An apparent similarity between the functioning of electric circuits and neural traces or engrams made memory appear unusually suitable for this enterprise. Engineers and mathematicians began to talk about computers, inorganic entities, in terms that had previously been more frequently applied to organic structures and events. Probably the most conspicuous of the terms used in this way is the word memory (von Neumann, 1958). Psychologists, in turn, began to refer to organic processes with words that are customarily applied in the inorganic domain, and material to be memorized, for example, came to be called input and is said to be encoded. Atkinson and Shiffrin (1968) describe a scheme in which information is conceptualized as entering the human system through a sensory register, then flowing into a short-term store, and then into a long-term store or repository.

The hypothetical nature of memory as a processing phenomenon prohibits direct access to these events, and experimenters use a number of compensatory tactics. One involves analyzing changes in the material as encoded and as retrieved. Some researchers augment this information by asking subjects to describe how they recall. Evidence is accumulating that the organization of the material, particularly at the input stage, is more important than had been previously realized. Recall also appears to be influenced by the mode in which a person represents the material, as, for example, in images versus formal, verbal propositions.

Since the middle to late 1970s previously unavailable data about extended periods of retention have been reported. One of these experiments also points up the enhancing effects of knowledge and understanding at the time the material is learned. In this research Bahrick (1984) measured the remembering of Spanish that had been studied in academic courses, in the case of some subjects as long as fifty years previously—a rare design in that it assesses the long-term retention of normal, extralaboratory educational experiences. The results disclosed that recall declines during the first six years after courses are completed, remains at a constant level for about twenty-five years, and then again declines. Bahrick locates this long-term retention in a "permastore," and the laboratory data indicate that few people rehearse this material in significant amounts. Subjects who remember the larger amounts of permastore content are those who had the most instruction and received high grades.

A second research procedure that does not use direct observations involves measuring different aspects of processing. This is accomplished in various ways, and a popular one is to use REACTION TIME as an index of the time required for retrieval (Westcourt & Atkinson, 1976). Another commonly used strategy consists of ascertaining the level of agreement between postulated and observed events. Several comparisons of this nature have been made, and they are illustrated here by a brief reference to attempts to determine the validity of the assumption that the capacity of memory is limited. One experimental technique, called shadowing, requires subjects to repeat a message—in some experiments a short one, in others a long one—as it is delivered to one ear—sometimes slowly, sometimes rapidly—while at the same time ignoring material that is being delivered to the other ear or, less frequently, to the eyes. This procedure is based on the premise that limited capacity would interfere with information coming from more than one channel. Cofer's (1979) review of the relevant literature allowed him to conclude that there is support for the assumption of limited capacity inasmuch as the retention of the secondary message is minimal.

Recent evidence is weakening the certainty about the comparability of human and computer memory. Estes (1980) lists some differences in the two mechanisms, pointing out that computer memory is activated when ordered and fails only when purposefully eradicated or when equipment fails. Engineered mechanisms have a high fidelity, and the specifications for preserving the original are known. Human memory, in contrast, is initiated both by the self and by others, fails unpredictably, especially in the case of minor disruptions, and distorts in directions that are far from fully comprehended.

These discrepancies hamper the devising of a concept of memory that is analogous to electronics. Furthermore, there are cues that this strategy may be displaced by concepts that acknowledge the changes in recall that were observed during the first quarter of the century as well as the interbehavioral interpretation of memory as a process of change. Estes illustrates this shift by expressing doubts about some of the traditional attributes: "It [memory] seems to be not at all like a storeroom, a library, or a computer core memory, a place where items of information are stored and kept until wanted, but rather presents a picture of a complex, dynamic system. . . . In fact, human memory does not, in a literal sense, store anything; it simply changes as a function of experience" (p. 68).

References

Atkinson, R. C., & Shiffrin, R. M. (1968). Human memory: A proposed system and its control processes. In K. W. Spence & J. T. Spence (Eds.), *The psychology of learning and motivation: Advances in research and theory* (Vol. 2, pp. 89–195). New York: Academic Press.

Bahrick, H. P. (1984). Semantic memory content in permastore: Fifty years of memory for Spanish learned in school. *Journal of Experimental Psychology: General, 113*, 1–29.

Baldwin, J. M., & Shaw, W. J. (1895). Memory for square size. *Psychological Review, 2*, 236–259.

Bartlett, F. C. (1932). *Remembering: A study in experimental and social psychology*. Cambridge: Cambridge University Press. Bartlett's research design included successive reproductions of visual stimuli by the same person as well as reproductions

of auditory material by several people. The latter simulates the way in which
information about the past is distorted as it is spread through a group.

Calkins, M. W. (1894). Association. *Psychological Review, 1*, 476–483.

Cofer, C. N. (1979). Human learning and memory. In E. Hearst (Ed.), *The first century
of experimental psychology* (pp. 323–369). Hillsdale, NJ: Lawrence Erlbaum.

Ebbinghaus, H. (1913). *Memory: A contribution to experimental psychology*. (H. A.
Ruger & C. E. Bussenius, Trans.). New York: Teacher's College, Columbia
University. (Original work published 1885). Ebbinghaus writes in a clear, straightforward manner and clarifies why he chose particular procedures. He was aware
of erratic and uncontrolled errors, and he estimated statistically their probable
size.

English, H. B., & English, A. C. (1958). *A comprehensive dictionary of psychological
and psychoanalytical terms*. New York: Longmans, Green.

Estes, W. K. (1980). Is human memory obsolete? *American Scientist, 68*, 62–69. Estes'
conclusion that there are basic differences between computer and human memory
seems obvious. The fact of making such a point indicates the depth to which the
metaphor with electronics has intruded into the study of memory.

Kuhlmann, F. (1906). On the analysis of the memory consciousness: A study in the
mental imagery and memory of meaningless visual forms. *Psychological Review,
13*, 316–348. Kuhlmann's research is carefully controlled and more precise than
was typical of the era.

Murphy, G. (1956). The current impact of Freud upon psychology. *American Psychologist, 11*, 663–672. This is an invited address to the Division of Clinical Psychology of the American Psychological Association. Murphy assesses Freud's
influence on the broad field of psychology, including the concept of memory.

Rapaport, D. (1943). Emotions and memory. *Psychological Review, 50*, 234–243.

Underwood, B. J. (1957). Interference and forgetting. *Psychological Review, 64*, 49–
60.

Verplanck, W. S. (1983). Remembering: Reflections upon reading a dissertation. *The
Psychological Record, 33*, 421–425. Verplanck develops the argument that theories of memory are based *not* on behavior, but on the technology the culture
uses to make and preserve physical records.

von Neumann, J. (1958). *The computer and the brain*. New Haven CT: Yale University
Press.

Westcourt, K. T., & Atkinson, R. C. (1976). Fact retrieval processes in human memory.
In W. K. Estes (Ed.), *Handbook of learning and cognitive processes: Vol. 4.
Attention and memory* (pp. 363–413). Hillsdale, NJ: Lawrence Erlbaum. The
authors suggest that the demands for accurate retrieval restrict investigations to
error-free retention.

Wulf, F. (1938). Tendencies in figural variation. In W. D. Ellis (Ed.), *A source book
of Gestalt psychology* (pp. 136–148). London: Routledge & Kegan Paul. (Original
work published 1922). A classic paper that provoked arguments—both pro and
con. It is a bit difficult to read and may be more frequently cited than read.

Yates, F. A. (1966). *The art of memory*. London: Routledge & Kegan Paul. The author
begins this survey for improving memory with an account of the techniques that
the Greeks used. "Mnemotechnics" was important before the advent of printing
because it was the only available "record."

Sources of Additional Information

Blankenship, A. B. (1938). Memory span: A review of the literature. *Psychological Bulletin, 35*, 1–25. Early research disclosed a relationship between age and grade level and memory span (the maximum number of units that can be recalled from a single presentation). As a result, memory span was included in intelligence tests, and modern psychometrists continue to use this measure. Ericsson, K. A. & Chase, W. G. (1982). Exceptional memory. *American Scientist, 70*, 607–615. "It appears that normal people's memory for prose involves the same mechanisms that underlie expert memory" (p. 614). A discussion of unusual memory feats. Miller, G. A. (1956). The magical number seven, plus or minus two: Some limits on our capacity for processing information. *Psychological Review, 63*, 81–97. This is a frequently cited experiment on the capacity of human memory. Miller, accepting seven as the number of discrete stimuli a normal adult can grasp at one time, found that when items are "chunked" (organized), capacity is expanded to seven "chunks." Tulving, E. (1972). Episodic and semantic memory. In E. Tulving & W. Donaldson (Eds.), *Organization of memory* (pp. 381–403). New York: Academic Press. Tulving elaborates the differences between episodic memory, the recall of personal or dated events, and semantic memory, the recall of facts or relationships. He ascribes the original formulation of semantic memory to M. R. Quillian as part of the work on a doctoral dissertation completed in 1966. Tulving sees semantic memory as outside the Ebbinghaus tradition.

METHODOLOGICAL BEHAVIORISM. See BEHAVIORISM.

MOTIVATION. 1. The initiating and directing of behavior. **MOTIVE.** 1. An hypothesized force—such as an instinct, drive, need, goal, or incentive—that is believed to guide, or at least to bias, the organism toward specific ends.

Motivation refers to the activation of behavior and the guiding of it toward particular objects or events. Motive designates the particular agent or force that is assumed to energize and to regulate. The directing property of a motive distinguishes it from a STIMULUS, an immediate instigator of behavior.

The concept of motivation has, with few exceptions, involved a combination of real events and suppositions. Many of the latter are residuals of the custom in prescientific eras of seeking explanations in the supernatural rather than in the natural realm. This heritage teaches that organisms are activated, guided, and even controlled by gods, demons, and spirits, with specific ones identified variously by era. Convictions about this matter were so throughtly entrenched that would-be scientists had difficulty repudiating them. Supernatural agents were relatively readily discarded, but the idea that an organism is energized by an auxiliary force was not excised, and as a result, even modern theories contain both material and immaterial components. To illustrate—Harvey A. Carr, a proponent of FUNCTIONAL PSYCHOLOGY, began a discussion of motivation with the naturalistic position that reactivity is inherent: "Organisms are necessarily active because they are alive and are continually being subjected to sensory stimulations. There is no need to postulate the existence of an 'instinct of activity' in order to account for the activity of living organisms" (1925, p. 72). Carr then decided that this vitality does not apply to adaptive responses, and as a scholar of the era and a legatee of philosophical doctrine, he decided that activation does occur: "The motivating stimulus . . . *arouses and energizes* [italics added] the act" (1925, p. 72).

A decade later P. T. Young published *Motivation of Behavior*, and the first sentence in that volume reveals how unrestrained the belief in activation became: "All behavior is motivated" (1936, p. 1). The text also asserts that the phenomenon is material: "The *arousal* of behavior necessarily implies a release of physical energy from the tissues" (1936, p. 45). The durability of this conviction is documented in a passage in a second book by Young, published twenty five years after the original: "The two most important aspects are the *energetic* aspect and the aspect of *regulation and direction*" (1961, p. 24).

Some additional nonempirically based ideas about motivation came from philosophy. Probably the most influential of these is the ethical principle that people have a duty to seek pleasure and avoid pain (McTeer, 1972). Self-defeating reactions, such as explicit and observable disobedience, gambling, and smoking, should cast doubt on the validity of this hedonic premise, but the doctrine is only seldom defeated. Its credence is so firmly established that one can find the habitual misbehavior of a child "explained" on the basis of the gratification that comes from the attention the child receives while being punished.

The early scientific literature supplemented philosophy as a source of some "facts" about motivation. One of the more familiar of these came from the heightened interest in survival that the study of evolution provoked. This view brought the question of why organisms behave in particular ways to the forefront, and this gave added attention to instincts. Although INSTINCT doctrine would later come under severe censure, its early persuasiveness appeared to assure the reality and efficacy of an internal vitalizing force (Russell, 1970).

A second scientific explanation that motivation theorists adopted is that of homeostasis, a principle that affirms that disruptions in equilibrium or imbalances in physiological processes stimulate activity that restores the balance. This biological principle was transposed to psychological events, and word was spread that organisms seek psychological stability (Cofer and Appley, 1964). It is believed, for example, that poverty in childhood leads to a strong motive to acquire wealth in adulthood. This assurance usually stands by itself, unsubstantiated by information about the number of instances in which this sequel does not develop, the number of times in which the aftereffect is not an unrelenting frugality, nor the number of people who do not act on this aspect of their history.

The concept of motivation implies that behavior is controlled and regulated, and this makes it attractive because the regularity gives off a kind of scientific aura (Cofer, 1981). These different vectors nurtured numerous investigations of such different motives as INSTINCT, DRIVE, NEED, COMPETENCE, INCENTIVE, and GOAL. This work led to the concept of SOCIAL MOTIVATION, motives that are activated and appeased by the behavior of others. The more conspicuous of these are NEED FOR ACHIEVEMENT, NEED FOR AFFILIATION, NEED FOR POWER, FEAR OF FAILURE, and FEAR OF SUCCESS.

This research spawned masses of data, most of which appeared in the journal literature in the form of reports of single experiments. The first textbook on human motivation was published in 1928 by Leonard Troland. In 1936 Paul T. Young published the previously cited *Motivation of Behavior*, a book also exclusively devoted to motivation, but dealing with both humans and animals. There have been many experiments and the literature is so massive that dichotomies that are intended to consolidate it are in circulation. These efforts reduce the bulk, but they also obscure many relevant variables.

One of these classifies motives as either internal, as in the case of instinct and drive, or external, as in the case of goal and incentive. Informally, the former are said to "push" the organism and the latter to "pull" it. This division overlooks the ineffectiveness of an external motive unless it is linked to variables within an organism. A second scheme categorizes the source of gratification of a motive as either intrinsic or extrinsic. In the former, satisfaction is assumed to come from indulging in the activity—the teacher who instructs for the pleasure of teaching and the toddler who jumps up and down for the sheer joy of jumping. Extrinsic motivation refers to the gaining of satisfaction from something unrelated to the activity—a person who works in order to obtain financial rewards and a child who tidies up the playroom in order to please Mother. A third classification, confined to human motivation, characterizes the awareness of reasons for behaving as either CONSCIOUS or UNCONSCIOUS. This polarity neglects the fact that people are frequently neither clearly cognizant of all that spurs them to action nor completely unaware of any of their motives.

Beginning about the middle of the current century experimenters began to attend less to the activation of organisms and to attend more carefully to the variables that determine the particular direction that responses take. Much of the impetus for this shift came from COGNITIVE PSYCHOLOGY, a viewpoint that argues for the study of covert behavior and frequently casts psychological events as analogous to information processing. This orientation brings reactions within the organism into focus, particularly the sequence in which they occur. The cumulative effect of these various revisions is a reduction in the importance of the idea of activation. Taylor (1960) illustrates this modern stance and even reiterates Carr's 1925 comment that life and activity are concomitant. In Taylor's own words: "The central problem in motivation . . . is not that of explaining why the individual keeps moving through the maze—he keeps moving primarily because he is alive—but rather that of explaining why the individual, confronted with two or more alternatives of whose consequences he has at least partial knowledge, selects at each choice point the alternative which he does" (1960, p. 63).

Brown also illustrates a disdain of the traditional insistence on activation: "One of the current trends is to assert, *flatly and without explication* [italics added] that behaviors such as eating, drinking, and copulating are 'obviously motivated,' and that the motivational enterprise reduces to the delineation of the

variables of which such behaviors are functions'' (1979, p. 265). He also suggests that the knowledge that is currently available renders much of the original
concept inappropriate: ''Indeed, the new knowledge is so compelling as to provide strong support for the proposition that a clear understanding of the 'how'
of behavior makes further questions as to its 'why' rhetorical'' (1979, p. 265).

References

Brown, J. S. (1979). Motivation. In E. Hearst (Ed.), *The first century of experimental
    psychology* (pp. 231–272). New York: Lawrence Erlbaum. Brown criticizes the
    concept of motivation: ''Motivation is a multifaceted, culturally transmitted, folk-
    loristic idea concerning covert processes believed to initiate or to energize one or
    another form of behavior. The concept was not forged of explanatory necessity
    in the crucible of active experimentation, nor has it been retained for its sub-
    sumptive fertility'' (p. 232).
Carr, H. A. (1925). *Psychology: A study of mental activity*. New York: Longmans, Green.
    One of the chief proponents of functional psychology is emphatic about the ad-
    justive or utilitarian aspects of behavior.
Cofer, C. N. (1981). The history of the concept of motivation. *Journal of the History
    of the Behavioral Sciences, 17*, 48–53.
Cofer, C. N., & Appley, M. H. (1964). *Motivation: Theory and research*. New York:
    John Wiley. This volume offers a thorough coverage of the concept of motivation.
    The section on both physiological and psychological homeostasis is accurate and
    lucid.
McTeer, W. (1972). *The scope of motivation: Environmental, physiological, mental,
    social*. Monterey, CA: Brooks/Cole. ''Even though purposes point to the future,
    they are in reality anticipations *based on prior experiences* in this world of re-
    petitive cycles and recurring events'' (p. 163). The volume contains a succinct,
    but sharply focused discussion of hedonism.
Russell, W. A. (Ed.). (1970). *Milestones in motivation: Contributions to the psychology
    of drive and purpose*. New York: Appleton-Century-Crofts. A collection of papers.
    The editor's introduction to each of the six sections of the book adds coherence
    and continuity to the volume. The discussion of the influence of evolution on
    motivation is well done.
Taylor, D. W. (1960). Toward an information processing theory of motivation. In M. R.
    Jones (Ed.), *Nebraska symposium on motivation* (pp. 51–78). Lincoln: University
    of Nebraska Press.
Troland, L. T. (1967). *The fundamentals of human motivation*. New York: Hafner.
    (Original work published 1928). Troland addresses a variety of problems, in-
    cluding ''the foundations of 'happiness' . . . the explanation of typical modern
    interests: automobiles, radio, and the like'' (p. v).
Young, P. T. (1936). *Motivation of behavior: The fundamental determinants of human
    and animal activity*. New York: John Wiley. Young was adamant that motivational
    psychology be scientific and, for him, that meant an identity with biology: ''Stim-
    uli, from the environment and from the tissues, excite receptors and nerves; the
    nerve cells excite the muscles. From first to last, this process is a physical one,
    and the scientific description of it excludes such conceptions as *libido*, vital, and
    psychic forces unless they be identified with physical processes'' (p. 533).

Young, P. T. (1961) *Motivation and emotion: A survey of the determinants of human and animal activity*. New York: John Wiley.

Sources of Additional Information

Harlow, H. F. (1953). Mice, monkeys, men, and motives. *Psychological Review, 60*, 23–32. Harlow makes a strong case for extrinsic motivation. His criticisms of intrinsic motivation are cogent and written in a way that promotes remembering them: "In the course of human events many psychologists have children, and these children always behave in accord with the theoretical position of their parents" (p. 28). Harlow, H. F., Harlow, M. K., & Suomi, S. J. (1971). From thought to therapy: Lessons from a primate laboratory. *American Scientist, 59*, 538–549. A lucid account of a research program on affectional systems in monkeys, a landmark series of experiments and ones that, among many other things, indicate that an infant's need for bodily contact may be as strong or even stronger than the need to suckle. Holmes, W. G., & Sherman, P. W. (1983). Kin recognition in animals. *American Scientist, 71*, 46–55. The authors introduce their research topic in a manner that reflects both a modern and a traditional stance. They ask *how* animals distinguish intruders and strangers, and they describe the sensory and spatial cues that are used. They also ask *why* this discrimination occurs, but in this instance they adapt an "evolutionary" or "ultimate perspective," and find the motivation to be self-protective, such as avoiding close inbreeding. The article, written for the educated layman, is rich in facts and has an extensive reference list. Kantor, J. R. (1942). Toward a scientific analysis of motivation. *The Psychological Record, 5*, 225–275. A critique of motivational doctrine. Kantor draws attention to the vagueness of the topic, its metaphysical components, and the pervasive confusion between what can be observed and the conjectured causes. Munn, N. L. (1950). *Handbook of psychological research on the rat: An introduction to animal psychology*. Cambridge, MA: Houghton Mifflin. A compendium about one of psychology's most often observed subjects. There is an extended discussion of motives. Woodworth, R. S. (1918). *Dynamic psychology*. New York: Columbia University Press. Dynamic psychology, at this early publication date, paid a great deal of attention to why organisms behave in particular ways. The role of emotions and feelings was barely acknowledged, and the emphasis was on the sources of energy and the directing of behavior.

MOTIVATION, SOCIAL. See NEED and SOCIAL MOTIVATION.

MOTIVE. See MOTIVATION and MOTIVE.

N

NEED. 1. An hypothesized internal state that is believed to be caused by either physiological or psychological events, and one that activates the organism to seek gratification, in the first instance in the biological domain, and in the second, in relationships between the self and others. **SOCIAL MOTIVATION.** 1. Motivation that comes from needs that are activated, directed, appeased, and defeated by the behavior of others.

In everyday conversation the word need is often used in an evaluative rather than in a motivational sense in that the reference is to something ameliorative, for example, "She needs a reprimand" or "I need money." The clarity of the experience ranges from a vague uneasiness through a desire that is imperative, and indulging may or may not be salutary, for example, "I want reassurance" and "I'm going after a fix."

Initially the concepts of DRIVE and of need dealt with the effects of organic instabilities, especially insufficiencies, and thus sometimes these words are used synonymously. Psychologists interested in the study of PERSONALITY perceived that complex human motivation could not be understood by attending merely to biological phenomena, and they turned attention to needs that are generated and satisfied by psychological rather than physiological variables. This area of study came to be called social motivation; the word need came to be applied, frequently but not exclusively, to humans and the word drive pertained to animals.

Henry A. Murray generated one of the cardinal concepts of need (1937, 1938). His theory is complex, but it merits review because it contributes significantly to the definition of different social motives. He first divided needs into two categories, similar to the classification of drives, that is, as primary and secondary. He labeled the former viscerogenic and the latter psychogenic, and characterized viscerogenic needs as dependent on organic or physiological variables. He characterized psychogenic needs as activators or forces—some conscious, some unconscious or unrecognized—and described them as originating in and assuaged by interpersonal relationships.

Murray assumed that since both behavior and ideation are directed by needs, what an individual thinks and what he or she does disclose them. To illustrate— a person who *imagines* being bountiful, becoming a benefactor, and also *acts* in a generous and helpful manner is, in Murray's terminology, said to have a "need *for* nurturance." The need is not to be helped personally, but to be of assistance to others. One who personally wants help is said to have a "need for succorance." This may be disclosed covertly, for example, by imagining that one is receiving care, and/or overtly, for example, actually asking for help or actively seeking sympathy.

Murray, assisted by a team of colleagues, probed the life histories of a group of undergraduates and catalogued the needs they displayed. He also classified what he called press, the ways in which the environment had treated them. For example, the statement "My mother was always generous and understanding" is identified as a nurturant press. Murray retained the same spelling for both the singular and the plural of press, and he labeled each need-press interaction a thema.

Murray and his staff then investigated different methods of studying themas and came to the conclusion that it would be both feasible and practical to replace direct observations of behavior with analyses of stories that subjects make up when they are asked, first, to describe what is going on in each of a series of ambiguous pictures and, then, to relate events that might have preceded and might follow the scene. The vagueness of the pictures and the failures to specify the sequence of events result in content that comes mainly from the narrator. Because the amount of autobiographical information is increased when the scenes portray people of a similar age and the same sex as the subject, four sets of pictures were devised, one for boys, girls, men, and women. A "hero" is identified in each story, and the needs and press of this character are assumed to be those of the narrator.

This procedure is called the Thematic Apperception Test, and the techniques for administering it and comprehensive instructions for judging or scoring the content have been devised (Morgan & Murray, 1935; Murray, 1943). The title of this test reactivated an obsolete term in psychology (Rooper, 1891). Both PERCEPTION and apperception refer to the integration of previous experiences with current ones, but apperception is conceptualized as less dependent than perception on the immediate stimulus and more dependent than perception on personal convictions about the outcome of events. To illustrate—an automobile driver, perceiving that the car he is driving is out of control, predicts extensive injuries and apperceives the administering of medical miracles, whereas a second, also perceiving that the vehicle is out of control, predicts maneuvering that is so skillful that he regains control of the vehicle and apperceives commendations from the passengers. In both of these stories the hero discloses a press of physical danger, but there are differences in motives, including the first person's need for succorance and the second's need for exhibition (Murray, 1943).

Psychological research is sustained by methodology, and before Murray the experimental work on psychogenic needs had been handicapped by the absence of appropriate methods. His method of assessment provided a tool and was, and continues to be, used extensively. There are critics, but in general those who have adopted the method have exerted more influence than the opposition. Only a few fault the conjectural status of needs, and references are rare to the serious limitations that may be imposed by the possible failure to identify all existing needs (Marx & Hillix, 1979; Woodworth, 1958).

The concept of social motivation, in many respects a direct outgrowth of Murray's work on thematic apperception, was initiated during a period in which more credence was placed in physiological than in psychological phenomena, and the research started in a conservative way, specifically by means of an experiment on the effects of hunger. The concept of need as a variety of social motivation can best be understood by a recital of the main steps that were taken to break away from the biological constraints.

The inaugural experiment, conducted by McClelland and Atkinson (1948), included measuring the influence of different periods of food deprivation on perception. The subjects, shown an illuminated but blank projection screen, were told that very faint pictures were being projected, and they were asked to write their impressions of each. The results disclosed that as hunger intensified, the number of food and food-related replies increased, and the references to efforts to procure nourishment and to objects related to food increased more than the references to obtaining food. The latter difference suggested that the technique was tapping desire rather than gratification, and this trend in the data helped to orient the concept of social motivation to what is wanted rather than to what is obtained. In a second study the same investigators (Atkinson & McClelland, 1948) once more varied levels of hunger, but this time they used ambiguously sketched pictures, and found that the evidence of the need for food changed with the level of hunger in essentially the same pattern they had found in the previous experiment.

One of the next steps was that of ascertaining whether or not a social motive could alter the narratives in ways similar to the effects of a biological deficit. For this phase of the experimental program the investigators (McClelland, Clark, Roby & Atkinson, 1949) used the NEED FOR ACHIEVEMENT. The specific purpose was to find out if there are thematic differences among subjects whose social motive has been aroused to different levels of intensity. They asked male undergraduates, before writing stories about a series of pictures, to perform a few simple tasks, such as rearranging letters to form anagrams and unscrambling words. The experimenters then interpreted the purpose of the tasks in ways that were designed to vary the need for achievement. For example, in one group an effort was made to induce a relaxed attitude by informing the participants that they were assisting a graduate student in the development of a test and that the test items, rather than the students, were on trial. In another group the subjects were informed that the tasks had been assigned in order to identify colleges with the highest number of potential leaders and that the scores they had obtained were low. Analyses of the stories indicated that those made up by the relaxed group differed from those in the "failing" or motivated group in ways similar to the changes that accompany varying levels of hunger.

This inaugural work set the pattern for much of the research on social motivation. It consists of obtaining a series of ambiguous pictures; procuring stories for each of these scenes from subjects in whom a particular social motive has been aroused and from those who are not similarly motivated, but are otherwise comparable; carefully examining all stories in order to make certain that there is adequate evidence that the need in question is present; tallying the number of times the need that is being studied is encountered in each story; and comparing the scores of the experimental or aroused groups with those in the control or neutral groups. This procedure, called the thematic apperception method, differs from the Thematic Apperception Test in that the scenes that are shown are related to the motive that is being investigated, and the needs of all the characters in the story, not just the "hero," are taken into consideration. Each of these steps is essential, but the principles for judging the presence of a need are crucial because these directions help researchers to agree with one another in the way they analyze the narratives. They also provide a definition of each concept that is technical, cohesive, and clearly bounded. The research has resulted in the formulation of several social motives, but some appear to be tautological and have attracted little attention. Those that are viable, and appear to be able to remain so are the NEED FOR ACHIEVEMENT, FEAR OF FAILURE, FEAR OF SUCCESS, NEED FOR AFFILIATION, and NEED FOR POWER.

Although the thematic apperception method is a dominant one in the field of social motivation, it is not the only method, and different procedures often yield results that vary from those obtained by the thematic method. Probably the most common discrepancy is found between apperceptively determined needs and those that are based on self-reports, such as by the use of questionnaires as well as those observed in interviews. A person may, for example, describe himself or herself as having a need for others, and support this with comments that he or she is drawn to others, is highly desirous of companionship, and is intolerant of being alone. Acquaintances may agree with this assessment. The thematic material may concur with these opinions, *or* it may disclose that what appears behaviorally as a need for affiliation is more a need for power because relating to others involves both attempts and plans to control and manipulate. In other words, the concept of need as a variable discerned from the way a person thinks and acts and is not necessarily identical with the way the self is described.

References

Atkinson, J. W., & McClelland, D. C. (1948). The projective expression of needs: 2. The effect of different intensities of the hunger drive on thematic apperception. *Journal of Experimental Psychology, 38*, 643–658. A reference experiment.

Marx, M. H., & Hillix, W. A. (1979). *Systems and theories in psychology* (3rd ed.). New York: McGraw-Hill.

McClelland, D. C., & Atkinson, J. W. (1948). The projective expression of needs: 1. The effect of different intensities of the hunger drive on perception. *Journal of Psychology, 25*, 205–222. The title is a bit misleading in that the subjects were told that a scene was projected on a screen when the screen was actually blank. An argument could be developed that this was more a study of suggestion than of perception, but laboring that issue is, in this context, less important than the results.

McClelland, D. C., Clark, R. A., Roby, T. B., & Atkinson, J. W. (1949). The projective expression of needs: 4. The effect of the need for achievement on thematic apperception. *Journal of Experimental Psychology, 39*, 242–255.

Morgan, C. D., & Murray, H. A. (1935). A method for investigating fantasies. *Archives of Neurology and Psychiatry, 34*, 289–306. "When some one attempts to interpret a complex social situation he is apt to tell as much about himself as he is about the phenomena on which attention is focused. At such times the person is off his guard, since he believes that he is merely explaining objective occurrences" (p. 289).

Murray, H. A. (1937). Facts which support the concept of need or drive. *Journal of Psychology, 3*, 27–42.

Murray, H. A. (1938). *Explorations in personality: A clinical and experimental study of fifty men of college age.* New York: Oxford University Press. Murray criticizes laboratory paraphernalia and, by implication, defends his search for elusive but significant variables: "Some psychologists have an almost religious attachment to physical apparatus . . . Working with such contrivances they have the 'feel' of being purely scientific . . . Sometimes this is nothing but a groundless fantasy . . . It is dubious whether many crucial problems in psychology can be solved by instruments. Certainly if physical appliances do not give results which lead to conceptual understanding, it is not scientific to employ them" (p. 26).

Murray, H. A. (1943). *Thematic Apperception Test Manual.* Cambridge, MA: Harvard University Press.

Rooper, T. G. (1891). *Apperception;—or—the essential mental operation in the act of learning.* Syracuse, NY: C. W. Bardeen. A discussion of the contribution of "modern" psychologists to the acquisition of knowledge. Rooper explains to parents and teachers how to help children relate the new to the familiar.

Woodworth, R. S. (1958). *Dynamics of behavior.* New York: Henry Holt. Woodworth states that relating motivation to internal needs is more parsimonious than relating motivation to environmental manipulation but doubts if the former "could possibly be stretched to cover the play motives of children and the absorbing interests of adults" (p. 102).

Sources of Additional Information

Koch, S. (1951). The current status of motivational psychology. *Psychological Review, 58*, 147–154. Koch discusses needs, and the problems and questions surrounding the concept at the date of writing. Solomon, R. L. (1980). The opponent-process theory of acquired motivation: The costs of pleasure and the benefits of pain. *American Psychologist, 35*, 691–712. An effort to account for dangerous and unpleasant behavior as well as affection and social attachment. The explanation is intricate. Tolman, E. C. (1949). The nature and functioning of wants. *Psychological Review, 56*, 357–369. Tolman discusses the differences between "want, *as an immediate event*" (p. 357) and "a complex of underlying 'drives' or 'needs' " (p. 359).Veroff, J., & Veroff, J. B. (1980). *Social Incentives: A life-span developmental approach*. New York: Academic Press. A discussion of motives at various developmental levels.

NEED FOR ACHIEVEMENT.   See ACHIEVEMENT.

NEED FOR AFFILIATION.   1. Desires for friendly, companionate and/or intimate interpersonal contacts.

The need for affiliation is a variety of SOCIAL MOTIVATION, and research on the topic first appeared three years after the inaugural account in the literature of the NEED FOR ACHIEVEMENT. Interest in this NEED was precipitated when a group of undergraduate males, who believed that they had made a poor showing on a personality test, were observed to disclose some concerns about socializing and having friends. These remarks suggested that a need for affiliation had been aroused, and in order to learn more about such a motive, Shipley and Veroff (1952) designed and conducted a formal experiment. In this they analyzed the responses to a request to describe each picture in a series of ambiguous scenes and to imagine what has happened before the scene occurred as well as what will happen next. The assumption is made that what the characters in the stories do is directed by their motives, and what the subject reports that the environment does—called the press—constitutes apperception, that is, opinions about the important, long-term consequences of environmental action. Each need-press interaction is called a thema, and the procedure is called the thematic apperception method. The vagueness of the scenes as well as the absence of information about the sequence of events elicit material that draws heavily from the personality of the subject and therefore discloses his or her needs and apperceptions.

In order to ascertain the effects of different levels of intensity of the need for affiliation, Shipley and Veroff compared the stories made up by two groups of fraternity members; one in which the members rated one another on a series of personality traits and a second in which no attention was drawn to personality. They also compared the responses of a sample of undergraduates who had joined a fraternity with a second that consisted of students who had sought membership but had been denied it and gave some evidence of being disappointed. In both comparisons the students whose social skills were questioned showed more concern in their stories about separation from others and more unhappiness because of rejection, being ignored, and/or being lonely.

The identification of thematic content that indicates the presence of various needs in the narrator's thoughts is a complex task, and experimental rigor demands the establishing of clear-cut guidelines for judging, typically referred to as scoring, the presence of each need. These principles make it possible for researchers to agree with one another, and define the motive in a comprehensive and explicit manner. Establishing scoring guides has turned out to be particularly difficult in the case of the need for affiliation. Various rules have been devised, but none has gained widespread sanction. As a result the definition of the need for affiliation is not in a form that is accepted as final.

The scoring criteria that Shipley and Veroff devised failed in a second experiment to differentiate groups that varied in the intensity of the motive. In order to accommodate to this failure the guidelines were extended to include thinking about and/or reaching out for friendly, convivial relationships (Atkinson, Heyns, & Veroff, 1954). Thus the affiliation motive came to involve both approaches to and retreats from others. In 1958 a second revision of the criteria was published but identified as a version that would probably be further refined (Heyns, Veroff, & Atkinson). The evidence demanded in this last scheme centers around the concept of friendship. References to behavior that comes from merely a sense of obligation, kinship, or marriage are not considered sufficiently strong in affiliation to be scored. Neither does sexual activity per se qualify. A wish or striving to relate to another person(s) is the crucial factor.

The combining into a single score of both retrenching and reaching out drew criticism, and the proposed corrections brought about various modifications in experimental procedures as well as suggested alterations in the scoring criteria. Boyatzis concludes from a review of the two decades of research on the need for affiliation that "unfortunately, it is difficult to draw any conclusions from the data except that something is not right" (1973, p. 261). Boyatzis ascribes much of the confusion to the original vagueness about the concept because this ambiguity left the door open for researchers, confronted with unforeseen results, to assume that the source of the irregularity was in the scoring rather than in some other aspect of the design.

One of the more recent innovations is the formulation of a need for intimacy, "complementary but related" to the need for affiliation (McAdams, 1980, p. 413). The data on which this need is based were obtained by the thematic apperception method, but the scoring principles for the need for intimacy give more weight to affective reactions than to overt behavior (McAdams, 1982). Following are examples of this kind of content: "They're just sitting there enjoying being together," "Discussing their future together as a couple," "He feels responsible for their well-being," "They have a kind of rapport that spans time and generations" (McAdams, 1982, pp. 143–144).

The early work on the need for affiliation was, as in the case of the need for achievement, based almost exclusively on male undergraduate subjects. Stewart and Chester (1982) compiled a review of the sex differences that have been reported, and they judge none of these as important. Their overall appraisal of the research is positive, but they are not explicit about the particular version of the concept they endorse: "In general, affiliation motivation appears to be a valid measure for both men and women. It is aroused in similar ways and expressed in fantasy by similar imagery. For both sexes, the motive appears to be related to behavior that is meant to establish and maintain relationships, particularly among one's peers" (Stewart & Chester, 1982, p. 196).

There is additional research on affiliation that is noteworthy. It does not follow the standard social motivation procedures, but rather emerged in experiments conducted by Schachter (1959) in a search for the purposes that gregariousness serves. Schachter assembled relevant evidence from a variety of sources, and concluded that isolation induces anxiety and this in turn induces a need for affiliation. This information led him to design an experiment that would arouse anxiety and also offer varying opportunities for affiliation. Some subjects were told that they would receive painful shocks, and others were told that the shocks they would receive would not be distressing. These instructions were intended to intimidate, and they were conveyed by a person surrounded by a great deal of apparatus and identified as a physician who experiments on the effects of electric shocks.

The subjects rated the strength of both their desire for companionship and their fears at various steps in the procedure as well as at the conclusion, (when they were advised of the contrived nature of the experimental situation and assured that electric shocks would not be administered to anyone). During the experiment some participants were assigned to work alone, others joined individuals who were also awaiting shock, and still others were in groups assembled for reasons unrelated to the experimental procedure. The amount of conversation and its relevance to the anticipated shocks were monitored. The data indicate that anxiety had indeed been aroused, and the greater the apprehension, the stronger the preference for companions who are also anxious. Similarity, however, seems to be important in that the subjects preferred to be alone rather than to be with people who were not involved in the research. "Misery doesn't love just any kind of company, it loves only miserable company" (Schachter, 1959, p. 24).

Schachter concludes that people in the same plight do not seek others in order to plot escapes or even to share speculations about what is transpiring. Rather, they seem to be seeking information as to how others in a comparable predicament behave. The spread of the distress throughout the group increases the probability of acquiring information as to what is appropriate, what is beneficial, and what is unfortunate—information that helps one to understand and to guide the self.

The literature dealing with social support groups seldom refers to Schachter, and when it does, the citation often appears to be more "for the record" than as a rationale for the experiment (Sarason, 1981). Nonetheless, this research helps to clarify why mutual assistance groups are so popular, why so many troubled people affiliate with the similarly distressed.

References

Atkinson, J. W., Heyns, R. W., & Veroff, J. (1954). The effect of experimental arousal of the affiliation motive on thematic apperception. *Journal of Abnormal and Social Psychology, 49*, 405–410. These researchers used a different set of pictures than those used by Shipley and Veroff in the original study (1952), and they also obtained different results. The discrepancy provoked "a broader definition of affiliation imagery" (p. 405).

Boyatzis, R. E. (1973). Affiliation motivation. In D. C. McClelland & R. S. Steele (Eds.), *Human motivation: A book of readings* (pp. 252–277). Morristown, NJ: General Learning Press.

Heyns, R. W., Veroff, J., & Atkinson, J. W. (1958). A scoring manual for the affiliation motive. In J. W. Atkinson (Ed.), *Motives in fantasy, action, and society: A method of assessment and study* (pp. 205–218). Princeton, NJ: Van Nostrand. The authors characterize the assumptions underlying thematic scoring: "The subject is asked to write a four minute story . . . If his thoughts are saturated with imagery concerning one particular goal . . . it is assumed that his motivation for that particular goal is sufficiently strong to prevent competing associations in his imaginative story for that period of time" (p. 217).

McAdams, D. P. (1980). A thematic coding system for the intimacy motive. *Journal of Research in Personality, 14,* 413–432.

McAdams, D. P. (1982). Intimacy motivation. In A. J. Stewart (Ed.), *Motivation and society: A volume in honor of David C. McClelland* (pp. 133–171). San Francisco: Jossey-Bass.

Sarason, I. G. (1981). Test anxiety, stress, and social support. *Journal of Personality, 49,* 101–114. The author speculates about possible reasons why affiliation facilitates test performance: "Social support may be effective because the presence of an interested other shakes the individual's assumption that he or she must face a challenge alone" (p. 112).

Schachter, S. (1959). *The psychology of affiliation: Experimental studies of the sources of gregariousness.* Stanford, CA: Stanford University Press.

Shipley, T. E., Jr. & Veroff, J. (1952). A projective measure of need for affiliation. *Journal of Experimental Psychology, 43,* 349–356.

Stewart, A. J., & Chester, N. L. (1982). Sex differences in human social motives: Achievement, affiliation, and power. In A. J. Stewart (Ed.), *Motivation in society: A volume in honor of David C. McClelland* (pp. 172–218). San Francisco: Jossey-Bass.

Sources of Additional Information

Aronson, E. (1980). *The social animal* (3rd ed.). San Francisco: Freeman. The author's goal is to interpret research on "the influences that people have upon the beliefs or behavior of others" (p. 6). It is written for undergraduates and is easily read. Chapter 7, "Attraction: Why People Like Each Other," discusses various facets of affiliation, with the information drawn from literature of social psychology and by a methodology quite different from the thematic apperception method. deCharms, R. (1957). Affiliation motivation and productivity in small groups. *Journal of Abnormal and Social Psychology, 55,* 222–226. An experimental demonstration of the differential effects on cooperative efforts of being motivated to make friends rather than motivated to avoid rejection. "The group discussion facilitated cooperative productivity in general, but among Ss high in affiliation motivation this effect was counteracted by the threat of rejection" (p. 226). French, E. G., & Chadwick, I. (1956). Some characteristics of affiliation motivation. *Journal of Abnormal and Social Psychology, 52,* 296–300. This was one of the early efforts to distinguish between affiliation that is based on both a concern with establishing friendly relationships and avoiding rejection. The experimental results indicated that popularity and the level of the need for affiliation are not correlated, but popularity is correlated with an increased number of positive statements made about others. Sullivan,

H. S. (1953). *The interpersonal theory of psychiatry*. (H. S. Perry & M. L. Gawel, Eds.). New York: W. W. Norton. Sullivan, a psychiatrist, has developed a theory of personality development in which interpersonal relationships are given the importance that psychiatrists more often assign to strivings and impulses. A crucial variable in this theory is a need for collaboration with an intimate.

NEED FOR POWER. 1. Wishes to acquire and maintain influence in order to mitigate weakness. 2. A disposition to acquire power and to enjoy exercising it. 3. An attraction, tempered by fears, to the impact of power, to the effectiveness of dealing with others. 4. Wishes to feel strong or powerful and, less importantly, to act powerfully.

Many of the observations that psychologists make are obscured by cultural beliefs, and distinguishing between tradition and actual events is often difficult and seldom complete. The coexistence in the same person of both envy and fear of power makes separating myth from fact particularly troublesome. As a result, there is to date no sovereign definition of the need for power, but there are, at least, four formulations. Each of these is structured as a NEED, a form of SOCIAL MOTIVATION, and while they overlap in meaning, each posits a different basis for the motive.

The research on this topic has been conducted in a pattern that is standard in the study of social motivation. This demands segregating subjects into groups that are believed to reflect varying levels of intensity of the need for power, and comparing their responses to a request to describe each picture in a series of ambiguous scenes and to imagine what happened before the scene and what will happen subsequently. The assumption is made that what the characters in the stories do is directed by their motives and what the environment does to the characters—called the press—reveals their apperception, that is, opinions they hold about the important long-term consequences of environmental action. The need-press interactions are called thema, and the procedure is referred to as the thematic apperception method. The lack of clarity of the scenes, as well as the lack of any information about the sequence of events, produces content that originates within the narrator, and hence discloses his or her needs and apperceptions. Care is taken to formulate criteria for judging the existence of the need in the narrator's thoughts. These principles make it possible for different experimenters to agree with one another, and they also provide an empirically based definition of the motive.

The first formulation of the concept of the need for power relates its attractiveness to its protective and strengthening function. This explanation grew out of a doctoral dissertation by Veroff that was published in 1957. Veroff assumed that different intensities of the need for power would be found in two groups of students—one consisting of male candidates for elective offices in campus organizations and the other of politically inactive students. The former were asked to write stories while they were awaiting the counting of ballots. The control group consisted of undergraduate males who were asked to devise stories as part of regular course work for the purpose of augmenting an accumulation of normative data.

The narratives differed in many respects. The sample with the higher need for power showed more concern about acquiring, maintaining, or losing influence. They described more episodes of control, made more references to their emotions, such as gratification about winning an argument, humiliation about loss of status, resentment about the authority of another, or were bothered about the lack of opportunity to be assertive.

Additional researchers began to study the need for power, and a 1972 review by Veroff and Veroff of this work prompted them to amend the original definition by specifying that power is desired as a means of compensating for a sense of weakness and one that markedly increases when status is threatened or decision making is blocked. According to this version the need for power has more of a protective than an assertive or dominating function.

A second definition of power, published by Winter in 1968, was also first conceptualized in a doctoral dissertation. This research was initially considered to be a study of the effects of a charismatic leader, and in order to measure these, a film of John F. Kennedy's 1961 inaugural ceremony and speech was projected as a portrayal of power and triumph. The film was shown in 1965, only two years after the Kennedy assassination, to male MBA students. Their stories were compared with those written by a group that had merely seen a movie in which laboratory equipment was described. The difference between the narratives written by the two groups suggested to Winter that the documentary had unexpectedly aroused a need for power, and he compiled a scoring scheme to use in additional research.

While this was under way a third investigator, Uleman, also was working on a doctoral dissertation, which was completed in 1966 but not published until 1972, the year of Veroff and Veroff's literature review. Uleman started out to study a need for influence. He endeavored to arouse this motive by requesting male undergraduates to pretend to be experimenters and by arranging for them to win two card games as well as a stick matching game. They were urged to frustrate opponents and were provided with marked cards to assist them in the enterprise. These manipulations were intended to help each so-called experimenter see himself as a power holder licensed to dominate without reservation or shame. Stories were written during the neutrality at the beginning of the experiment and after acting as an experimenter.

The stories that were made up under instructions to be victors contained references to pleasure in procuring and using influence. This led to a second definition of the need for power, one that specifies that it is gratifying in its own right and not inevitably involving a protective element. Uleman suggested that the need for power and influence are different, but other psychologists tend to overlook this distinction and consider Uleman's work as dealing with power.

Winter (1973) endeavored to develop a scoring system that would integrate his research results with the attributes that Veroff and Uleman had developed.

The guidelines that reflect these varied interpretations yield a third version of power, one that includes both desires for and reservations about power. The thinking of people with this kind of need discloses that the allure may outweigh the doubts and include some urgency to attain, hold, or restore power. These people are concerned about their impact on others and a recurring goal is that of arranging matters so that the world conforms to their own images or desires. They vary in the skill they have in interpersonal relationships, but many have a knack for defining a problem clearly while taking care to delegate the solution to others (Veroff, 1982; Winter & Stewart, 1978).

David McClelland, one of the most productive researchers and theoreticians in social motivation, devised yet a fourth interpretation of the need for power, a combination of desires to feel strong and only secondarily to act powerfully (1975). This definition is a product of experimental results obtained by the social motivation format, observations of the behavior of subjects who have a high need for power, and analyses of both the fears that power holders experience and the restrictions that are placed on their behavior. These include ambivalence about being in command, an awareness that one's win is unavoidably another's loss, as well as a fear that having an authoritative position exposes one, potentially at least, to attack. Such guarded attitudes as these influenced McClelland to conclude that a sense of strength takes priority over a desire to act forcefully.

McClelland became curious as to why wishes to feel strong are expressed overtly in so many different ways, and he decided that the diversity comes from the residuals in the adult of the different ideas about power that are entertained at various stages of growth. McClelland suggests that the dependency of an infant provokes an idea that power comes from outside the self, from the caretaker. The locus changes when the toddler discovers force within the self and joyfully tests and strengthens his or her personal vigor. The youngster learns that it is possible, for example, to run away from Mother and that one can get an upper hand merely by saying no. The schoolchild takes on the task of actually exploring his or her impact among equals, of ascertaining just how much control can be gained and maintained, learning how much aggression gets desired results and how much backfires. Emotionally healthy adults move beyond the selfish purpose of the individual and look favorably at altruism, duty, and expressing power through contributions to a common purpose—the state, the corporation, science. In other words, adults harbor at least some belief that power comes from a dependent relationship (invulnerability because one works for a strong foreman or a strong boss), a powerful self (gaining a sense of force from developing one's physique or from financial resources), forceful actions (gaining a feeling of control by impeding a political opponent or by instructing students), and pursuing the common welfare.

The research on the need for power, as in the case of other social motives, began as a male enterprise, but the barrier was broken, and numerous studies of sex differences have been completed. Stewart and Chester (1982) conclude from an appraisal of the research that men and women tend to react similarly to arousal procedures. There also appears to be some similarity in overt behavior—for example, both men and women tend to seek out high-level positions—but there are also sex differences in the way the power motive is expressed. These are currently interpreted as stemming from differences in sex role, but the mechanisms that underlie these variations have yet to be identified.

References

McClelland, D. C. (1975). *Power: The inner experience*. New York: Irvington. A treatment of numerous aspects of the power motive with, as the title suggests, considerable attention devoted to the private experiences of power. McClelland comments on the fascination with power: "Man . . . his history: a long succession of wars with interludes of peace in localized times and places . . . The Judaeo-Christian God is almighty" (p. 3). McClelland is certain that there are sex differences in the way the need for power is manifest in overt behavior: "Sex role is a key variable in determining how the power drive is expressed. It deflects the power drive into different channels" (p. 81).

Stewart, A. J., & Chester, N. L. (1982). Sex differences in human social motives: Achievement, affiliation, and power. In A. J. Stewart (Ed.), *Motivation and society: A volume in honor of David C. McClelland* (pp. 172–218). San Francisco: Jossey-Bass.

Uleman, J. S. (1972). The need for influence: Development and validation of a measure, and comparison with the need for power. *Genetic Psychology Monographs, 85*, 157–214. This paper is based in good part on Uleman's doctoral dissertation, completed at Harvard University in 1966.

Veroff, J. (1957). Development and validation of a projective measure of power motivation. *Journal of Abnormal and Social Psychology, 54*, 1–8. This is a report of Veroff's doctoral dissertation, completed at the University of Michigan in 1955.

Veroff, J. (1982). Assertive motivations: Achievement versus power. In A. J. Stewart (Ed.), *Motivation and society: A volume in honor of David C. McClelland* (pp. 99–132). San Francisco: Jossey-Bass.

Veroff, J., & Veroff, J. B. (1972). Reconsideration of a measure of power motivation. *Psychological Bulletin, 78*, 279–291.

Winter, D. G. (1968). Need for power in thought and action. *Proceedings of the 76th Annual Convention of the American Psychological Association, 3*, 429–430. This is based on Winter's doctoral dissertation, completed at Harvard University in 1967.

Winter, D. G. (1973). *The power motive*. New York: Free Press. This book includes detailed instructions for a revised scoring system for the need for power. They are clarified by numerous examples.

Winter D. G., & Stewart, A. J. (1978). The power motive. In H. London & J. E. Exner, Jr. (Eds.), *Dimensions of personality* (pp. 391–447). New York: John Wiley. This chapter defines the need for power and then summarizes ramifications of this motive for both the individual and society. The topics include power motivation in women as well as a review of the scores on need for achievement, affiliation, and power of fourteen presidents of the United States. These are derived from tallies of the imagery in their original speeches.

Sources of Additional Information

Guterman, S. S. (1970). *The Machiavellians: A social psychological study of moral character and organizational milieu.* Lincoln: University of Nebraska Press. "Machiavellianism" describes a personality that is amoral, manipulative, cynical, and emotionally indifferent to others. Such people gain and wield power and do not hesitate to treat others as pawns. Their own wishes are more influential than social morality. Guterman elaborates on these traits as well as many others. The reference list is quite comprehensive. Lindzey, G. (Ed.). (1958). *Assessment of human motives.* New York: Rinehart. In this multiauthored volume various methods of assessing social motives are described and evaluated. One chapter is written by Henry A. Murray, the architect of the Thematic Apperception Test and the thematic apperception method. Other authors comment on Murray's work. These remarks are interesting in that they assess this procedure twenty years after its introduction. These chapters help in the difficult task of distinguishing the effects of power from the myths about power. Maslow, A. H, (1970). *Motivation and personality* (2nd ed.). New York: Harper & Row. One of several books by this author. Maslow develops numerous aspects of healthy growth, and he relates it to a mature concept of power. May, R. (1972). *Power and innocence: A search for the sources of violence.* New York: W. W. Norton. This volume illustrates a clinical approach to the study of power. This provides enlightening information about this motive in individuals and particular situations, but the integration that characterizes research about the effects of power on social movements in missing.

NEOBEHAVIORISM.   See BEHAVIORISM.

O

OPEN MIND.   See DOGMATISM and OPEN MIND.

OPERANT BEHAVIORISM.   See BEHAVIORISM.

OPERANT CONDITIONING.   See CONDITIONING.

P

PERCEPTION. See PERCEPTUAL PHENOMENA.

PERCEPTUAL DEFENSE. See PERCEPTUAL PHENOMENA.

PERCEPTUAL PHENOMENA have interested psychologists for a long time, with much of the initial emphasis on the relationship between sensation, defined as the awareness of stimulation, and perception, defined as the immediate, rapid interpreting of sensations. By the middle of the current century, research disclosed that the perception of stimuli that arouse emotion may on occasion be either accelerated or delayed, and that the recognition of such stimuli may be distorted. These discoveries, referred to as the "New Look" in perception, were enthusiastically received, and two concepts that amend the traditional version of perception were devised. Criticisms were also voiced and the impact of the innovative concepts was weakened, but they are, nonetheless, part of modern psychology.

The original concept and its amendments are as follows:

Perception. 1. The quick, unwitting appreciation and integration of immediate stimulation with prior experiences. 2. An appreciation of objects and events that is primarily determined by the configuration or pattern of the stimuli. 3. An apprehending of events that is colored by prior cognitive and affective experiences. 4. A synonym for sensation.

Perceptual Defense. 1. Irregularities in perception that deflect affectively unpleasant stimuli and enhance affectively pleasant ones.

Subception. 1. Responding physiologically and emotionally prior to the accurate perception of affect arousing stimuli.

Perception is often conceptualized as the second phase in a sequence that starts with SENSATION, the awareness of being stimulated, and culminates in action. Perception is assigned a crucial role inasmuch as behavior is commonly assumed to be contingent upon it. Thus a person who perceives a flash of light as a bolt of lightning is expected to react differently from one who perceives the flash as a sign that an extraterrestrial vehicle has landed on earth.

This sensation-perception-action sequence, however, has only limited psychological justification. The responses occur in extremely rapid succession, and it is difficult to distinguish between sensation and perception or to extract either from the totality of the experience. Furthermore, they are in continual interaction. To illustrate—one senses a sharp, spatially restricted pain and this triggers speculation about its cause, but as this reflection goes on a puncture point is sensed, an apprehending that strengthens an impression of having been bitten by an insect. Sensation and perception are on occasion treated as synonyms, and although this may appear to be logically inaccurate it may be psychologically accurate.

The history of perceptual phenomena has involved at least three phases: the first is distinguished by the importance assigned to sense organ reactions, the second emphasizes the configuration of the stimuli, and the third features complex prior experiences. The first of these views was in vogue during the nineteenth century, when considerable effort was expended in identifying cues that help one to sense various properties of the physical world. For example, perception of depth, or distance, was believed to result from a combination of sensations from eye movements as they bring objects into focus, muscular activity that adjusts the lens, and retinal disparity, that is, the slightly different view that each eye has of the visual field.

This approach was based on the belief that perception is not an appreciation of reality itself, but of receptor reactions, and it provoked questions about possible distortions of the physical world. The potential of visual illusions to mislead made them useful in the pursuit of this matter. The discrepancies that were found were, in the custom of the era, explained by reference to sense organ activity. To illustrate—a vertical line is customarily seen as longer than a horizontal one of the same length. One explanation of this held that eye movements, when inspecting the vertical, demand more effort than when inspecting the horizontal. As a result, sighting the vertical appears to require more time, and this makes the line seem longer (Boring, 1942).

The task of discovering the cues that guide perception was criticized, shortly after the turn of the century, when GESTALT PSYCHOLOGY emerged. This viewpoint postulates that a Gestalt—a whole, a configuration—is the basic variable, and Gestalt psychologists, asserting that perception is dependent on the configuration of stimuli, identified numerous patterns in which the integrity endures under varying conditions. A melody offers a clear example of organization in that the auditory pattern is preserved and is readily recognized even when the melody is played by different musical instruments and at different tempos. The research conducted by the Gestaltists generated an impressive sophistication: "The facts of perception are nearly all gestalt facts" (Attneave, 1962, p. 648).

The insistence of BEHAVIORISM that behavior is the only legitimate subject matter of psychology not only deflected the Gestaltists' focus on configuration, but also suspended various other kinds of research on perception until the middle of the current century when psychologists, defying the behaviorist's prohibitions, began to argue effectively that implicit responses are legitimate topics of scientific inquiry. This turnabout reactivated the interest in perception, but in a revised form, inasmuch as the cognitive and affective repertoires of perceivers were assigned more weight than in the earlier interpretations. As a result of these changes perception came to be construed as an inferential process and as economical for the organism. To illustrate—members of modern society assume that there is a motor in every automobile. This is a gamble based on information that has been learned, but efficiency would be intolerably impaired if it were necessary to confirm the presence of a motor in every vehicle.

There were some precedents for conceptualizing perception as dependent on complex previous experiences. William James, for example, called attention to the importance of the beliefs held by the perceivers: "Every new experience must be disposed of under *some* old head. The great point is to find the head which has to be least altered to take it in. Certain Polynesian natives, seeing horses for the first time, called them pigs, that being the nearest head. My child of two played for a week with the first orange that was given him, calling it a 'ball' " (1892/1908, p. 327).

A few of James' successors entertained similar views, but these impressions remained diffused and were rarely related to perceptual theory until the late 1940s when research on the role of emotions in perception began to flourish. The initial experimental steps that were undertaken to identify specific experiential sources of perceptual inferences were cautious ones. Scientists are customarily more interested in general trends than in heterogeneous details, and this bias led them to look for the effects of shared or common experiences. Hunger, a cyclical phenomenon, falls into this category, and several investigators studied the influence of deprivation. Gilchrest and Nesberg (1952), typical of this group, observed some subjects when they were thirsty and others when they were hungry. They were examined in the latter state immediately after they had completed a meal, again six hours later, and for the third time twenty hours after food intake. During each session the participants, seated in a darkened room, were shown a series of slides of different kinds of nourishment. After the projection of each the screen was darkened for a brief interval and then again lighted, in some instances brighter than the original and in others dimmer. The subjects were required to adjust the illumination so that it appeared equal to that of the first exposure. Hungry individuals, as compared with control subjects, adjusted the brightness of food related stimuli to higher levels but did not increase neutral stimuli. Such action suggests that individuals, when deprived, perceive food and drink as more striking than they do when satiated.

Money, a cultural property, has also been used in similar experiments. Dukes and Bevan (1952), for example, in an investigation of its influence, found that participants in a simulated raffle increase or decrease their estimates of the size of blank cards in a manner that varies with the amount of currency they believe they have just lost or won.

Clinical psychologists were less cautious than their experimental colleagues in assessing the role of personality in perception. They began research on this matter as early as 1930, when Beck published a study of the ink blots that Rorschach had devised. This kind of experimentation is still continuing (Lerner, 1984). The clinicians discovered that perceivers disclose more individuality when interpreting ambiguous rather than clear-cut, well-defined stimuli. The responses to a request to describe a chair, for example, are generally restricted to culturally widespread comments about cost, durability, aesthetics, and comfort. In contrast, a request to react to an ink blot elicits more varied reactions. The same blot may be described, for example, as "an individual in a gray wool uniform," "a billowing puff of black smoke," "a beam of light in a glass lantern," and "a crackled, broken hour glass." Because the blot does not actually represent anything these perceptions are presumed to come from within the perceiver, and thus they mirror each respondent's personality. This is a form of projection, a variety of perception, in which the perceiver's own characteristics determine what is discerned. The technique is commonly identified as the projective method of personality assessment. Piotrowski (1957/1979), in recognition of the linkage with perception, used the label perceptanalysis, but this practice was not generally adopted.

Experimental psychologists deferred exploring the relationship between personality and perception until the 1940s, but once underway, the work culminated in the "New Look," an interpretation of perception as influenced by emotional as well as cognitive factors. The research of Postman, Bruner, and McGinnies (1948) is typical of this kind of experimentation. These investigators had undergraduates complete a questionnaire that identified in each respondent the relative strength of different values, such as theoretical, economic, or social factors. The researchers also compiled lists of words that are associated with each of these specialized interests. The terms chosen for the aesthetic value, for example, were beauty, artist, poetry, elegant, literary, and graceful. The words were displayed by means of a tachistoscope, a device that exposes visual material at various speeds, starting with an interval that is too brief to allow accurate perception and gradually increasing in duration until accurate perception occurs.

The results disclosed three variations: a rapid appreciation of the words that suggest preferred values; a slow pick up of words that suggest nonpreferred values; and a misperceiving of words, frequently in ways that are related to their meaning (reading "reverence" as "divinity") or to their form (reading "theory" as "turkey"). These erraticisms point to perceptual acceleration for stimuli that are attractive and perceptual interference for those that are aversive. The authors referred to this monitoring function as perceptual defense.

In 1949 McGinnies endeavored to ascertain how successfully perceptual defense insulates a subject. He presented undergraduates with tachistoscopically displayed neutral words as well as some that, at the date of this particular experiment, were socially unacceptable. As each of these words was exposed, measurements were also made of the subjects' galvanic skin responses, GSRs, minute changes in electrical potential of the skin that occur during emotional reactions. The results indicated that the subjects required more time to recognize the offensive than the neutral words, and that the GSRs for these words, even prior to their recognition, were larger. In other words the discrimination of taboo stimuli appeared to be deferred, but a physiological component of the EMOTIONS, they induce are not deflected. "Out of sight" may not necessarily be "out of mind."

McCleary and Lazarus, in 1949, the same year as the McGinnies paper, published a report of a preliminary experiment, and a refinement of it appeared two years later (Lazarus & McCleary, 1951). By means of a tachistoscope they determined for each subject five recognition intervals that ranged from 100 percent accuracy to as low as chance, for ten five-letter nonsense syllables (for example, VECYD). During the experiment five of these syllables were emotionally charged by means of CLASSICAL CONDITIONING. Specifically, each syllable was repeatedly paired with an unpleasant, but not dangerous, electric shock until the sight of the syllable alone produced an increase in the GSR. The results disclosed that the GSRs were larger for incorrectly perceived syllables that had been conditioned. The authors concluded that they had demonstrated "*a process by which some kind of discrimination is made when the subject is unable to make a correct conscious discrimination*" (Lazarus & McCleary, 1951, p. 113). They were reluctant to apply the label of either unconscious or subconscious because of the numerous controversies about these terms, and they also resisted the word perception because of the connotation of awareness. They coined the word subception to designate the phenomenon.

Subception provoked even more examination than perceptual defense, and various experimenters corroborated the inaugural work. Others, however, found the grafting of a defensive function onto perception to be intolerably unorthodox and, assembling criticisms of both perceptual defense and subception, they proposed more conventional interpretations. Bitterman and Kniffin (1953), for example, interpreted the temporal difference as due to a reticence about repeating an unacceptable word rather than a failure to recognize it. Even the original proponents of perceptual defense joined in the criticisms. Postman, Bronson, and Gropper (1953) gave a negative response to the question posed in their title "Is There a Mechanism of Perceptual Defense?" Their conclusion was based on evidence procured by tachistoscopic exposure of a series of censored and neutral words under four kinds of instruction: no cues that taboo items would be displayed; information that distasteful content would be offered; encouragement to report the forbidden; and encouragement to withhold such reports. The results indicated that the longest intervals were required by the group who were not advised about the unsavory material, and the briefest ones, by those who were encouraged to verbalize whatever they perceived. The researchers interpreted this difference as due not to perceptual defense, but to such variables as the SET of the subjects that the instructions induced and to variations in the familiarity of the words.

The critics were criticized. Jenkin, observing that the faultfinding was premature, commented: " 'Selective sensitization' . . . appears to be well established, and not wholly due to artifacts of experimental procedure" (1957, p. 122). Lazarus reports a lack of convincing evidence and suggested that the "extensive controversy" (1966, p. 84) is concerned more with the mechanism(s) than with the existence of perceptual defense.

A review of the arguments and counterarguments is found in a paper by Erdelyi (1974), who converts the "New Look" into an information-processing structure. He equates the reactions with selectivity, and points out that this is not an either-or phenomenon, but is one that occurs at different times and in various ways. The perceiver may, for example, ward off unpleasant stimuli by simply closing the eyes or looking in another direction. The instructions to the research participants may foster reacting to only certain kinds of stimuli or with a particular style. A subject who becomes aware of socially disapproved stimuli and pauses before reporting them is demonstrating a response rather than a perceptual postponement. Receptor restraint is cast as input selectivity and delay in responding as output selectivity. For Erdelyi, this multiplicity prohibits an existence-nonexistence dichotomy.

The currently popular technique of devising metaphors between psychological behavior and information processing seems to gain more approval for perceptual mechanisms than in the past (Hilgard, 1987). The capability of an information-processing frame to accommodate various kinds of selection suggests that this format may also be more productive than those that were formerly used. If these trends continue the concept of perception as a relatively static, predominantly rational phenomena may become obsolete.

References

Attneave, F. (1962). Perception and related areas. In S. Koch (Ed.), *Psychology: A study of a science* (Vol. 4, pp. 619-659). New York: McGraw-Hill.

Beck, S. J. (1930). Personality diagnosis by means of the Rorschach test. *American Journal of Orthopsychiatry, 1,* 81–88. This is said to be the first publication in English of research on the Rorschach, the now famous ink blot test.

Bitterman, M. E. & Kniffen, C. W. (1953). Manifest anxiety and "perceptual defense." *Journal of Abnormal and Social Psychology, 48,* 248–252.

Boring, E. G. (1942). *Sensation and perception in the history of experimental psychology.* New York: Appleton-Century-Crofts.

Dukes, W. F., & Bevan, W., Jr. (1952). Size estimation and monetary value: A correlation. *Journal of Psychology, 34,* 43–53. The authors comment that many studies of motivation and perception fail to report quantified data. Their goal is to furnish these so as to demonstrate that perceptual accentuation varies directly in relation to the value of the perceived object.

Erdelyi, M. H. (1974). A new look at the new look: Perceptual defense and vigilance. *Psychological Review, 81*, 1–25. Erdelyi dates the beginning of as the revision 1947–1949. He describes it "the perception of external stimuli is not free of the shackles of internal events: attitudes, values, expectancies, needs, and psychodynamic defenses all impinge upon perception" (p. 1).

Gilchrist, J. C., & Nesberg, L. S. (1952). Need and perceptual change in need-related objects. *Journal of Experimental Psychology, 44*, 369–376.

Hilgard, E. R. (1987). *Psychology in America: A historical survey*. San Diego, CA: Harcourt Brace Jovanovich. Hilgard suggests that the "New Look" is still viable: "While the excitement lasted for only a few years, the influence can be traced in the later conceptions of information processing in perception" (p. 172).

James, W. (1908). *Psychology, briefer course*. New York: Holt. (Original work published 1892). This was a widely used text for a number of years, and is famous for its scope, content, and writing style.

Jenkin, N. (1957). Affective processes in perception. *Psychological Bulletin, 54*, 100–127.

Lazarus, R. S. (1966). *Psychological stress and the coping process*. New York: McGraw-Hill.

Lazarus, R. S., & McCleary, R. A. (1951). Autonomic discrimination without awareness: A study of subception. *Psychological Review, 58*, 113–122. In discussing the results of the experiment the authors note that the mechanism for subception has yet to be clarified.

Lerner, P. M. (1984). Projective techniques and personality assessment: The current perspective. In N. S. Endler & J. McV. Hunt (Eds.), *Personality and the behavioral disorders* (2nd ed.) (Vol. 1, pp. 283–309). New York: John Wiley. This is a review of research and current uses of the Rorschach and Thematic Apperception Test—two of the most popular projective techniques.

McCleary, R. A. & Lazarus, R. S. (1949). Autonomic discrimination without awareness: An interim report. *Journal of Personality, 18*, 171–179. One of the first experiments on subception.

McGinnies, E. (1949). Emotionality and perceptual defense. *Psychological Review, 56*, 244–251. An experimental demonstration that triggered research, criticism, counterarguments, and rejection of the term perceptual defense.

Piotrowski, Z. A. (1979). *Perceptanalysis*. New York: Macmillan. (Original work published 1957). Piotrowski, one of the most eminent authorities on the Rorschach (ink blot) technique, devised a title that emphasizes the role of perception in this procedure.

Postman, L., Bronson, W. C., & Gropper, G. L. (1953). Is there a mechanism of perceptual defense? *Journal of Abnormal and Social Psychology, 48*, 215–224.

Postman, L., Bruner, J. S., & McGinnies, E. (1948). Personal values as selective factors in perception. *Journal of Abnormal and Social Psychology, 43*, 142–154.

Sources of Additional Information

Dick, M., Ullman, S., & Sagi, D. (1987). Parallel and serial processes in motion duration. *Science, 237* (No. 4813), 400–402. This experiment exemplifies the currently popular research technique of using REACTION TIME as a measure of "processing time." Increases in time are assumed to indicate serial rather than parallel or simultaneous processing. This technique is patterned after information processing, and this particular experiment deals with the conditions that give rise to apparent motion, a perceptual phenomenon that came to the forefront in the early days of GESTALT PSYCHOLOGY. Gibson, E. J., & Walk, R. D. (1960). The "visual cliff." *Scientific American, 202*(4), 64–71. This apparatus consists of a large sheet of heavy glass, directly under half of which is a board divided into light and dark squares. In the other half the board is on the floor, several feet below the glass. The depth perception of young and/or sensory-deprived organisms is studied by observing their reactions to this cliff. A refusal to move onto the glass that covers the floor board suggests that the subject is perceiving depth. Haber, R. N. (1978). Visual perception. In M. R. Rosenzweig & L. W. Porter (Eds.), *Annual review of psychology, 29* 31–60. A review of research on visual perception 1974 to 1977. The author characterizes this interval as "incredibly productive" but lacking "any great revolution or break-through" (p. 31). Henle, M. (1942). An experimental investigation of past experience as a determinant of visual form perception. *Journal of Experimental Psychology, 30*, 1–22. A Gestalt psychologist provides experimental evidence that the history of the organism influences perception. Vanderplas, J. M. & Blake, R. R. (1950). Selective sensitization in auditory perception. *Journal of Personality, 18*, 252–266. These investigators used the same words that Postman, Bruner, and McGinnies (1948) used, but the presentation was auditory rather than visual. The results pointed to the same kind of perceptual selectivity as was found in vision.

PERSONALITY. 1. The person—recognizably consistent and singular by virtue of a particular pattern of traits. 2. The person—recognizably consistent and singular by virtue of a pattern of inner dynamics. 3. An obsolete synonym for character.

Popular thinking about personality often features social skills, conspicuous or rare characteristics, and even emotional difficulties, thus "great personality and a sharp piano player," "he's sure got a personality problem," "an accountant's mind in all places at all times," or even "no personality at all." Psychologists are usually not concerned with these social assessments or, at most, treat them as minor, peripheral entries, and place the emphasis on those elements of the behavioral repertoire that convey individuality.

The focus in the concept of personality on a unique individual contrasted with the more common practice of studying specific responses (such as learning, emotion, and perception), and like many innovations, it required time to develop. As a result, personality did not become a recognized topic in psychology until the 1930s, but once initiated, it gained momentum and did so with an extraordinary rapidity. The word personality began to displace the German word *Charakter*, or character, "the sum total of those features, properties, or qualities of an individual organism" (McDougall, 1932, p. 4). In 1932 the inaugural issue of a journal appeared under a title that acknowledged the transition, *Character and Personality*. New, but generally short-lived, labels such as "personalistic psychology" and "personology" were devised. In 1937 Gordon W. Allport (1897–1967) published *Personality: A Psychological Interpretation*. Although a few volumes dealing with some similar subject matter were in print, this book was comprehensive, and it soon became a popular text. Courses in the psychology of personality burgeoned.

Important among the reasons for the acceleration once the topic was under way is its relevance to a variety of problems that people face, such as choosing an occupation and correcting a learning problem. An increasing number of psychologists became interested in rectifying these difficulties, and the concept of personality offers guides for organizing pertinent information. Whatever the catalysts may be, the field flourished, and an unwarranted number of definitions of personality were devised. Unfortunately many of them failed to limit the concept. The expansiveness, generally unacknowledged, started early and still persists: *"Personality* is the sum total of all the biological innate dispositions, impulses, tendencies, appetites and instincts of the individual and of all the *acquired* dispositions and tendencies—acquired by experience. And to these it is limited" (Prince, 1921, p. 532); and, "The study of personality may be approached through a study of the determinants and consequences of responses to stimulating conditions. There are many psychologists who mean by this *all* human behavior" (Gordon, 1963, p. 14). The concept has even been stretched beyond the immediately given: *"Personality is the organized system of potentialities for behavior"* (Crowne, 1979, p. 10).

One way of bringing some order into these definitions is to search out similarities among them. There seem to be two varieties: those that define personality as an aggregate of TRAITS and those that define personality in terms of internal dynamics, such as an interplay between wishes and fears or the dominance of a particular motive. To deal first with the former—many theorists see traits as the basic elements of personality, and they ascribe the uniqueness of each person to the configuration peculiar to that individual.

The presence or absence of particular traits is commonly measured by pencil-and-paper tests. Typically these consist of a series of questions or statements about a diversity of topics, and the examinee indicates his or her level of agreement or disagreement with each item. These instruments are called "objective" because the techniques for administering and scoring them are uniform. The label is, however, misleading inasmuch as there is no effective control of the subjects' interpretations of the test items. Neither is there information about either the respondent's level of candor or his or her sophistication about the self and others. To illustrate—an accurate reply to the statement "I lose my temper quicker than most" requires knowledge of the speed of anger arousal in the population at large, a willingness to disclose a personal reaction, and to do so for the perusal of people whom the examinee may not personally know. Confusion also accrues to the use of questions in which more than one topic is involved. For example, "I like parties just to be with people" poses a problem for subjects who enjoy social gatherings but are highly selective about their companions. The net effect of all these unknowns is, of course, an unknown, but the lack of controls diffuses the definition of personality and provides one instance in which measurement does not refine, but rather attenuates the concept.

Some theorists attend more to the effect a person has on others than to a pattern of traits. For them, personality is in the eyes of the beholders and in the ears of the listeners. In this frame of reference the selfishness of a person is measured in terms of how selfish his or her acquaintances think the person is. In this kind of assessment psychological variables are quantified not in terms of tangents such as the timing and intensity of the stimuli, but in terms of judgments about psychological attributes. For many psychologists this is the preferred method because it is "uncontaminated psychology." This reasoning is convincing, but there are some technical limitations that may distort experimental results (Norman, 1969). One additional source of erraticism is the denial of personality to neonates and hermits, even though one is granted to pets and infants (Allport, 1924/1975). Organizing data around the perspective of spectators also allows distortion in that memory and legend can intensify personality after death, particularly in the case of religious and political leaders (Mowrer & Kluckhohn, 1944).

The collective perceptions of acquaintances were used as a measure of personality in an investigation conducted in 1915 in relation to the concept of the SELF. R. R. Sears (1936), however, is generally credited with initiating this kind of measurement, and a sketch of his procedures clarifies a method of relying on beholders. Sears, working with undergraduates who were well known to one another, obtained the self-ratings of each subject as well as the ratings assigned to all members of the group on the traits of stinginess, obstinacy, disorderliness, and bashfulness. He interpreted the average of the ratings that the group assigned to each person as the actual strength of the trait. Sears also calculated the distance between the self-rating and the average peer rating, and ascribed insight to people whose personal appraisal approximated the ratings of others, and ascribed lack of insight to those in whom there is a discrepancy. Sears then reviewed the ranking of others by people who do and who do not meet this criterion of insight. He found that those in the latter category tended to project personally unacknowledged attributes onto others; that is, the failure to recognize a trait in oneself is concomitant with attributing more than the average of that characteristic to other people.

This procedure was adopted by others, and more refined statistical treatments were devised. The information that was generated was challenged by the finding that the ratings by college students of people to whom they had just been introduced are distributed in patterns similar to those of people with whom the raters are well acquainted (Passini & Norman, 1966). The attempts to explain this paradox frequently assume that opinions about others are weighted as much or more by cultural expectations than by actual observations.

A second popular way of defining personality is organized around the configuration of dynamic inner variables. The best known of these formulations are the psychoanalytic doctrines of the unconscious. One of the most popular techniques in psychology is the thematic apperception method, devised by H. A. Murray (1938) for research in personality, particularly in the areas of NEED and SOCIAL MOTIVATION. This is a complex procedure, and the component of immediate interest is Murray's relating the needs of a person to what he calls the press, the way the person believes the environment reacts. The interactions between the needs and press are called thema, and uncovering these brings the personality into focus. To illustrate—a individual who reacts to being treated generously with annoyance because the gift cannot be reciprocated is construed by Murray as reacting to a press of nurturance with a need for autonomy. The same person strengthens this nurturance-autonomy thema when he or she perceives a superior's lengthy explanation as more restraining than informative. Analogous thema in different situations would yield a personality that imposes distance from others when help is given.

The belief that the crucial components of personality are the result of inner dynamics encouraged the use of projective methods of personality assessment. In these procedures the examinee is presented with ambiguous stimuli and requested to assign meaning to them. Because there is no readily identifiable structure in the stimuli, the PERCEPTION, that is, the meaning that is assigned to the stimuli, is considered to come from within the person. In other words, personality is inferred from the way the respondent perceives. The Rorschach Test, a series of ink blots, is the best known of the projective methods. Murray's technique for measuring personality has also been compiled as an examination. It is called the Thematic Apperception Test (TAT) and it consists of twenty pictures of vague scenes. In accord with laboratory procedures, the examinee is asked to describe each scene and to imagine what happened prior to the picture and what will happen next. Each of the stories that is made up is generated more by the narrator than by the scenes, and thus the procedure discloses the personality of the narrator.

Projective techniques have been used both to postdict and to predict behavior, to infer the presence of conscious and unconscious variables, and to formulate a host of constructs about both covert events and the influence of infantile experiences on personality. Unfortunately these inferences are difficult to verify. For example, there is little possibility of either confirming or denying the accuracy of the proposition that a particular interpretation of an ink blot by a thirty-year-old indicates that her mother's handling of her in childhood was hard, cold, and controlling.

The concept of personality is, for a variety of reasons, in disarray, and psychologists are concerned about it. Some hard-core experimentalists condemn the field because it lacks rigor, whereas those who endorse the HUMAN POTENTIAL MOVEMENT see the individual concealed by scientism. The dissatisfaction of some is extensive: "The conventional science of personality is close to its limits. No major, generally-accepted advances have been made in recent years. In fact, neither investigators nor theorists have much consensus on anything" (Fiske, 1974, p. 1). Lamiell reviews some criticisms that are found in the literature:

"The general failure of personality research to come to grips with the concepts of identity and individuality . . . despite the proliferation of empirical research, personality psychology has failed to achieve any major theoretical advances in decades" (1981, p. 287).

But such discouragement does not imply imminent demise, and various concepts of personality, even if not maturing, endure. Textbooks of varying quality continue to be published. Courses entitled "Personality" or "Personality Theory" are still being offered in universities. The traffic in pencil-and-paper tests continues; in fact a revision is under way of the forty-five-year-old Minnesota Multiphasic Personality Inventory, a pencil-and-paper test identified as "the most heavily used test of its kind *in the world* [italics added]" (Holden, 1986, p. 1249).

References

Allport, F. H. (1975). *Social Psychology*. New York: Johnson Reprint (Original work published 1924). This early text emphasizes the relationship between personality and social interactions.

Allport, G. W. (1937). *Personality: A psychological interpretation*. New York: Holt.

Crowne, D. P. (1979). *The experimental study of personality*. Hillsdale, NJ: Lawrence Erlbaum.

Fiske, D. W. (1974). The limits for the conventional science of personality. *Journal of Personality, 42*, 1–11.

Gordon, J. E. (1963). *Personality and behavior*. New York: Macmillan.

Holden, C. (1986). Researchers grapple with problems of updating classical psychological test. *Science, 233*, 1249–1251. This is the MMPI, originally designed as an objective test of psychopathology. It is still used for that purpose, but it is also used in the study of normal personality. It has been translated into several foreign languages.

Lamiell, J. T. (1981). Toward an idiothetic psychology of personality. *American Psychologist, 36*, 276–289. The author suggests that the study of individual differences is less profitable than the study of the development of personal identity.

McDougall, W. (1932). Of the words character and personality. *Character and Personality, 1*, 3–16.

Mowrer, O. H., & Kluckhohn, C. (1944). Dynamic theory of personality. In J. McV. Hunt (Ed.), *Personality and the behavior disorders: A handbook based on experimental and clinical research* (Vol. 1, pp. 69–135). New York: Ronald Press.

Murray, H. A. (1938). *Explorations in personality: A clinical and experimental study of fifty men of college age*. New York: Oxford University Press.

Norman, W. T. (1969). "To see oursels as ithers see us!": Relations among self-perceptions, peer-perceptions, and expected peer-perceptions of personality attributes. *Multivariate Behavioral Research, 4*, 417–443. Norman criticizes the careless use of pencil-and-paper tests: "The day has passed when anything of much value is going to be learned by 'one-shot' studies using just any conveniently available inventory, sample and data analysis procedure" (p. 441).

Passini, F. T., & Norman, W. T. (1966). A universal conception of personality structure? *Journal of Personality and Social Psychology, 4*, 44–49. The authors suggest that the similarity between the ratings of intimate friends and those of strangers may be explained by "implicit personality theory". This states that people casually build up ideas about which traits go together in individuals of similar backgrounds. The ratings of others may reflect these opinions as much as, or even more than, what is personally observed.

Prince, M. (1921). *The unconscious: The fundamentals of human personality normal and abnormal* (2nd ed. rev.). New York: Macmillan.

Sears, R. R. (1936). Experimental studies of projection: 1. Attribution of traits. *Journal of Social Psychology, 7*, 151–163. This study uses, but does not acknowledge, a method used in 1915 by Cogan, Conklin, & Hollingworth in "An Experimental Study of Self-analysis, Estimates of Associates, and the Results of Tests." This method is discussed in the section on the concept of the SELF.

Sources of Additional Information

Endler, N. S. (1984). Interactionism. In N. S. Endler & J. McV. Hunt (Eds.), *Personality and the behavioral disorders* (2nd ed.) (Vol. 1, pp. 183–217). New York: John Wiley. A penetrating assessment of the major approaches to the study of personality. There is an emphasis on a relatively recent view, that is, interactionism: "a continuous and ongoing process whereby situations affect persons, who in turn affect situations" (p. 185). Kantor, J. R. (1937). Character and personality: Their nature and interrelations. *Character and Personality, 6*, 306–320. Kantor points out that character traits have the same origins and functions as other kinds of personality traits. The concern with morality and social standards does not endow them with any special attributes. Lewin, K. (1935). *A dynamic theory of personality: Selected Papers* (D. K. Adams & K. E. Zener, Trans.). New York: McGraw-Hill. A landmark theorist and the instigator of many experiments in the study of personality. McReynolds, P., & Ludwig, K. (1984). Christian Thomasius and the origin of psychological rating scales. *Isis, 75*, 546–553. The authors describe Thomasius' (1655–1728) methods of personality assessment. They interpret his collection of quantitative data as "the first documented use of numerical values to represent psychological variables" (p. 546).

PERSONALITY, AUTHORITARIAN.   See AUTHORITARIAN PERSONALITY.

PHENOMENOLOGICAL PSYCHOLOGY.   See HUMAN POTENTIAL MOVEMENT.

PHENOMENOLOGY.   1. A method in psychology that features observation and descriptions of experience, just as it occurs—naturally.

Phenomenology is an approach to psychology that is held by psychologists who may endorse different theoretical positions but who share an appreciation of experience as it appears to the experiencing individual, without dividing it into parts (Landsmann, 1958). Analytical procedures are considered to be logically valid, possibly compelling, but inappropriate inasmuch as the breaking of consciousness into segments may do more to destroy than to clarify. For example, the tonal quality of loudness in isolation from other auditory properties (such as pitch and timbre) is experientially meaningless, and a color is seen as a unitary whole rather than as a combination of different hues (purple is seen as purple, *not* as a mixture of red and blue).

Even advocates of the method concede that dividing the subject matter into elements may have advanced physical science, but insist that dissecting serves a "preference for simplicity and elegance over relevance" (MacLeod, 1973, p. 122). There are also criticisms of other kinds of differentiation, for example, "the belief that something small is more fundamental than something large" and the assumption that "that which is genetically early is more fundamental than that which is genetically late" (MacLeod, 1947, p. 195).

One of the most influential proponents of phenomenology was David Katz (1884–1953), a psychologist who was educated and worked in Germany until after the rise of Hitler, when he moved first to England and then to Sweden. He conducted research on a diversity of topics, the best known of which are studies of the perception of color (Katz, 1911/1970). Some personal reminiscences about this phenomenologist also throw light on phenomenology: "For Katz the most fascinating thing to wonder about was a human experience. It might be a simple color or sound, or the strange beauty of an El Greco picture, or the peculiar sensations that accompany the crunching of a nut between the teeth . . . the first task of the psychologist—not really a task, but a pleasure—was to observe and describe without bias both the salient characteristics and the subtle nuances of ordinary human experience" (MacLeod, 1954, p. 3).

Phenomenology is one of the few methods that is unique to psychology. Another is INTROSPECTION, the procedure devised by STRUCTURAL PSYCHOLOGY for observing the elements of consciousness. Both of these procedures are concerned with awareness, and they both came into use during the inaugural days of experimental psychology. Their similarity is, however, limited to the timing and to the concern with awareness, and there are two differences that overwhelm their comparability. One involves the reliance on analysis. The goal of the structuralists is to resolve consciousness into basic elements, whereas the goal of phenomenology is to capture unanalyzed consciousness. The second discrepancy, also crucial, centers around the importance of meaning. Introspection tries to deal with the elements that constitute awareness, a task that is analogous to the one in chemistry of identifying basic elements. In the framework of structural psychology this meant discovering the building blocks of the mind without considering their significance to the person. This is in marked contrast to the phenomenologists' conviction that experience cannot be separated into components, even one as important as meaning.

GESTALT PSYCHOLOGY asserts that a configuration, that is, a Gestalt, is the important variable in psychology, and the phenomenological method is a preferred way of describing Gestalten. Beginning in the 1910s they used the technique to study PERCEPTION, and one of their first discoveries documents its fruitfulness. At issue here is the phi phenomenon, the perception of motion when stationary stimuli are successively exposed (three arrows lighted in sequence so as to be seen as moving). Gestalt psychologists affirm that the psychological datum is the perception of this motion, and this *experience*, rather than the nature of the physical stimulation, is the appropriate subject matter of psychology.

The Gestaltists have applied the concept of phenomenology to several other topics, including social psychology. Heider (1944, 1946), for example, transferred some of the principles of the organization of the perceptual field to the perception of social relationships. He proposed that the relationships among people may be perceived as in balance, that is, as in accord with expectations, or they may be perceived as unbalanced. Heider assumed that perceivers prefer stable fields, and that inconsistent ones provoke change. This idea was extended in various ways by different theorists, probably gaining the most visibility in the concept of COGNITIVE DISSONANCE.

MacLeod (1947) suggests that the effectiveness of handling social problems might be enhanced if phenomenological data were used. He describes how the neglect of perspective hampers the understanding of other people and, in illustration, draws attention to the differences in the concept of China that American laborers and American students of Chinese literature hold. He predicts that these discrepancies will not be reconciled until the variations in meaning are known to all parties.

The method of phenomenology was also applied to the study of personality, with one major impetus for this coming in Snygg and Comb's *Individual Behavior: A New Frame of Reference for Psychology*, published in 1949, and revised in 1959 as *Individual Behavior: A Perceptual Approach to Behavior* by Combs and Snygg. Sections of these books are devoted to reinterpretations of conventional psychology. For example, Dunlap's discovery (1932) that practicing an error, such as typing repetitively h-t-e, not t-h-e, facilitates correcting it, is cast into a phenomenological frame of reference and then explained as due to the moving of the inaccuracy into the foreground, that is, increasing its distinctiveness from the background of the field.

Combs and Snygg join MacLeod in advising psychologists to focus on the point of view of the individual, often designated as the phenomenal or perceived SELF. They mobilize evidence that perception controls action, and point out that a thorough knowledge of the phenomenal self would not only allow understanding the perspective of each person, but would also increase the accuracy with which behavior is predicted.

A decline in interest in Gestalt psychology brought with it some decline in the use of phenomenology, but this was an interruption rather than a renunciation, and the technique regained popularity in the various approaches to psychology that emerged in the decade 1960 to 1970 and came to be known as the human potential movement. This group includes EXISTENTIAL PSYCHOLOGY, HUMANISTIC PSYCHOLOGY, TRANSPERSONAL PSYCHOLOGY, and a fourth that is specifically labeled PHENOMENOLOGICAL PSYCHOLOGY. This last group elevated the method of phenomenology to the position of a pivot around which to organize the field. This particular extension may have been an inevitable outcome of the emphasis in these viewpoints on the enhancement of the whole human being and on the interpretation of the personal, private world as the moderator and guide to action.

Endorsements of phenomenology have always been countered by censure, and the resurgence of the method within the subjective framework that characterizes the human potential movement may well have increased both the amount and the intensity of the faulting. The most common objections, of course, center around the lack of objectivity (Skinner, 1963). This overall theory-based opposition is also supplemented by criticisms of some of the details. Smith (1950), for example, reacting to some proposals to apply phenomenology to the study of personality, comments that the technique is selective in that it deals with conscious variables and excludes unconscious vectors. He notes that she is not aware of all the stimuli to which one reacts, and therefore "a psychology of experience or consciousness has distinct explanatory limits" (p. 517).

Despite the faultfinding, phenomenology is beginning to attract enough approbation in orthodox research circles to prompt arguments that the objective orientation of psychology should be modified so as to include the "development of a broadened behavioral psychology which will embrace phenomenological data" (Lichtenstein, 1971, p. 7). Lichtenstein lists various assets of phenomenology, including a fidelity to experience, incorporativeness so that all awareness can be accommodated, and the status of being the only medium in which to examine what is experienced. On the liability side of the ledger he includes the privacy of consciousness. This inaccessibility to the public has, in the past, been considered a serious obstacle for a variety of reasons, but the most significant censure seems to emerge from the assumption that phenomenological experiences are not identical with physical events. Lichtenstein reminds readers that this postulate is more historic than valid, and that PERCEPTION actually involves real objects and activities. On a more positive note he remarks that self-observations constitute real and significant events, and that the privacy or idiosyncracy can, to some extent at least, be penetrated. One way to accomplish this is to learn a great deal about the life history of a person because that information throws light on why that person interprets a particular experience in a specific way.

In conclusion, at this point in time the method of phenomenology appears to be gaining ground, to be a candidate for membership in mainstream psychology. However, the recency of this move and the vigor of the debates about it prohibit any trustworthy prediction of the ultimate fate.

References

Combs, A. W., & Snygg, D. (1959). *Individual behavior: A perceptual approach to behavior* (rev. ed.). New York: Harper & Bros. Combs claims the major credit for this revision of Snygg & Combs' 1949 volume. This edition is intended to bring the original up to date, that is, to present the phenomenological approach a decade after it was presented as innovative.

Dunlap, K. (1932). *Habits: Their making and unmaking*. New York: Liveright. Dunlap develops explanations for different kinds of learning, and the relevant one here is the effectiveness of negative practice, that is, practicing an error that is habitually made. The classic example is the advice to typists to practice errors that they persistently make in typing. This technique does help one to stop making the same mistake.

Heider, F. (1944). Social perception and phenomenal causality. *Psychological Review, 51*, 358–374.

Heider, F. (1946). Attitudes and cognitive organization. *Journal of Psychology, 21*, 107–112.

Katz, D. (1970). *The world of colour* (R. B. MacLeod & C. W. Fox, Trans.). New York: Johnson Reprint. (Original work published 1911)

Landsman, T. (1958). Four phenomenologies. *Journal of Individual Psychology, 14*, 29–37.

Lichtenstein, P. (1971). A behavioral approach to "phenomenological data." *The Psychological Record, 21*, 1–16.

MacLeod, R. B. (1947). The phenomenological approach to social psychology. *Psychological Review, 54*, 193–210. This is a classic, probably the sine qua non of phenomenology.

MacLeod, R. B. (1954). David Katz 1884–1953. *Psychological Review, 61*, 1–4. A necrology that not only reports biographical details, but also portrays Katz as a person.

MacLeod, R. B. (1973). Concluding remarks. In D. Krech (Ed.), *The MacLeod symposium: June 2-3, 1972* (pp. 117–125). Ithaca, NY: Department of Psychology, Cornell University. This volume presents the proceedings of a symposium in honor of MacLeod's retirement from Cornell University. MacLeod died two weeks after this event, and the papers prepared for it were published as a memorial.

Skinner, B. F. (1963). Behaviorism at fifty. *Science, 140* (No. 3570), 951–958.

Smith, M. B. (1950). The phenomenological approach in personality theory: Some critical remarks. *Journal of Abnormal and Social Psychology, 45*, 516–522. Smith, an advocate of humanistic psychology, criticizes some of the devotees because they "misconstrue the appropriate role of a phenomenological approach in a way that invites the critical to reject a humanized psychology lock, stock, and barrel" (p. 516). Smith pleads for maintaining a perspective on both the assets and liabilities of phenomenology.

Snygg, D., & Combs, A. W. (1949). *Individual behavior: A new frame of reference for psychology*. New York: Harper & Bros.

Sources of Additional Information

Marx, M. H., & Cronan-Hillix, W. A. (1987). *Systems and theories in psychology* (4th ed.). New York: McGraw-Hill. This text covers the history of the field of psychology, and the account of phenomenology is unusually specific in its comparison and contrast of phenomenology and introspection. Rogers, C. R. (1964). Toward a science of the person. In T. W. Wann (Ed.), *Behaviorism and phenomenology: Contrasting bases for modern psychology* (pp. 109–133). Chicago: University of Chicago Press. A leading therapist endorses phenomenology and predicts that psychology will come to focus "on a broader reality, which will include not only behavior but the person and perspective of the observer and the person and perspective of the observed" (p. 118). Sargent, S. S. (1967). Humanistic methodology in personality and social psychology. In J. F. T. Bugental (Ed.), *Challenges of humanistic psychology* (pp. 127–133). New York: McGraw-Hill. Sargent reviews the "focus on the experiencing person" that several psychologists have advocated (pp. 129). Snygg, D., & Combs, A. W. (1950). The phenomenological approach and the problem of "unconscious" behavior: A reply to Dr. Smith. *Journal of Abnormal and Social Psychology, 45*, 523–528. As the title implies, this is a rebuttal of the M. B. Smith (1950) reference. It is an effort to justify excluding unconscious variables from explanations of behavior. Woodworth, R. S., & Sheehan, M. R. (1964). *Contemporary schools of psychology* (3rd. ed.). New York: Ronald Press. A clear and accurate account of phenomenology with an emphasis on the relationship to Gestalt psychology.

POWER. See NEED FOR POWER.

PSYCHOPHYSICS. 1. The study of the relationship between physical energy and sensation. **THRESHOLD.** 1. The minimal amount of physical energy that is sensed in a specific proportion of stimulations. 2. The minimal difference in amounts of energy that is sensed in a specified proportion of stimulations. 3. A synonym for limen.

Both the laity and scientists have long recognized that we do not appreciate very low levels of physical energy, nor are we able to discriminate small differences in amount (Collier, 1950). Interest in this topic gained momentum during the nineteenth century when philosophers elaborated various ideas about variations in awareness and physiologists devised techniques for quantifying the relationship between varying amounts of energy and sensory experiences.

J. F. Herbart (1776–1841), a philosopher, is one of the key figures in this history. Herbart assumed that the mind is made up of ideas, that these are active, and that some of them are compatible and others are incompatible. He also construed the mind as partly CONSCIOUS and partly UNCONSCIOUS, with these two domains separated by a boundary or threshold. Concordant ideas struggle to remain conscious, but they are countered by conflicting ones. In the course of these battles some ideas are forced into unconsciousness, but they remain viable and continue to try to reenter consciousness. As a result, ideas were believed to vary in intensity or force, and thus the threshold also varies (Peters, 1962).

Scientists began research on thresholds by stimulating various sense organs with different amounts of energy and recording the levels that are and are not sensed. They rejected Herbart's premises about mental activity in favor of the proposition that sensory reactions are immediate products of arousal and that they terminate when the excitation is withdrawn. The scientists, however, adhered to Herbart's belief that a threshold varies after they discovered that there are bands or ranges of energy in which identical excitation is sensed in some applications and in others it is not. This led to the defining of a threshold in terms of the amount of physical energy that elicits a response in a specified proportion of the times it is applied. As the research continued, varied opinions were expressed as to just what proportion best defines a threshold. The figure that is commonly, but not universally, adopted is .50. In other words, a threshold is not a psychological measurement, but it is a statistical statement of the magnitude of energy that results in sensibility, commonly 50 percent of the time (Guilford, 1954).

One of the trailblazers of sensory thresholds was E. H. Weber (1795–1878), a German anatomist and physiologist, who was particularly interested in tactual sensations. A sketch of some of his work both describes the concept of threshold and fills in some of its history. Weber was aware that the simultaneous touching of the skin at two points, in proximity, produces the sensation of only a single contact, and he undertook to find out just how large the separation of the points must be for two sensations to be experienced. Weber discovered that increasing the distance between the points elicits reports of both single and double stimulation, and he reported the widths of the separation at which "impressions begin to be distinguished as two" (cited in Diamond, 1974, p. 679). These data indicate that thresholds vary in different parts of the body, and that the tip of the tongue and the tips of the fingers are, for example, more sensitive than the upper arm.

Weber also explored how much objects must differ in weight in order for them to be judged unequal. He discovered that the amount is a proportion of the magnitude of the stimulus. To illustrate—if the ratio should be 1/20, an object would have to weigh twenty-one ounces to be discriminated as heavier than a similar one weighing twenty ounces, and another object would have to weigh forty-two ounces to be judged heavier than one of forty ounces (Boring, 1942). The minimal difference that is appreciated has been labeled and translated variously as the "just" or "least", "noticeable" or "perceptible," "difference" or "discrimination" (Baldwin, 1901/1960). The combination of words that has endured is "just noticeable difference," commonly abbreviated as "jnd." Weber apparently did not attach great importance to this work, and he went on to study other aspects of the sense of touch (Murphy & Kovach, 1972).

Other scientists were less indifferent, and G. T. Fechner (1801–1887) became intrigued with Weber's figures when he discerned the feasibility of relating them to a problem that was troubling him. Fechner—both a scientist and a mystic—yearned for idealism, and believed that this could be approached if a regular relationship between the material and the spiritual could be established. He was attracted to the regularity in Weber's data, and his reflections led him to assume that all jnd's are equal; that they therefore quantify the distance between sensations and thus they are units on a sensory scale. Fechner used these units to formulate a principle or law that he stated as a mathematical formula in which the intensity of sensation is expressed as a predictable function of the intensity of the stimulus (Peters, 1962). Fechner believed that this expressed the relationship between mind and body, and he referred to it as Weber's law. Initially others followed this practice, but with the passage of time, authors began to refer to it as the Weber-Fechner law, and current writers are prone to speak of Fechner's law and Weber's ratio or fraction (English & English, 1958).

Fechner coined the word psychophysics to designate the study of the relationship between the physical properties of stimuli and sensation, and in 1860 he published a landmark volume, *Elements of Psychophysics*. "By *psychophysics*. . . . I mean a theory which, although ancient as a problem, is new here insofar as its formulation and treatment are concerned; in short, it is an exact theory of the relationship of body and mind. Thus one finds its novel name neither unfitting nor unnecessary'' (Fechner, 1860/1966, p. xxvii).

An active interest in assessing the validity of these relationships developed, and Fechner's work, combined with the research that it prompted, generated a technical vocabulary, one that reflects its Germanic origin. The word threshold is often replaced with the synonym limen, and abbreviated as L. The differences in the amounts of physical energy that are discernible are called differential or difference limens, or DLs. The threshold at which minimal amounts of energy are sensed is called the absolute or stimulus limen, and abbreviated as RLs. In the psychological literature the letter R is usually a symbol for response, but in the psychophysical literature R stands for the German word *Reiz* or stimulus. This terminology was adopted because it is the stimulus rather than the sensation that is graduated and measured (Guilford, 1954).

Psychophysics was enthusiastically received in the early psychological laboratories, particularly those devoted to STRUCTURAL PSYCHOLOGY because it appeared to be so pertinent to their concern about the fidelity with which the mind represents the physical world. Various ways of stimulating subjects as well as various ways of responding were devised, and by means of these different psychophysical procedures different aspects of physical energy were isolated and related to different sensory attributes. Both DLs and RLs were calculated, and a diversity of questions were answered quantitatively.

A few illustrations follow: How much of an odoriferous substance must be added to a solution of perfume to produce a jnd? How much must the amplitude of sound be increased in order to double its loudness? What is the threshold of pain? What is the faintest amount of light that can be seen? How many shades can be discriminated on the continuum from black to white? How much of a particular therapeutic drug can be added to a solution before the change in taste is discernible? (Boring, 1942).

The techniques that were used to quantify sensory thresholds were also found to be feasible for measurements of other responses. Fernberger (1921), for example, suggested quantifying the span of visual apprehension by one of the psychophysical methods, and he defined the span as the number of objects that has a probability of .50 of being apprehended in one glance. Guilford and Dallenbach also used a psychophysical procedure to define memory span that they identified as one ''which is as likely to be remembered as not'' (1925, p. 626). English and English comment: ''The concept of threshold is fundamental to all measurement, even when it is not explicitly mentioned. Originally limited to the *dimensions* of sensation, it is now freely applied to any aspect of the stimulus broadly conceived. Thus, it is proper to speak of the threshold of social mobility'' (1958, p. 554).

The idea that a response has a probability, rather than a certainty, of appearing or not appearing is pervasive even though as English and English suggest, this variability may not be referred to directly. To illustrate—most psychologists do not think of a person as being either honest or dishonest, as fair or unfair, as loving or hating, but prefer to assume that a reaction resonates with the intensity of the stimulation. One who is customarily honest may, when subjected to enough stress (hunger, cold, fear, etc.), resort to dishonesty. Organisms do not react in a twofold "either or" manner. Rather, there is a range, a probability of reacting.

When BEHAVIORISM with its denial of the validity of implicit behavior gained momentum, psychophysics was downgraded, but this renunciation was temporary and, in fact, the psychophysical methods were applied on an ad hoc basis when they were appropriate. For example, the research on VIGILANCE, that is, the detection of faint and erratic signals, that began during World War II included computations of both DLs and RLs. The study of PERCEPTUAL DEFENSE and SUBCEPTION that developed during the middle of the twentieth century used increases in RLs as evidence of the effect of emotional material on perception.

Organized efforts to reinstate psychophysics came during the 1960s and 1970s. The journal *Perception and Psychophysics* was founded in 1966, and a decade later the periodical *Sensory Processes* also began publication. This resurgence was due in part to the influence of COGNITIVE PSYCHOLOGY, a view that conceptualizes the organism as an active processor of information, and one starting point for this is sensation. The inaugural editorial in *Sensory Processes* highlights the shift from the traditional concept of sensory *receptors* by means of a comment about the "expanded understanding of how the senses operate on impinging stimuli" (Marks, 1976, p. 1).

The current date is too close to this revitalized interest to allow sound predictions about the future. But the relationship between the present and the past, although somewhat clouded, is a bit clearer, and what stands out in a retrospective view is continuity. The modern focus on the organism as a determiner appears to be supplementing, not replacing, existing knowledge. Several areas that were originally searched are now being re-searched. This is strikingly illustrated in reports (Stevens, 1979, 1982; Stevens & Green, 1978) of a sequence of experiments on the interaction between temperature and touch that are explicitly identified as a continuation of Weber's research. The first paper in this series begins: "In 1846 the physiologist E. H. Weber . . . noted that a cold coin . . . resting on the forehead feels heavier than a warm one. . . . This report has received little subsequent followup" (Stevens & Green, 1978, p. 206). The authors continue: "It is of historical interest that Weber's phenomenon was reported verified as early as 1865. . . . In our opinion the [critical] experimental evidence presented was far too weak to settle the matter, but is of sufficient interest to warrant fuller investigation" (Stevens & Green, 1978, p. 207).

References

Baldwin, J. M. (Ed.). (1960). *Dictionary of philosophy and psychology* (Vol. 1). Gloucester, MA: Peter Smith. (Original work published 1901)
Boring, E. G. (1942). *Sensation and perception in the history of experimental psychology.* New York: Appleton-Century.

Collier, R. M. (1950). The minima sensibilia in the history of the threshold concept. *Journal of General Psychology, 43*, 231–243. History of the topic during the prescientific period.

Diamond, S. (Ed.). (1974). *The roots of psychology: A sourcebook in the history of ideas*. New York: Basic Books. Diamond presents excerpts from an 1835 paper by Weber "On the Sense of Touch."

English, H. B., & English, A. C. (1958). *A comprehensive dictionary of psychological and psychoanalytical terms*. New York: Longmans, Green.

Fechner, G. (1966). *Elements of psychophysics* (Vol. 1) (H. E. Adler, Trans.; D. H. Howes & E. G. Boring, Eds.). New York: Holt, Rinehart & Winston. (Original work published 1860). Both the translator and the editors see Fechner's role in psychophysics as using and adapting the methods, but not originating them.

Fernberger, S. W. (1921). A preliminary study of the range of visual apprehension. *American Journal of Psychology, 32*, 121–133.

Guilford, J. P. (1954). *Psychometric methods*. (2nd ed.) New York: McGraw-Hill. First published in 1936, this book served as the definitive text on this topic for a number of years.

Guilford, J. P., & Dallenbach, K. M. (1925). The determination of memory span by the method of constant stimuli. *American Journal of Psychology, 36*, 621–628.

Marks, L. E. (1976). Editorial. *Sensory Processes, 1*, 1.

Murphy, G., & Kovach, J. K. (1972). *Historical introduction to modern psychology* (3rd ed.). New York: Harcourt Brace Jovanovich.

Peters, R. S. (Ed.). (1962). *Brett's history of psychology*. Cambridge, MA: MIT Press. This one-volume work is an edited and abridged version of Brett's original Volume 1 (published 1912), Volume 2 (1921), and Volume 3 (1921). These are widely commended for their erudition.

Stevens, J. C. (1979). Thermal intensification of touch sensation: Further extensions of the Weber phenomenon. *Sensory Processes, 3*, 240–248.

Stevens, J. C. (1982). Temperature can sharpen tactile acuity. *Perception and Psychophysics, 31*, 577–580. A study of the effects of the temperature of stimulating objects on the perception of spatial acuity of the skin. The study is at one and the same time a classic and modern.

Stevens, J. C., & Green, B. G. (1978). Temperature-touch interaction: Weber's phenomenon revisited. *Sensory Processes, 2*, 206–219.

Sources of Additional Information

Avery, D. D., & Cross, H. A., Jr. (1978). *Experimental methodology in psychology*. Monterey, CA: Brooks/Cole. This textbook includes an account of signal detection theory that is directed to the undergraduate, and hence is less technical than many discussions. Blackwell, H. R. (1953). Psychophysical thresholds: Experimental studies of methods of measurement. *Engineering Research Bulletin, No. 36*. Ann Arbor: University of Michigan Press. This bulletin illustrates the immense number of measurements that threshold determinations demand. It is an account of four series of experiments on sensory thresholds. In part #17 four research subjects made more than 60,000 observations; in part #2 four subjects made more than 34,000 observations; in parts #3 and #4 seventy-seven subjects made more than 183,000 observations. James, W. (1890). *Principles of Psychology* (Vol. 1). New York: Holt. James took strong exception to Fechner and to psychophysics, and his criticisms are stated in a colorful way. Following is only a fragment of them: "But it would be terrible if even such a dear old man as this could saddle our Science forever with his patient whimsies, and . . . compel all future students to plough through the difficulties, not only of his own works, but of the still drier ones written in his refutation. Those who desire this dreadful literature can find it . . . but I will not even enumerate it in a footnote" (p. 549). Luce, R. D. (1972). What sort of measurement is psychophysical measurement? *American Psychologist, 27*, 96–106. Luce argues that man per se is a measuring device and "each individual within a species is calibrated somewhat differently" (p. 96). This is technical paper, difficult to read but it does clarify the purposes of psychophysical measurements.

R

RADICAL BEHAVIORISM. See BEHAVIORISM.

REACTION TIME. 1. Response latency, or the time required for the initiation of a response, specifically the interval between the onset of a stimulus and the onset of a response. 2. Response speed or the time required to make a response.

Even though reaction time is a measure of time rather than of behavior, it has been considered important throughout the history of psychology. Although there are two varieties, they are both called reaction time, or RT. One is the speed of response, or the *time of* responding, and the second is the delay, or the *time before* responding. The research on response duration has occurred at two widely separated intervals: one at the beginning of the laboratory era and the second in the recent past. Response latency has been studied much more consistently, and as a result, many assume that reaction time means merely the period required for the initiation of a response.

The inaugural research on the time of responding is customarily credited to the German physiologist, H. F. Helmholtz (1821–1894), who tried to determine the speed of neural conduction from reaction time measurements. In one procedure he stimulated a nerve at various distances from the muscle to which it was attached and then inferred the transmission speed by subtracting the response lag for the shorter distance from the response lag for the longer distance. Helmholtz found the intervals ascertained in this and similar ways to be erratic, and other researchers, intrigued with the apparent feasibility of the technique, also tried it out, but by the turn of the current century they concurred with Helmholtz that the measurements are intolerably inconsistent (Woodworth, 1938).

Individual differences in the delay in reacting were observed as early as the close of the eighteenth century when the astronomer royal of the Greenwich

Observatory in England noticed that an assistant did not agree with him as to the second at which a star crosses the meridian. Various techniques for pinpointing the instant at which the interception occurred were tried, but disagreements were not eliminated. Even though these discrepancies were very small, they embarrassed astronomers, and the efforts to correct the problem helped to make scientists aware of reaction time (Sanford, 1888).

The Dutch physiologist F. C. Donders (1818–1889) investigated the timing of various psychological responses by means of a technique called mental chronometry. In one illustrative experiment Donders determined the period required to respond to a simple reaction, specifically the interval between a subject's hearing the syllable "Ki" spoken and his or her repetition of it. He then determined the interval before the repetition of "Ki" when the stimuli were varied as "Ka," "Ke," "Ko," or "Ku". Donders assumed that subtracting the latency of the simple reaction from the latency of the more complex one would yield a measure of the interval required for the discrimination of the syllable. Irregularities similar to those encountered in the measurement of neural transmission appeared. Temporal erraticisms occurred even within one experimental session, and the duration of a complicated response was found, on occasion, to be shorter than that required for a simple reaction (Woodworth, 1938). As a result, subtractive procedures as a measure of response time fell into disuse until the past two to three decades.

These problems in ascertaining response time did not block efforts to measure the delay in responding, and an abundance of experimentation on this variety of reaction time was forthcoming. One of the more commonly used designs requires subjects to press a telegrapher's key as soon as a stimulus is perceived, that is, is seen, heard, felt, smelled, or tasted. In other designs subjects are asked to respond verbally. This is accomplished by means of the voice key, an instrument that activates a timer when a person speaks.

The founding psychologists adulated laboratory equipment, in part because it signified a scientific status and a rejection of the earlier identification of psychology with philosophy. Reaction time fed this deference because it mandated precise measurements of very brief intervals. The chronoscope was the preferred apparatus. A satisfactory model was assembled in the 1860s, and several revisions soon followed (Popplestone & McPherson, 1980). Although it may have been a mechanical triumph of its time, the chronoscope demanded repetitive calibration and monitoring. The pride of ownership combined with these maintenance demands to permeate the literature on reaction time with discussions of apparatus. Titchener (1905), for example, devotes nearly half a chapter on "The Reaction Experiment" to a section on "The Electric Current and the Practical Units of Electrical Measurement."

The investigations that were conducted yielded a mass of minutiae. These include, but are far from limited to, the discovery that the time before reacting to painful stimuli is especially long. In taste, the pause is shortest for salt and longest for bitter. A stimulus applied to the forehead produces a longer delay than one applied to the hand. The pickup of a light stimulus is quickest when the fovea is stimulated. Binocular reactions begin more rapidly than monocular ones (Boring, Langfeld, & Weld, 1935).

When BEHAVIORISM began to dominate psychology, the number of experiments on response delay as an independent topic dropped precipitously, and the measurements that were taken were merely one facet of the response that was being studied. This integration is illustrated in procedures that were designed for the selection of such personnel as automobile drivers, industrial machine technicians, and telephone operators in that these include assessments of various skills as well as response latency (Maier, 1955). The readiness to react was also included in PERSONALITY assessments with both decreases and increases in time related to emotional blocking (Abt & Bellak, 1950).

A revival of interest in reaction time came shortly after World War II when scientists began to draw analogies between psychological behavior of people and information processing by machines in the hope of increasing the understanding of psychological processing. Researchers working in this frame of reference have the advantage over their predecessors of access to sensitive equipment, and this modernization is producing corrections of previously accepted intervals of time (McGuigan, 1984). These refinements have not, however, included noteworthy advances in understanding the qualitative properties of the variables related to reaction time. What they are yielding is a reiteration of the past, of both earlier evaluations of the concept and laboratory data. To illustrate—William James remarked, as early as 1890, about the allure at that time of reaction time research: "An immense amount of work has been done on reaction-time, of which I have cited but a small part. It is a sort of work which appeals particularly to patient and exact minds, and they have not failed to profit by the opportunity" (p. 97). In 1974 Pachella remarks about the current attraction to the topic. "Indeed, reaction time has become about as common a dependent variable as there is in human experimental psychology ... measures have sometimes been used as much for convenience as for any particular theoretical purpose" (p. 41).

In 1890 James also advised readers that the intensity of stimuli shortens response latency. In 1970 Murray reported that the delay in responding to three levels of auditory intensity shows "an inverse relation between RT and stimulus intensity" (p. 383).

A 1911 textbook advises: "To shorten the reaction-time as much as possible, the subject must know what place of the sensory organism is to be hit by the stimulus, and about when to expect it" (Ladd & Woodworth, p. 476). A modern investigator concludes: "Allocation of attention ... is a more important factor in observed RT than structural links between stimulus and response mechanisms" (Peters, 1983, p. 397).

Mental chronometry has also been reactivated, and the earlier discrediting of the technique is now attributed to failures to carefully analyze the processes. The attempts to rectify this deficit take various forms, and prominent among them is the separating of the responses on a logical basis into smaller units, often called "stages". Temporal measurements are then used to identify some of the properties of the stages, whether they are, for example, dependent or independent, concomitant or serial (Posner & Mitchell, 1967). This design has been applied to various responses and a brief outline of one measurement in memory (Sternberg, 1969) illustrates this approach even though it violates the complexity of the research design. Subjects were first required to memorize a set of stimuli and then asked to decide as quickly as possible whether or not particular stimuli are part of the original set. The delay in responding was found to increase as the number of stimuli to be identified increased, an increment that suggests that subjects process items serially rather than simultaneously.

The validity of using time to infer process is far from clear. The enthusiasm for the procedure is high, but it is also tempered. For example, "Mental chronometry provides both a set of techniques and an important theoretical framework that *can serve to* [italics added] unify diverse approaches to the study of mind . . . it does represent a significant *tool* [italics added] for unravelling the most basic and perplexing questions of the nature of mind" (Posner & Rogers, 1978, p. 184).

References

Abt, L. E., & Bellak, L. (Eds.). (1950). *Projective psychology: Clinical approaches to the total personality.* New York: Alfred Knopf.

Boring, E. G., Langfeld, H. S., & Weld, H. P. (1935). *Psychology: A factual textbook.* New York: John Wiley.

James, W. (1890). *The principles of psychology* (Vol. 1). New York: Henry Holt.

Ladd, G. T., & Woodworth, R. S. (1911). *Elements of physiological psychology: A treatise of the activities and nature of the mind.* New York: Charles Scribner's Sons.

Maier, N.R.F. (1955). *Psychology in industry* (2nd ed.). Cambridge, MA: Houghton Mifflin. Maier includes discussions of muscular and perceptual speed in relation to job proficiency and safety in this broad coverage of industrial psychology.

McGuigan, F. J. (1984). Psychophysiological methods in the assessment of nutritional adequacy. In J. Brožek & B. Schürch (Eds.), *Malnutrition and behavior: Critical assessment of key issues* (pp. 149–156). Lausanne, Switzerland: Nestlé Foundation. McGuigan reports that electromyographic measures of reaction time indicate that the traditional key pressing and voice key activating exceed the "true" reaction time by "at least 50 msec in the case of the former and by several hundred milliseconds in the case of the latter" (p. 151).

Murray, H. G. (1970). Stimulus intensity and reaction time: Evaluation of a decision-theory model. *Journal of Experimental Psychology, 84*, 383–391.

Pachella, R. G. (1974). The interpretation of reaction time in information-processing research. In B. H. Kantowitz (Ed.), *Human information processing: Tutorials in performance and cognition.* Hillsdale, NJ: Lawrence Erlbaum.

Peters, M. (1983). RT to tactile stimuli presented ipsi- and contralaterally to the responding hand. *Quarterly Journal of Experimental Psychology, 35A*, 397–410. This modern study questions the validity of interpreting difference in reaction time to crossed and uncrossed stimuli (react with the hand that is stimulated versus react with the opposite hand) as measures of the time required for neural transmission. Peters found that the reaction time varies with attention and not between crossed and uncrossed conditions. There are no references to similar early criticisms.

Popplestone, J. A. & McPherson, M. W. (1980). The vitality of the Leipzig model of 1880–1910 in the United States in 1950–1980. In W. G. Bringmann & R. D. Tweney (Eds.), *Wundt studies: A centennial collection* (pp. 226–257). Toronto: C. J. Hogrefe. This volume commemorates the centennial of the laboratory at the University of Leipzig in 1879, generally acknowledged to be the first psychology laboratory. It was the scene of a large amount of research on reaction time.

Posner, M. I., & Mitchell, R. F. (1967). Chronometric analysis of classification. *Psychological Review, 74*, 392–409. The authors apply Donders' subtractive procedures to a series of problems, but they state that "the emphasis is not placed upon the times themselves but upon their relevance for understanding the operations and mechanisms involved in perceptual matching, naming, and classifying" (p. 392).

Posner, M. I., & Rogers, M. G. K. (1978). Chronometric analysis of abstraction and recognition. In W. K. Estes (Ed.), *Handbook of learning and cognitive processes: Vol. 5. Human information processing* (pp. 143–188) Hillsdale, NJ: Lawrence Erlbaum.

Sanford, E. C. (1888). Personal equation. *American Journal of Psychology, 2*, 3–38, 271–298, 403–430. A detailed, meticulously worked out account of the astronomers' struggles to be precise, to gain control over the "personal equation." They believed, initially, that each astronomer's error was constant and the difference between any two individuals would therefore be reliable.

Sternberg, S. (1969). The discovery of processing stages: Extensions of Donders' method. *Acta Psychologica, 30*, 276–315.

Titchener, E. B. (1905). *Experimental psychology: A manual of laboratory practice: Vol. 2. Quantitative experiments: Pt. 1. Student's manual*. London: Macmillan.

Woodworth, R. S. (1938). *Experimental psychology*. New York: Holt. Woodworth's presentation of the history of reaction time is comprehensive, accurate, and relates different approaches. This treatment has been effective in keeping the inaugural days of reaction time research in view.

Sources of Additional Information

Brožek, J. (1970). Contributions to the history of psychology: XII. Wayward history: F. C. Donders (1818–1889) and the timing of mental operations. *Psychological Reports, 26*, 563–569. An account of Donders' work. It also calls attention to the unusual number of errors that are found in various citations of him. Gilbert, J. A. (1894). Researchers on the mental and physical development of schoolchildren. *Studies from the Yale Psychological Laboratory, 2*, 40–100. Gilbert administered tests to children at a time when studies of development were only beginning to appear and when psychological differences were sought in simple as well as complex responses. Gilbert's measures included reaction time, height, weight, but these tests of simple functions did not discriminate between bright and dull children. Goodman, E. S. (1971). Citation analysis as a tool in historical study: A case study based on F. C. Donders and mental reaction times. *Journal of the History of the Behavioral Sciences, 7*, 187–191. Goodman traces over a one hundred-year span the references to Donders' paper on the speed of psychological processes. Miller, J. M., Moody, D. B., & Stebbins, W. C. (1969). Evoked potentials and auditory reaction time in monkeys. *Science, 163* (No. 3867), 592–594. This article provides an illustration of the technical improvements that have developed during the course of reaction time study. Sound is delivered directly to the auditory cortex, and this yields a briefer response latency than when the animals are normally stimulated. Mueller, J. H., & Wherry, K. L. (1982). Test anxiety and reaction time for matching decisions. *Journal of Research in Personality, 16*, 281–289. This research is clearly of this era. The authors suggest that "anxiety differences observed in recall tasks do not involve solely access speed differences, but instead reflect differences in encoding, strategy utilization, and similar memory processes" (p. 289).

REINFORCEMENT. See EFFECT and REINFORCEMENT.

RESPONSE. See STIMULUS, RESPONSE, and BEHAVIOR.

RESPONSE FUNCTION. See STIMULUS FUNCTION, RESPONSE FUNCTION, and INTERBEHAVIORAL PSYCHOLOGY.

S

SELF. 1. A subjective summary of one's individuality. 2. A synonym for ego.

The self is a composite of a person's knowledge of and reactions to his or her individuality. This includes an awareness of the differences between the self and the not self, an appreciation of the coherence of an ongoing stream of experiences as well as evaluations of one's physical and psychological integrity. The words PERSONALITY and self both connote singularity, and this leads at times to their being used as equivalents. They are different, however, in that the concept of personality stresses the perception of others, whereas the concept of self stresses an individual's own perception. The terms ego (Latin for I) and self both denote uniqueness and are therefore, in some instances, also used synonymously. In others they are differentiated, most distinctly by psychoanalysts who typically define the ego as one component of a psyche that consists of different parts. The ego is commonly identified as the agent that mediates between a person's self-serving wishes and the constraints that society imposes on them (Klein, 1968). Neither ego, personality, nor self are used in scientific writing to designate a sense of personal importance, nor do they refer either to highly developed social skills or to a self-conscious shyness. Rather, all three highlight the singularity of each person.

The concept of the self was borrowed from philosophy by some early psychological theorists who believed it to be the nucleus of their subject matter: "After all, the consciousness of selfhood is the very core of our psychical being. . . . The fact of its existence is for each of us the one absolutely indubitable fact" (Angell, 1908, p. 457). "Psychology may be defined provisionally as science of consciousness . . . but, in the view of the writer of this book, it does not go far enough. For consciousness . . . always is a somebody-being-conscious.

... We may define psychology more exactly by naming it science of the self as consciousness'' (Calkins, 1911, p. 1).

These early endorsements of the concept of the self were repudiated by advocates of two dominant and opposed schools, or theories, of psychology. The criticisms came first from STRUCTURAL PSYCHOLOGY, after its influential proponent E. B. Titchener requested graduate students to observe "the psychological self" by the method of INTROSPECTION, an abstruse technique devised for the observation and analysis of CONSCIOUSNESS. Titchener (1911) concluded that psychology could not be defined as the science of the self because introspections disclose that one becomes aware of the self only intermittently, infrequently, and generally in a social context.

The second assault came from BEHAVIORISM, a very different theory from structuralism, and one that rejected the study of personal, private experiences because they seem to violate the requirement that a science deal only with public, observable phenomena. This dogma resulted in a boycott of the concept of the self that lasted from approximately the late 1920s through the 1960s when the influence of the HUMAN POTENTIAL MOVEMENT began to restore the self as the core of the field of psychology. Both the behaviorists' and the structuralists' doctrines were unusual, unique views of psychology, and their effect on the concept of the self was puzzling: "One of the oddest events in the history of modern psychology is the manner in which the ego (or self) became sidetracked and lost to view. I say it is odd, because the existence of one's own self is the one fact of which every mortal person—every psychologist included—is perfectly convinced. . . . They have before them, at the heart of their science, *a fact of perfect certainty . . . and yet they pay no attention to it* [italics added] (Allport, 1943, p. 451).

The problems that come from these theoretical disagreements have been augmented by the impossibility of establishing direct links among different aspects of the self (such as age or gender) and the concept as a whole. Researchers are forced to rely only on inference, and this drawback became apparent as early as 1897 in an analysis of the results of a questionnaire regarding children's ideas about themselves that was devised by G. Stanley Hall, one of the pioneer investigators of the psychology of childhood. Hall inquired about a variety of factors that he assumed influenced one's impressions of the self, and thus the actual data are personal interpretations rather than observed relationships. Among the items Hall studied are the informal names that children are given, their notions of the soul, and the age at which the concept of the self first emerges. In relation to this last topic he noted the anatomical parts to which infants pay attention and speculated that their attention to specific details of the body might signal the formation of the ego. This proposal may well be correct, but these responses may be more relevant to the BODY IMAGE component of the self.

None of Hall's successors has been successful in demonstrating conclusively how reactions to specific activities and parts of the self are linked to the perception of the whole. In fact, the history of the concept resonates with themes that were popular during the era in which the particular explanations were devised. Kagan's first sentence in a modern volume, with the subtitle "The Emergence of Self-Awareness," comments on these changes: "There is a glaring disparity between the uniformity that characterizes the growth of young children and the variability that observers from different historical periods and cultures have imposed on their descriptions of these universal phenomena. . . . All newborns with an intact central nervous system will tighten their tiny fingers around a pencil placed in their palms. Whereas nineteenth century observers were certain that this reaction was an early form of the adult proprietary instinct, modern observers who follow Piaget regard the same act as the initial structure in the growth of intelligence" (Kagan, 1981, p. 1).

There is a variation in emphasis even among explanations that draw from similar sources. Some of the psychologists who believe that sensory information provides the most important cues point to the role of both kinesthesia and audition. They note, for example, that shaking a rattle generates messages that are different from those that come from shaking merely the hand. Others emphasize the role of vision and audition, and in investigating this relationship observe infants' reactions to their mirror images as well as to photographs and videotapes (Lewis & Brooks-Gunn, 1979). The enthusiasm for this technique is, once again, tempered by reservations about the validity of the interpretation of the data: "We may be learning more about the infant's developing understanding of reflective surfaces and pictorial modes of representation than about the infant's emerging sense of self, more broadly defined and experienced" (Harter, 1983, p. 292).

The research on the concept of the self has dealt with numerous additional determiners, including, but not limited to, the accepting and rejecting of ethnic origin, occupational choice, gender, insight, self-deception, and self-esteem (Hilgard, 1949; Rosenberg & Kaplan, 1982). On the current scene the concept seems to be moving from the traditional view that the self functions passively, in the direction of one that directs and guides behavior; that is, the self is seen as a kind of cognitive organizer that seeks out particular experiences and interprets their meaning. This viewpoint was promoted earlier by advocates of PHENOM-ENOLOGY, but it was rejected, particularly by the behaviorists, since it suggests a selective or executive self inside the person, almost a homunculus. Currently, however, behaviorism is being challenged and, as previously mentioned, critics, waving such banners as humanistic and phenomenological psychology, are speaking loudly and clearly on behalf of the self. Opinion is being expressed that behavior can best be understood from the perspective of the actor, for example: "While people may behave strangely from another's viewpoint, the behavior is always reasonable from the viewpoint of the people doing the behaving, at least at the moment they are carrying out the behavior" (Epstein, 1980, p. 91). The enthusiasm for this orientation is high, particularly in the HUMAN POTENTIAL MOVEMENT, where the concept of the self is being aligned with so many other aspects of personality that the subject matter appears to approach the earlier equation of the self with the field of psychology.

In spite of both the elusiveness of information about the self and changes in theoretical fashions, research has yielded some enduring themes. One of these is the relationship between the "accuracy of self-analysis" and the accuracy of the assessments of others. Research on this started as early as 1915 when Cogan, Conklin, and Hollingworth asked undergraduate students to rate both themselves and acquaintances on a series of personality traits, such as sociability, conceit, intelligence, and vulgarity. The "true" measure of each of these traits for each subject in the experiment was considered to be the median of the ratings that members of the group assigned to the individual. In other words, a person was said to be as sociable as a composite of the judgments of acquaintances.

A comparison between the evaluations of the self and those assigned by others disclosed that the subjects did not consistently rate themselves in a manner that was markedly different from the ratings that peers a them, but there was a tendency to underestimate one's own undesirable qualities and to overestimate desirable ones. A second comparison, in this instance between the ratings assigned to an individual and those that the individual assigns, indicated that those who are judged as having a commendable trait often assess the trait accurately in others, but when the trait is reprehensible, the judgments of others are apt to be inaccurate. A similar demonstration of the projection of one's own PERSON-ALITY onto others was made in the 1930s, and since that time the topic has been investigated and the results supported in various additional experiments.

A second example of continuity is found in opinion about the compounding effect of the concept of the self. A 1925 textbook states: "The fact of growth means not only that the self changes during life, but that the nature of these changes and accretions is dependent in part upon previous conditions . . . the old adage that the tree grows as the twig is bent" (Carr, p. 339). And fifty-seven years later a 1982 article expresses the same view, but the adage is replaced by a modern metaphor between information processing and cognitive functioning: "As we accrue knowledge about ourselves and achieve cognitive representations of our experience in various behavioral domains, we become 'experts' about ourselves. We may come to understand that we are shy, or creative. . . . These generalizations about the self function as selective mechanisms in further processing" (Markus & Sentis, p. 45).

References

Allport, G. W. (1943). The ego in contemporary psychology. *Psychological Review, 50*, 451–478. Allport regrets the purging of the self from psychology and predicts its return, a forecast that turned out to be accurate.

Angell, J. R. (1908). *Psychology: An introductory study of the structure and function of human consciousness* (4th ed., rev.). New York: Holt.

Calkins, M. W. (1911). *A first book in psychology*. New York: Macmillan.

Carr, H. A. (1925). *Psychology: A study of mental activity*. New York: Longmans, Green.

Cogan, L. C., Conklin, A. M., & Hollingworth, H. L. (1915). An experimental study of self-analysis, estimates of associates, and the results of tests. *School and Society, 2*, 171–179. The method that these investigators used was similar to that used by

R. R. Sears in 1936 in what is often identified as the original experimental demonstration of projection.

Epstein, S. (1980). The self-concept: A review and the proposal of an integrated theory
of personality. In E. Staub (Ed.), *Personality: Basic aspects and current research*
(pp. 81–132). Englewood Cliffs, NJ: Prentice-Hall.

Hall, G. S. (1897). Some aspects of the early sense of self. *American Journal of Psychology, 9*, 351–395. Hall used questionnaires extensively, and the discussions
of both FEAR and ANGER in this volume refer to other questionnaires he distributed.
These portray the psychology of the era.

Harter, S. (1983). Developmental perspectives on the self-system. In P. H. Mussen (Ed.),
*Handbook of child psychology: Vol. 4. Socialization, personality, and social
development* (4th ed., pp. 275–386). New York: John Wiley.

Hilgard, E. R. (1949). Human motives and the concept of the self. *American Psychologist, 4*, 374–382. This is Hilgard's presidential address to the American Psychological Association. A strong argument for the importance of the self concept,
particularly in relation to both motivation and self-understanding.

Kagan, J. (1981). *The second year: The emergence of self-awareness.* Cambridge, MA:
Harvard University Press. This volume is outstanding because of the author's
integration of various lines of evidence about the development of self-awareness.
Sophisticated attention is devoted to various complexities of the phenomenon.

Klein, G. S. (1968). Psychoanalysis: Ego psychology. *International encyclopedia of the
social sciences* (pp. 11–31). New York: Macmillan. This is an accurate, reasonably comprehensive account written for the educated lay person. A psychoanalytic
concept is described with a minimum of jargon.

Lewis, M., & Brooks-Gunn, J. (1979). *Social cognition and the acquisition of self.* New
York: Plenum Press. The authors use both videotapes and mirrors to study the
concept of the self.

Markus, H., & Sentis, K. (1982). The self in social information processing. In J. Suls
(Ed.), *Psychological perspectives on the self* (Vol. 1, pp. 41–70). Hillsdale, NJ:
Lawrence Erlbaum. In this chapter the self is construed as crucial in influencing
one's social behavior.

Rosenberg, M, & Kaplan, H. B. (Eds.). (1982). *Social psychology of the self-concept.*
Arlington Heights, IL: Harlan Davidson. This volume contains forty-two chapters
by various authors. It represents the wide range of variables with which the concept
of the self is aligned, ranging from professional self-images of Greek military
personnel through the effects of parental attitudes on children's self-esteem.

Titchener, E. B. (1911). A note of the consciousness of self. *American Journal of
Psychology, 22*, 540–552.

Sources of Additional Information

Horowitz, E. L. (1935). Spatial localization of the self. *Journal of Social Psychology,
6*, 379–387. This is a study that illustrates earlier research on where in the body children
and young adults localize the self. The specifications are diverse. For example, in one
sample sixty areas were reported, thirty-six of which were in the head and the others
miscellaneous—lungs, hair, fingers, etc. Smith, M. B. (1978). Perspectives on selfhood.
American Psychologist, 33, 1053–1063. This is Smith's presidential address to the American Psychological Association. The discussion is in the vein of both humanistic and
phenomenological psychology. Viney, L. (1969). Self: The history of a concept. *Journal*

of the History of the Behavioral Sciences, 5, 349–359. The strength of this article is in the prescientific history. Wylie, R. C. (1968). The present status of self theory. In E. F. Borgatta and W. W. Lambert (Eds.), *Handbook of personality theory and research* (pp. 728–787). Chicago: Rand McNally. This chapter reviews the early history of the concept and assesses the experimental data at the time of publication. Ziv, A. (1981). The self concept of adolescent humorists. *Journal of Adolescence, 4,* 187–197. Ziv compared the self concept of high school students who were classified as humorists with those classified as nonhumorists. This research is interesting because humor, particularly in females, has received only a scant amount of attention. Ziv concluded that there are some sex differences, and that humorists of both sexes see themselves as more sociable and active than their sober-minded peers.

SENSATION.   1. An image or representation of the physical world, said to be created by the impinging of sufficient and appropriate stimulation on sense organs. 2. An awareness of objects or events, with the apprehending occasioned by the interaction of an organism with an object or an event. 3. A synonym for perception.

Traditionally, sensations are said to be initiated when receptors are activated, and the ensuing experiences are believed to vary both with the particular sensory apparatus that is stimulated (the ear versus the eye) and with the physical properties of the energy (sound versus light). The experiential history of the individual is customarily allocated only a limited influence. Training, for example, cannot induce a sensation of pitch in a deaf person or one of color in a blind person, but training in music and in art can refine pitch and hue discriminations in people with normal sensory receptors.

Classically, the senses are classified as sight, hearing, touch, taste, and smell, but this scheme omits the appreciation of temperature, pain, dizziness, and kinesthesis, or movement of parts of the body. Sense organs are also categorized by reference either to their anatomical location or to the energy to which they respond. The former includes exteroceptors, structures that are on or near the surface of the body; proprioceptors, located in the muscles, tendons, joints, and inner ear; and interoceptors, or enteroceptors, in the viscera. If the effective energy is applied directly, the sense organ is called a contact receptor, but if the energy is radiant, it is called a distance receptor or telereceptor. Adults react readily to telereception, but infants are probably stimulated more by contact. The temperature and texture of nourishment, for example, appear to be more clearly sensed by infants than the sight of food.

Many psychologists prefer to use the word sensation to refer to the awareness of stimulation, and PERCEPTION to refer to its interpretation, to the recognizing of its causes, role, and sequels. One *senses* a ringing but *perceives* it as produced by a telephone, often inferring the identity and purpose of the caller. The misinterpretation of the sound of an approaching tornado as the more familiar sound of a train whistle is more a perceptual than a sensory event.

The difference between the two concepts is not, however, consistently made, and in fact many psychologists use the words perception and sensation interchangeably (Graham, 1958). Numerous authors replace the noun sensation with a phrase composed of the adjective sensory coupled to a specific item, for example, "sensory deprivation" and "sensory data." These amendments are not made consistently, as documented in a volume entitled *Introduction to Sensation/Perception* (McBurney & Collings, 1977), in which the Index, in contrast to the title of the volume, lacks an entry for sensation but does use phrases beginning with the word sensory.

Sensation was a salient topic during the ground-breaking days of experimental psychology, with its visibility reflecting the importance of the concept in each of the two dominant historical roots of psychology—physiology and philosophy. By the time the first psychological laboratories were established, physiology had already conducted a considerable amount of research on sensation, and psychologists, eager to demonstrate their scientific credentials, found it easy to build on their procedures.

The inaugural psychological formulations were patterned in accord with the philosophical proposition that sensations are mental or ethereal representations of the external world, excited when physical energy impinges upon sensory and neural structures. This doctrine of sensationism asserted that what is sensed is independent of the stimulus and is determined by the sense organ that is activated and/or the specific nerves that react. These psychic units were also assumed to comprise all that organisms can know about reality. These intangible mental entities violate the scientific mandate to address only tangibles, but scientists have not been completely successful in excluding them, in part because it is exceedingly difficult to distinguish between the actual and the described. One factor that has also helped to sustain them is the opinion that sensations are basically neurological phenomena. Advocates of this position assert that they will be understood and their impalpability erased when the nervous system is fully understood (Smith, 1983).

Some theorists, exerting great care to adhere to scientific principles, reject the proposition that sensations are nonsubstantive and illusory, and they structure them as responses rather than images or representations. From this point of view, an organism does not see light or hear sound waves, but when the light is satisfactory, an organism sees the real or actual entity, such as a bird, a house, or a printed word. In the case of adequate auditory stimulation one hears a violin, the spoken word, or a motor. This interpretation of sensation is most thoroughly developed in the school or system of INTERBEHAVIORAL PSYCHOLOGY but this is not a dominant view, and much of the history of the concept of sensation is a chronicle of the concept of illusory experiences. Hochberg comments on this course of events in his concluding remarks about the history of the first century of research in sensation: "In summary, the present scene generally looks much like the one with which we started. . . . There is hot pursuit, at both physiological and psychophysical levels, for units of sensory analysis (what were once called 'specific nerve energies'), and there is recourse to 'mental structure' (schemas, etc.) to which those units eventually contribute'' (1979, p. 138).

To direct attention to some of the nuances of this tradition—the concept acquired unusual importance when Titchener, the eminent systematist of STRUCTURAL PSYCHOLOGY, identified sensations as one of the basic units of the mind. This role made it necessary to examine them with great care and the main method used to accomplish this was INTROSPECTION. This is an esoteric technique of observing one's own consciousness, and it yields meticulous details about such sensation-related factors as variations in the saturation of colors, different pitches and loudness of tones, the existence of saline, sour, sweet, and bitter tastes as well as the nuances of hunger experiences, the nature of small variations in sensations in the circulatory, respiratory, digestive, genital, and urinary systems. There were probes of the relationship between different physical phenomena and various sensations, for example, wave length and color or wave amplitude and loudness (Titchener, 1911). The standard research design was a one-to-one treatment, for example, stimulating the fixated eye of a subject passively awaiting the event and neglecting the simultaneous contributions to vision of such variables as touch, head movements, and successive views. The information generated by the structural psychologists constituted many facts about sensation, but many of the theories concerning the relationship among energy, structure, and sensation were controversial (Boring, 1942).

Exceptions to this format gradually began to appear. An important figure in this movement is James J. Gibson, a psychologist, who began work on sensation and perception in the 1930s. As he continued to experiment, Gibson (1966, 1979) became convinced of the merits of dealing with sensing rather than with the interplay between physiological and physical events. He proposed bypassing the physiological and physical events and proceeding directly to the study of psychological phenomena, with an emphasis on relating what is perceived to the stimulation. He came to see some laboratory procedures as so artificial that they interfered with rather than disclosed the normal ways of becoming acquainted with one's surroundings. He constructed a convincing argument that important determiners of sensing are in the environment, such as moving patterns or gradients of light and texture.

Although Gibson highlights what is perceived, he also construes perceivers as active. He notes that the eyes, ears, nose, mouth, and skin are not merely passive receptors, but are ''mobile, exploratory, orienting'' (1966, p. 33). His discussion of audition, for example, centers around listening, not hearing. He also amends the venerated analogy between the camera and the eye in a way that makes the latter an active contributor to visual sensations: ''But the eye is not a camera; it is a self-focusing, self-setting, and self-orienting camera whose image becomes optimal because the system compensates for blur, for extremes of illumination, and for being aimed at something uninteresting'' (1966, p. 33).

Gibson also deals at length with the means by which sensory information from different sources compounds. He calls attention, for example, to how a person in the dark gropes with hands and fingers. He also discusses the mutuality between sensory and motor acts, how, for example, the mouth and the hands feel and act reciprocally, and he also mentions the alternation of both olfactory and gustatory sensations that come from chewing and sniffing.

The modern investigator of sensation faces many of the problems of the pioneers but is better equipped to handle them. Improvements in laboratory apparatus allow more efficient monitoring of the multiplicity of sensations that are continually being experienced. The development of COGNITIVE PSYCHOLOGY has increased the notice that is paid to the actions of the organism, and the orienting function of sensation led to its ready inclusion in the recently adopted custom of drawing analogies between behavior and electronic information processing. These changes have generated a great deal of enthusiasm, fostered the discovery of some previously unknown nuances, but as the previous quotation of Hochberg implies, there are as yet no stellar improvements in the understanding of sensing.

There is, however, one aspect of sensing in which dramatic progress appears to be under way. This incipient victory involves the replacing of biologically defective sensory equipment with devices that permit a sensory handicapped person to sense physical energy. Electronic implants in the ear and the eye now allow sound to be heard and light to be seen, although the discrimination of differences in what is heard and what is seen is still very unsatisfactory (Solomon, 1982). These are replacements for biological parts, and in that respect they do not involve psychology, but they do make it possible for psychological behavior to develop. One must hear in order to learn to speak. One must see in order to grasp distance and appreciate variations in the density of the atmosphere. But the ability to hear does not assure discrimination between the sound of an electronic organ and a pipe organ. Neither does the ability to see the variegated colors in the sky assure the ability to reproduce them in a painting.

References

Boring, E. G. (1942). *Sensation and perception in the history of experimental psychology.* New York: Appleton-Century-Crofts. This is a classic, frequently cited presentation of the dominant tradition of research in sensation and perception.

Gibson, J. J. (1966). *The senses considered as perceptual systems.* Boston: Houghton Mifflin. The title reflects Gibson's innovative view.

Gibson, J. J. (1979). *The ecological approach to visual perception.* Boston: Houghton Mifflin. This is a technical presentation of a complex subject matter. Gibson uses the word ecology to refer to such details of the visual field as arrays of light and gradients of texture. This is a highly specialized meaning, and much more restricted than the concept of ECOLOGICAL PSYCHOLOGY.

Graham, C. H. (1958). Sensation and perception in an objective psychology. *Psychological Review, 65,* 65–76. A statement of some of the behaviorist's problems when dealing with sensation and perception. Graham entertains substituting "discrimination" for "sensation" but then recognizes that this would probably involve only a change in vocabulary.

Hochberg, J. (1979). Sensation and perception. In E. Hearst (Ed.), *The first century of experimental psychology* (pp. 89–142). Hillsdale, NJ: Lawrence Erlbaum. Hochberg's level of scholarship is referred to as "unrivaled," and this is a remarkable review of the field.

McBurney, D., & Collings, V. (1977). *Introduction to sensation/perception.* Englewood Cliffs, NJ: Prentice-Hall. This book is cited in the current discussion only in order to illustrate terminology.

Smith, N. W. (1983). Sensing is perceiving: An alternative to the doctrine of the double world. In N. W. Smith, P. T. Mountjoy, & D. H. Reuben (Eds.), *Reassessment in psychology: The interbehavioral alternative* (pp. 161–211). Washington, DC: The University Press of America. The author reviews theories about sensation and perception from Medieval theology to the present. He offers a scientifically acceptable explanation to replace this non-scientific tradition.

Solomon, S. (1982, November 28). Spare-parts medicine. *New York Times Magazine* (pp. 120–123, 134, 140). This article includes a description of the sensations induced when electronic implants are used to compensate for anatomical deficits in the eye and ear. The procedures generate some sensations, but the technology does not yet allow refined discriminations; for example, sound is heard, but different speech sounds are not distinguished. The author also reports progress in compensating for deficits in various nonsensory anatomical parts.

Titchener, E. B. (1911). *A text book of psychology.* New York: Macmillan.

Sources of Additional Information

Collins, W. E. (1966). Vestibular responses from figure skaters. *Aerospace Medicine, 37,* 1098–1104. An experimental demonstration of the interaction between two kinds of sensory stimulation. When executing on-ice spins, professional skaters induce a great deal of vestibular stimulation. The skaters who keep their eyes open retain their balance, but if these visual cues are absent, they are prone to stagger. Crafts, L. W., Schneirla, T. C., Robinson, E. E., & Gilbert, R. W. (1950). *Recent experiments in psychology* (2nd ed.). New York: McGraw Hill. This volume reports various research programs, including the so-called facial vision experiments that were conducted at Cornell University. The description is well written, in nontechnical language, and it illustrates psychologists' interest in how sensing in one system can compensate for deficits in another. Comparisons were made of people who are blind, blindfolded but normally sighted, and blind-deaf in avoiding obstacles and judging the distance of a sound source. The blind are more adept than the others and more sensitive to auditory cues. They appear to rely on changes in reflected sounds as they approach objects. This skill, of course, creates an anomaly in that the blind person experiences sensory interference in a noisy environment. Makous, W. L. (1966). Cutaneous color sensitivity: Explanation and demonstration. *Psychological Review, 73,* 280–294. This research demonstrates the discrimination of unpainted from painted surfaces on the basis of cutaneous temperature. It also points up the limitations of such sensitivity. Myers, T. I., Murphy, D. B., Smith, Steward, & Goffard, S. J. (1966). *Experimental studies of sensory deprivation and social isolation.* Alexandria, VA: The George Washington University Human Resource Office, Technical Report 66–8. This includes a report of a study of the effects of sensory deprivation and social isolation on various psychological phenomena. In general, the results indicate deleterious effects of deprivation or, conversely, that sensory stimulation facilitates psychological behavior. Palmer, R. D. (1970). Visual actuity and stimulus-seeking behavior.

Psychosomatic Medicine, 32, 277–284. The featuring of the active capabilities of sense organs led investigators to look into the relationship between sensory acuity and preferred level of stimulation. The results of this experiment suggest that high visual acuity increases the probability of including exciting and novel content when asked to make up a story. Some of the research on optimal levels of stimulation has been converted by other investigators into studies of excitement and thrills. These are referred to as research in sensation, but this use of the word has little or no affinity with the concept elaborated in this discussion.

SET. 1. A readiness to react to an anticipated stimulus or to respond in a particular way. 2. A synonym for attention and vigilance.

The concepts of set, ATTENTION, and VIGILANCE denote a disposition to react, and they are on occasion used as equivalents. Vigilance stands apart from the others in that it is a relatively new concept and is mainly concerned with reactions to faint and weak stimuli. But set and attention have a long history of synonymous use. Dashiell's textbook, for example, informs students that "set goes by the name of attending or attention" (1937, p. 322), and Munn's textbook claims that "attending may be considered a form of set" (1951, p. 385). This identity is not, however, all-inclusive, and there are differences in emphasis between the two words. Attention is frequently applied when the clarity of an ongoing experience is the topic (a reader absorbed in a novel), and set is often applied when the referent is an organism tuned either to a specific stimulus (an automobile driver anticipating a green light) or a particular response (a copy editor on the lookout for errors).

Initially set attracted attention in psychology not in its own right, but as a concept that was invoked to resolve discrepancies between laboratory results and theory (Allport, 1955). STRUCTURAL PSYCHOLOGY, one of the inaugural viewpoints in the discipline, assumed that the mind is made up of mental elements. These were investigated by the method of INTROSPECTION, a technique in which participants observe in meticulous detail the nuances and subtleties of their own consciousness. Some early introspective data suggested that THINKING might proceed in the absence of discernible mental elements. To illustrate—introspectionists instructed to respond to a stimulus word with a word of opposite meaning readily complied even when they were not aware of an element that represented the relationship that was expressed. This suggested activity without a structure, and thus provoked controversy. The difficulty was handled by postulating a mechanism that guides or regulates thinking. This has been defined in different ways and given different names, including the obsolete labels of *Aufgabe* or instruction, *Einstellung* or predisposition, conscious attitude, and determining tendency as well as set, the label that endures to the present (Gibson, 1941; Ruckmick, 1928). The problems with "imageless thought" were, however, not resolved, and the issue was shelved when BEHAVIORISM began to argue that all mental concepts be eradicated.

The concept of set survived this renunciation, in part at least because of the conspicuousness of muscular activity. It is not easy, for example, to dismiss as unreal the set that is disclosed in the posture of a runner awaiting a starting signal. Whatever the reasons, the concept gained in importance, and in 1940 Dashiell went so far as to suggest that the three variables on which behavior was then believed to depend—the stimulus complex, habits, and heredity—be amended by adding set as a fourth and equally important determiner.

In 1941 Gibson compiled a 125-item bibliography on the topic, and he described the concept of set as "a nearly universal one in psychological thinking despite the fact that the underlying meaning is indefinite, the terminology chaotic, and the usage by psychologists highly individualistic" (p. 781). Gibson reviewed the relationship between set and various concepts such as REACTION TIME, association, PERCEPTION, THINKING, and LEARNING—including conditioning—and enumerated twenty-nine variants or forms, such as voluntary set, mental set, anticipation, and unconscious set.

As the research accumulated, an earlier trend of dividing these variables into two parts was strengthened. One stresses the perception of the stimulus and the other stresses the execution of the response. In stimulus set the focus is on the expectation of a cue, such as a mother's receptivity to signals of her infant's distress. In response set there is a preparedness to respond, such as the ready salutes of military personnel. These two varieties vary in the relative dominance of overt and covert components, and their history is different.

The covert component of stimulus set made it particularly vulnerable to attacks from behaviorism, and the topic was placed on the back burner until the middle of the current century when it began to reappear on an ad hoc basis in research on the effects of set on PERCEPTION and VIGILANCE (Haber, 1966). Investigations of the influence of the intrusion of set into various responses was accelerated when cognitive psychology began to investigate what an organism does, how it handles information. Sekuler and Ball illustrate this kind of probing. First, they report experimental evidence obtained by others that "a sound will be easier to hear if beforehand the listener can be certain what sound to expect and when to expect it" (1977, p. 60). On the basis of their own research they conclude that information in advance about the direction and speed of motion also enhances success in detecting it. They are adamant that this improvement is not due to such auxiliary reactions as increasing muscle tone and decreasing reaction time, and they demonstrate that "mental set—foreknowledge about the character of the upcoming stimulus—affects visibility directly" (p. 61). These researchers also speculate about the reduced visual efficiency of drivers, pedestrians, and pilots in real-life situations in which advance information is lacking.

Response set is measured by changes in overt responses, and thus the topic was not only relatively immune to the faulting by behaviorism, but the general favoring of behavior enhanced its importance. In the 1970s the *Psychological Abstracts* replaced the generic "set" as an Index entry with "response set." This was also the practice in the first edition of the *Thesaurus of Psychological*

Index Terms (Kinkade, 1974), and it persists to the present (*American Psychological Association*, 1985).

As research goes on, more and more special response sets are identified, and illustrations of them follow. Positive and negative response sets refer to a person's tendency to react automatically in an agreeable or a disagreeable manner. A positive response set indicates a predilection to concur, to accept directives, and a negative response set indicates a proneness to disagree. There are many assumptions, and some experimental evidence, that positive and negative response sets may have a capability to contaminate the measurements of various responses. One of the more suspect of these is examination scores. There is speculation, for example, that a child who has a negative response set might well receive a misleadingly low score on a test in which the questions are framed in positive terms. In a measure of "attitude toward school" an aversive frame of reference could lead a child to disagree with such statements as "I like school," "I think my teacher is nice," and even to deny the sentence "I like recess." Psychologists who are involved in the examination of underprivileged people have, for an extended period of time, been alerted to this source of attenuation (Deutsch, Fishman, Kogan, North, & Whiteman, 1964).

Another variety of set is called learning set. This was described in 1949 by Harry Harlow (1905–1981) in connection with the discovery that the learning rate of monkeys increases as they gain experience on a series of problems in which they must learn which of two objects is the one that brings a reward. He supplemented the animal data with analogous observations of young children, and obtained comparable results. Harlow interpreted these increases as evidence that organisms acquire a set to discriminate; that is, they "learn how to learn." Harlow proposes that "the behavior of the human being is not to be understood in terms of the results of single learning situations but rather in terms of the changes which are affected through multiple, though comparable, learning problems" (1949, p. 51).

Controversy arose as to whether improvement in one kind of problem promotes the learning of those that vary from the original ones. At about the same time, LEARNING THEORY data were also producing evidence that the personal history of memorizing influences the amount that one remembers (Hilgard, 1987). The details of the arguments about these prolonged effects exceed the scope of this discussion, but they point to the probability that set may not be merely an episodic phenomenon.

References

Allport, F. H. (1955). *Theories of perception and the concept of structure: A review and critical analysis with an introduction to a dynamic-structural theory of behavior.* New York: John Wiley. Although this book focuses on perception, there is an impressive review of the concept of set during various eras in experimental psychology.

American Psychological Association. (1985). *Thesaurus of psychological index terms* (4th ed.). Washington, DC: Author.

Dashiell, J. F. (1937). *Fundamentals of general psychology*. Boston: Houghton Mifflin.

Dashiell, J. F. (1940). A neglected fourth dimension to psychological research. *Psychological Review, 47*, 289–305. This is the address of the retiring vice-president of the Psychology Section of the American Association for the Advancement of Science, 1939.

Deutsch, M., Fishman, J. A., Kogan, L., North, R., & Whiteman, M. (1964). Guidelines for testing minority group children. *Journal of Social Issues, 20*, 129–145.

Gibson, J. J. (1941). A critical review of the concept of set in contemporary experimental psychology. *Psychological Bulletin, 38*, 781–817. This article delineates various formulations, including the role of set in conditioning. Gibson was unable to find a common meaning for the concept, and he spells out several ambiguities and contradictions. Gibson uses attitude as a synonym for set, but this is unusual in that attitude connotes evaluation more than a readiness to respond.

Haber, R. N. (1966). Nature of the effect of set on perception. *Psychological Review, 73*, 335–351. Haber commends Gibson's earlier review and updates the study of the relationship between set and perception. He outlines arguments that set affects perception directly and that it enhances recall of perception.

Harlow, H. F. (1949). The formation of learning sets. *Psychological Review, 56*, 51–65. This was Harlow's presidential address of the Midwestern Psychological Association in 1948.

Hilgard, E. R. (1987). *Psychology in America: A historical survey*. San Diego: Harcourt Brace Jovanovich. Hilgard presents a concise history of the concept of learning set.

Kinkade, R. G. (Ed.). (1974). *Thesaurus of psychological index terms*. Washington, DC: American Psychological Association.

Munn, N. L. (1951). *Psychology: The fundamentals of human adjustment* (2nd ed.). Cambridge, MA: Houghton Mifflin.

Ruckmick, C. A. (1928). *A German-English dictionary of psychological terms*. (2nd ed.). Author. Iowa City, IA: Athens Press. Germany was the scene of one of the first laboratories for experimental psychology and most of the early American psychologists were fluent in German.

Sekuler, R., & Ball, K. (1977). Mental set alters visibility of moving targets. *Science, 198* (No. 4312), 60–62.

Sources of Additional Information

Berlyne, D. E. (1974). Attention. In E. C. Carterette & M. P. Friedman (Eds.), *Handbook of Perception* (Vol. 1), *Historical and philosophical roots of perception* (pp. 126–142). New York: Academic Press. This chapter contains a brief account of set, but one that sharpens the historical perspective. Foster, H. (1962). The operation of set in a visual search task. *Journal of Experimental Psychology, 63*, 74–83. This research, under the auspices of the United States Army Signal Corps, illustrates the search by the military for the facilitating effects of "mental sets" (stimulus set) on critical elements in a visual field. It also documents a reliance of set research on reaction time. Harlow, H. F., & Warren, J. M. (1952). Formation and transfer of discrimination learning sets. *Journal of Comparative and Physiological Psychology, 45*, 482–489. Another demonstration from Harlow's laboratory that practice progressively improves the learning of monkeys in a series of similar problems. The phenomena has been demonstrated in other species, including humans, but the role of learning sets remains controversial. Hoisington, L. B.

(1935). *Psychology: An elementary text*. New York: Macmillan. This textbook illustrates an early struggle with the meaning of determining tendency and set. Janis, I. L. (1962). Psychological effects of warnings. In G. W. Baker & D. W. Chapman (Eds.), *Man and society in disaster* (pp. 55–92). New York: Basic Books. This is one chapter in a volume dealing with research on disaster. The probability of a "vigilance set" is increased by many variables including information about impending disaster that indicates that an available escape route may become inaccessible, learning that self-initiated reaction will be required but at the same time restricted and that opportunities for contact with authorities will be reduced.

SKINNERIAN BEHAVIORISM. See BEHAVIORISM.

SOCIAL MOTIVATION. See NEED and SOCIAL MOTIVATION.

STIMULUS. 1. Instigators of action; some are internal, such as physiological processes and bodily movements, and others are external, such as objects, events, or places. **RESPONSE.** 1. Functional units including both muscular activities (eyelid reflex, talking, etc.) and an array of implicit psychological actions (perceiving, thinking, dreaming, etc.). **BEHAVIOR.** 1. An aggregate of responses.

Each of these concepts is commonly stated in the singular even though each stands for a multiple. Organisms are complex, and there is seldom, if ever, only one stimulus, a single response, or an isolated bit of behavior. Although the words stimulus, response, and behavior are indispensable in psychology, their meanings have not been carefully delimited, and in the main they are understood on a commonsense or self-evident basis. This casualness has fostered certain preferences. One is the restricting of both stimulus and response to immediate events, a practice that distinguishes them from MOTIVATION. Another is the categorizing of withholding as a response. Intentionally refraining from speaking, for example, is indeed a response. Another custom involves the term performance, and in many contexts this word is the equivalent of behavior. It is, however, preferred in situations in which a particular task is specified, for example, arithmetic or music performance. In relation to psychological tests the term designates manual rather than verbal tasks. Reaction and response are frequently used synonymously, but reaction was in vogue for some time before response, and it then generally designated simple, externally stimulated acts, such as a reaction to sound.

Each of the concepts—stimulus, response, and behavior—has diverse attributes. Stimulation, for example, embraces a broad spectrum of timing, familiarity, and quality. The temporal patterns range from the constancy of the days of the week to the rarity of a catastrophe. The familiarity extends from the ever-present experiences of body position through extremely rare direct contacts with the surface of the moon. Stimuli are both impersonal and personal, with the latter emerging both from other people and from one's own repertoire—another person provokes greetings and a frightening dream elicits crying. The impersonal agents are myriad: organic variables such as satiation, fatigue, and hormonal secretions; muscular activities such as walking and breathing; such energy changes as sound waves and odorous gases; both common and unique objects; and geographical features. As might be expected, the ubiquity of stimuli has fostered both ambiguous definitions and inconsistent terminology. Gibson, for example, enumerates eight areas of disagreement and comments: "The ways of conceiving the stimulus are often in flat contradiction. Occasionally one book can be quoted against itself" (1960, p. 695).

The concept of response has also been modified by a series of amendments that are best presented in a chronological sequence. During an early era a response was considered as movement, was equated with life, and was believed to be a manifestation of the supernatural—the soul, spirits (Skinner, 1931). Interpretations of this genre were threatened by laboratory disclosures of phenomena that are incompatible with supernatural explanations, such as discovering that an extirpated muscle contracts when an attached nerve is stimulated. The search for the naturalistic determiners of this response called attention both to conductivity, that is, to the nervous system and to the existence of a material stimulus. This was followed by the identification for a period of time of a response with neural activity, and at one point this was elaborated into opinion that different nerves produce different sensations, and neural activity is what is experienced. Physiologists soon, however, rejected specific nerve energies, and the modern view is one of similarity among all nerves (Fearing, 1930/1970; Langfeld, 1933).

The person who most successfully advocated the centrality of responses in psychological events is John B. Watson, the pioneer champion of BEHAVIORISM. Watson saw motor behavior as a means of meeting the scientific mandate to deal with palpables and thereby differentiating psychology from the mentalism that his predecessors had studied. Space-filling, observable actions are obviously real, and ones that involve contractions so minute that they have to be amplified to be discerned are also substantive. To Watson, responses are both objective and orderly, and in his opinion a mastery of psychology would yield details of the relationships between stimuli and responses: "In a system of psychology completely worked out, given the response the stimuli can be predicted; given the stimuli the response can be predicted" (1913, p. 167).

Watson appears to have based this statement more on logical than on psychological principles inasmuch as the proposal of a regular relationship between a stimulus and a response ignores the variations among the responses of different individuals to the same stimulus. The paradigm S(timulus) → R(esponse) implies regularity, but unfortunately it overlooks this heterogeneity. A cup, for example, will elicit drinking, serving, washing, stacking, purchasing, throwing, and/or breaking. Running, for instance, may be precipitated by fear, eagerness, tardiness, or a desire for exercise. There are also discrepancies between the timing and the strength of a stimulus and a response. The latter may be as immediate as exclaiming at the onset of pain, or it may emerge after prolonged reflection about the most effective action to take in a perplexing situation. A controlled, matter-of-fact announcement of a fire by one person can be the stimulus that sets off panic behavior in many.

All these inequalities are well recognized, and various recommendations for acknowledging them have been made. Woodworth (1929) included the organism in the paradigm S → O(rganism) → R as a way of indicating that a stimulus acts on an organism and that the organism molds the response. Several variations of this formula have been devised, and practically all of them incorporate the influence of the organism.

It is an easy step from the concept of response to that of behavior. Although the latter has been defined at different times in somewhat different ways, the underlying theme is what organisms do, conjoint responses. In Watson's words: "Several complex responses taking place simultaneously . . . the whole group of responses is integrated in such a way (instinct or habit) that the individual does something which we have a name for, that is, "takes food," "builds a house," "swims," "writes a letter," "talks" (1919, pp. 11–12). It is noteworthy that Watson used the word responses but illustrated "responding," for example, "talks" and "swims."

Other psychologists were impressed by the role of behavior and, once again, irresolute about number, they began to replace behavior with the word behaviors. The date when this practice started is elusive, but as early as 1926 Tolman commented: "A rat running a maze . . . a child hiding from a stranger; a woman doing her washing or gossiping over the phone . . . myself and my friend telling one another our thoughts and feelings. These are *behaviors*" (1926/1958, p. 49). The discrepancy between the language and the concept is repeated—the word is "behavior" but the event is "behaving."

These conceptual developments were concomitant with advances in experimentation. One of the most consequential starting points in the research came from the demonstrations of reflexes in the laboratories of physiology. These intrigued psychologists, and they began to relate and integrate them into both theories and concepts in psychology (Dewey, 1896). These elaborations came to include the conditioning of reflexes, and Watson saw CLASSICAL CONDITIONING as the means by which psychological behavior evolves. This involves presenting an organism with paired stimuli, such as exposing a dog both to the sound of a tone and the sight of food. These dyads are repeated until the tone, when presented alone, evokes the drooling that originally was elicited only by the food. The discovery of conditioning set off a profusion of experimentation, and by 1937 Razran was able to compile a bibliography of 1,111 titles. This burgeoning included the landmark change in vocabulary from conditioned reflexes to conditioned responses (Smith & Guthrie, 1921).

One incidental application of conditioning is very relevant to a discussion of stimulus and response. This is its use in the determination of the limits of energy that different species are able to detect, a strategy in which a response is used to identify a stimulus. Experiments are conducted on different animals to discover, for example, the lowest frequency of tone or the dimmest light to which a response in any particular species can be conditioned. The minimal level of energy at which a conditioned response can be established indicates that lesser amounts of energy are not sensed by the animal being observed, that is, this reduced level of energy is not an effective stimulus.

Watson's promotion of behavior and the broadening of its scope that came with conditioning had a strong impact on the field of psychology. Behaviorism in various forms dominated American psychology until after World War II. At that time COGNITIVE PSYCHOLOGY and the HUMAN POTENTIAL MOVEMENT rebelled against the behaviorists' restrictions and set out to redefine psychology so as to include mentation. The criticism was directed toward the neglect of subject matter, and it did not impugn responses or behavior. In fact, this facet of psychological events is embedded, a fundamental on the current scene and rarely, if ever, questioned.

One of the significant deviations of modern psychology from Watsonian behaviorism is a playing down of the efficacy of the stimulus. For Watson, it was the determiner of behavior, but the most recent variety, SKINNERIAN BEHAVIORISM, places control in reinforcement, in the outcome of behavior. In some versions of cognitive psychology that are modeled on an information-processing metaphor, control is invested in processing per se.

The role of behavior, in whatever way it may be governed, is paradoxical in that it is conceptualized as a basic unit but is only seldom studied in its own right, and is much more frequently used as a means of measuring the effects of different variables. Qualitative analyses of behavior per se are rare, and many specifications do not extend beyond dichotomies, such as voluntary versus involuntary, learned versus unlearned, and molar versus molecular behavior. There is also the custom of making single measurements of behavior when, in fact, it is a composite of qualitatively different units, as, for example, measuring changes in the speed of responses but ignoring changes in their amplitude. This slighting persists even though it is episodically faulted. Logan (1956), for example, commented on it thirty years ago, and in the recent past Bolles (1983) calls attention to the still prevailing neglect. He provides various illustrations of what is left out when nuances are ignored. One of his examples lightens the discussion by describing the different means that rats use to pull and to depress the same lever. One moved it one way with its teeth and the other with its paws. Another pulled the lever with the front paws, but depressed it by using a hind leg stretched over its ear. Accomplishing ends by difficult means is not restricted to rodents, but formal studies both of ingenuity and its lack are generally slighted in all species.

Merely the frequency, a tangential aspect of behavior, may be its most commonly documented property. This popularity is promulgated by the operant behaviorist Skinner, who decided to study frequency rather than substance: "The rat would often wait an inordinately long time . . . before starting . . . on the next run. There seemed to be no explanation for this. When I timed these delays with a stop watch . . . and plotted them, they seemed to show orderly changes. . . . This was, of course, the kind of thing I was looking for. I forgot all about the movements of the substratum and began to run rats *for the sake of the delay measurements alone* [italics added]'' (1956, p. 224).

In summary, stimulus, response, and behavior have been interpreted in various ways. Stimuli have been conceptualized in an extraordinary number of ways. Responses have been construed as manifestations of the supernatural, of neurological activity, as simple muscular phenomena, and as discrete and sequential acts or behavior. All but the first of these features are found in contemporary psychology.

References

Bolles, R. C. (1983). The explanation of behavior. *The Psychological Record, 33*, 31–48. An incisive account of the current state of neglect of behavior. Bolles deals at some length with researchers' reliance on only certain aspects of it, such as its frequency. He points out that laboratory apparatus has been adapted to the animals' capabilities as much or more than the animal adapts to the equipment.

Dewey, J. (1896). The reflex arc concept in psychology. *Psychological Review, 3*, 357–370. This article is cited extensively, frequently quoted, but read in its entirety probably by only a few scholars. Dewey depicts psychological behavior as an intricate complex, not a sequence of discrete units such as stimulus and response. The latter are logical, not behavioral, constructs.

Fearing, F. (1970). *Reflex action: A study in the history of physiological psychology*. Cambridge, MA: MIT Press. One of the more detailed chronologies of this topic. (Original work published 1930)

Gibson, J. J. (1960). The concept of the stimulus in psychology. *American Psychologist, 15*, 694–703. A critique of the inadequacies of the concept of stimulus: "We constantly use the word but seldom define it. We take it for granted" (p. 694).

Langfeld, H. S. (1933). The historical development of response psychology. *Science, 77*, (No. 1993), 243–250. Langfeld reviews briefly, but comprehensively pre-scientific and scientific notions of the relationship between motor responses and consciousness.

Logan, F. A. (1956). A micromolar approach to behavior theory. *Psychological Review, 63*, 63–73.

Razran, G. H. S. (1937). Conditioned responses: A classified bibliography. *Psychological Bulletin, 34*; 191–256.

Skinner, B. F. (1931). The concept of the reflex in the description of behavior. *Journal of General Psychology, 5*, 427–458.

Skinner, B. F. (1956). A case history in scientific method. *American Psychologist, 11*, 221–233. An interesting and personal account of some of the pitfalls and fortuitous events that a researcher encounters.

Smith, S. & Guthrie, E. R. (1921). *General psychology in terms of behavior*. New York: Appleton. An innovative approach at the time of publication.

Tolman, E. C. (1958). *Behavior and psychological man: Essays in motivation and learning*. Berkeley: University of California Press. (Original work published 1926). This offers the reader an opportunity to grasp the depth of concern about mentalism: "I am under compulsion to discuss ideas only from the one point of view of attempting to reduce them to a workable causal scheme" (p. 48).

Watson, J. B. (1913). Psychology as the behaviorist views it. *Psychological Review, 20*, 158–177. Watson is straightforward and does not hesitate to disclose his sense of his own correctness and the incorrectness of others.

Watson, J B. (1919). *Psychology from the standpoint of a behaviorist*. Philadelphia: J. B. Lippincott.

Woodworth, R. S. (1929). *Psychology* (rev. ed.). New York: Henry Holt. Woodworth writes with a remarkable clarity, as evidenced by this excerpt from his discussion about the importance of the organism when relating a stimulus to a response: "If you hear some creature stirring in a hedge, and 'coo' to it, it will probably fly away if it is a bird, and rush toward you if it is a dog. If it is a human being, it would be hard to predict the response, without knowing the age, sex, and training of the individual, and the mood he or she happened to be in at the moment" (p. 226).

Sources of Additional Information

Diamond, S. (1971). Gestation of the instinct concept. *Journal of the History of the Behavioral Sciences, 7*, 323–336. Diamond reports that the word stimulus is a descendant of stig-mulus, "originally a prod for mules and slaves and now applied with the same bland indifference to rats and students" (p. 324). Epstein, S. (1980). The stability of behavior: 2. Implications for psychological research. *American Psychologist, 35*, 790–806. Epstein is interested in raising the level of generalization of research results. He believes that the present level is unduly low, partly because humans respond to so many incidental sources of stimulation. "One solution lies in aggregating behavior . . . thereby canceling out incidental, uncontrollable factors" (p. 790). This proposal is in line with the common attitude of slighting the details of behavior. Hunter, W. S. (1932). The psychological study of behavior. *Psychological Review, 39*, 1–24. This is Hunter's presidential address to the American Psychological Association. In it he comments that physiology deals with functions which are intrinsic to various structures of the organism. In contrast, "*psychology seeks to describe and explain, to predict and control, the extrinsic behavior of the organism to an external environment which is predominantly social*" (p. 24). Notterman, J. M., & Mintz, D. E. (1965). *Dynamics of response*. New York: John Wiley. The authors reflect both the modern behaviorists' identification of psychology with learning as well as Skinner's reliance on reinforcement rather than stimulation: "The psychological concept deals with stimulus-response correlations that have to be established by training procedures: those in which the stimulus initially is neither necessary nor sufficient as the antecedent of a specific response" (p. 2). Thurstone, L. L. (1923). The stimulus-response fallacy in psychology. *Psychological Review, 30*, 354–369. An early, classic argument that organisms rather than stimuli mold responses.

STIMULUS FUNCTION. 1. The use that is made of a stimulus. **RESPONSE FUNCTION.** 1. The purpose that a response serves. **INTERBEHAVIORAL PSYCHOLOGY.** 1. A viewpoint that identifies the subject matter of psychology as the interdependent interplay among organisms, objects, and their surroundings.

These concepts were formulated by J. R. Kantor (1888–1984), a psychologist whose scholarship extends from 1917 through 1984. Kantor stands apart from colleagues in various ways but most conspicuously in his unrelenting determination to eliminate mentalism from psychology. Most psychologists share this goal, and in honor of it they are solicitous about using only precise methods. Kantor insists that, in a scientific enterprise, the subject matter as well as the procedures must be objective. He succeeds in bringing to light what he refers to informally as "spooks," that is, impalpable concepts that are still embedded in psychology. These are residuals of the theological and philosophical concepts from which prescientific psychology drew explanations, and some of these have not been purged, but remain, although disguised in modern terms. Examples of these include the idea of the UNCONSCIOUS as an internal force that directs behavior, and the idea of MEMORY as a warehouse that contains prior experiences. Interbehavioral psychology was conceptualized to remedy such defects. The system was first described in detail by Kantor in 1924 and in 1926 in a two-volume treatise that covers the entire subject matter. He supplemented this with presentation with elaborations of special topics, for example, grammar and linguistics (1936, 1977), physiological psychology (1947), history of psychology (1963, 1969), social and cultural psychology (1929, 1982).

Stimulus and response functions, integral components of interbehaviorism, are characteristic of the theory as a whole in that they highlight psychological rather than physical properties. Stimulus function refers to the use that is made of a STIMULUS. The structure of a stimulus may contribute to its use, but it does not determine it. A ruler, for example, may be shaken as a toy, may serve as a guide in drawing a straight line or in measuring the length of one, or may be placed as a prop to support an open window.

Response function refers to the purpose of a RESPONSE, and there is no identity between action and function inasmuch as a similar performance may serve different purposes and different performances may serve similar purposes. A watch is looked at, for example, to assure the owner that it is working, to learn the interval before an appointment, or to confirm an impression that the time for taking medication is at hand. An art instructor may demonstrate principles of perspective by drawing sketches on the blackboard, by projecting appropriate slides, or by having students look at a scene from different angles.

Most psychologists agree with Kantor that any particular stimulus may be aligned with different responses and that similar responses are occasioned by different stimuli, but theorists tend to describe rather than to account for this state of affairs. For example, Koffka, an advocate of GESTALT PSYCHOLOGY, affirms that "the things in our environment tell us what to do with them; they may do so more or less urgently and with any degree of specificity. But their doing so indicates a field of force between these objects and our Egos" (1935, p. 353).

At a more recent date Gibson suggested that the environment "affords" the organism various items and coined the term "affordance" to express this: "An elongated object of moderate size and weight affords *wielding*. If used to hit or strike it is a *club* or *hammer*. . . . A rigid staff also affords leverage and in that use is a *lever*. A pointed elongated object affords piercing; if large it is a *spear*, if small a *needle* or *awl* (1977, pp. 74–75).

Interbehavioral psychology depicts the relationship between stimulus and response functions as derivatives of personal experiences. A toddler, for example, initially attracted to a toy car by its bright color, picks it up, handles it, and discovers that pushing the car causes it to move smoothly. He or she may also observe that the tires are black, that the wheels move in a circular pattern, one that is different from the path that the car follows. Most toddlers manipulate a particular toy for only a brief period before abandoning it in favor of some other object. These apparently trivial contacts are actually consequential because as a result of them the child no longer sees merely a colored object, but discerns a number of uses or stimulus functions.

The stimulus and response functions that are brought into play at any one time are significantly influenced by the context in which the organism is functioning. To illustrate—a preschooler pushes a toy car along a floor, but when he or she finds some water the car may become a boat. The formality of the name that a college student uses when referring to an instructor varies with the presence or absence of the instructor.

The fact that stimulus and response functions are by-products of personal histories makes them peculiar to each person. Thus a schoolteacher's remarks about a circus stimulate one child who recently enjoyed attending a circus very differently than they stimulate a second child who was not so privileged. The first supplements the teacher's words by recalling the event and volunteering enthusiastic descriptions of it, but the second supplements the teacher's remarks with a private, unspoken nourishing of resentment.

The existence of various stimulus and response functions distinguishes psychological responses from the ever-present physiological ones. To illustrate—a person who is thinking, daydreaming, or reminiscing is also breathing, maintaining a certain posture, and focusing the eyes. These physiological reactions are readily predictable and sequential; that is, food as a physiological stimulus provokes ingesting, digesting, absorbing, and excreting. In contrast, food as a psychological stimulus elicits a variety of unrelated activities, such as selecting, purchasing, storing, washing, cooking, eating, serving, giving, receiving, and rejecting.

There is overlap among the sciences, but there is also specialization, and the existence of stimulus and response functions helps to identify the domain of psychology. Physiology is responsible for developing information about biological reactions, whereas psychology assumes the task of accounting for versatility. It is the discipline that takes on the problem, for example, of explaining why the same sound is recognized as "to," "too," or "two." The jurisdiction of psychology is the understanding of how variable behavior evolves, both simple and complex. It is responsible for explaining, for example, why cats reared by rat-killing mothers also kill, but those reared by non-killers do not; why children speak the language and the dialect of their parents; and how an attorney learns to distinguish between direct and both hearsay and circumstantial evidence and to restrict arguments to the first of these categories.

Interbehaviorism is a field theory, and it locates the subject matter of psychology in infrangible interactions between the response functions of the organism and the stimulus functions of the context. This places psychological events in the field rather than in the organism, and this feature of the theory led Kantor at one time to refer to it as interactional psychology or interactionism. But this name was changed when psychologists began to use the term interaction to designate mutual or reciprocal variables, such as explaining generosity as due both to a personality trait of the donor and the recipient's need of a gift. In interbehavioral psychology the interaction is between the organism and the context, not between stimuli.

This perspective is unique in psychology, and it requires some explanations. In providing this the current discussion takes advantage of the reader's familiarity with field theories in natural science, and compares some of the ways in which physical scientists approach a topic—using the flying of aircraft as an example—with an interbehavioral approach—using the seeing of humans as an example.

Physical scientists recognize that flying is a function of all the factors operative at the time the flying occurs. These include, but are not restricted to, the condition of the motor, the quality of the fuel, the weight, shape, and surface of the aircraft, atmospheric conditions, as well as the performance of the crew. Interbehavioral psychologists recognize that psychological activities are a function of all variables operative at the time the seeing occurs. These fall into three categories: the biological condition of the organism, the experiential history of the individual, and the conditions under which the interbehavior takes place. Thus seeing stimuli as an unfamiliar pattern of thin lines, or as a hieroglyphic, or as a familiar word in a sutra depends on the adequacy of the visual apparatus, the culture and education of the viewer, and the clarity of the drawing, with the latter varying according to the distance between the viewer and the viewed as well as with the illumination.

Physical scientists also recognize that flying is a composite of specific events, not an abstract entity such as flight, and that the variables are so interdependent that a change in any of them changes the event. Flying is modified, for example, by pilot fatigue, by mechanical malfunctioning, by air turbulence, and by the density of air traffic. By the same token, seeing is a composite of events, not an entity such as sight, and a change in any variable alters the seeing. It is modified, for example, by variations in the lighting, by what is being looked at, and by the preferences of the viewer.

Physical scientists recognize that no one variable—no matter how crucial it may appear to be—accounts for flying. Consequences, even catastrophes, do not alter this role. Thus, when a fuel line breaks and flying stops, no one identifies the fuel, the fuel line, or their combination as either the locus or the cause of flying. Interbehavioral psychologists also recognize the integrity of the plurality even when seeing is no longer possible, as in the case either of the removal of light or of damage to the eye. It is relatively easy in modern society to correct a power failure, but difficult, if not impossible, to replace anatomy. This is a differential in technology, and it does not indicate that the eye is either the locus or the cause of the seeing. The whole cannot be reduced to one of its parts.

Interbehavioral psychology is an acknowledged but not a conspicuous viewpoint in psychology (Smith & Ray, 1981). This results from several factors, and one of these is the failure of the theory to endorse either specialized research topics or methods. Experimenters are attracted to clearly bounded problems and feasible procedures, but interbehavioral psychology is so broad, so encompassing that it does not bring singulars to the forefront. A second factor that contributes to the status of the theory comes from its nontraditional approach to the discipline. Many who know about the viewpoint do not understand it, but in contrast, those who are the most familiar with it, Kantor's students, are loyal and grateful. In fact, their appreciation is sensed by some as more intense than that of many mentors (Verplanck, 1983; Woodworth, 1948). This stronghold is strengthened by a second factor, one that hinges on Kantor's role as a psychologists' psychologist. The Establishment, if not the profession as a whole, is cognizant of his contributions (Schoenfeld, 1969). Even Skinner, the outstanding proponent of OPERANT BEHAVIORISM and one of the most militant advocates of a scientfic psychology, confesses that Kantor "convinced me that I had not wholly exorcised all the 'spooks' in my thinking" (1967, p. 411).

References

Gibson, J. J. (1977). The theory of affordances. In R. Shaw & J. Bransford (Eds.), *Perceiving, acting, and knowing: Toward an ecological psychology* (pp. 67–82). Hillsdale, NJ: Lawrence Erlbaum.

Kantor, J. R. (1917). *Functional nature of the philosophical categories*. Unpublished doctoral dissertation, University of Chicago, Chicago.

Kantor, J. R. (1924–1926). *Principles of psychology* (Vols. 1 & 2). New York: Alfred Knopf. A treatment of the discipline of psychology from an interbehavioral point of view. This coverage was abridged and published in 1933 as an undergraduate text, *A Survey of the Science of Psychology*. This was revised by J R. Kantor & N. W. Smith in 1975 and published as *The science of psychology: An interbehavioral survey*.

Kantor, J. R. (1929). *An outline of social psychology*. Chicago: Follett. Social psychology is defined as the study of response functions that are shared or common within a culture, for example, dietary customs, professional manners, religious practices.

Kantor, J. R. (1936). *An objective psychology of grammar*. Bloomington: Indiana University Publications.

Kantor, J. R. (1947). *Problems of physiological psychology*. Bloomington, IN: Principia Press. This is an extensive description of the mentalism that characterizes much of the study of physiological psychology.

Kantor, J. R. (1963–1969). *The scientific evolution of psychology* (Vols. 1 & 2). Chicago: Principia Press.

Kantor, J. R. (1977). *Psychological linguistics*. Chicago: Principia Press.

Kantor, J. R. (1982). *Cultural psychology*. Chicago: Principia Press.

Kantor, J. R. (1984). The relation of scientists to events in physics and in psychology. *The Psychological Record, 34*, 165–174.

Koffka, K. (1935). *Principles of Gestalt psychology.* New York: Harcourt, Brace. A presentation of Gestalt psychology by one of the founders.

Schoenfeld, W. N. (1969). J. R. Kantor's *Objective psychology of grammar* and *Psychology and logic: A retrospective appreciation. Journal of the Experimental Analysis of Behavior, 12*, 329–347. Schoenfeld suggests that "perhaps the darkness surrounding Kantor is beginning to lift, and we may soon be discovering that he has been a 'great' scientist all along. The historical development of psychology has already paid him the compliment that some of his views are accepted today more widely than when he set them down, though it may not be known that he is their source" (p. 330).

Skinner, B. F. (1967). B. F. Skinner. In E. G. Boring & G. Lindzey (Eds.), *A history of psychology in autobiography* (Vol. 5, pp. 387–413). New York: Appleton-Century-Crofts.

Smith, N. W., & Ray, C. E. (1981). A citation study of the interbehavioral field psychology of J. R. Kantor. *Revista Mexicana de Análisis de la Conducta, 7*, 117–134. The authors tabulated the citations to Kantor during a sixty-year period, and reported many references between 1917 and the early 1920s. During the next thirty years there was a steady, but low level of acknowledgment, but about 1950 an increase started and this was continuing at the date the analysis ended.

Verplanck, W. S. (1983). Preface. In N. W. Smith, P. T. Mountjoy, & D. H. Ruben (Eds.), *Reassessment in psychology: The interbehavioral alternative* (pp. xi–xxv). Washington, DC: University Press of America. A multi-authored volume in honor of J. R. Kantor.

Woodworth, R. S. (1948). *Contemporary schools of psychology* (rev. ed.). New York: Ronald Press.

Sources of Additional Information

Carter, J. W., Jr. (1938). An experimental study of psychological stimulus-response. *The Psychological Record, 2*, 36–91. The author relates experimental results to various theories, and finds interbehaviorism to be the most satisfactory. A lengthy article, but it discloses a great deal about psychology during the 1930s. Mountjoy, P. T. (1976). Science in psychology: J. R. Kantor's field theory. *Mexican Journal of Behavior Analysis, 2*, 3–21. An overall account of interbehaviorism. The author relates Kantor's and Skinner's approach to the field. Pronko, N. H. (1980). *Psychology from the standpoint of an interbehaviorist.* Monterey, CA: Brooks/Cole. Pronko refers to traditional psychology as self-actional, that is, explanations are sought *within* the organism. He contrasts this approach with that of interbehaviorism on a variety of topics. This is an undergraduate text. Pronko published earlier versions in 1951, 1969, 1973. These texts are both accurate and interesting. Smith, N. W. (1973). Interbehavioral psychology: Roots and branches. *The Psychological Record, 23*, 153–167. The author describes interbehaviorism and relates it to other theories in psychology. Wolf, I. S. (1958). Stimulus variables in aphasia: 1. Setting conditions. *Journal of the Scientific Laboratories, 44*, 203–217. 2. Stimulus objects. *Journal of the Scientific Laboratories, 44*, 218–228. These experiments contrast with the traditional restriction of the study of aphasia to neurological events in that they include the effects of specific stimuli and the context on speech behavior.

STRESS. 1. A constellation of responses, typically involving decrements in the quality and/or speed of performance as well as subjective feelings of tension, and provoked when a person believes that he or she cannot manage the demands being made.

The idea of an overburdened organism is a time-honored one, but its introduction into science was delayed until the recent past. The scientist responsible for promoting it is Hans Selye, a physician and researcher, who, in 1936, reported a pattern of biochemical changes that accrue to reactions to both the ordinary and the extraordinary vicissitudes of living. Selye discovered that a wide array of heterogenous variables, including pleasant as well as unpleasant ones, induce these physiological effects. In other words, a "nice" surprise and a "bad" surprise may both function as stressors. Utilizing an analogy with mechanics he labeled these consequences the biological stress syndrome, and this configuration soon acquired the label the *General Adaptation Syndrome*. Selye devoted years to ascertaining the details of this configuration, particularly the interaction among neural, hormonal, and metabolic factors. He procured detailed information about the medical consequences of accumulated stress as well as ways of preventing or, at least, of limiting the mal-effects (Selye, 1956, 1973).

Stress engaged the attention of numerous biologists and psychologists, and the latter were keen to transfer the concept from the systemic to the psychological domain. Their enthusiasm far outweighed reflection, and the psychological versions lost the refinement that characterizes the formulation in biology. As a result, stress, when used in a psychological context, is diffuse and elusive: "It is as though, when the word stress came into vogue, each investigator, who had been working with a concept he felt was closely related, substituted the word stress for it and continued in his same line of investigation" (Cofer & Appley, 1964, p. 449).

This unrestrained diffusion embraced relatively inconsequential, mild strain and thereby nourished a belief that stress is widely distributed throughout the population at large. For example, it is said to pervade occupational competition, crucial academic examinations, the carrying out of demanding vocations (surgery, performing arts, air traffic control), as well as working in hazardous occupations or even some hobbies (firefighting, sky diving). The level of stress tends to be elevated when the recipient fails to predict the stressor, feels unable to control its duration, judges himself or herself as incompetent to cope, and assesses the adversity as severe (Dohrenwend & Dohrenwend, 1974; Monat & Lazarus, 1985).

The enthusiasm for the concept has resulted in the interpretation of stress as a stimulus, as a response, and as a condition. It is considered by some to be a synonym for ANXIETY, conflict, emotionality, and FRUSTRATION. The reaction is said to be caused both by traumatic events (tornado, flood) and by chronic problems (famine, prolonged marital conflict). The stressors are conceptualized both as immediately effective and as delayed. Some theorists highlight internal sources (worry, jealousy), whereas others pinpoint externals (riots, drought). Some feature uncontrolled, unusual events (accidents) whereas others target irritants that are sustained long enough to become customary (chronic pain). Some dwell on interpersonal problems (rivalry), some on intrapersonal strain (envy), and still others emphasize the impersonal (extreme environmental temperatures). Some definitions focus on anticipation of stress (financial forecasts) and others on its actuality (poverty) (Cohen, 1980; McGrath, 1970). A pervasive theme throughout all formulations is that of overload, an imbalance between challenge and capability.

Despite a lack of consensus about the meaning of the concept, psychologists diligently investigate it, both by interviewing and by observing people in real-life situations in which they are experiencing adversity as well as in controlled laboratory situations. In the latter context stress is induced in various ways, such as creating time pressure, carrying on close and critical surveillance, assigning tasks that are deemed to be important but also ones on which failure is highly probable (Hackman, 1970; Lazarus, Deese, & Osler, 1952).

Some complications of designing experiments are illustrated in the results of one investigation in which college students drove a car for thirty-two trips through an elliptical course (Finkelman, Zeitlin, Filippi & Friend, 1977). While driving, each subject was required at intervals to recall a digit that had been paired with another and was also subjected to blasts of a loud sound. Hearing the noise and recalling digits increased driving time, but driving accuracy decreased only when the subjects were confronted simultaneously with the request to remember and with noise. The authors suggest that the low-risk environment that characterized this experiment may have lifted much of the ordinary burden of driving and may even have prompted the subjects to interpret recalling the digits as the primary assignment. They speculate that the results might have changed had the rubber pylons used to mark the course been made of concrete and thus, been potentially much more damaging.

A sample of the effects of prolonged stimulation is detailed in a study of the reactions of residents living within five miles of Three Mile Island approximately seventeen months after the nuclear accident at that plant (Baum, Gatchel, & Schaeffer, 1983). The efficiency on two tasks and some self-reported emotional reactions of these subjects were compared with three other groups, comparable in all respects except for not having been in the vicinity of a nuclear accident: one living within five miles of an undamaged nuclear plant, another at the same distance from a coal-fired installation, and a third residing twenty miles from any such facility. The Three Mile Island residents were found to be less efficient than the other groups both in reading proof and in discerning figures embedded in complex geometric designs. They also reported more somatic complaints, anxiety, and symptoms of depression. These signs of stress, however, are only slightly higher than those in the other groups, but the authors point out that the pressure continues and the final level has yet to be ascertained.

Individual differences in susceptibility to stress are among the most commonly reported laboratory findings, and numerous searches have been made for the factors that underwrite resistance. A study by Mullen and Suls (1982) exemplifies one of these investigations, and also points to a complicated interplay among the stressors that may impair health. The researchers asked undergraduates to list the ailments they had experienced during the prior three weeks, to identify on a list of forty-five events (change of residence, death of a relative) those that they had personally recently experienced, and to indicate whether they assessed each of the episodes as desirable or undesirable and whether they were controllable in that the respondent had or had not caused the event. The subjects were also asked to reply to a series of questions regarding the monitoring of their own feelings ("I'm alert to changes in my mood"; "I reflect about myself a lot"). Finally the students returned to the laboratory three weeks later and the data concerning recent sickness and experiences were brought up to date. The results indicate that undergraduates who pay attention to their own feelings may not be affected by the number of unpleasant, uncontrolled episodes, but that undergraduates whose self-appreciation is limited report more illness. The authors suggest that those who are tuned to themselves take ameliorative action, such as seeking social support and carefully evaluating stressors. In contrast, subjects who lack this awareness continue to tolerate the discomfort so that the tautness continues: "Commitment to self may be a stress resistance resource" (Mullen & Suls, 1982, p. 51).

References

Baum, A., Gatchel, R. J., & Schaeffer, M. A. (1983). Emotional, behavioral, and physiological effects of chronic stress at Three Mile Island. *Journal of Consulting and Clinical Psychology, 51*, 565–572. An experiment that deals with a modern, technologically potent stressor. The authors begin the article with the phrase, "Cataclysmic phenomena . . ." (p. 565).

Cofer, C. N., & Appley, M. H. (1964). *Motivation: Theory and research.* New York: John Wiley.

Cohen, S. (1980). Aftereffects of stress on human performance and social behavior: A review of research and theory. *Psychological Bulletin, 88*, 82–108. This is a sophisticated appraisal, emphasizing multiple causation.

Dohrenwend, B. S., & Dohrenwend, B. P. (Eds.). (1974). *Stressful life events: Their nature and effects.* New York: John Wiley. This volume consists of chapters written by various authors, representing various disciplines. Each is based on participation in a 1973 conference of the same name as the title.

Finkelman, J. M., Zeitlin, L. R., Filippi, J. A., & Friend, M. A. (1977). Noise and driver performance. *Journal of Applied Psychology, 62*, 713–718.

Hackman, J. R. (1970). Tasks and task performance in research on stress. In J. E. McGrath (Ed.), *Social and psychological factors in stress* (pp. 202–237). New York: Holt, Rinehart & Winston.

Lazarus, R. S., Deese, J., & Osler, S. F. (1952). The effects of psychological stress upon performance. *Psychological Bulletin, 49*, 293–317. One of the first systematic reviews. It is frequently cited.

McGrath, J. E. (Ed.). (1970). *Social and psychological factors in stress*. New York: Holt, Rinehart & Winston. The chapters in this multi-authored book are mainly based on papers prepared for a conference sponsored by the Air Force Office of Scientific Research, and they are designed to probe psychological stress. The discussion goes beyond military applications.

Monat, A. & Lazarus, R. S. (Eds.). (1985). *Stress and coping: An anthology* (2nd ed.). New York: Columbia University Press.

Mullen, B., & Suls, J. (1982). "Know Thyself": Stressful life changes and the ameliorative effect of private self-consciousness. *Journal of Experimental Social Psychology, 18*, 43–55.

Selye, H. (1956). *The stress of life*. New York: McGraw-Hill. This volume is intended to inform the intelligent lay person about medicine's knowledge of stress.

Selye, H. (1973). The evolution of the stress concept. *American Scientist, 61*, 692–699. This article reviews the concept to the date of publication.

Sources of Additional Information

Basowitz, H., Persky, H., Korchin, S. J., & Grinker, R. R. (1955). *Anxiety and stress. An interdisciplinary study of a life situation*. New York: McGraw-Hill. This book reports the details of a comprehensive assessment of the reactions of paratroopers to their training. Burnham, W. H. (1926). *The normal mind: An introduction to mental hygiene*. New York: D. Appleton. A classic volume and one that, as expected, omits a discussion of stress under that name. The "Practical Rules for Mental Health" imply the topic and advise how to avoid stress. For example, "Do not drive your tacks with a sledgehammer. There is a better, less fatiguing way . . . Do not accept hurry as a necessary part of modern life" (p. 671). Grinker, R. R., & Spiegel, J. P. (1945). *Men under stress*. Philadelphia: Blakiston. The authors describe the psychological weaknessess and strengths of air combat crews during World War II. Postman, L., & Bruner, J. S. (1948). Perception under stress. *Psychological Review, 55*, 314–323. In this research the authors identify stress with frustration, specifically by requiring subjects to describe a picture they could not see clearly and criticizing them for their failures. No reason is given for the use of the word stress rather than frustration in the title. Sarason, I. G., de Monchaux, C., & Hunt, T. (1975). Methodological issues in the assessment of life stress. In L. Levi (Ed.), *Emotions: Their parameters and measurement* (pp. 499–510). New York: Raven Press. A brief, but critical account of the problems of accurately assessing stress in extralaboratory contexts.

STRUCTURAL PSYCHOLOGY. 1. A theory that defines psychology as the study of the structure of the mind. 2. A synonym for the obsolete concept of existential psychology.

Structural psychology, or structuralism, one of the first systematic viewpoints or schools of psychology, is now obsolete. It was promoted in the United States by Edward B. Titchener (1867–1927) as an extension of a viewpoint promulgated by Wilhelm Wundt (1832–1920) at the University of Leipzig, in Germany. This was called "experimental," "physiological," or the "new" psychology, modifiers that were used to designate the separation of the subject matter from philosophy. These terms were not intended to imply that psychology was to be reduced to physiology, but rather to signify a research enterprise. In 1892 Titchener completed a doctorate at Leipzig and came to Cornell University to begin a lengthy tenure. Psychology in the 1890s was a small, unformed enterprise, and it was possible for a single authority to dominate the field. Titchener did so. He was unusually knowledgeable and his erudition attracted students; for thirty-five years he directed a laboratory, masterminded contributions to the psychological literature, and awarded more than fifty doctoral degrees. Structuralism remained the official doctrine at Cornell University until Titchener's death, but after his demise the system moved rapidly in the direction of antiquarianism (Boring, 1927, 1937).

Titchener's formulations are most unusual, and to many on the current scene they appear artificial, sterile, even incredible. This assessment is, however, in error in that it imposes a perspective of the present on the past. Structuralism was one of the inaugural attempts to be scientific and it was in vogue for a considerable period of time. It merits discussion not only because it is a historic event, but also because residuals of the theory persist in modern psychology and because it colored the opposition that replaced it and grew into modern psychology.

Titchener was adamant that psychology must become a natural science, and he was very aware that attaining this status demanded the acquiring of knowledge by means of empirical laboratory work. In his opinion the primary responsibility of psychology was neither to improve nor to assist individuals or society, but to procure verifiable information. For Titchener, this consisted of ascertaining the structure of the normal adult human mind. He believed that it consisted of momentary processes and that these are substantive elements that scientists can observe and analyze. The label "existential psychology" highlights this imputed reality. Titchener also assumed that the mind and the body parallel each other and that the two phenomena do not interact. This explanatory device strengthened the substantive base of the mind and also made it possible to bypass the physical in favor of tracing out mental structures (Heidbreder, 1933).

Titchener was certain that consciousness is a compound and that a detailed, precise analysis of awareness would disclose the basic elements that make up the compound. INTROSPECTION was chosen as the most appropriate method for accomplishing this goal. This is an erudite technique in which laboratory personnel are trained in observing their own consciousness. These participants were called observers, and the charge to examine their own awareness was interpreted in a strict, exacting manner. Observers were instructed to attend only to their experiences and not to the stimuli that provoked them. To report, for example, that one sees a chair is erroneous in that this describes a stimulus, not an experience. It is a report of what is known, an interpretation rather than an observation. For the introspectionist, a chair is a composite of an awareness of color, brightness, form, and similar variables.

The detachment from the stimulation comes from the goal of discovering the fundamental nature of the mental elements, not as they are sensed in a particular setting. The task is analogous to the one that chemists took on when they sought to identify basic elements. Introspection disclosed that the units or the building blocks of the human mind are sensations, images, and feelings, and that each of these possesses various attributes, such as duration and intensity.

Introspection, when conducted under the restraints of structural psychology, yields information that is not easily related to extralaboratory experiences. The method discloses a spectrum of subtleties of awareness to which a person ordinarily pays no heed. To illustrate—descriptions of the afterimages that come from looking at a bright white light indicate a sequence of many colors, and most hues have been reported, with yellow probably the most predominant early in the sequence, followed by red, then blue, then purple, and dark green. These hues are apt to appear as a core of color that is surrounded by a ring of another color, sometimes with a halo of yet another hue. When clicks of sound are delivered simultaneously through tubes to the ears, they are sensed as coming from the median plane, but a difference in the time of stimulation as short as one one thousandth of a second changes the location to one side. Smelling also activates touch and taste, so that odors may be accompanied by sensations of pain, warmth, cold, sweet, or sour. Trained observers are able to distinguish these different nuances (Woodworth, 1938).

Structural psychologists were attracted to the study of illusions, or mistaken perceptions, because they appeared to violate the assumption that the image of an object on the retina is a copy of the object. The implications of this were of commanding importance inasmuch as they suggested that the mind might not be reflecting, but rather might be distorting reality. The structuralists investigated illusions in various modalities, but the emphasis was on vision. They tried to find out why, for example, a row of dots is perceived as more extensive than a blank space of the same length, and why a vertical line is judged longer than one that is horizontal, and why >———< is seen as longer than <———>.

Numerous theories were devised to account for the discrepancies between the content of the mind and the physical properties of stimuli. The variables that were assumed to be responsible included eye movements, the nature of the excitation of the retina, as well as the actual task that is undertaken. The role of this last factor is exemplified in the drawings presented above by judging the distance between the wings rather than the length of the lines. The perplexities were not resolved before the theory of structural psychology faded (Boring, 1942).

Titchener patterned his laboratory after those in German university science departments, and he was adamant about exerting rigid controls over experimental variables. This meant relying on laboratory equipment for many purposes. To illustrate—the exposure of stimuli had to be regulated, the fixation point of the eyes had to be stable, research in audition had to be conducted in a soundproof room, and the speed of responses had to be accurately measured. In other words, instrumentation became the sine qua non of the laboratory, and meeting this demand was looked on with pride. The equipment increased the accuracy, but perhaps even more important it signified scientific status, and did so in a visible, impressive manner. At that time many of the instruments were imported from Europe, and in addition to this prestigious origin their design was elegant. What they lacked in precision they made up for in bulk and ornateness. Many were large, imposing pieces, made of brass (Popplestone & McPherson, 1971, 1980). In fact, the field during that era came to be referred to as Brass Instrument Psychology. Structural psychology provided the discipline with this paraphernalia of science, and the custom of using appurtenances in psychological research has undoubtedly been responsible for much of the progress.

Titchener's bibliography is extensive (Dallenbach, 1928), and a major part of it constitutes reports of experiments, but it also reflect struggles to clarify the viewpoint that he considers to be the only appropriate formulation for the discipline. He tolerated others who dealt with topics that he did not deal with, but resisted calling these efforts psychology because, in his view, they were not part of basic, scientific psychology. He preferred to call his own system "psychology," and he entitled only two journal articles and one note for an encyclopedia structural psychology (1898, 1899, 1914). In some discussions (for example, 1909) he used the adjective existential as a means of stressing the existence of mental elements or content. Titchener's claim to the field of psychology was not honored, and colleagues called attention to its specialized nature by referring to it as structural or existential psychology (Marx & Cronan-Hillix, 1987).

The recipients of the doctorates that were awarded under Titchener at Cornell held some of the most respected academic posts in the United States, and thus were in a position to spread the theory. A few continued to teach as they were taught, but many more began to examine, accept, and teach other views. The reasons for their defection are numerous, but prominent among them is the aridity that came from Titchener's insistence on being scientific. In his opinion, if a problem could not be handled with the controls that science mandates, it should not be considered. "It was a system with a definite form and a definite code. Aggressively pure, pointedly aloof, consciously correct" (Heidbreder, 1933, p. 144).

This priority of methodology over subject matter is very restrictive, and it was inevitable that people would break out of the mold and study what appeared important in the most accurate, precise way they could. This did not mean abandoning science, but it did mean striving to devise ways of monitoring and regulating the observations of the phenomena of interest. Titchener's students undertook these endeavors with the advantages of a thorough training in laboratory procedures and with a keen awareness of both the importance and feasibility of being objective about psychological events.

References

Boring, E. G. (1927). Edward Bradford Titchener: 1867–1927. *American Journal of Psychology, 38,* 489–506. Boring was Titchener's student, a role he filled throughout both their lives with gratification and with duty. He was ever willing to interpret and to explain the master.

Boring, E. G. (1937). Titchener and the existential. *American Journal of Psychology, 50*, 470–483. Boring prints excerpts of letters that Titchener wrote to him. They illustrate not only Titchener's point of view, but also his meticulous attention to details and the sharpness of his criticisms.

Boring, E. G. (1942). *Sensation and perception in the history of experimental psychology.* New York: Appleton-Century.

Dallenbach, K. M. (1928). Bibliography of the writings of Edward Bradford Titchener. *American Journal of Psychology, 40*, 121–125. This article updates a 1917 listing of Titchener's writings. Dallenbach reports the following totals: 27 books, 216 articles, notes, or discussions, 5 editorials, 176 papers published by students working in the laboratory during Titchener's directorship. In addition to these, Titchener has translated twelve professional publications and reviewed numerous books.

Heidbreder, E. (1933). *Seven psychologies.* New York: Appleton-Century.

Marx, M. H., & Cronan-Hillix, W. A. (1987). *Systems and theories in psychology* (4th ed.). New York: McGraw-Hill. "About half of America's psychologists are Wundtian by descent, but not by conviction" (p. 103).

Popplestone, J. A., & McPherson, M. W. (1971). Prolegomenon to the study of historic apparatus, circa 1875–1915. *American Psychologist, 26*, 656–657.

Popplestone, J. A., & McPherson, M. W. (1980). The vitality of the Leipzig model of 1880–1910 in the United States in 1950–1980. In W. G. Bringmann & R. D. Tweney (Eds.), *Wundt Studies: A centennial collection.* Toronto: Hogrefe. Historic apparatus is illustrated, including some pieces that are in use in modern laboratories and have undergone only minor changes.

Titchener, E. B. (1898). The postulates of a structural psychology. *The Philosophical Review, 7*, 449–465. This lengthy discussion documents Titchener's absorption with psychology. It is obviously an exhilarating, fascinating topic for him.

Titchener, E. B. (1899). Structural and functional psychology. *The Philosophical Review, 8*, 290–299.

Titchener, E. B. (1909). *Lectures on the experimental psychology of the thought-processes.* New York: Macmillan. This is a series of lectures in which Titchener struggles with several problems, including imageless thought. The latter refers to introspective failures to discern images, as in the case of solving a problem but experiencing no image while doing it. This vacuum implied action without a basis, and hence was impossible.

Titchener, E. B. (1914). Structural psychology. In P. Monroe (Ed.), *A cyclopedia of education* (Vol. 5, pp. 67–68). Titchener comments that the adjectives structural and functional were first used by William James in 1884, and then criticizes James' interpretation.

Woodworth, R. S. (1938). *Experimental psychology.* New York: Henry Holt. This was the standard text for a considerable period of time. The third edition was published in 1971 as J. W. Kling & L. A. Riggs (Eds.), *Woodworth & Schlosberg's Experimental Psychology.* New York: Holt, Rinehart & Winston. This first edition was published at a time when structural psychology laboratory data were still considered to be relevant to research design. Woodworth describes the experiments in a manner that is more readily understood than is a technical introspective treatise.

Sources of Additional Information

Barnholt, S. E., & Bentley, M. (1911). Thermal intensity and the area of stimulus. *American Journal of Psychology, 22*, 325–332. This illustrates the modus operandi in the Cornell laboratory. The researchers are interested in confirming one of four possible reasons why the intensity of a sensation of warmth or cold increases with increases in the area of the skin that is stimulated. Following is one procedure: "The observer's eight fingers were ringed with indelible ink 1/2 inch and 2 inches from the tips. The forearm was supported and the hand was allowed to hang down in a natural position. Water was kept at a constant temperature (45° C.) in a small vessel, and the vessel was raised by the experimenter until the water reached the first or the second ring upon a single finger . . . Immersion lasted one second. After it, the finger was dried gently . . . Then the same or another finger was immersed in the same way . . . The usual precautions against the constant errors of space and time were taken. The observer was asked to report which sensation was the stronger" (p. 327). Boring, E. G. (1929). *A history of experimental psychology*. New York: Appleton-Century. This book is written by an advocate of structural psychology, and it was, for many years, the most widely circulated textbook in the history of psychology. The second edition was published in 1950. Evans, R. B. (1972). E. B. Titchener and his lost system. *Journal of the History of the Behavioral Sciences, 8*, 168–180. The author reviews some of Titchener's modifications of his system. These started as early as 1913 and were known to his contemporaries but have been slighted by historians. Sullivan, A. H. (1921). An experimental study of kinaesthetic imagery. *American Journal of Psychology, 32*, 54–80. The article is a report of a doctoral dissertation, and it offers another account of life in the Cornell laboratory. Kinaesthetic sensations were found to differ from kinaesthetic images in various ways: sensations include dull pressure, light pressure, smooth pressure, strain, and ache, but images include only pressure. The image is generally weaker and briefer and more apt to be two-dimensional than three-dimensional. Titchener, E. B. (1972). *Systematic psychology: Prolegomena*. Ithaca, NY: Cornell University Press. (Original work published 1929). This is a posthumous publication of a manuscript Titchener was working on at the time of his death.

SUBCEPTION. See PERCEPTUAL PHENOMENA.

SUCCESS. See FEAR OF SUCCESS.

T

TEMPERAMENT. 1. The style of an individual; the mode, vitality, spirit of the person; the *way* in which situations are approached and things are done rather than *what* is done.

Temperament is a traditional concept and one that began very early. Hippocrates (c. 460–377 B.C.E.) believed that blood, phlegm, red bile, and black bile constitute the humors of the body, and that imbalances among these fluids give rise to some illnesses and some personality characteristics. Although Galen (131–200) is customarily given credit, it was probably Vindician, a fourth-century C.E. physician, who originated the idea that temperament varies with these humors (Diamond, 1974). He asserted that blood is responsible for various traits, including goodwill and cheerfulness, that phlegm is the cause of passivity, that red bile induces irascibility, and that black bile gives rise to melancholy.

Although temperament has never been a dominant concept in psychology, it has consistently attracted some attention, and much of the scientific work has been carried on by one of three methods, listed here in the temporal order in which they were devised: the relating of temperament to physique, the statistical processing of psychological tests, and the longitudinal method, that is, the repeating of observations of the same individuals at different ages. This discussion illustrates each of these three techniques, but first a few comments about the similarities among them are in order. Many investigators who use the latter two procedures share the assumption of those who use the first method that temperament has a biological cause. Advocates of all these methods also assume that temperament is consistent in different situations and at different times, even though sound research support for this belief has yet to be established (Rutter, 1982). Experimenters, whatever the particular method they use, are remarkably uniform in the way in which they organize the study of temperament. They first formulate a very broad definition and then supplement it with a list of specific traits. These tend to vary from researcher to researcher, and thus the definitions of temperament tend to vary from researcher to researcher.

William H. Sheldon (1899–1977), a modern advocate of a biologically based theory, began work in the 1920s but did not publish an integrated account of the results until the 1940s (Sheldon, 1944). He clearly illustrates the custom of relying on a vague definition: "By temperament we shall mean, roughly, the level of personality just above physiological function and below acquired attitudes and beliefs" (Sheldon & Stevens, 1945, p. 4). Starting with this kind of formulation he developed an intricate classification of both body structure and psychological variables. He devised the former (Sheldon, Stevens, & Tucker, 1940/1970) by categorizing approximately 4,000 photographs of naked men, each posed in three ways, into three morphological forms: endomorphy, a predominantly spherical and soft body structure; mesomorphy, a sturdy and firm body; and ectomorphy, a frame in which long extremities and linearity are outstanding. He rated the dominance in each subject of each of these structures on a seven-point scale and then combined these ranks into a three-digit expression, for example, 6-2-2 or 1-7-1. He called this the somatotype, but the relationship that it quantifies is often ignored, and the person is categorized in terms of the most prominent body TYPE.

Sheldon and Stevens (1945) next classified the psychological concomitants of the three morphologies. They started by assembling 650 alleged temperament traits, and by eliminating duplicates and similarities reduced the number to 50. They then rated thirty-three males on these traits in a number of different situations during a twelve-month period. The next step was a statistical analysis that yielded three major groups of traits, which they identified as a variety of temperament. Following is the name of each, its constitutional basis, and a few illustrative traits; viscerotonia, the dominance of digestive viscera, an endomorphic physique, and traits of amiability, sociability, and a fondness for eating and for comfort; somatotonia, a preponderance of muscular activity, congruent with mesomorphy and a preference for physical activity and assertiveness; and cerebrotonia, well-developed intellectual functions, identified with ectomorphy and with restraint in behavioral space as well as in social contacts.

Sheldon provoked a number of criticisms—many of them appropriate—and this censure fed a growing dissatisfaction with constitutional theories of temperament. Sheldon, however, merits commendation, since he is one of the few investigators to accumulate observations of people over an extended period and under various circumstances (Hall, Lindzey, Loehlin, & Manosevitz, 1985). Sheldon admonished his co-workers to "observe the subject closely for at least a year in as many different situations as possible. Conduct a series of not less than 20 analytic interviews" (Sheldon & Stevens, 1945, p. 27). Such repetitive scrutiny of psychological behavior is not highly visible again in investigations of temperament until 1968 (Thomas, Chess, & Birch).

The disapproval of a body type-temperament alignment was increasing at about the time factor analysis was gaining approval. This is a complex statistical procedure that identifies variables that cluster together. In the case of temperament the data consist of responses to pencil-and-paper tests. Following is an oversimplified example of this partitioning: Some people would be prone to agree with the three following statements: "I feel happy," "I am carefree," and "I'm eager," and they would disagree with a second trio composed of "I am desperate," "I want to cry," and "I'm very blue." Factor analysis has the power to identify these alignments or factors in masses of data, for example, the responses of 3,000 or more subjects to 400 or more test items. Each factor is assigned a name that best describes the dominant content of the items in each cluster.

The capability of factor analysis to handle large amounts of data prompted the incorporating of the superabundant pencil-and-paper tests of personality into research on temperament. Factor analysts, unrestrained by a clearly limited definition of temperament, have taken advantage of the available resources and even used tests that tap numerous aspects of personality other than temperament. Some of the specifies that follow illustrate how this has expanded temperament, an aspect of personality, into a concept of personality.

L. L. Thurstone, one of the better known factor analysts, developed some procedures in the early 1930s and continued factor analytic work throughout his lifetime. He joins other investigators of temperament by beginning with a vague definition: "Each of us has relatively permanent personality characteristics or traits known as our temperament. These aspects of personality are important for an understanding of the way we will act in school or industrial situations . . . stable traits which describe how normal, well adjusted people differ from each other" (1950, p. 1).

Thurstone (1950) factor analyzed a combination of some already existing tests and some that he personally compiled. He found seven factors that he identified as follows: active, vigorous, impulsive, dominant, stable, sociable, and reflective. These components illustrate the previously noted variations in the definitions of temperament in that a prior factor analysis, based on many of the same test items, yielded six additional components, or a total of thirteen factors. Thurstone's data also illustrate the practice of blending the concepts of temperament and of personality. The factors "active" and "vigorous" appear to be attributes of the style of responding, but "reflective" and "social" appear to designate sources of stimulation and of satisfaction rather than modes of reacting. This kind of fusion is explicitly acknowledged, often by emphasizing the relationship between temperament and normal adjustment. This is clearly illustrated in Thurstone's previously quoted reference to traits "which describe how normal, well adjusted people differ from each other." In most research designs normality is not actively pursued as much as pathology is avoided, both by administering tests to subjects who have no known emotional disorders and by restricting the test items to everyday matters.

A second recurring theme is stability of temperament, and this is also apparent in the reference in Thurstone's definition to "relatively permanent personality characteristics or traits." The consistency appears to stem from a belief that temperament is biologically based inasmuch as there is little or no empirical support for consistency in the single administration of a questionnaire.

One particular factor of analytic study merits attention because of its astonishing combination of the ancient concept of temperament and modern factor analysis. In 1963 Eysenck published a report of an experiment in which he reactivated the four temperaments that were identified by "the great medieval physician Galen" (1963, p. 1032). Eysenck considers two factor analytically identified personality variables—extraversion-introversion and stability-instability—to be basic dimensions of personality. He combined these with the four classic temperaments in a diagram that is reminiscent of Renaissance cosmological charts. It consists of two concentric, quartered circles. Each section of the inner circle is labeled with one of Galen's cardinal temperaments, and one of each of the four factor-analytic dimensions is identified on the outer circle at the end of each of four diameters. Between these perimeter points and in the quadrant corresponding to each of the prototypical temperaments is an array of eight, for a total of thirty-two factor analytically derived traits. Eysenck comments: "There is considerable agreement at this descriptive level between medieval theory and modern discovery" (1963, p. 1032). Apparently science can be circular as well as linear, in this instance both literally and figuratively.

The third and most effective method of studying temperament consists of observing the same individuals over a time span. This design was not used extensively in the study of temperament until the mid-1950s, when Thomas and Chess began a long-term investigation in which infants and children were observed in different situations, given individual clinical examinations, and also described by both parents and teachers (Thomas, Chess, & Birch, 1968; Thomas & Chess, 1977, 1980).

The experimenters followed the usual pattern of starting from a broad base, in this instance from interviews with parents. These accounts were used to identify nine variables to be examined. These appear to be related to the style or manner of responding; that is, they are temperamental rather than personality variables. They are activity level, regularity of repetitive biological functions, approach or withdrawal from new stimuli, adaptability, intensity of reaction, threshold of responsiveness, quality of mood, distractibility, and attention span or persistence.

The investigators were not content to assume that these factors are the cause of certain responses, but rather took on the task of tracing out how these might affect not only the child, but also the parents, peer relationships, and adjustment to school. An important research goal was to determine the influence on personal development of "the child's own characteristics as a reactive organism" (Thomas, Chess, & Birch, 1968, p. 5). This focus extends the subject matter from analyses of the temperament of a person to analyses of how temperament influences the reactions of other people to the individual, and this interaction frees temperament from the control of merely biological variables.

The authors do not assume that temperament is consistent, but rather try to measure the amount of consistency. This is arduous because functionally equivalent behavior takes various forms at different ages; for example, a dysphoric mood in an infant may be manifest in loud wailing, whereas a teenager would only seldom resort to this but would use another equally extreme way of expressing distress. The authors made impressive inroads on the very difficult task of identifying and confirming these infant-child analogies. The conclusions they reach are, like the subject matter of the research, complex. There are indications that "temperamental individuality is well established by the time the infant is two to three months old" (Thomas & Chess, 1977, p. 153). On the other hand, "continuity and predictability can thus not be assumed. . . . Consistency in development will come from continuity over time in the organism and significant features of the environment. Discontinuity will result from changes in one or the other" (Thomas & Chess, 1977, p. 174).

Among the more important effects of these experiments are the modification of temperament and its reappearance on the research stage. There is an increased awareness among professionals that temperamental variables do exert a significant influence on the treatment that one receives from others. An intense child—one who is enthusiastic, vigorous, crying, and excitable—solicits reactions from those around him or her that are quite different from those provoked by a less intense child—one who is not particularly interested in the surroundings, more apt to sulk than to cry, and hard to stir to action. This interplay depicts the child as not merely buffeted—benefited or victimized—but construes the child as an active contributor to his or her own fate.

Longitudinal research is complicated and expensive, and thus relatively uncommon, but despite these handicaps some data are being collected by other investigators, although often over a briefer time span than that covered by Thomas and Chess (Rutter, 1982). A 1984 study (Garrison, Earls & Kindlon), for example, reports data concerning temperamental consistency in the interval between three years of age and the time of entering school.

In conclusion, even though the style of responding has been extensively investigated, conclusions about it tend to vary with the method that is used to study the phenomenon. The early search for a direct relationship between constitutional and psychological factors has faded. The case for the consistency of temperament is still being built, and appreciation that temperament is psychological in nature, and not merely a manifestation of biology, has taken hold.

References

Diamond, S. (Ed.). (1974). *The roots of psychology: A sourcebook in the history of ideas.* New York: Basic Books.
Eysenck, H. J. (1963). Biological basis of personality. *Nature, 199,* 1031–1034. The title would be more accurate if the word temperament replaced personality.

Garrison, W., Earls, F., & Kindlon, D. (1984). Temperament characteristics in the third year of life and behavioral adjustment at school entry. *Journal of Clinical Child Psychology, 13*, 298–303.

Hall, C. S., Lindzey, G., Loehlin, J. C., & Manosevitz, M. (1985). *Introduction to theories of personality*. New York: John Wiley.

Rutter, M. (1982). Temperament: Concepts, issues and problems. In R. Porter & G. M. Collins (Eds.), *Temperamental differences in infants and young children* (pp. 1–19). Ciba Foundation Symposium 89. London: Pitman. This entire volume presents the papers that were delivered at a symposium devoted to temperament. Rutter wrote not only the chapter cited here, but as chairman of the symposium he made some "closing remarks" in which he reviews some pros and cons of the consistency of temperament. He discerns progress: "It is striking that we have been able to take for granted the resolution of many issues that would have provoked controversy a mere 20 years ago. We have assumed the importance of behavioural individuality . . . it was possible for us to start with the presumption that these differences *matter*; that they predict future disorders, patterns of personal interaction and responses to life change or stress" (p. 294).

Sheldon, W. H. (1944). Constitutional factors in personality. In J. McV. Hunt (Ed.), *Personality and the behavior disorders: A handbook based on experimental and clinical research* (Vol. 1) (pp. 526–549). New York: Ronald Press.

Sheldon, W. H., & Stevens, S. S. (1945). *The varieties of temperament: A psychology of constitutional differences* (3rd ed.). New York: Harper & Bros.

Sheldon, W. H., Stevens, S. S., & Tucker, W. B. (1970). *The varieties of human physique: An introduction to constitutional psychology*. Darien, CT: Hafner. (Original work published 1940)

Thomas, A., & Chess, S. (1977). *Temperament and development*. New York: Brunner/Mazel.

Thomas, A., & Chess, S. (1980). *The dynamics of psychological development*. New York: Brunner/Mazel. The authors relate the data from a longitudinal study to numerous aspects of personality.

Thomas, A., Chess, S., & Birch, H. G. (1968). *Temperament and behavior disorders in children*. New York: New York University Press. The authors note "the general disrepute of earlier constitutionalist views that had ascribed heredity and constitution as causes for complex personality structures" (pp. 5–6).

Thurstone, L. L. (1950). *Examiner manual for the Thurstone Temperament Schedule*. Chicago: Science Research Associates. Thurstone's definition of the sociable factor illustrates the confusion between personality and temperament. "Persons with high scores in this area enjoy the company of others, make friends easily, and are sympathetic, cooperative, and agreeable in their relations with people. Strangers readily tell them about their personal troubles" (p. 2).

Sources of Additional Information

Diamond, S. (1957). *Personality and temperament*. New York: Harper & Bros. This book includes a comprehensive and critical review of the literature. Downey, J. E. (1923). *The will-temperament and its testing*. Yonkers-on-Hudson, NY: World Book. This test involves the unusual method of having subjects write under varying directions, for example, as rapidly as possible as well as in imitation. The method was adopted because handwriting is a record of muscular activity, and for Downey, this was a direct expression of temperament. LaHaye, B. (1977). *How to develop your child's temperament*. Eugene, OR: Harvest House. This is one in a series of recent publications that present Galenic typology as a valid theory and, guided by a doctrine of biblical inerrancy, provide directives for daily living. This volume, for example, advises parents that a "San Chlor" child (Sanguine-Choleric) is a manipulator and most effectively punished by confinement to a room. This fosters contemplation, whereas spanking is conducive to immediate and transient regret. Pavlov, I. P. (1967). *Lectures on conditioned reflexes: Twenty-five years of objective study of the higher nervous activity (behaviour) of animals* (vol. 1). (W. H. Gantt, Ed. and Trans.). New York: International Publishers. (Original work published 1928). Pavlov entitles a chapter "A Physiological Study of the Types of Nervous Systems, i.e., of Temperaments" (p. 370). In this he relates the differences in conditioning among dogs to the four classic temperaments—sanguine, phlegmatic, choleric, and melancholic.

THINKING. 1. Implicit behavior that is reflective, rational, and frequently requires substituting symbols for stimuli that are not immediately present. **CONCEPT FORMATION.** 1. Gaining an appreciation of the characteristics of a class or category of events by observing, comparing, and contrasting an array of specimens.

Each of these concepts is concerned with behavior that entails very little gross motor activity. In fact, a person who is "thinking hard" often appears to be "doing nothing." This apparent inactivity is in striking contrast to the active, although implicit, struggles that may be going on when a person is striving to understand a situation that is complex, and cannot be handled by techniques that have worked in the past. In order to arrive at a solution the thinker may be forced to attend *to relationships* among various elements in the situation or to rearrange and manipulate symbols ideationally. This covert behavior is so complicated and so obscure that psychologists do not agree about the distinctions among such similar phenomena as abstracting, concept formation, creativity, decision making, insight, judgment, planning, problem solving, productive thinking, reasoning, and thinking. We have selected from these concepts two that overlap in meaning but are conceptualized in contrasting ways: thinking that is often diffuse and vaguely defined, and concept formation, relatively specific and more clearly defined.

Until the twentieth century, thinking was generally believed to follow the principles of formal logic and to be as orderly as syllogistic reasoning. Skepticism about this regularity emerged when INTROSPECTION—an esoteric method of analyzing subtle and minute nuances of awareness—failed, on some occasions, to discover a mental structure that represented the thinking. For example, introspectionists would report that their judgment was clear, but they were not aware of just how the decision was made, even in instances in which it was correct. This was theoretically very disturbing because it denied the regularity that had been an assumed characteristic of thinking, and it also pointed to reactivity in the absence of a structure. The search for a satisfactory explanation deflected attention away from analyses of the experience of thinking in favor of speculations about underlying mechanisms, and the topic of thinking per se has yet to return to center stage.

The questions about mental structures were not resolved and, in fact, lost their importance when BEHAVIORISM, with its militant rejection of mentalism, became influential. John B. Watson, a pioneer behaviorist, was convinced that thinking is a muscular phenomenon, primarily localized in the laryngeal area. In Watson's view, thinking is a derivative of language habits, and he italicized his summary of the process: *"What the psychologists have hitherto called thought is in short nothing but talking to ourselves"* (1925, p. 191). The sequence starts when the sounds an infant first vocalizes spontaneously come to be associated with particular stimuli; for example, the infant learns to vocalize "ma ma" at the approach of the mother and "bye bye" at her departure. Social pressures induce children to convert these overt responses into silent speech, but some minute, residual muscular activities in the throat area persist, and for the early behaviorists these constituted thinking.

The advocacy of a peripheral location drew criticism from those who believe that psychological behavior is localized in the central nervous system. Researchers initiated experimental work—and it currently continues in the same vein—on the influence on thinking of several biological variables, particularly brain structure and physiology (Morgan & Stellar, 1950; Stevens, 1971). An impressive body of knowledge has been accumulated, but data concerning the role of particular areas of the brain fall short of clarifying the psychological nature of the concept.

A recent innovation in the study of thinking is the drawing of analogies between electronic information processing and psychological events. The successes of the former enterprise suggested that familiarity with psychological events that intervene between stimuli and responses could be enhanced by using a flow chart as a model. This format becomes yet another instance in which research is deflected away from the direct study of thinking, in this case in favor of assessing the comparability between electronic and psychological activities. One of the ways of doing this has involved the reactivation of a historic method known as mental chronometry, the measuring of the time required to make different psychological responses.

Mental chronometry was first used by Donders in the nineteenth century, and in one variety of this procedure the REACTION TIME required for a simple reaction ("Say 'Ki' as soon as the sound 'Ki' is heard") is subtracted from that required for a more complex one ("Say 'Ki' only in response to 'Ki', and not to similar sounds such as 'Ka' and 'Ko'). The difference between these two intervals was believed to be the time required to discriminate the sounds, but the time differences were found to vary with stimuli as well as with variables within the subject, such as fatigue and SET. Researchers have recently revived these methods and are now using them to identify some of the cognitive processes (Mayer, 1983).

A modern example is encountered in an investigation of the way children add (Groen & Parkman, 1972). These investigators assume that children do not rely on memorized sums the way adults do, but that they use what they call a reconstructive process. They outlined five processes that they believe children might use in adding single digits, and they found that the actual and predicted temporal patterns were closest when "setting" and "incrementing" are assumed. It is plausible that a child, requested to compute the sum of 5 + 3, starts with a setting of 5 and then adds increments of 1 + 1 + 1. When asked to add 7 + 1, the setting may be 7 and thus only one increment is necessary. The second problem appears, logically, to require less time than the first, and measurements of the intervals that children actually require to complete a number of problems agree more closely with those projected for "setting" and "incrementing" than for any of the other reconstructive processes the investigators thought might have been used.

The qualitative differences between information processing (by a machine) and thinking (by a person) may be more critical than any procedural shortcomings. Machines adhere without deviation to a program, whereas thinking is flexible (Henle, 1962). Technicians do not yet know how to program the computer to reflect the many subtleties that are in the repertoire of the thinker. They are not able to register the nuances that organisms perceive, nor are they able to mirror how the human being compensates for incomplete information or how differentiated effects of actions are predicted. A flow chart is a scheme for methodological, step-by-step compliance, whereas thinking bypasses fidelity in favor of selectivity, organization, and choice (Denning, 1986). Despite these differences, the information-processing model has fostered some understanding of the relationships among various reactions that are part of thinking. There has been an increased appreciation of the importance of memory in thinking, more sophistication about how associations are formed, and a better comprehension of the role of meaning (Revlin & Mayer, 1978).

The history of research in concept formation is more clear-cut than is the history of thinking, in part because the forming of a concept is a more clearly limited process than thinking. It is an intellectual challenge for every person in that it demands the identification of critical features that are common among diverse stimuli. A concept is not built from rules, but is constructed from examples; these offer irregularities as well as regularities, and mastery is usually gradual. Some of the perplexity can be discerned in a list of some of the heterogeneous phenomena that a young child encounters as he or she tries to grasp the concept of motion, tries to learn what moves and what does not. These may well include a ball rolling down a hill, cars traversing both short and long distances—sometimes in rapid and sometimes in slow motion—adults walking, infants creeping, frogs hopping, birds and airplanes flying, fish swimming in water, ships moving on the surface of the water, plants swaying in the wind, and fireworks exploding. These suggest that motion could be intrinsic to a hill, a motor and/or fuel, even to human legs, animal legs, bird wings, aircraft wings, fish gills, and/or invisible forces. The research on concept formation is designed to learn how such aggregates are systematized.

In order to accomplish this, investigators often ask subjects to categorize unfamiliar or meaningless stimuli, for example, to segregate the following six groups of marks into three categories: (1) '°', (2) -°°, (3) xxx, (4) °-°, (5) ***, (6) °'°. Another similar technique is to assign nonsense names ("Fevif" and "Cipus") to a series of heterogeneous objects (usually pictures) and to request a report when the communality is grasped, that is, when, for example, the subject realizes that the pictures associated with "Fevif" are flowers and those associated with "Cipus" are leaves. Participants are often asked for verbal reports about their implicit experiences at the time they are forming a concept. They are queried, for example, about the cues they believe to be the most salient, the factors that are particularly helpful in extracting homogeneous elements, and the confidence they have in their decisions. The research on concept formation started in the 1920s, a time when INTROSPECTION was losing its appeal, and the verbal reports are a substitute for introspections, or perhaps more accurately a residual of them.

English (1922) was one of the earliest investigators, and he studied the tactics that adults use in the initial phases of forming a concept, in this instance grouping abstract designs into categories. He procured meticulous descriptions of the subjects' "train of associations" (p. 312) and concluded from these that people begin early in concept formation to relate material they are trying to comprehend to something they already know. He observed that they tend to approach the task in similar ways but since they are also guided by previous personal knowledge, diversity is unavoidable.

A series of studies conducted by Edna Heidbreder (assisted on occasion by Bensley, Ivy, & Overstreet, 1946, 1947, 1948, 1949) provide an impressive amount of information about concept attainment. This supports English's finding that people normally relate novel stimuli to already existing knowledge. The results also disclosed that certain properties of the stimuli tend to be integrated in a particular order. To illustrate—a person probably first isolates an object, then conceptualizes it as a cube, then as a red cube, and finally integrates the number that it bears. Heidbreder also notes that this sequence may be violated when some aspects of the stimuli are unusually conspicuous.

Numerous additional experimental papers have added many details about how a concept is formed, and in general they elaborate prior laboratory data much more frequently than they correct them. Reed (1972) illustrates one of these amendments. He observed individuals classifying a series of schematic faces into similar groups. He also recorded verbal reports during the matching. Most subjects were found to conceptualize a prototype for each category, to classify each drawing on the basis of its similarity to the standard, and to place more reliance on the features that most clearly distinguish each category. These results suggest that, in continuity with English's early experiment, people may resort to a generality in order to generalize.

It is beyond the scope of this discussion to review the numerous details and the qualifications of them that have come from the experimental work on concept formation. They are, nonetheless, available in the literature (Newell & Simon, 1972; Mayer, 1983; Vinacke, 1974).

References

Denning, P. J. (1986). The science of computing: Will machines ever think? *American Scientist, 74*, 344–346. This brief article is readily intelligible, and the author refers readers to recently published book-length treatments of the topic.

English, H. B. (1922). An experimental study of certain initial phases of the process of abstraction. *American Journal of Psychology, 33*, 305–350. Some of English's research participants were trained introspectionists and they added some introspective data to the larger collection of verbal reports.

Groen, G. J., & Parkman, J. M. (1972). A chronometric analysis of simple addition. *Psychological Review, 79*, 329–343. The authors end the paper on a cautious note: "The present paper merely points to some promising possibilities and some potentially useful experimental results" (p. 342).

Heidbreder, E. (1946, 1946, 1947, 1948, 1949, 1949). The attainment of concepts. I. *Journal of General Psychology, 35*, 173–189; II. *35*, 191–223; III. *Journal of Psychology, 24*, 93–138; VI. *26*, 193–216; VII. *27*, 3–39; VIII. *27*, 263–309.

Heidbreder, E., & Bensley, M. L., & Ivy, M. (1948). The attainment of concepts. *Journal of Psychology, 25*, (Pt. 4) 299–329.

Heidbreder, E., & Overstreet, P. (1948). The attainment of concepts. *Journal of Psychology, 26*, (Pt. 5) 45–69.

Henle, M. (1962). On the relation between logic and thinking. *Psychological Review, 69*, 366–378.

Mayer, R. E. (1983). *Thinking, problem solving, cognition.* New York: W. H. Freeman. This is an authoritative review of various facets of thinking. The conclusion to the chapter on mental chronometry summarizes the weaknesses in this procedure.

Morgan, C. T., & Stellar, E. (1950). *Physiological psychology* (2nd ed.). New York: McGraw-Hill. This textbook was in wide use. It is comprehensive and reflects many of the beliefs about the relationship between the psychological behavior and physiology, particularly the location of psychological behavior in the nervous system. The first edition was published in 1943.

Newell, A., & Simon, H. A. (1972). *Human problem solving.* Englewood Cliffs, NJ: Prentice-Hall.

Reed, S. K. (1972). Pattern recognition and categorization. *Cognitive Psychology, 3*, 382–407.

Revlin, R., & Mayer, R. E. (1978). *Human reasoning.* Washington, DC: V. H. Winston. This book emphasizes syllogistic reasoning and utilizes an information-processing model. The perspective of the volume is sharpened by a foreward by Mary Henle.

Stevens, C. F. (1971). Basic mechanisms of neural function. In J. W. Kling & L. A. Riggs (Eds.), *Woodworth and Schlosberg's experimental psychology* (3rd ed., pp. 87–116). New York: Holt, Rinehart & Winston.

Vinacke, W. E. (1974). *The psychology of thinking* (2nd ed.). New York: McGraw-Hill. The first edition of the volume was published in 1952, and at that time it was one of only a few books devoted to thinking.

Watson, J. B. (1925). *Behaviorism.* New York: The People's Institute Publishing Co. Watson's writing style is to the point and not intended to placate; for example:

"Behaviorism claims that 'consciousness' is neither a definable nor a usable concept; that it is merely another word for the 'soul' of more ancient times. The old psychology is thus dominated by a kind of subtle religious philosophy" (p. 3).

Sources of Additional Information

Hayes, J. R. (1978). *Cognitive psychology: Thinking and creating.* Homewood, IL: Dorsey. This volume offers an overview of cognitive psychology, but there are two chapters devoted to problem solving and one to creativity. It is written at the level of the beginning student. Posner, M. I. (1973). *Cognition: An introduction.* Glenview, IL: Scott, Foresman. The historical section of this text begins with Greek philosophy. The account is concise, but accurate and readily intelligible. It includes a description of the controversy over the relative importance in thinking of structure versus operations or acts. Rose, F. (1984). *Into the heart of the mind: An American quest for artificial intelligence.* New York: Harper & Row. This is written for a lay audience, and it clarifies the limitations of technology in the simulation of intelligence. Scheerer, M. (1963). Problem-solving. *Scientific American, 208,* 118–128. This article describes experiments on how humans solve problems. There is some emphasis on how the perspective on a problem facilitates its solution. Wertheimer, Max. (1959). Productive thinking. In M.[ichael] Wertheimer (Ed.), *Productive thinking* (enlarged ed.). New York: Harper & Bros. Max Wertheimer completed the manuscript for this book shortly before his death, and he intended to supplement it with two volumes. His colleagues first published it in 1945. This 1959 version, edited by his son, Michael Wertheimer, includes some additional relevant manuscripts that were found among his papers. The book describes the process of thinking in a meticulous manner.

THRESHOLD. See PSYCHOPHYSICS and THRESHOLD.

TRAIT. 1. An attribute that is believed to be characteristic of a person and consistent even in different contexts and throughout life.

The customary sequence in research is one in which a phenomenon is first discovered and then named and investigated by conducting experiments on the role of the relevant variables, but many scientists who study traits start with descriptions of behavior rather than with behavior. As early as 1884 Francis Galton, a British gentleman-scientist, attempted "to gain an idea of the number of the more conspicuous aspects of the character by counting in an appropriate dictionary the words used to express them" (p. 181).

A similar practice was adopted by Gordon Allport (1897–1967), the master traitologist and the psychologist who so effectively promoted the concept that his work frames most of the research on the subject (Hall, Lindzey, Loehlin, & Manosevitz, 1985). His initial paper on the topic appeared in 1930, and in this he enumerated various specifications of a trait and identified it as the basic element of personality. In 1936, with the assistance of Odbert, he reviewed the prior work of six investigators who had obtained data from sources similar to the one Galton used. They extracted from the 1925 *Webster's Dictionary* 17,953 words that had "the capacity . . . to distinguish the behavior of one human being from that of another'' (p. 24). They then identified, merely by inspection, 4,504 ''real'' traits of personality. Allport (1937) suggests that some of these are styles of adaptation, for example, politeness and restraint, but others are dynamic, for example, aggression and sociability.

Allport conceptualized traits as hypothesized entities, and he also assumed that they are responsible for the consistency of personality at different times and in different places: ''Traits are not directly observable; they are inferred. . . . Without such an inference the stability and consistency of personal behavior could not possibly be explained'' (Allport, 1937, p. 340). Much of the history of traits has involved a defense of this assumed reliability, and this effort is apparent as early as 1937 when Allport attempted to resolve a conflict between trait theory and the laboratory results obtained by Hartshorne and May in a 1928 investigation of the morality of children. The subjects in this experiment were given various opportunities to be dishonest, that is, to cheat at games, to lie about their cheating, to correct their own examination papers, and to steal coins. Individual children were found to be honest in some situations but dishonest in others. Allport endeavored to deflect interpretations of this variability as evidence of trait inconsistency by invoking a single underlying covert entity. He remarks, for example, that ''Child D does not steal pennies, but he lies about his cheating, not because he has a general trait of dishonesty, but because he has a general trait of *timidity* (fear of consequences)'' (1937, p. 251).

Others have joined Allport in proposing concealed traits. These are typically dichotomized, with one described as expressive and the other as causal. Lewin (1935), for example, transposed the biological notions of genotype and phenotype onto psychological traits, and depicted the latter as directly observable and the genotype as a determiner of overt behavior. Baumgarten (1936), another illustrative figure, proposed ''genuine and non-genuine character qualities'' (1936, p. 291). This scheme allows goodness, for example, to be expressed both in friendliness and ''in a harsh rudeness'' (1936, p. 294). Incidentally, Baumgarten, like Allport, procured the inventory of potential traits, in this instance 1,093 of them, from lexical sources.

One of the more popular modern techniques of identifying traits is the use of factor analysis, a practice that also conceptualizes them on two levels. This method involves a complex of statistical operations that reduces large masses of data—in this instance traits assessed by means of pencil-and-paper tests of personality—into a manageable number of relatively homogeneous clusters. Each of these is called a factor, and is given a name that reflects the dominant content of the test items that make up each group or cluster. Cattell identifies the yield from these procedures as ''surface'' traits, that is, what a person does or experiences, and ''source'' traits, that is, the reasons for the surface traits. To illustrate—and in the interests of clarity to oversimplify—personality questionnaires indicate that people who describe themselves as suspicious also tend to blame others rather than themselves for failures, and the correlation between these two reactions is ascribed to a source trait, a lack of trust in others. These people stand apart from another group, one that is guided by an underlying trait of sensitivity and thus prone to worry about offending others, and to strive to understand their motives.

Cattell reduced the 4,504 traits that Allport and Odbert had singled out to 171 entries. He factor analyzed tests that measure these traits, including examinations that others had administered as well as some he had personally collected. He also processed additional tests and reported that these various treatments distilled the original list into primary factors or source traits that vary somewhat in number but do not exceed twenty (Cattell, 1946, 1957; Cattell & Dreger, 1977). Other factor analysts report different numbers and assign different names to the factors that they discover, but these discrepancies in conclusions about the basic traits have not arrested the factor analytic method of studying traits, and similar research is continuing (Sells & Murphy, 1984).

Several criticisms are leveled against the concept of trait, irrespective of the method of measurement, and conspicuous among these is the assumed consistency. This is seen as deflecting the study of changes that come from different experiences as well as explorations of how individuality is achieved. Allport (1937) and several other theorists have tried to solve this latter problem by directing attention to the *pattern* of traits. Few psychologists argue against this view, but on the other hand few even attempt to confirm it experimentally, and as a result, little or no information is forthcoming about the truism that each person is unique. Reflection suggests that the configuration that is assumed to be responsible may be less relevant than consistency. To illustrate—a person who displays both courtesy and agreeableness is similar to many people, but a person who, without exception, is courteous and agreeable might well be unique.

By the 1950s the deficits in the concept of trait prompted many psychologists to turn to an examination of behavior per se and to neglect the early formulation of "*a generalized and focalized neuropsychic system (peculiar to the individual)*" (Allport, 1937, p. 295). Consistency was not included in this transfer but its persistance is represented by McClelland, who defines trait as "a recurrent similar response *pattern* (italics added)" (1951, p. 156).

Direct assaults on the assumed reliability and generality of traits were inevitable. One example of these is found in a conclusion Mischel drew from a critical survey of the research literature: "Highly generalized behavioral consistencies have not been demonstrated, and the concept of personality traits as broad response dispositions is thus untenable" (1968, p. 146).

The dismissals did not convince one and all, but increased recognition began to emerge (Endler, 1973). This did not, however, obliterate the tradition, and a recent definition documents the still persisting idea of uniformity: "*A trait is a consistent and persistent pattern of behavior and experience (cognitive and affective) characteristic of a particular individual*" (Stagner, 1984, p. 7).

The arguments—both pro and con—have not produced remarkably persuasive results, and the heyday of the concept of trait may well have passed. The concept lends itself to measurement and, as a result, it is said to enrich descriptions of people and to be useful in describing different groups. Apparently these assets have sustained it even though it neglects the influence of personal experiences as well as the impact of different situations (Mischel, 1986).

References

Allport, G. W. (1930). What is a trait of personality? *Journal of Abnormal and Social Psychology, 25*, 368–372.

Allport, G. W. (1937). *Personality: A psychological interpretation*. New York: Henry Holt. A classic text and one that promoted an equation between the concepts of trait and personality.

Allport, G. W., & Odbert, H. S. (1936). Trait-names: A psycho-lexical study. *Psychological Monographs, 47*, (Whole No. 211).

Baumgarten, F. (1936). Character qualities. *British Journal of Psychology, 26*, 289–298. At the time this article was written the term trait was just coming into use and Baumgarten uses "trait," "character trait," and "character quality" as synonyms.

Cattell, R. B. (1946). *Description and measurement of personality*. Yonkers-on-Hudson, NY: World Book.

Cattell, R. B. (1957). *Personality and motivation: Structure and measurement*. Yonkers-on-Hudson, NY: World Book.

Cattell, R. B. & Dreger, R. M. (Eds.). (1977). *Handbook of modern personality theory*. Washington, DC: Hemisphere.

Endler, N. S. (1973). The person versus the situation—a pseudo issue? A response to Alker. *Journal of Personality, 41*, 287–303. A review of the controversy over the relative importance of what a person brings to a situation versus the situation.

Galton, F. (1884). Measurement of character. *Fortnightly Review, 36*, 179–185.

Hall, C. S., Lindzey, G., Loehlin, J. C., & Manosevitz, M. (1985). *Introduction to theories of personality*. New York: John Wiley.

Hartshorne, H., & May, M. A. (1928). *Studies in the nature of character. Studies in deceit: Book one: General methods and results; Book two: Statistical Methods and Results*. New York: Macmillan. This is a report of the Character Education Inquiry, conducted at Teachers College, Columbia University. Deception was assessed in the classroom, in homework, in athletic contests, and in party situations. Lying, both to avoid disapproval and to gain approval, was also scrutinized. More than 170,000 deception tests were conducted.

Lewin, K. (1935). *A dynamic theory of personality. Selected papers* (D. K. Adams & K. E. Zener, Trans.). New York: McGraw-Hill. Lewin's first treatment of genotype and phenotype was "Gesetz und Experiment in der Psychologie." *Symposion*, 1927, *5*, 375–421. Allport and other early personologists refer to this paper more often than Lewin and his biographers.

McClelland, D. (1951). *Personality*. New York: William Sloane Associates.

Mischel, W. (1968). *Personality and assessment*. New York: John Wiley.

Mischel, W. (1986). *Introduction to personality: A new look* (4th ed.). New York: Holt, Rinehart & Winston. This text is unusually successful in placing numerous details in perspective. The strengths and weaknesses of different interpretations of traits are clearly outlined.

Sells, S. B., & Murphy, D. (1984). Factor theories of personality. In N. S. Endler & J. McV. Hunt (Eds.), *Personality and the behavioral disorders*. (2nd ed., Vol. 1, pp. 39–72). New York: John Wiley. The first edition of this two-volume work, appearing in 1944, was a landmark publication. At that time psychology was just beginning to become deeply involved in problems of adjustment, and the first edition documented the scholarship of the discipline in this area. This revision is impressive, but it has much keener competition than the initial book.

Stagner, R. (1984). Trait psychology. In N. S. Endler & J. McV. Hunt (Eds.), *Personality and the behavioral disorders* (2nd ed., Vol. 1, pp. 3–38). New York: John Wiley.

Sources of Additional Information

Allport, G. W. (1966). Traits revisited. *American Psychologist, 21,* 1–10. This is Allport's address at the time the American Psychological Association honored him with a Distinguished Scientific Contribution Award. He affirms an intention to reexamine the concept of trait that he has advocated for nearly forty years, but the body of the address is more a censure of critics than a reformulation. Feshbach, S., & Weiner, B. (1982). *Personality.* Lexington, MA: D. C. Heath. The authors attempt to settle the question of specificity versus generality of behavior by affirming that "the individual, the trait, and the situation must all be considered" (p. 9). Rosenzweig, S. (1944). Converging approaches to personality: Murray, Allport, Lewin. *Psychological Review, 51,* 248–256. There are interesting historical details in this comparison of three theorists. Stagner, R. (1984). Traits are relevant: Theoretical analysis and empirical evidence. In N. S. Endler & D. Magnusson (Eds.), *Interactional psychology and personality* (pp. 109–124). Washington, DC: Hemisphere. Stagner sees traits as valid and necessary. He argues that they determine what is and is not a reward, what is learned and what is rejected. They also support predictions about behavior over time.

TRANSPERSONAL PSYCHOLOGY. See HUMAN POTENTIAL MOVEMENT.

TYPE. 1. A distinctive feature, or cluster of them, that is believed to be characteristic of a group of individuals.

The core of the concept of type is either a single attribute, or a combination of them, that is perceived as a distinguishing mark, a kind of insignia for a group of individuals. The concept is organized around opinions about behavior, and a person does not display a type, but rather fits, or fails to fit, one. The distinctive qualities are generally considered to be stable and compelling in that the characteristic responses resist control or inhibition.

Individuals who conform to a type are assumed to indulge in extremes ("the talkative type" versus "the silent type") or to possess a large number of salient characteristics ("the typical sophomore"). This premise violates the more commonly held opinion that the majority of people exhibit only a moderate number of one kind of response and only a few display extreme amounts. Most people, for example, speak at a normal level, and only a few talk with an unduly high frequency and an equally small number talk only rarely. The concept of type denies this distribution, which is, incidentally, called the normal distribution curve, in favor of one in which the largest number of people are at either end of a continuum with only a few, if any, in the center. This reduction in the middle range suggests that the behavior of types is mutually exclusive. Silence, for example, is believed only rarely to interrupt or interfere with the high verbal output of "the talkative type."

A classification of types may be helpful, possibly even indispensable, in some intellectual endeavors, but psychological categories are artificial, since they ignore the variability that is induced by different kinds and amounts of stimulation. In the early days of experimental psychology the concept of type was widely circulated, and although the shortcomings were recognized, they were not considered to be serious flaws. Their limitations were also countered by the illusion of predictability and by the sense of having captured something complex that the concept of type suggests. As the discipline matured the concept became less acceptable and, with a few highly visible exceptions, the word is not now used. Beginning in the 1970s and continuing to the present the *Psychological Abstracts* omits the generic term type from the Index and uses the word only when it is modified, that is, only when a particular type is indicated. The initial *Thesaurus of Psychological Index Terms* (Kinkade, 1974) as well as later editions (American Psychological Association, 1985) also enter only specific varieties of type.

The research on psychological types gained momentum in the United States in the 1920s when three formulations appeared, either written or translated into English. Each of these theories came to be called a typology even though each is in part like and in part unlike a typology.

One of the early schemes deals with both body build and TEMPERAMENT. Its creator, William H. Sheldon (1899–1977), quantified the relative prominence within any one person of three components of physique (Humphreys, 1957). He expressed the rank of each in a sequence of three digits, but these multiple entries are commonly slighted in favor of spotting the highest rank and identifying this component as the "body type." Sheldon believed that each of these anatomical configurations is closely related to a different temperament, and with the assistance of colleagues, he made numerous measurements and observations of temperament. The formulation was, however, soon overwhelmed by criticism, and it currently appears to be confined to the past, to be merely an illustration of the early appeal of the concept of type.

A second scheme, translated into English in the 1920s, was devised by Eduard Spranger (1882–1963), a German psychologist, who complied a rational rather than an empirical classification of six ideals or values that he believed are held by humans. Each of these is a kind of master sentiment, a principle that the individual searches for or reads into the various contexts in which he or she functions. The six values are theoretical, assigning priority to knowledge; economic, a bias toward practicality; aesthetic, a partiality for beauty; social, a fondness for altruism; political, an intrigue with power; and religious, an attraction to spirituality. Although Spranger entitled his book *Types of Men* (1913/ 1928) he is explicit that the values are not mutually exclusive and that a person favors at least two of them, often more. These qualifications did not fend off either the attraction of the era for types or the suggestion conveyed by the title of the book, and the label "Spranger's types" came into active circulation.

The classification is still in service in the form of a pencil-and-paper test, "Study of Values: A Scale for Measuring the Dominant Interests in Personality." This test, first published in 1931, quantifies the relative strength of Spranger's six ideals. The vocabulary level makes the test most appropriate for the college educated, and the instrument is popular, particularly for classroom demonstrations of the measurement of personality. It has been revised twice and is still being sold and used (Mitchell, 1985). The label type is seldom applied to the "study of values," and Spranger's original system has not been altered in any significant way but has, in fact, endured—albeit in recent years in phantom form—for more than five decades.

The analyst Carl Jung (1875–1961), the third of the early theorists, is frequently identified as the prototypical typologist. Although Jung published *Psychological Types* (1921/1933), his theory emphasizes complex interrelationships. The initial formulations grew out of Jung's observations that psychiatric patients assume two general attitudes; one he called extraversion, an orientation toward the outer world, and the second he called introversion, an orientation toward the self. Jung used the word type to refer to the dominance of either extraversion or introversion, but he denied the exclusion of either reaction: "There can never occur a pure type in the sense that he is entirely possessed of the one mechanism with a complete atrophy of the other" (Jung, 1921/1933, p. 13).

There is much more to Jung's theory than this dichotomy. He defined extraversion and introversion, not as autonomous entities, but combined each of them with a propensity to think, to feel, to sense, and to intuit. Thus there are eight reaction patterns: extraverted thinking, introverted feeling, and so on.

Psychologists, critical both of the restricting of the observations to patients and of the impressionistic quality of much of the information, began to try to improve on Jung by constructing tests designed to measure extraversion-introversion. Soon quantity exceeded quality, and an unwieldy number were constructed, with the productivity still continuing (Loomis, 1982). In fact, the measurement became so popular that for an extended period of time, the concept of type was equated with extraversion-introversion, both yoked to Jung.

The tests are too numerous to be reviewed here, but it is feasible to look at two typical characteristics. One of these is a widely acknowledged improvement in population sampling. Many normals were examined, and they were selected by techniques that are believed to represent the population at large. The second is a generally unrecognized, but nonetheless real modification of Jung's concepts. Psychologists, in pursuit of objectivity, devised test items that deal with specific situations. In the beginning they emulated Jung in that they used a diversity of contexts, but gradually they emphasized questions that feature an inclination either to engage in or to avoid social contacts. In other words extraversion-introversion was reduced to a preference for or against socializing. Excerpts from a fifty-five year span of the literature illustrate this trend. As early as 1927

Guthrie was able to locate seven discussions of extraversion-introversion, an impressive number for that era. Even at that date he was distressed about the casual way in which definitions are formulated: "The total impression gained is decidedly reminiscent of the accounts of the phrenological faculties" (p. 83). Three decades later Cronbach offers the same kind of criticism but illustrates it in relation to socializing: "The meaning of 'introvert' is twisted and turned so that it represents for one author a brooding neurotic, for another anyone who would rather be a clerk than a carnival barker" (1960, pp. 467–468). A remark twenty-two years later points out the restriction to interpersonal relations: "The introversion-extroversion continuum refers to two rather opposite styles in dealing with one's social environment. At one extreme introverts would be shy and anxious in all novel social situations and would much prefer to withdraw from people than to approach them" (Liebert & Spiegler, 1982, p. 190).

There are two tests in modern psychology that are exceptions to the unidimensional definition of extraversion-introversion, and both of these are mentioned because their alignment with Jung is exaggerated. One of them was devised by Hans Eysenck, a psychologist who became interested in Jung's classification in the 1940s. Initially Eysenck set about to verify Jung's contention that extraverted and introverted people who become psychiatrically disabled develop different disorders. The statistical analyses of masses of tests of many aspects of personality convinced him that all personality traits are a manifestation of merely two independent dimensions: stability-instability and extraversion-introversion. As the research progressed, Eysenck began to concentrate on the underlying causes of extraversion-introversion, and he shared Sheldon's opinion that temperament is the critical determiner. He later added other biological factors to the explanatory matrix, and currently the system is referred to as a biological typology. It is mainly concerned with how organisms are aroused, and this is depicted both as stable and different in extraverts and introverts (Monte, 1987).

A second test, The Myers-Briggs Type Indicator, promotes the concept of type by including that word in the title, and it also exaggerates the Jungian tradition by repeatedly advising that the instrument mirrors his theory. The advice, although only partially true, appears to carry weight inasmuch as one author begins a review of the test with the following: "The Myers-Briggs Type Indicator represents a major effort to capture the Jungian personality typology in a psychometric instrument" (Coan, 1978, p. 973). Work on this test started during the 1940s, and there has been a series of revisions (Mendelsohn, 1965; Myers & McCaulley, 1985). It now consists of four scales: Extraversion-Introversion, Thinking-Feeling, Sensation-Intuition, and Judgment-Perception. These represent, to some degree at least, Jungian formulations, but in the original theory the attitudes of extraversion-introversion did not stand alone and were related to other responses.

By the 1970s the connotation of the word type had changed dramatically. This modification was initiated outside the field of psychology when two physicians, Friedman and Rosenman, reported at the annual meeting of the American Heart

Association that there is a link between some forms of coronary pathology and "a specific overt behavior pattern" (1959, p. 1286). The investigators based this conclusion on the differences in incidence of certain cardiovascular symptoms among three groups of men differentiated on the basis of their occupational behavior. Each of these groups was referred to with the neutral letters A, B, and C. Group A, the one with a number of physiological problems, consisted of men who had several psychological characteristics in common, including being competitive, having a strong desire for achievement, repeatedly facing deadlines, and being unusually alert, both mentally and physically. At that time the investigators called this constellation Pattern A. A program of research was begun, and in 1974 Friedman and Rosenman published an account for the general public. By this time "Pattern" was replaced with "Type" and the latter, was incorporated into the title of the book written for the laity—*Type A Behavior and Your Heart*. The authors, like their predecessors, combine attributes of a typology with those that are alien to this kind of organization. In line with the former they report a higher incidence at the extreme than at the middle of a distribution; specifically, that the majority of the population belongs to Type A and that only approximately 10 percent of the population displays both Type A and Type B behavior patterns. But these two types are not depicted as mutually exclusive or immutable inasmuch as the authors identify one of their purposes as showing how Type A behavior "can be drastically altered—even abolished" (1974, p. ix).

Friedman and Rosenman's formulation prompted a show of interest in psychological circles, and research on both overt and covert aspects of Type A and Type B personalities is flourishing. Experiments are conducted not only with the medically disabled, but also with healthy people of both sexes and various ages, and their reactions to a wide variety of situations are observed (Goldberg, 1985; Price, 1982).

We do not query the validity of this research, but we do query the terminology. The label invokes the assumptions that underlie a typology, and many psychologists believe that these are invalid, and prefer to relate the phenomenon to the normal distribution curve. This bias is illustrated in a review of the literature by Goldberg (1985) in which he reports that laboratory results suggest that males who are both categorized as Type A and whose NEED FOR ACHIEVEMENT is concomitant with a hope of success rather than a FEAR OF FAILURE may not have any more biopathology than Type B men. Experimental support of the accuracy or inaccuracy of this amendment is not as important for this discussion as is the existence of the search for variables that form a typical frequency curve. Goldberg states explicitly: "There is a definite need to refine both the concept and assessment of Type-A behavior" (1985, p. 8).

References

American Psychological Association. (1985). *Thesaurus of psychological index terms* (4th ed.). Washington, DC: Author.

Coan, R. W. (1978). The Myers-Briggs Type Indicator. In O. K. Buros (Ed.), *The eighth mental measurements yearbook* (pp. 973–975). Highland Park, NJ: Gryphon Press.

Cronbach, L. J. (1960). *Essentials of psychological testing* (2nd ed.). New York: Harper & Row. A reference source that evaluates a wide variety of tests.

Friedman, M., & Rosenman, R. H. (1959). Association of specific overt behavior pattern with blood and cardiovascular findings. *Journal of the American Medical Association, 169*, 1286–1296. The authors report that "clinical coronary artery disease was seven times more frequent . . . in the men of Group A than in those of Group B or Group C" (p. 1295).

Friedman, M., & Rosenman, R. H. (1974). *Type A behavior and your heart.*New York: Alfred Knopf. Although this book is primarily written for the patient, it is also comprehensive.

Goldberg, C. (1985). On the relationship between Type-A behavior and coronary heart disease: Association and assessment. *Psychological Documents, 15*, 8. (Ms. No. 2686)

Guthrie, E. R. (1927). Measuring introversion and extroversion. *Journal of Abnormal and Social Psychology, 22*, 82–88. Guthrie correlated the scores of undergraduates on various tests that were assumed to measure extraversion and introversion. Some of these measures did not agree, and on this basis Guthrie questioned the validity of characterizing normals as either extraversive or introversive.

Humphreys, L. G. (1957). Characteristics of type concepts with special reference to Sheldon's typology. *Psychological Bulletin, 54*, 218–228. This article sharpens the perspective on the concept of type. It also documents how a theory of this nature is converted to a typology.

Jung, C. (1933). *Psychological types or the psychology of individuation* (H. G. Baynes, Trans.). London: Kegan Paul, Trench, Trubner. (Original work published 1921)

Kinkade, R. G. (Ed.). (1974). *Thesaurus of psychological index terms*. Washington, DC: American Psychological Association.

Liebert, R. M., & Spiegler, M. D. (1982). *Personality: Strategies and issues* (4th ed.). Homewood, IL: Dorsey Press.

Loomis, M. (1982). A new perspective for Jung's typology: The Singer-Loomis inventory of personality. *Journal of Analytical Psychology, 27*, 59–69. This is a modern attempt to build a valid scale. Such a test is needed because "previous inventories which were designed to measure *Jung's typology* [italics added] failed to substantiate that the instruments were measuring what they purported to measure" (p. 59). The author understands Jung's formulation, and the test content reflects this.

Mendelsohn, G. A. (1965). The Myers-Briggs Type Indicator. In O. K. Buros (Ed.), *The sixth mental measurements yearbook* (pp. 321–322). Highland Park, NJ: Gryphon Press.

Mitchell, J. V., Jr. (1985). Study of values: A scale for measuring the dominant interests in personality. (3rd ed.) In J. V. Mitchell, Jr. (Ed.), *The ninth mental measurements yearbook* (Vol. 2, p. 1499). Lincoln: University of Nebraska Press. This is a thumbnail sketch of the various versions of the test. A list of seven recent studies in which it is used is included. The authors are G. W. Allport, P. E. Vernon & G. Lindzey.

Monte, C. F. (1987). *Beneath the mask: An introduction to theories of personality* (3rd ed.). New York: Holt, Rinehart, & Winston.

Myers, I. B., & McCaulley, M. H. (1985). *Manual: A guide to the development and use of The Myers-Briggs Type Indicator.* Palo Alto, CA: Consulting Psychologists Press.

Price, V. A. (1982). *Type A behavior pattern: A model for research and practice.* New York: Academic Press.

Spranger, E. (1928). *Types of men: The psychology and ethics of personality* (5th German ed.). (P. J. W. Pigors, Trans.). Halle: Niemeyer. (Original work published 1913). Spranger's "ideal" values or "types" refer to preferences that people look for in their experiences. The searching for a particular value is said to unify experiences.

Sources of Additional Information

Bellak, L. (1956). Psychoanalytic theory of personality. In J. L. McCary (Ed.), *Psychology of personality: Six modern approaches* (pp. 1–62). New York: Grove Press. The author contrasts types and traits in psychoanalytic theory. Boder, D. P. (1946). Nazi science. In P. L. Harriman (Ed.), *Twentieth century psychology: Recent developments in psychology* (pp. 10–21). Boder describes how E. R. Jaensch, a German psychologist, converted a typology, based on perceptual consistency and inconsistency, into a pro-Nazi doctrine. Unstable perception was expanded into unstable or degenerate personality, labeled the Anti-Type and contrasted with the Nordic type. Haller, J. S., Jr. (1981). *American medicine in transition 1840–1910.* Urbana: University of Illinois Press. The emphasis is on constitutional types, but a brief section on behavioral types is also included. Matthews, K. A., & Volkin, J. I. (1981). Efforts to excel and the Type A behavior pattern in children. *Child Development, 52,* 1283–1289. An illustration of research on type with children, in this instance those in the fifth and sixth grades. Type A children solved more arithmetic problems, supported a weight for longer intervals, and reported less fatigue than other children. Sheldon, W. (1971). The New York study of physical constitution and psychotic pattern. *Journal of the History of the Behavioral Sciences, 7,* 115–126. This is an autobiographical account of Sheldon's education and research. He talks about his mentors, including Ernest Kretschmer, a German psychiatrist, and one of the trailblazers in theories of body type.

U

UNCONSCIOUS. See IMPERCEPTION.

UNCONSCIOUSNESS. See IMPERCEPTION.

V

VIGILANCE. 1. Readiness to detect, during an extended period of time, irregular changes in faint and/or brief stimuli in a relatively homogenous stimulus configuration. 2. The interpreting of automatically displayed data and, when appropriate, the adjusting of the system that is generating the information.

During World War II military personnel experienced enough difficulty in reacting accurately intermittent radar signals to prompt laboratory research into the human capability to recognize very weak changes in stimulation, particularly visual and auditory signals. Mackworth (1950) applied the term vigilance to the sustained alertness that this task seems to require. The word was borrowed from neurology, where it is used to refer to a condition of heightened neural excitability that occurs in some physical illnesses.

The research on vigilance should not be confused with that on the determination of a THRESHOLD. The central problems in threshold measurement are to find the smallest *amount* of physical energy and the least *change* in the amount of energy that is sensed. In contrast, the central problems in vigilance research are to discover the factors that facilitate or improve the sensing of inconspicuous stimuli, such as ascertaining the optimal length of a watch, identifying personal attributes that distinguish those who are vigilant from those who are not, and determining the physical properties (size, color, brightness, etc.) that are the most and the least accurately detected.

Many psychologists classify vigilance as a variety of ATTENTION or of SET. Lapses in these reactions have long been recognized, and lamented, but only a few, relatively isolated exprimental attacks on the problems of reacting to attenuated stimuli were made until military requirements called attention to the need of more sophisticated information. Shortly after this work was under way vigilance was also investigated in relation to other tasks, for example, driving an automobile, piloting an aircraft, inspecting products as they come off an assembly line, controlling air traffic, monitoring electronic signals that are generated by machines as well as those that display a patient's physiological status.

In the laboratory the level of vigilance is measured in several ways, including the frequency of correctly detected stimulus changes, the number of subjects who pick up a signal correctly, the total of missed cues, the sum of all incorrect reports, and the length of delays in responding. Generally the sentinels' responses have no effect on stimulus events.

In order to convey the flavor of the research methods, capsule descriptions of some of the specifics of a few experiments are presented here. Davies and Griew (1963) requested participants to press a button when they heard three consecutive odd numbers in a series of digits spoken at the rate of one per second for seventy-five minutes. Osborn, Sheldon, and Baker (1963) required subjects during a three-hour interval to acknowledge interruptions in a light in the center of box in direct view by pressing a button at their left side; offsets of a steady noise delivered through a headset by pressing a button on their right side; and the simultaneous stopping of light and sound by activating both buttons. There were twenty-four signals per hour, the duration of each was .041 seconds, and the intervals between interruptions were irregular. Each person worked in isolation and had no access to a watch, a pen, or reading material. Jerison and Pickett (1964) asked subjects during an eighty-minute session to watch a bar of light, two millimeters wide and eighteen millimeters high, as it appeared to move twenty-nine millimeters to the right, return to the starting position, and then repeat the sequence. The signal was an increase in the length of the second deflection from twenty-nine to thirty-five millimeters. A noise that masked sounds made by the equipment was broadcast throughout the trials.

The emphasis in much of the research is on the causes of decrements in vigilance as the monitoring continues (Fisk & Schneider, 1981). There is consensus that failures appear relatively early and, with only a few exceptions, are commonplace. Fallibility has many causes, and no thoroughly dependable, preventive means are in sight, but there are some measures that are often effective. These include selecting personnel who are adept at the task, keeping them informed of their accuracy, and arranging for them to work in pairs or groups with irregularly scheduled periods of supervision (Bergum, 1963). Such features of the stimulus pattern as a relatively high frequency of signals and a restricted exposure area increase accuracy, but these variables usually cannot be controlled in real-life situations, the ones in which performance is the most critical.

Researchers originally assumed that an obvious cause—fatigue—is the actual cause of the decrements, but as information accumulated this explanation lost favor, in good measure because drops in accuracy develop early, show only limited progression, and are at times reversed. Several alternative explanations have been put forth. One, for example, proposes that subjects, starting out enthusiastically, begin in a hypervigilant state, and as boredom develops they return to normal vigilance. Another suggests that knowing the duration of the vigil promotes accuracy at the end of the period (Bergum & Lehr, 1963).

One explanation that has gained a considerable following is called signal detection theory. This asserts that surveillance requires making judgements or decisions, as well as sensory discriminations, and as the lookout progresses, subjects may change their ideas about what constitutes a signal. If such modifications occur, the decrements would reflect either decreases in sensory sensitivity (fatigue) or revisions in the criteria used to decide that a critical stimulus is present. The proponents of signal detection theory propose that these two conditions can be distinguished by the use of *statistical* procedures that were originally developed in electrical engineering for a theory of statistical decision (Swets, Tanner, & Birdsall, 1961). Even though this interpretation relies more on statistics than on behavior, it offers some potential to differentiate judgement and sensation, and thus was welcomed with enthusiasm.

Modern refinements in technology include the designing of instruments that indicate the way the equipment is functioning, including announcements of irregularities, or even the actual shutting down of operations (Kantowitz & Hanson, 1981). This automation has improved human efficiency, but it has also changed the responsibility of the individual from that of merely sensing signals to that of interpreting the reasons for the changes in them and, when necessary, intervening in the functioning of the equipment. A relatively simple example of this is an annunciator panel that discloses when sensors have cut off an engine. Probably the most complex system is a nuclear power plant.

Safety is frequently paramount in these human-machine systems, but personnel must react to a large array of information, and they must make a variety of expert appraisals. Abnormal conditions are difficult to model, and as a result, personnel may receive the least adequate information at a time when it is most needed. Some authors retain the word vigilance to designate the response made to these complex demands, but this meaning is quite different from the original references to the monitoring of a single kind of weak and aperiodic cue (Rasmussen & Rouse, 1981).

Operating an automobile demands an array of skills, and the dangers involved in driving point to the necessity of understanding the task thoroughly. Some of the skills that are used in driving a car appear merely to resemble those that are required in watchkeeping, and others may actually be the same (Stroh, 1971). In driving, both weak and strong as well as regular and irregular signals are in play. The visual backdrop is usually complex, but on long stretches of uninhabited areas it can be relatively homogeneous. Further, the criteria on which decisions are based may change. Under time pressure, for example, caution may become less compelling and taking chances may become more attractive. Laboratory results indicate that risky overtaking may actually increase toward the end of relatively long driving periods (Brown, Tickner, & Simmonds, 1970). Some experiments, however, fail to yield results that concur with those that the concept of vigilance predicts. One of these is a lack of decrement in vigilance. One study, for example, reported improvements when vigilance was measured by the time required to detect low-intensity light signals coming from apertures in three mirrors on a car (Brown, Simmonds, & Tickner, 1967). The research on automobile driving is voluminous, and a review of it is not appropriate in this discussion, but these few comments illustrate the intricacies that characterize vigilance, a concept that at first glance appears simple and straightforward.

Despite its importance, the enthusiasm for filling in the blanks in the knowledge about vigilance appears to be faltering. In a review of a recent book on the topic, Wilkinson comments: ''A glance at the date of the references reveals that vigilance is not a bushy-tailed new field of research; very few of the papers cited fall within the last 10 years; the book reflects this feeling of spent effort'' (1986, p. 514). Wilkinson concludes with a reminder of the significance of the concept: ''After all, it is arguable that some quite important things depend on human vigilance—such as who wins at bingo and whether humankind survives'' (1986, p. 515).

References

Bergum, B. O. (1963). Vigilance: A guide to improved performance. *Human Resources Research Office, Research Bulletin*, No. 10. As the title implies, this bulletin provides a list of suggestions for maintaining vigilance, and it was compiled on the basis of the results of a series of experiments. The account is technically accurate and readily intelligible.

Bergum, B. O., & Lehr, D. J. (1963). End-spurt in vigilance. *Journal of Experimental Psychology, 66*, 383–385. These researchers found that subjects who are informed of the duration of the watch and are also allowed to wear timepieces improved their detection accuracy during the final phase of the vigil. Subjects deprived of this information did not do so.

Brown, I. D., Simmonds, D. C. V., & Tickner, A. H. (1967). Measurement of control skills, vigilance, and performance on a subsidiary task during 12 hours of car driving. *Ergonomics, 10*, 665–673.

Brown, I. D., Tickner, A. H., & Simmonds, D. C. V. (1970). Effect of prolonged driving on overtaking criteria. *Ergonomics, 13*, 239–242.

Davies, D. R., & Griew, S. (1963). A further note on the effect of aging on auditory vigilance performance: The effect of low signal frequency. *Journal of Gerontology, 18*, 370–371. This is the second experiment by these investigators in which auditory vigilance was found to be unaffected by age, at least between seventeen and fifty-eight years.

Fisk, A. D., & Schneider, W. (1981). Control and automatic processing during tasks requiring sustained attention: A new approach to vigilance. *Human Factors, 23*, 737–750. The authors describe various factors that help to sustain vigilance.

Jerison, H. J., & Pickett, R. M. (1964). Vigilance: The importance of the elicited observing rate. *Science, 143* (No. 3609), 970–971.

Kantowitz, B. H., & Hanson, R. H. (1981). Models and experimental results concerning the detection of operator failures in display monitoring. In J. Rasmussen & W. B. Rouse (Eds.), *Human detection and diagnosis of system failures: NATO Conference Series: III* (Vol. 15, pp. 301–315). New York: Plenum Press.

Mackworth, N. H. (1950). Researches on the measurement of human performance. *Medical Research Council Special Report Series, No. 268*. London: His Majesty's Stationery Office. Mackworth's researches were first reported in a series of unpublished military reports. They include interference with efficiency that is induced by a variety of conditions, including lachrymators, heat, high humidity, and various drugs.

Osborn, W. C., Sheldon, R. W., & Baker, R. A. (1963). Vigilance performance under conditions of redundant and nonredundant signal presentation. *Journal of Applied Psychology, 47*, 130–134. Simultaneous visual and auditory signals are referred to as redundant, and the detection of redundant signals is generally more accurate than the monitoring of single ones.

Rasmussen, J., & Rouse, W. B. (1981). (Eds.). *Human detection and diagnosis of system failures: NATO Conference Series: III* (Vol. 15). New York: Plenum Press. This volume includes the papers presented at an international symposium. These are all technical accounts, and they bring a diversity of problems to light. Some attention is devoted to the inability to gain intellectual control over the increases in complexity that confront the human, the responsible agent, as automation increases. The observation is made that there is no adequate model currently available for keeping pace with these changes.

Stroh, C. M. (1971). *Vigilance: The problem of sustained attention*. Oxford: Pergamon Press.

Swets, J. A., Tanner, W. P., Jr., & Birdsall, T. G. (1961). Decision processes in perception. *Psychological Review, 68*, 301–340. This paper clarifies signal detection theory. This theory assumes that the threshold is variable because noise (irrelevant factors) is/are always present. The strategy is to ascertain the number of both the correct judgments and the "false alarms" and to infer from these when the subjects' expectations result in deviations from statistically identified accuracy.

Wilkinson, R. T. (1986). Human vigilance at the crossroads [Review of *Sustained attention in human performance*]. *Contemporary Psychology, 31*, 514–515.

Sources of Additional Information

Buckner, D. N., & McGrath, J. J. (Eds.). (1963). *Vigilance: A symposium*. New York: McGraw-Hill. A series of papers by different scientists; authoritative accounts of the topic. Jerison, H. J., & Pickett, R. M. (1963). Vigilance: A review and re-evaluation. *Human Factors, 5*, 211–238. Although such practical goals as minimizing accidents and avoiding military assaults have dominated the study of vigilance, there has also been some theory construction. Jerison and Pickett attempt to integrate vigilance and decision making in relation to manned space systems. Mackworth, N. H. (1948). The breakdown of vigilance during prolonged visual search. *Quarterly Journal of Experimental Psychology, 1*, 6–21. Mackworth details the original experiments. The first suspected cause of inefficiency was length of watch, and in this connection he cites Shakespeare. " 'For now they are opress'd with travel, they/Will not, nor cannot, use such vigilance/As when they are fresh.'—(*The Tempest*, Act 3, Scene 3.)" (p. 7). Stroh, C. M. (1977). The influence of personality and age on the relationship between vigilance performance and arousal level. In R. R. Mackie (Ed.), *Vigilance: Theory, operational performance, and physiological correlates* (pp. 617–622). New York: Plenum Press. This study illustrates the interactive effects of selected personality traits on signal certainty, arousal level, monitoring, and age. These results are in line with previous evidence that skill in surveillance is multidetermined.

Author Index

Note: The italic numerals signify the page where an author's work is cited.

Subject Index

Note: the italic numerals signify the pages where the main entry can be found.

About the Authors

JOHN A. POPPLESTONE is Director of Archives of the History of American Psychology and Professor of Psychology at the University of Akron.

MARION WHITE MCPHERSON is Associate Director of the Archives of the History of American Psychology at the University of Akron.

DATE DUE